The Green Agenda
in American Politics

STUDIES IN GOVERNMENT
AND PUBLIC POLICY

The Green Agenda
in American Politics

New Strategies for the Twenty-first Century

Robert J. Duffy

 University Press of Kansas

*52133213

Published by the University Press of Kansas (Lawrence, Kansas 66049), which was
organized by the Kansas Board of Regents and is operated and funded by Emporia State
University, Fort Hays State University, Kansas State University, Pittsburg State
University, the University of Kansas, and Wichita State University

Library of Congress Cataloging-in-Publication Data
Duffy, Robert J.
    The green agenda in American politics : new strategies for the
twenty-first century / Robert J. Duffy.
        p. cm. — (Studies in government and public policy)
Includes bibliographical references and index.
    ISBN 0-7006-1277-7 (cloth : alk. paper) — ISBN 0-7006-1278-5 (pbk. :
alk. paper)
    1. Environmentalism—United States.   2. Environmental policy—United States.
I. Title. II. Series.
    GE197.D84 2003
333.7'2—dc21   2003008803

British Library Cataloguing in Publication Data is available.

Printed in the United States of America

10 9 8 7 6 5 4 3 2 1

The paper used in this publication meets the minimum requirements of the American
National Standard for Permanence of Paper for Printed Library Materials Z39.48-1984.

*To Debra and Julie, whose patience, understanding,
and unswerving devotion mean the world to me,
and to Marissa, whose recent arrival
was eagerly anticipated*

Contents

Preface and Acknowledgments

The idea for this book began to take shape in the weeks leading up to the 1996 election. Every day, it seemed, my mailbox was filled with a deluge of campaign flyers, mostly negative in tone and substance. What caught my attention, though, was the steady barrage of ads, all of them attacking Democratic Congressman Frank Pallone, from some organization known as Americans for Job Security. As someone who teaches courses in American politics, I had thought I was pretty familiar with the candidates, parties, and interest groups involved in the campaign. Although I believe job security is a good thing, I had never heard of this organization. Who were they? What did they stand for? Why would a group in favor of job security attack Pallone for being against Social Security and environmental protection? And where did they get the money to send me—and plenty of other folks—all of those mailings? That the ads were wildly misleading only added to my sense of intrigue. I began to wonder if other organizations were also conducting these so-called issue ad campaigns. It turns out that they were, and so I decided to combine an investigation into this new form of political activity with a long-standing interest in environmental politics.

Although my name alone appears on the front of the book, this was really a collaborative effort. I am especially grateful to the many individuals associated with environmental groups for speaking with me and answering my many questions. Although it may not be directly reflected in these pages, I learned quite a bit from the people who spoke or corresponded with me. Much of the early research for this book took place while I was teaching at Rider University, where my colleagues, especially Frank Rusciano, offered great support and encouragement. In particular, I would like to thank the Faculty Research and Patent Committee for granting me a sabbatical so that I could undertake the early research and the writing of several chapters. Midway through this project, I joined the faculty at Colorado State University, in large part because I found the idea of joining a vital community of scholars with similar interests too good to resist. My thanks also go to Michael Briggs of the University Press of Kansas, who graciously allowed me the time to complete this manuscript. I would also like to thank Michael Kraft and the anonymous readers who reviewed the manuscript for the University Press of Kansas, for their detailed insights and suggestions. Kenneth Godwin, Shanto Iyengar, Chris Bosso, and Mike Roloff also read sections of the manuscript and offered valuable advice.

The Green Agenda
in American Politics

1

Environmental Activism in
the United States

The environmental movement historically has been a minor, rather ineffectual
player in the political process. Its engagement has been tentative and diffident—
it plays at politics rather than going to war.
—Philip Shabecoff, *Earth Rising*

On January 5, 2001, after a lengthy rule-making proceeding involving more than
six hundred public hearings and a record 1.6 million official public comments, the
Forest Service issued the Roadless Area Conservation Rule. The rule prohibited
most commercial logging and road building in almost 58.5 million acres of roadless areas in the national forests. Although the newly elected Bush administration
soon announced plans to review the Forest Service's decision, the issuance of the
rule was a major victory for the coalition of conservation organizations who had
sought it. The Roadless Area Conservation Rule was significant for several reasons, not the least of which was that it was the largest land protection measure
since the 1980 Alaska National Interest Lands Conservation Act. More importantly, though, the campaign for the roadless forest rule provides a glimpse into
the future of environmental advocacy.[1]

It was a collaborative effort, involving more than five hundred national, regional, state, and local environmental groups. It was also very sophisticated, using
public opinion polling to ascertain attitudes about forests, and thereby shape a
consistent and effective message. To that end, the Heritage Forest Campaign, the
national group spearheading the effort, conducted weekly conference calls with
local groups, enabling them to coordinate their actions with groups in other states.
For over two years, the roadless forest campaign combined traditional and online
organizing, with groups educating and mobilizing their memberships through
community meetings as well as email action alerts and websites. And, because the
campaign was exceptionally well financed, groups were able to communicate
their message broadly, and in a variety of ways, including door-to-door contacts,
direct mail, the Internet, video, telephone, and radio and television advertising.[2]

The campaign to protect roadless areas had its roots in a decades-long effort
by conservation organizations seeking greater protections for the national forests.[3]
The creation of the Heritage Forest Campaign in 1998 was, however, a turning

point in making the rule change possible. The Heritage Forest Campaign was launched by a $1.4 million grant from the Pew Charitable Trusts to the National Audubon Society. Over the next two years, a dozen foundations gave more than $10 million to more than three dozen environmental groups seeking to protect roadless areas.[4]

Environmental activists say the money, the bulk of which came from the Pew Charitable Trusts, was unprecedented for a public lands issue. The money enabled the participating groups to mail thousands of form letters and postcards to the White House and to Forest Service officials asking that all logging be banned in roadless areas and that the new protections be extended to the Tongass region in Alaska. A number of groups produced and distributed brochures and videotapes explaining the proposed rule and urging viewers to take action. The Heritage Forest Campaign bought television and newspaper ads, commissioned numerous public opinion polls throughout the nation, manned phone banks, and created its own website, which was created by the Technology Project. The website included links to the participating groups, some of which prepared reports on the issue and encouraged visitors to take immediate action. At one point, visitors to the site needed to send an electronic postcard to policymakers before gaining access to the rest of the site. Perhaps the most controversial expenditure, however, was for a hospitality suite at the Hyatt Hotel in Alexandria, Virginia, in 1999, when the Forest Service held one of its first public meetings on the proposed rule. In fact, the groups spent so much that the House Subcommittee on forests and forest health later convened a hearing to look into the matter.[5]

The Heritage Forest Campaign also illustrates the technological sophistication of contemporary advocacy efforts. As a case in point, ONE/Northwest, a nonprofit organization based in Seattle that provides technology assistance to conservation activists and organizations, provided training and assistance to more than half the groups in the Heritage Forests Campaign. The group also conducted major technology upgrade projects for the Oregon Natural Resources Council and the Washington Wilderness Coalition, both key players in the campaign.[6] For both organizations, ONE/Northwest installed new computers, trained the staff in their use, and helped strategize on how to make the best use of the new technology. A key part of the plan was to use email and the Internet as a means of educating the public and generating public comments for the rule making. According to Ken Raitt, conservation director of the Oregon Natural Resources Council and an architect of the Heritage Forests Campaign, "Internet organizing has been a major component of the Heritage Forests Campaign strategy. The technology infrastructure that ONE/Northwest created for ONRC played a significant role in moving this effort forward to success." John Leary, director of the Washington Wilderness Coalition, claimed, "Improved technology is making it possible for us to inform and activate our members in order to achieve permanent protection for all of Washington's wildlands, and to coordinate our efforts with a larger national roadless area campaign."[7]

Pew's initial grant to Audubon came about as a result of conversations between Steve Kallick, assistant director of Pew's environmental programs, and a handful of forest activists. Many of the activists believed that the Forest Service's 1999 announcement of its intent to study the possibility of a permanent road building ban in several regional forests created an opportunity for an even greater policy shift. Kallick said, "We thought it should be a national rule. We wondered whether or not it was possible, since it had never been done, to change a Forest Service planning process in midstream. I had to do some fast-talking within our institution to convince people we weren't crazy." Responding to complaints from industry groups about being outspent, Kallick said, "The bottom line here is not what we did was wrong, but they're angry that what we did was so effective. They don't mind if foundations support environmental groups as long as they don't accomplish great change. What is unusual here was this unprecedented historical scale of great change." And it was effective. The number of public comments generated by the campaign was a record for a federal rule-making proceeding, and Forest Service data on the 1.1 million comments received during the first public comment period showed that supporters of the new rule outnumbered opponents by an incredible margin of twenty-eight to one.[8] In addition, the campaign was highly effective in mobilizing citizens to attend the many public hearings convened by the Forest Service. In most instances, the overwhelming majority of people speaking at those hearings supported greater forest protection.

Although the Heritage Forest Campaign may prove to be unique, especially in its funding, it seems likely that it will be a model for future advocacy and public education campaigns. For starters, the campaign did not just happen. It was carefully planned and executed. In fact, Kallick noted, "For ten years, we've been working closely with members of the environmental community to set up projects that are different and to set up paradigms for advocacy. This campaign is an exceptional example of a model we've been tinkering with and improving upon for ten years."[9] The reliance on computer and communications technology, the use of focus groups and public opinion polling to develop persuasive conservation messages, and greater coalition building among environmental groups will increasingly become the norm. Similarly, groups will resort more often to indirect lobbying techniques designed to shape public perceptions of environmental issues and to encourage their members, and others, to contact policymakers.

AMERICAN ENVIRONMENTALISM TODAY

Compared to thirty years ago, the environmental movement is clearly larger, better funded, more sophisticated, and more active politically. Despite these advances, many observers argue that the movement has very little to show for it. Mark Dowie, for example, contends that environmental groups lack the resources to compete with either corporate lobbyists or corporate campaign contributions.[10]

Others put the blame squarely on environmental groups themselves. In some ways, leading an environmental organization these days must be like managing a baseball team or driving a car—everybody thinks they can do it better.

Consider for a moment some of the familiar charges directed at environmental groups in recent years. One set of critics, mostly corporate and conservative, contends that environmentalists are too strident, too confrontational, too narrowly focused on their own particular issues, and too litigious.[11] In their view, environmental groups are powerful and effective. Many of these critics also say that environmental groups cynically rely on distorted or sensational claims in their fundraising and membership appeals, and are actually more interested in selling books, T-shirts, and calendars than in protecting the environment. At the same time, some environmental activists contend that the national groups have grown so dependent on donations from corporations and foundations that they are either unable or unwilling to take principled stands on important issues. According to this camp, the national groups lack passion, are too tame, and are too eager to compromise. In their view, the environmental lobby is weak and ineffective. The contradictory nature of these criticisms suggests that not all of them can be true.

This book tries to sort out these claims. My aim is to provide an overview of environmental group activity in American politics, not to offer an exhaustive account of every political tactic or strategy ever used by an environmental organization. Consequently, some important topics will not receive the detailed treatment scholars might expect—that would be another book, one written primarily for a more specialized audience. For this reason, I have opted to omit any extended discussion of litigation, which has been perhaps the most effective weapon in the arsenal of environmental groups. Litigation, in fact, is such an important tool that it could (and should) be the basis for an entirely separate book. Similarly, I do not pay much attention to the activities of more confrontational groups such as Earth Liberation Front. It is my impression that although such groups have attracted a considerable amount of attention from the media and law enforcement, they have not had much effect on either policy or elections and would thus add little to the issues discussed here. Again, something has to be left out, and what is omitted tells as much about my focus as what is included.

What is included here is a discussion of emerging trends in the ways in which American environmental groups approach electoral politics, and in the strategies they use to affect government decisions. More specifically, I seek to document and explain recent changes in the political behavior of such groups, including more aggressive participation in elections at all levels, as well as the use of new communication technologies to educate and mobilize their grass roots and to influence policymakers. I argue that the new forms of behavior are best understood as exercises in agenda setting, and are intended to raise the prominence of environmental issues and to shape voter perceptions of candidates. Put simply, environmental groups are devoting unprecedented resources and energy to framing issues and perceptions of candidates, in the hope that their preferred policies will be adopted and that their preferred candidates will be elected. Along the way, I will also assess the effectiveness of the new strategies and their impact on both elections and environmental policy.

To be sure, even the most casual observer of environmental groups knows that they have long been engaged in issue framing and agenda setting.[12] In debates over wilderness in the 1960s, for example, environmentalists worked to frame the policy alternatives as an either-or choice, between preservation of wilderness on the one hand, or its complete and utter destruction on the other. In that case, environmentalists deliberately constructed a narrow list of policy options that included their preferred policy option—preservation—and one decidedly less attractive alternative. The lesson of such framing, which political actors have known for some time, is that policy options are judged by the company they keep, and the best way to ensure that your preferred solution is adopted is to surround it with less attractive alternatives.[13] Consequently, it is not my intention to claim that environmental groups have only recently discovered the importance of issue definition.

Rather, my argument is that many groups are now experimenting with new *methods* of issue definition and agenda setting, and are now placing more emphasis on this task than in previous years. Groups are also devoting more attention to framing issues in a strategic manner. This shift is most apparent in elections, which environmental groups ignored twenty-five years ago, and in the large-scale public education campaigns routinely waged by the National Environmental Trust, the Sierra Club, and others. Groups are now communicating with vastly larger audiences in an effort to force environmental issues onto the political and electoral agenda. Whether or not these tactics have been effective is an open question, one that I hope to shed some light on in this book.

THE CONTEXT OF CONTEMPORARY ENVIRONMENTAL POLITICS

By almost any measure, the economic, political, and social contexts in which environmental groups operate have changed considerably since the first Earth Day in 1970. For one thing, many of the "third-generation" issues that groups confront today, such as climate change, are global in scale, and more complicated than the issues that dominated the early stages of American environmentalism.[14] In some ways, the easier problems were addressed first, but even in many of those cases, such as water and air pollution, solutions have been hard to find and costs have been prohibitive. In the economic realm, decades of deficit spending, and deficit budget politics, took their toll on environmental agencies and accomplishments. In the face of constant budget shortfalls, politicians often sacrificed environmental programs in favor of more pressing economic priorities. The political context is also very different, because the environment is now a partisan issue, with Democrats generally far more supportive of environmental laws and regulations than are most Republicans. Bipartisanship, once common in the early 1970s, is now the exception. Of course, the environment is not the only issue that divides the parties, but it is emblematic of a larger ideological split that marks modern American politics. Since the early 1980s, the Republican Party has waged relentless attacks on government in general, and on regulation in particular. Those attacks contributed in no small way to declining public trust in government and to the Republican takeover of Congress in 1994. In the end, argues Phil Shabecoff, those events ultimately hurt environment groups because they had relied so heavily on government to address environmental problems.[15] With oversight and appropriations under Republican control, faith in free markets and private sector solutions displaced government regulation as the preferred instruments of public policy.

For all of these reasons, and several others to be discussed later, environmental groups have been playing defense for much of the last twenty years. Indeed, it is frequently pointed out that although environmental groups have been very effective in beating back most efforts to repeal or weaken environmental laws, they have been unable to secure many significant policy gains. While that claim is certainly true, it also applies to almost all progressive interest groups. What sort of policy breakthroughs, for example, can labor unions claim as their own in the last twenty years? What about women's groups? Consumer advocates? Civil rights organizations? Now that you're done wracking your brains—probably in a futile attempt to conjure any meaningful policy victories by those groups—it should be clear that environmental groups just might have done all that they could hope for, given the difficult political and economic circumstances in which they have been operating. With either the White House or one branch of Congress under Republican control for all but two of the last twenty-two years, progressive groups have had little choice but to play defense. Sometimes the best offense is a good defense.

It should be clear by now that I think some of the criticisms directed at environmental groups are inaccurate. I tend to side with Christopher Bosso, who argues that the national environmental groups, despite their troubles, play a crucial role in a political system dominated by pressure groups. For example, one complaint commonly made by environmental activists about the mainstream organizations is that they have become conventional lobby groups who have sacrificed their ideals for the desire to retain their status as "players" in the Washington political game. In the best of all possible worlds, such behavior would not be desirable. But, as Bosso notes, we don't live in such a world, and until we do only the national organizations have the resources and expertise to stand up against governments and entrenched corporate interests, pursue complex lawsuits in the courts, and offer financial and technical assistance to activists in the local, state, and global arenas.[16] If the national groups did not lobby or litigate, does anyone really believe that the environment would be in better condition? This is not to suggest, however, that environmental groups are immune from criticism.

By the early 1990s, for example, it was apparent that many of the groups had emphasized other issues at the expense of grassroots organizing. When wise use and property rights groups, with considerable financial assistance from extractive businesses and conservative interests, turned out a considerable number of supporters in the congressional elections of 1992 and 1994, the environmental community got the message. A Washington presence, while important, was clearly insufficient, especially with the Republican takeover of Congress and an increasing shift of policy responsibility to the states. Without Democratic allies in their familiar leadership positions, environmental and other progressive groups confronted a much less hospitable Congress. And despite record fundraising, the groups could never hope to match the resources their opponents can bring to bear on the legislature, courts, or the federal bureaucracy. This became even more apparent when the 104th Congress unleashed an unprecedented assault on environmental laws and regulations. Every day, it seemed, a new series of budget cuts, appropriations riders, or legislative reauthorizations threatened a different program or agency.[17] Lobbyists for environmental groups were nearly overwhelmed by the need to fight so many battles, and it is unlikely that they would have succeeded without waging a massive, well-orchestrated grassroots campaign. Letters, phone calls, and faxes from angry constituents compelled a number of moderate Republicans, mostly from the Northeast, to backtrack from earlier votes, at least in part because of the possible electoral ramifications. That experience showed groups that, for both political and policy reasons, it made abundant sense to do the hard work of rebuilding the grass roots.

The hard times of the early 1990s clearly spurred some soul searching among many of the national groups. The Sierra Club, for example, chose to devote more resources to community outreach and to its local chapters and groups. It now does much more to assist chapters with training sessions for politics, media skills, and community organizing. The Audubon Society and the National Wildlife Federation (NWF) also decentralized their operations and diverted more money to support their local and regional chapters. Compared to ten years ago, the NWF pays considerably more attention to skills training and building the grass roots. The Environmental Defense Fund (now Environmental Defense) conducted a strategic plan in 1997 that, in addition to urging a commitment to community work, concluded that the group had spread itself too thin and recommended that the group focus its efforts on just four issues: climate change, oceans, protecting human health from toxics, and biodiversity. The Wilderness Society, which had been hurt by wise use groups' efforts to fight wilderness designations, opted in the early 1990s to build its grass roots with a specially funded "New Voices for the American West" campaign, which had its own newsletter, and by making grants to local conservation groups.[18] Finally, in the mid-1990s the Natural Resources Defense Council began to conduct media and grassroots campaigns in addition to its traditional focus on lobbying and litigation.[19]

Environmental writer Phil Shabecoff has even suggested that the mainstream groups need help from the grassroots community more than vice versa.[20] Although I agree with Shabecoff that the national groups could do a much better job in understanding and addressing environmental problems that affect people where they "live, work, and play," we shouldn't minimize the ways in which those groups can help grassroots organizations. For example, beginning in the mid-1990s some of the national groups and environmental donors set out to build the capacity of local and state-based organizations through grants, technological assistance, and other services. One of the most common forms of capacity building involved the provision of computers, software, databases, and other communication tools, as well as training on how to use them effectively. Armed with the new technology, leaders of state and local groups now use email lists to communicate with one another and with their members. Many groups have created websites to educate and mobilize their members, and the use of Internet-based "action alerts" to generate grassroots pressure on policymakers is now common. None of this would have been possible without the national groups and foundations.[21]

The Pew Charitable Trusts were among the donors that played a key role in this endeavor. Joshua Reichert, who managed Pew's environmental programs, was concerned that the national groups simply weren't very good at organizing at the state and local level, where decisionmaking power was devolving. Reichert also faulted the national groups for not making effective use of information and media tools to achieve their goals. So Pew began to fund the creation of new environmental organizations, like the National Environmental Trust and Environmental Media Services, who brought valuable organizing, communication, and media skills to the environmental cause.[22] Although there is still considerable room for improvement, in the last five years environmental groups have, for the most part, become much better at developing and communicating their messages. This is largely a direct result of the capacity-building efforts mentioned above. Hundreds of individuals have attended training sessions sponsored by the national groups and donors, and thousands more have access to the same information via the Internet and email. As a result, groups are learning what type of communication strategies work to frame issues and shape public and elite understandings of environmental issues. Despite these improvements, though, some argue that the national groups still do not devote enough resources to media campaigns, especially on television, and that grassroots campaigns are hindered by a lack of expertise in and resources for getting stories to the media. Obviously, groups will need money—and plenty of it—if they are to engage in expensive television advertising campaigns.[23]

Fortunately, business has never been better for many of the nation's environmental groups. Thanks to a booming stock market through much of the past decade, donations to environmental groups reached $3.5 billion in 1999, nearly double that of 1992. According to the National Center for Charitable Statistics, which monitors nonprofit fundraising, individuals, companies, and foundations gave an average of $9.6 million per day to environmental groups in 1999. As one might expect, though, some groups do better than others. The nation's twenty largest groups received almost 30 percent of the contributions in 1999, and the top group, the Nature Conservancy, received $402 million, more than the combined totals of the next six groups.[24] Whether environmental groups can expect to do as well in a bear market and in the aftermath of September 11 is doubtful, at least in the short term. But clearly, environmental groups have more money than ever before, and this has allowed them to do more things, and to do them in a more professional manner.

Knudson and others have also criticized environmental groups for relying too heavily on gloom-and-doom fundraising appeals. As anyone who receives mail from environmental groups well knows, most of their direct mail features one impending disaster or another. The reason for this, notes Daniel Beard, chief operating officer of the Audubon Society, is that it works. "So," says Beard, "what you get in your mailbox is a never-ending stream of crisis-related shrill material designed to evoke emotions so you will sit down and write a check. I think it's a slow walk down a dead-end road. You reach the point where people get turned off."[25] To be sure, groups do exploit issues to raise money and attract new members. And yet, as many groups know, it is often necessary to shout in order to get people's attention and, more importantly, to move them to take action. And it's not like environmental groups are the only ones guilty of hyping issues. Supporters of drilling in ANWR, for example, routinely cited the "thousands of jobs" that drilling would create and the "thousands of lives" that would be lost by raising CAFE standards. As Ronald Libby argues, many environmental groups believe that the long-term effects of hyperbolic advocacy ads are innocuous. Those who support the group will, in his view, tolerate sensationalism, and only those who disagree with the groups will be upset.[26]

ENVIRONMENTAL GROUPS AND ELECTIONS

With respect to electoral politics, it has frequently been noted that environmental issues—and environmental organizations—are rarely significant factors in American political campaigns, especially at the national level.[27] And although a clear majority of Americans claim to be environmentalists, other issues typically figure more prominently in both campaign rhetoric and voter decisions. In explaining this phenomenon, Christopher Bosso and Deborah Lynn Guber argue that the low salience of environmental issues creates a "permissive consensus" that, in the absence of obvious popular dissent or electoral reprisal, gives political leaders wide latitude in designing policies. They also suggest that environmental groups need to become much better at issue framing and mobilizing public concern if environmental issues are to become important in elections.[28]

Others have suggested that a lack of money, strategic thinking, and political infrastructure have also hampered the electoral success of environmental groups. Shabecoff, for example, in a stinging critique of the political activities of the environmental movement, offers a veritable laundry list of its shortcomings. He argues, for example, that the national environmental groups devote only 1 percent of their budgets to politics, an amount that is dwarfed by their corporate opponents.[29] As a result, any attempt to "buy influence" through direct contributions is a game environmentalists cannot hope to win. Shabecoff states that the national environmental organizations need to "organize for political power" and become far more aggressive in elections. In his view, this would require raising much more money and concentrating it on the electoral process, albeit in new ways. It would also require building an army of grassroots political organizers, made up of both volunteers and paid staff, who would operate in all states and in many communities, going door to door, educating citizens, and getting out the vote. To be effective in electoral politics, groups would clearly need to build an infrastructure by training large numbers of campaign organizers, media specialists, and political fundraisers. Media specialists are a critically important need, he suggests, and although there has been a distinct improvement in recent years, many groups still lack public relations and lobbying skills. Given the national media's lack of interest in environmental issues, it is critically important for groups to be able to explain how their agendas link with the real needs of everyday citizens, and why those issues should matter on election day.[30]

Shabecoff and others have also suggested that environmentalists need to become better at building electoral coalitions with one another and with other groups.[31] The goal would be to construct a larger, broader, and potentially more successful political coalition, one that would win more often at the polls. While noting that the so-called Green Group of about twenty organizations does meet to discuss issues and tactics, Shabecoff argues that it "does not represent an organized core of the environmental movement—certainly not when it comes to electoral politics."[32] Although there have been specific circumstances in which environmentalists have tried to mobilize grassroots activists at the state and local level, these efforts have been sporadic and ad hoc. Real success would instead utilize the many local groups, which have not only some political skills but also passion, an important element in elections, especially in those characterized by low turnout.[33]

Some of these criticisms are accurate, but others are not. For example, although environmental issues are not significant factors in presidential elections, they can and have played an important and in some cases decisive role in congressional elections, as well as in state and local races. In part, this is because environmental groups have become more active in recent election cycles, and have raised and spent record amounts of money. More importantly, some of the largest groups have been spending their political money in new ways. In addition to contributing directly to candidates for federal office, as had been their usual practice, the League of Conservation Voters and the Sierra Club now use most of their money to mount less tightly regulated independent expenditure and issue advocacy campaigns. And after years of inaction and neglect, a rapidly growing number of organizations have also begun to devote considerable time and resources to influencing state and local elections, including a number of important statewide ballot initiatives.

In addition to their political spending, many environmental groups have also become involved in a range of activities typically associated with political parties, including voter registration drives, candidate recruitment and training, and fund-raising. Indeed, some of the national environmental groups have become sophisticated players in electoral politics. They concentrate their efforts and resources on competitive races, they carefully target voters, and, in some cases, they provide candidates with polling and precinct data, as well as the assistance of professional campaign staff and volunteers. In addition to registering and targeting voters, groups routinely utilize phone banks and extensive public education campaigns to inform and mobilize voters and have even conducted elaborate get-out-the-vote efforts on election day. In close contests, these "ground war" campaigns can make the difference between winning and losing.[34]

The Republican takeover of Congress in 1994 prompted environmental groups to alter their electoral strategies and political spending in an effort to play a larger role in national elections. In the early days of the 104th Congress, Republicans proposed sweeping changes to existing environmental policy, including gutting the Endangered Species and Clean Water Acts, selling off or privatizing the public lands, and opening huge tracts of wilderness areas and wildlife refuges to drilling, mining, and logging. Faced with the most serious threat to environmental laws and regulations in decades, environmental groups ratcheted up their lobbying, fundraising, and public education efforts. Although typically short of money, environmental groups do possess some valuable resources, such as politically savvy national organizations and dedicated grassroots activists who can educate the public about issues, provide volunteers for campaigns, and get out the vote.

Although environmental groups are raising and spending more money, their direct contributions to candidates have significantly declined. So where is all the money going? At least some of it takes the form of independent expenditures supporting or opposing particular candidates, an increasingly popular form of campaign spending since the 1990s. Environmental groups did not begin making independent expenditures until 1994, and then only in relatively small amounts. But after the League of Conservation Voters (LCV) and the Sierra Club combined to spend $200,000 in a special Oregon Senate race in January of 1996, independent expenditures by the two groups skyrocketed. In fact, the LCV opted to use the vast majority of the $1.3 million it raised for independent expenditures rather than direct contributions to candidates.

Environmental groups also broke new ground in 1996 with the use of issue advocacy advertising. Issue ads are often thinly disguised campaign ads designed to encourage a vote for or against a specific candidate. Initially, Citizen Action and the Sierra Club were the only environmental groups to engage in such activity, but their success has encouraged others to follow suit. In subsequent elections, groups spent millions trying to force environmental issues onto the campaign agenda in select congressional races. Total issue advocacy spending by environmental groups in 2000 has been estimated as high as $20 million dollars; but since such spending is not disclosed, that figure is only an educated guess.

Campaigns since the 1990s are increasingly marked by the involvement of individuals and groups not formally affiliated with either the candidates or the parties. This is because federal election laws limit direct contributions by both individuals and groups. Such actors can, however, spend unlimited amounts independently or on issue advocacy campaigns. In a departure, environmental groups are now playing this game by relying less on direct contributions and more on the newer forms of political spending. The explanation for this shift in tactics is quite simple: environmental groups have never been able to match direct contributions from corporate interests, so they have decided to spend their scarce resources in ways that leverage their political influence. The virtue of independent expenditures and issue advocacy is that they allow the groups themselves to inject environmental issues into campaigns, rather than waiting passively for the candidates to raise them. In short, the new forms of spending increase the ability of environmental groups to define the issues in campaigns and drive the debate.

All forms of political spending, including the newly popular varieties, should be viewed in this light. Environmental groups, like other political actors, struggle to define the nature of political issues, lest others define them first. The increased use of issue advocacy and independent expenditures demonstrates that environmental groups are trying to adapt their behavior in response to two significant changes in the political environment. The first was the collapse of the campaign finance rules, which opened the door even wider to wealthy donors, while the second was the Republican takeover of Congress. In conjunction, these two developments have altered the political landscape and forced environmental groups to adapt their approach to electoral politics.

WHAT'S NEW IN ENVIRONMENTAL ADVOCACY?

New forms of political spending are not the only departures from previous practice. Environmental organizations are now engaged in more types of behavior to influence policy outcomes. As a case in point, the Sierra Club has sponsored highly aggressive, and expensive, lobbying and public education campaigns in an effort to shape public opinion and influence government decisions. These campaigns have utilized new communication technologies and strategies as they seek to frame policy debates. For example, expensive television issue advocacy campaigns on pending environmental issues, patterned after election ad campaigns, seek to influence policymakers by raising public awareness of the environment as a political issue. Efforts to shape public opinion are not limited to specific legislative or regulatory proposals; rather, environmental groups also try to encourage the public to "think green" as a means of shaping public opinion and thus the political agenda.

A number of scholars have noted that advocacy by environmental groups began to change in the early 1990s. As a case in point, Mitchell, Mertig, and Dunlap suggested that although groups were using the same tactics as in earlier periods, there was something different about environmental advocacy. What was new, they argued, was "the scale of the environmental movement's advocacy, its sophistication, and especially its continuity," as groups can now be involved in all stages of policymaking.[35] Those trends have not only continued; they have gained momentum.

Compared to even ten years ago, advocacy by environmental groups has changed in several ways. First, lobbying efforts by environmental groups of all sizes today are more professional and strategic. In large part, that is the result of a concerted capacity-building effort by foundations and others, which have boosted the resources and skills of many groups. Second, the large national groups now put greater emphasis on their grass roots and do more indirect lobbying than ten years ago. According to Kraft and Wuertz, environmental groups increased the frequency and sophistication of their indirect lobbying as they discovered that direct lobbying was becoming less effective in a changed political environment.[36] Grassroots campaigns serve a variety of organizational goals, such as attracting new members, energizing existing members, and stimulating media coverage. Perhaps more importantly, such campaigns can generate public pressure for groups' policy agendas and, as the messages from the grass roots echo the sentiments of group leaders, can help reinforce and legitimize the arguments of the groups' lobbyists. When the public is mobilized, the thinking goes, officials will see that the group's position has support and will thus act accordingly. This is especially true if a previously uninvolved segment of society expresses its views.[37]

The methods of generating and coordinating grassroots campaigns have also shifted, thanks to advances in communication technology, which makes communication quicker and cheaper. Today, mainstream environmental groups use web magazines and the Internet to create and mobilize activist networks. These tools are designed to educate grassroots members on local issues, train local activists, and establish more meaningful relationships with legislators at the state and federal levels. In fact, technology has made it possible for some groups to create a "cybergrassroots" consisting of large numbers of people linked through the Internet, rather than through local chapters.[38]

Environmental groups also monitor many more issues than before, at all levels of government, and are capable of alerting their activist networks of pending votes on very short notice. Consequently, the groups can not only do more to educate their members and the public about issues, they can also generate large numbers of phone calls, emails, faxes, and letters to public officials within hours. Local chapters of groups like the Sierra Club now routinely coordinate "letters to the editor" campaigns in an effort to call attention to environmental issues and to influence the way the public thinks about them.

Another recent development is that environmental organizations now lobby everyone—their own members, other interest groups, the general public, and the media—instead of just the usual suspects in legislatures, the executive branch, and the courts. To a significant degree, this "all-directional lobbying" is based on the recognition that all of these targets are linked. Success in policymaking now demands that groups stay in almost constant communication with everyone. Yet another trend is that environmental groups are now building coalitions more often and, in some cases, establishing permanent links that allow them to take advantage of each other's unique strengths and resources. Again, technological advances have made it easier for groups to work together and to piggyback their messages on one another, spreading them more quickly and to a broader audience.

There is also considerable evidence that many organizations are devoting more attention to crafting better conservation messages and to communicating them more effectively. In the words of one activist, "None but the most scrappy grassroots groups would dare invest in a major communications campaign without 'field testing' the message first."[39] Environmental activists have embraced the value of strategic communications. Many are putting a higher priority on gaining and holding public attention, an important factor as they try to define environmental issues and shape the public agenda.

Finally, technology has had a profound effect on how some environmental groups pursue their goals. Groups can use the Internet, for example, to provide enhanced services to existing members, or as a tool to recruit new members. Groups can also use their websites to raise money, either by soliciting donations or by selling products, such as calendars, books, and T-shirts. Besides these ends, groups can and have used the Internet to publicize their activities, to disseminate research findings to the public, media, and policymakers, and to encourage citizens to become more politically active. As such, technology has become a critical element in group outreach and advocacy. Thanks to the spread of computer and communications technologies, leaders can communicate with each other, group members, and policymakers more quickly. More generally, technology allows conservation groups to exercise greater control over the content and timing of their messages, to communicate them cheaper, and to a broader audience. In fact, the use of sophisticated databases, software, direct mail, websites, phone banks, toll-free numbers, television and radio advertising, video, and email allows groups to send different messages to different audiences.[40] The same technologies that make it easier for groups to communicate with the public also provide the public with additional tools for communicating with one another and with policymakers.

In many ways, then, environmental advocacy is in flux. The argument offered here is not that environmental groups are doing anything completely new. Rather, they continue to do many of the same things they have always done, but in different ways and with more intensity. Depending on their own particular expertise, some environmental groups seek to educate and mobilize the public, others engage in policy analysis and research, and still others litigate. A few groups try to do it all.[41] Today, there is also a growing awareness that these tasks are inextricably linked. In the words of a Wilderness Society activist, "Our economic and ecologic analyses inform the work we do in advocacy and public education."[42] In the end, environmental advocacy is still about the communication of policy information. Current technology, though, allows groups to make policy information available to a broader audience, in the hope that the audience will use that information to push for stronger environmental programs.

That said, it should also be noted that the trends described above do not apply equally to all environmental groups. There are thousands of groups active in the United States today, with different resources at their disposal, and there are wide variations in the technology, tactics, and strategies they employ. Although many groups have embraced sophisticated new methods of advocacy, many others have not. Most of the large national groups, for example, have resources that are not available to smaller groups, and have been able to purchase technology and the expertise to use it effectively. Similarly, the record on coalition building is mixed as well. Generally speaking, groups of all types are forging links among themselves, and in some places there are renewed efforts to construct a broad-based movement linking environmentalists with groups representing labor, women, the poor, farmers and ranchers, sportsmen, and churches. There is scant evidence of similar trends in other locations, however. It may be that there is more talk about coalition building than there are actual, sustained examples, but even if that is so, it represents a shift from the early 1990s.

WHAT EXPLAINS THE CHANGES IN ENVIRONMENTAL ADVOCACY?

The evolution in strategies and tactics shows that environmental groups have adapted to their own changing political circumstances and to broader institutional developments in American politics. Most notably, after the 1994 midterm election environmentalists had fewer friends in Congress, especially at the top of the key committees and subcommittees. For the first time in a generation, most national environmental organizations found themselves without direct access to the congressional majority in at least one chamber. Under these new circumstances, the groups could no longer rely so heavily on an "inside" approach to congressional lobbying because the Republicans, who now controlled both chambers, were much less receptive to their policy goals. A greater emphasis on an "outside" or indirect strategy of grassroots lobbying, in which groups would mobilize public opinion in an attempt to resist congressional efforts to weaken environmental laws, was thus in order. At the same time, twelve years of Republican presidents had rendered the federal courts decidedly less receptive to suits brought by environmental organizations. This was especially true of the D.C. Circuit, which plays a crucial role in overseeing the actions of key regulatory agencies. Not wanting to risk losing in court and thus setting bad precedent, a number of groups decided that they needed to explore options to litigation.

As an example of the new approach, shortly after the election a number of the national groups met to plan their response to what was called the "Republican War on the Environment." The strategy they developed involved mobilizing their members by way of a massive grassroots lobbying campaign, which was communicated through direct mail, television advertising, and the Internet. The groups prepared and distributed "Breach of Faith," a report detailing the Contract with America's impact on the nation's environmental laws. One version of the report was distributed via email to thousands of members nationwide.

The loss of congressional access, coupled with an increasingly skeptical federal judiciary, meant that the only thing standing between environmental groups and their worst policy nightmares was the Clinton White House, which had profoundly disappointed many activists by failing to act more aggressively in support of environmental programs. Nevertheless, a quick reading of the new political landscape convinced many in the movement to shift greater attention to lobbying the White House and executive branch agencies. Even if the groups failed to prevent Congress from weakening environmental protections, perhaps they could convince the president to use his veto pen or other administrative powers to accomplish their policy goals. Ultimately, this is what happened, as Clinton used the powers granted him by the Antiquities Act to create numerous new national monuments.

Another lesson gleaned from the 1994 elections was that the large national groups had relied too heavily on litigation and on their Washington lobbyists and had allowed the grass roots to wither away. This perspective was reinforced by the striking success of the "wise use" and property rights groups that year, who were important factors in a number of congressional elections. Many of these groups had engaged in extensive grassroots organizing utilizing methods developed years before, ironically enough, by progressive organizations. A growing number of national and statewide organizations responded to these developments by trying to rebuild their own grass roots through the traditional means of community organizing. As a case in point, in the late 1990s the Sierra Club launched a new effort to strengthen the links between its national offices and its local chapters and groups. The initiative had three central elements: to restore the group's activist culture by involving more members in the political process; to improve communication and coordination by encouraging Club volunteers to take advantage of new information technologies; and training in grassroots organizing skills. According to former Sierra Club president Robbie Cox, "To the degree that we invest in healthy groups and chapters and training for grassroots effectiveness, the Sierra Club's national priority goals also will be met."[43] In this sense, the national groups were acknowledging the criticisms leveled by many local activists, who had never forgotten the importance of grassroots organizing.

In addition to tending to their own base, several state, regional, and national organizations, along with prominent environmental foundations, launched programs to build the capacity of local conservation groups. These programs, which provided technology, training, and other resources, were aimed at increasing the ability of local groups to influence policymaking, enhance collaboration between conservation groups, and communicate more effective and consistent conservation messages.[44] The renewed effort to rebuild the grass roots reflects the belief that the movement needs to supplement its Washington lobbying efforts, and its televised advocacy campaigns, with a real presence on the ground. Simply put, environmentalists need people in communities working to put environmental issues on the agenda and to hold public officials accountable. Without real people in local communities, environmental groups are vulnerable to charges of being outsiders with little understanding of local conditions or problems.

2
Interest Groups, Issue Definition, and Agenda Setting

Use language that speaks to your audience.
—Biodiversity Project "Tip Sheet: Crafting Effective Messages"

Interest group lobbying has changed profoundly in recent decades as groups have adapted to dramatic shifts in the nation's political and institutional environment. The 1960s and 1970s were marked by significant institutional change and shifting patterns of interest group mobilization, which fundamentally altered the context in which policymaking, and thus interest group lobbying, took place. The new environment was more crowded, fragmented, and conflictual, and rewarded different types of group behavior. Although still necessary for groups seeking to influence policy, direct or inside lobbying was no longer sufficient. Instead, "all-directional lobbying," in which groups lobby the public, the media, and other groups, in addition to policymakers, became the norm.[1]

In addition to a significant expansion of the nation's policy agenda in the 1960s and 1970s, there was a profound change in patterns of interest group mobilization. There is compelling evidence to suggest that for much of the early part of the century American politics was characterized by a one-sided mobilization of interests. Quite simply, the vast majority of organized groups seeking to influence government were business groups. Organizations seeking to protect consumers, the environment, and other broad interests were greatly outnumbered. As a number of scholars have shown, however, there was a profound transformation in mobilization patterns in the 1960s and 1970s, when the number of organized interests, especially those representing consumer, environmental, and other so-called public lobby groups, grew exponentially. The result of this new mobilization pattern was that policy communities were more crowded than in the past. Issues that had once been of interest to a mere handful of actors were now of interest to many. Naturally, this growth in the number of groups contributed to a greater diversity of views in policy communities, which in turn contributed to greater policy conflict.

At the same time, there were significant reforms in policymaking institutions and processes. Congressional reforms, such as the weakening of seniority, increases in staff, and the growth in the number and power of subcommittees, rendered an already fragmented institution more so. Committee chairs lost power, jurisdictions were shuffled, and Congress became more open, democratic, and entrepreneurial. In many policy areas, like the environment, new committees competed for and claimed jurisdiction. Ambitious members of Congress urged their committees and subcommittees to become active in areas where political rewards might be expected. For groups that had been excluded from policymaking, the new, more open environment made it easier to find allies. If one committee proved to be unsympathetic, groups could simply shop for another. Antinuclear groups, for example, found it much easier to gain access to Congress after the Joint Committee on Atomic Energy, a strong supporter of nuclear power, was abolished and its responsibilities were parceled out to multiple committees.[2]

Similarly, the rise of the public lobby movement and its commitment to participatory democracy led to reforms that significantly increased public participation in administrative proceedings. Under pressure from both Congress and the federal courts, administrative agencies were required to hold public hearings before issuing new rules or revising existing ones; to provide opportunities for interested parties to comment on the proposed rules; and to provide careful explanations of their decisions for the public record. Congress enacted new laws, such as the National Environmental Policy Act, which required federal agencies to prepare environmental impact statements; these statements gave environmental activists an important tool for challenging agency decisions in court. At the end of the day, interests that had previously been excluded had greater access to agency deliberations and had an easier time monitoring their decisions.

SUBGOVERNMENTS AND POLICY CHANGE

Ultimately, these important structural changes transformed the shape of many policy communities, especially subgovernments. These policy communities, also known as iron triangles or policy monopolies, are small, stable groups of actors that dominate policy in a specific issue area, and were once thought to be descriptive of many policy areas. The typical iron triangle consists of three parts: the organized groups interested in a particular policy, the congressional committees and subcommittees with jurisdiction over the issue, and the executive agency bureaucrats responsible for that policy. Because each of the groups of actors benefits in some tangible way from the relationship, they are assumed to have complementary goals. In addition, these shared interests create strong incentives for the actors to cooperate, compromise, and reach agreements among themselves. Consequently, policymaking within subgovernments tends to be marked by incrementalism, because dramatic or abrupt policy changes could attract the attention of outsiders and thus jeopardize its autonomy. The chances of policy change increase dramatically when new actors and new perspectives are attracted to an issue.[3]

Policy monopolies were once thought to be autonomous and enduring, but even the most powerful policy monopoly does not operate in a vacuum. The exponential growth in the number of organized interest groups, together with congressional and administrative reforms, transformed the traditional patterns of interaction between agencies, committees, and interest groups and contributed to the demise of many subgovernments. According to Jeffrey Berry and others, policy monopolies simply cannot function in today's more open and conflictual policy environment. Constant policy battles and the glare of publicity mean that policy monopolies, which thrive on being left alone, can no longer control the flow of information about issues.[4]

Whether issue networks, advocacy coalitions, or other entities have replaced policy monopolies is a matter of considerable debate.[5] What is clear, though, is that compared to subgovernments, policy communities today are larger and less exclusive, in that they grant access to a broader range of participants. These same traits increase the likelihood of conflict, which can be quite intense. Furthermore, actors in subgovernments were presumed to have complementary goals that gave them a strong incentive to cooperate. In contemporary politics, on the other hand, actors often have competing policy goals and it sometimes makes sense for them to pursue a strategy of deliberate conflict, an approach that would have been quite risky in earlier times.

The environment in which organized groups seek to influence policy has changed quite a bit in recent years. For one, it is much more crowded. Compared to just twenty years ago, there are now more groups seeking to influence policy, and they engage in a much broader range of activities. In fact, groups are now so active that some claim there is little distinction between inside and outside lobbying strategies. William Browne, for example, argues that the emergence of a larger, more open, and more crowded policy environment, especially in Congress, created more work for groups, who had to lobby more people. "To lobby most successfully," argues Browne, "quite often means lobbying in all directions."[6] Learning what to do, who to speak with, and what to tell them took more time, more discussion, and more money. At the same time, groups could engage in lobbying tasks, techniques, and tactics that were once discouraged. Because Congress was more open, groups were free to criticize committees and their handling of policies without fear of retribution. Environmental groups, for example, could use the media to help push their issues, attack unhelpful policymakers, and reward their legislative allies. Lawsuits and protests could also be used to publicize issues and to generate grassroots pressure for policy goals.[7] It was during this period, for example, that the League of Conservation Voters began compiling and publicizing its "Dirty Dozen" list of candidates with poor environmental voting records.

As the new political environment encouraged organized interests to conduct more campaigns aimed at multiple targets, new communication and computer technologies gave groups additional and better means of communicating with their members and the public. Initially, groups communicated through the use of direct mail, newsletters, and glossy magazines; by the mid-1990s, groups employed television, faxes, email, and websites. Organized interests also began to make more of an effort to lobby the media, who were often useful allies in efforts to raise the prominence of a group's issues. Indeed, one estimate suggests that approximately half of the stories in the news originate with interest groups. Not surprisingly, it has been suggested that the chief target of group lobbying is often the media rather than the public.[8] As opinion leaders, the media can play a key role in reaching the public. Knowing this, groups provide reporters with information and try to frame it in ways that are conducive to the group's policy goals. In the last twenty years, accordingly, television, radio, and other forms of mass media communication have become essential elements of group lobbying strategies. In 1989, for example, the Natural Resources Defense Council employed a sophisticated and successful media campaign that was designed to persuade the EPA to impose an immediate ban on the use of Alar, a chemical used to ripen red apples. The NRDC prepared a report on the issue and hired a public relations firm to publicize it. According to the firm's president, "Our goal was to create so many repetitions of NRDC's message that average consumers (not just the policy elite in Washington) could not avoid hearing it. . . . The idea was for the 'story' to achieve a life of its own, and continue for weeks and months to affect policy and consumer habits."[9] Despite considerable disagreement over whether Alar really posed a significant danger to human health, sales of the product fell precipitously, and the EPA was forced into a lengthy and contentious dispute.

As might be expected, some interest groups adapted more readily to this new environment than others. Access to the money and expertise needed to employ the new communications tools, for example, is not equally distributed. Although technology costs have declined considerably in the last twenty years, and practically anyone can afford to create a website, the fact remains that some of the grassroots tools are not available to every interest group. Some groups were able to buy computers before others. Similarly, the emphasis on communications confers advantages on groups with experienced staff and resources in that area. Smaller environmental groups, it bears reminding, often rely on volunteers or part-time staffers for many vital tasks. Thus the need to lobby practically everyone helps those interests with professional lobbyists, deep pockets, or both. Furthermore, although indirect lobbying via television and radio advertising has become more prevalent, it remains very expensive, and many organized interests simply cannot afford it. Those that can may therefore have unrivaled opportunities to communicate their policy positions to mass audiences, and to do it in ways that can be quite compelling. For public interest groups, then, the onset of all-directional lobbying offers both opportunities and obstacles.

As we shall see, some environmental groups have adapted readily to these new circumstances. For the most part, though, the mainstream organizations have responded by changing their lobbying and electoral activities. A growing number of groups are becoming involved in elections, at all levels, and several have become quite aggressive in seeking to inject environmental issues into campaigns. As noted earlier, the new forms of behavior are best understood as exercises in agenda setting.

THE CHANGING ROLE OF INTEREST GROUPS IN ELECTIONS

By almost any measure, organized interest groups have become more active in recent elections. In fact, the increase in group activity in the 1990s has been so profound that a number of scholars argue that we are witnessing the birth of a new era in American politics, one marked by new relationships among political parties and interest groups and by the transformation of electoral politics itself. Paul Herrnson, for example, claims that the collapse of federal election campaign finance rules ushered in a new "postreform era" for political parties and interest groups that has the potential to "drastically alter the dynamics of congressional election politics." Similarly, Rozell and Wilcox contend that the American electoral system is in the process of shifting from a candidate-centered system to one that may focus increasingly on the agendas of coalitions of interest groups. Cigler and Loomis argue that, in this new era, the distinction between the politics of elections and the politics of policymaking is disappearing. Increasingly, they suggest, organized groups have come to see that electoral politics and policy are linked, and so now engage in "permanent campaigns" to secure the policy results they desire.[10]

Although these scholars disagree on the defining traits of the emerging era, the different analyses do yield some common elements. Compared to earlier periods, there are now more organized groups spending money to influence elections. In addition, the amount of interest group money in elections has increased dramatically, and much of this money is raised and spent in ways that are designed to evade the limits imposed by federal election law. The exponential growth of independent expenditures and issue advocacy by interest groups is an example of this trend. Significantly, a considerable portion of group electoral activity, including the new forms of political spending, is independent of the efforts of candidates and political parties. Lastly, the new era is marked by a "blurring" of the traditional roles of political parties and organized groups in elections. Instead of being rivals, political parties now act as group patrons, using so-called soft money to fund group electoral activities, such as voter registration drives and phone banks. In fact, some interest groups now routinely engage in activities that had previously been carried out by the parties, such as recruiting candidates, organizing campaigns, and running campaign ads. There is evidence that interest groups are now more important in educating and mobilizing voters, especially at the grass roots.[11]

Several factors are responsible for the emergence of this new era. One is the escalating cost of federal elections. With the rise of candidate-centered elections in the 1970s and 1980s, candidates increasingly turned to political consultants, pollsters, and other specialists rather than to the parties for help with their campaigns. Political parties eventually began to play the role of brokers by forming loose fundraising alliances with groups and by offering them assistance in directing contributions to particular candidates. At the same time, high reelection rates among congressional incumbents led many political actions committees to abandon their election-oriented strategy of contributing mostly to candidates who shared their policy views. Instead, PACs seeking to influence policy shifted their approach and began contributing mostly to incumbents, who were in a better position to help groups with their policy concerns. The desire for privileged access to policymakers subsequently led PACs to become more involved in areas of campaigning that had traditionally been carried out by political parties. Some groups, for example, began providing candidates with a range of campaign services, such as precinct targeting data, public opinion polls, fundraising help, voter mobilization, and grassroots organizing.[12] Both the League of Conservation Voters and the Sierra Club have provided candidates with trained field organizers and other professional assistance.

With campaign costs rapidly escalating, candidates, political parties, and interest groups began looking for new ways of overcoming the spending and contribution limits imposed by federal election law. As a case in point, after contributing the legal maximum to its candidates, the parties began channeling money from their various campaign committees to allied political action committees, which in turn made contributions to those candidates involved in tight races. Some groups also used party money to wage independent expenditure and issue advocacy campaigns. The parties also steered PAC money to state party organizations to assist in the party's generic advertising, voter registration, and get-out-the-vote efforts. In essence, these tactics allowed parties to spend additional money to help candidates without breaking laws that regulate the amount of soft money that parties can spend in individual states.[13]

As Herrnson and others note, these money-sharing arrangements provide mutual benefits to parties and their affiliated interest groups. To begin, groups often have greater credibility with the public among targeted populations, who are skeptical of claims made by political parties. In addition, most organized groups have mailing lists, newsletters, websites, and other resources that parties can use to communicate with group members and other voters. Today, parties often work with allied groups to develop and communicate specialized messages aimed at the group's members. By giving money to the groups, the parties gain access to these resources. Party contributions can also help cement the allegiance of weakly allied groups and keep them from bolting the party coalition. As for interest groups, they can shift money back and forth among themselves and any umbrella organizations they create in order to engage in partisan activity, while still enjoying the benefits of tax-exempt status and avoiding Federal Election Commission reporting requirements.[14]

Political parties have also turned to interest groups because, in many areas of the nation, the parties' grassroots infrastructures have crumbled. In Pennsylvania, for example, the Democratic Party no longer has a viable field organization or get-out-the-vote capabilities. Interest groups, in particular labor unions, have stepped in to fill the void. In Philadelphia, which once had a formidable political machine, "the labor movement basically is the party," says Joe Rauscher, president of the Central Labor Council in the city. According to Steve Rosenthal, the AFL-CIO's political director, "The parties have become shells to move money. It used to be that the party had someone on your block, in your workplace, in your district, reminding you to go out and vote. That doesn't exist anymore." In an era of low turnout and close partisan divisions in Congress, interest groups that are capable of mobilizing their members thus become vitally important and can make the difference between winning and losing.[15] In these circumstances, interest groups have a strong incentive to support candidates from their preferred party. Presumably, groups would have an easier time securing their policy goals if that party controls one or both chambers of Congress.[16]

Although both parties rely on interest groups to help reach voters, the Democrats seem particularly dependent on their affiliated groups. In addition to labor unions, environmental groups and civil rights organizations have played important roles in mobilizing voters on behalf of Democratic candidates in recent elections. The vast majority of candidates, parties, and organized groups now use computer technology and databases to target voters. The candidates and party organizations, however, tend to concentrate their efforts on those most likely to vote and on specific categories of swing voters. Increasingly, though, organized groups are supplementing these programs, with some making a special effort to communicate with infrequent voters. With sophisticated software, interest groups can merge their membership lists with information from dozens of separate databases, such as voter registration lists, voting records, census data, and magazine subscription lists. Groups can also use information from member surveys to add information about their attitudes and issue preferences. All of this information can then be organized into a computerized display of neighborhoods, precincts, and legislative districts. With all of this information available at the push of a button, organized groups can help candidates by targeting particular households for direct mail, telephone calls, and personal visits. As we will see in Chapter 4, the League of Conservation Voters Education Fund has in recent years been devoting considerable resources to this task.

New Forms of Political Spending

One of the most important aspects of the postreform era involves the growing use of independent spending by interest groups and political parties. Such spending increased dramatically after a number of court rulings in the middle of the past decade. In 1996, for example, the U.S. Supreme Court ruled in *Colorado Republican Federal Campaign Committee v. Federal Election Commission* that political parties could make unlimited independent expenditures. The term *independent expenditures* refers to spending on campaign activities, such as advertising, which expressly advocates the election or defeat of a specific candidate, but which is made without prior consultation with the candidates. Under the law, individuals and groups making independent expenditures may spend as much as they like, so long as the spending is not coordinated in any way with the candidate's campaigns. Although such spending faces no limits, it is subject to disclosure under FEC regulations.

Genuine issue advocacy refers to communications to the public whose primary purpose is to promote a set of ideas or policies. These sorts of ads usually focus on important policy issues or pending legislative matters. Electioneering issue advocacy, on the other hand, is often indistinguishable from the ads aired by candidates, and is designed to influence election results. Electioneering issue ads differ from genuine issue ads in several respects. First, election ads tend to focus on individual candidates rather than on issues, and they often seemed aimed at shaping the viewer's image of the candidate. Genuine issue ads, on the other hand, usually avoid depicting a candidate by name, voice, or appearance. They focus on issues. Secondly, electioneering issue ads are typically much more negative in tone, and make negative references to the personal traits of candidates and/or their positions. Genuine issue ads avoid personal references. Thirdly, genuine issue ads often offer toll-free phone numbers, encouraging viewers to call policymakers, while electioneering ads feature only regular phone numbers and addresses. According to the Brennan Center for Justice, these differences suggest that the sponsors of election ads are primarily interested in shaping viewers' images of candidates, while sponsors of genuine issue ads want the public to actually get involved in the issue, by writing a letter or making a call to a legislator. Finally, genuine issue ads air throughout the year, while electioneering ads, not surprisingly, air in the weeks before elections.[17]

Unlike independent expenditures, issue advocacy ads cannot explicitly advocate the defeat or election of a particular candidate. According to the Supreme Court, campaign finance restrictions apply only to "communications that in express terms advocate the election or defeat of a clearly identified candidate for federal office." According to the Court those express terms include "vote for," "elect," "support," "defeat," or "vote against." If a communication does not contain those "magic words," it is classified as issue advocacy and thus does not fall within the purview of federal campaign finance law. So long as interest groups avoid using the "magic words," their issue advocacy ads are therefore not subject to any spending and contribution limits, or even disclosure requirements. Groups sponsoring issue campaigns may spend as much they like without having to disclose the amount of their spending. Moreover, groups sponsoring issue ads do not have to disclose their contributors, so the public often does not know who is behind the ads. The "magic words" standard is thus a major loophole in federal election law. Even candidate ads, which by any standard are election ads, use magic words only 10 percent of the time, thus illustrating how unnecessary such words are to conveying an explicit electioneering message.[18]

Until quite recently, those seeking to influence electoral results did not widely employ issue advocacy campaigns. Rather, most used direct contributions or independent expenditures. The first use of issue advocacy to sway elections was in 1980, when the National Conservative Political Action Committee (NCPAC) spent $1.2 million to defeat six Democratic senatorial candidates. Despite the NCPAC's success, it was not until the early 1990s, when members of the religious right and term limit advocates sponsored issue campaigns, that the tactic was widely used in elections.[19] In 1992, for example, the Christian Action Network ran issue ads in twenty-four cities denouncing candidate Bill Clinton's "homosexual agenda." The Federal Election Commission challenged the ads, arguing that their timing, content, and sinister depiction of Clinton amounted to express advocacy. The court of appeals disagreed, however, ruling that the ads were intended to inform the public about political topics and were not an exhortation to vote against Clinton.[20]

The court decision sanctioning issue advocacy threw open the floodgates to similar campaigns by other groups. In the next election cycle, several term limits groups ran issue campaigns. Americans for Limited Terms, for example, spent $1 million nationwide, including $300,000 against House Speaker Tom Foley.[21] Another group, U.S. Term Limits, spent $75,000 in eighty-nine congressional districts that same year.

Traditionally, the FEC has viewed issue advocacy more skeptically than the courts. A 1992 FEC advisory opinion on the matter said that the "magic words" listed in Buckley are not required to prove express advocacy when the message is "read as a whole . . . with limited reference to external events [and when] susceptible to no other reasonable interpretation but as an exhortation to vote for or against a specific candidate."[22] Because the courts have generally not supported the FEC's position, issue advocacy campaigns have proliferated in recent election cycles.

Since 1996, both genuine and electioneering issue ads have become increasingly common. In the 1995–96 election cycle, for example, more than two dozen groups engaged in issue advocacy advertising, spending an estimated total of $135 to 150 million. To put that in context, all candidates for federal office that year spent an estimated $400 million for advertising, which means that advocacy groups spent more than a third of what the candidates themselves spent. Issue advocacy spending increased dramatically in the next two election cycles, to more than $500 million.[23] In 2000, issue ad spending by environmental groups amounted to approximately $20 million. According to figures compiled by the Brennan Center for Justice, in the 2000 elections organized groups spent an estimated $98 million to air 142,000 television ads, of which more than half was for electioneering ads. The total spending represents a ninefold increase from 1998, when groups spent less than $11 million to air 22,000 ads.[24] But these figures are merely estimates—the amount of money spent on issue advocacy is impossible to track with precision because such spending does not have to be reported to the Federal Election Commission.

Questions Raised by the New Forms of Political Spending

Because such spending is relatively new, it is difficult to draw any firm conclusions about its effects on elections. According to Rozell and Wilcox, it is possible that coalitions of interest groups will assume even more quasi-party functions in the future, including specialization in particular electoral activities. If that happens, they say, the worry is that "interest groups may establish themselves as the primary source of communications with voters, drowning out the voices of political parties and even the candidates themselves. Such a shift would damage the accountability of candidates in American elections and further weaken the parties."[25]

Others worry about the consequences of the parties' surrendering their traditional roles in voter education and mobilization to organized groups, especially because resource disparities mean that not all groups can participate in those efforts. In a representative democracy, political parties provide an important and perhaps essential vehicle for the representation of mass interests. This is particularly important for those segments of society that traditionally lack resources and have been underrepresented in the interest group competition that characterizes U.S. policymaking. But because the emerging system places so much emphasis on the ability to raise and spend large sums of money, some groups will be able to exercise even greater influence over our electoral system. And that is worrisome.[26]

Still others have expressed concerns that unregulated spending by groups has the potential to undermine the viability of the current candidate-centered system. More and more, office seekers are forced to share the stage with other actors who face no spending limits or disclosure requirements. With groups spending so much money, it is possible that candidates may lose the ability to set the agenda in their own campaigns. In a small but growing number of cases, congressional candidates have been outspent by outside groups, which made it quite difficult for the candidates to be heard above the fray. In many respects, agenda setting in a growing number of congressional districts now resembles a free-for-all, with the candidates themselves playing smaller roles.

Another worrisome outcome of the rise of independent expenditures and issue advocacy is that with the airwaves full of advertisements about national issues such as abortion, term limits, and gun control, there may be little room for discussions of local matters. Indeed, many worry that the new forms of political spending may be "nationalizing" local elections and, in the process, transforming them into "ideological battlegrounds for forces much bigger than individual candidates." In short, some fear that candidates may lose their ability to frame the issues to outside groups with national agendas. At the very least, it seems clear that the less regulated forms of spending can deprive candidates of their ability to dominate the campaign agenda in their districts. In such cases, as a result, there is greater uncertainty in congressional elections. Candidates, and their political consultants, dislike uncertainty because it makes planning campaigns much harder.

As an example, Herrnson notes that "candidates can no longer estimate the funds that are going to be spent against them by merely checking FEC records of their opponents' cash on hand."[27] Candidates in such an environment would have an even greater incentive to raise money to ensure their election, further ratcheting up the money race in American elections.

To date, only a handful of national environmental groups have undertaken independent expenditure and issue advocacy campaigns, but their success has led others, including a growing number of state organizations, to do so as well. Given their nonprofit status, many have been surprised at the group's ability to raise and spend large sums of money in elections. How nonprofit public interest groups have been able to do this is the focus of the next section.

EXPRESSIVE AND INSTRUMENTAL INTEREST GROUPS

Some scholars have suggested that there are two types of organized groups: those that seek exclusive and material benefits for their members, and those that don't. Most organized groups are assumed to be of the first type and to pursue policies that will materially benefit their members. Accordingly, much of their political activity is said to be "instrumental" in nature; that is, the group's activity is motivated primarily by the desire to influence policy outcomes. Although "expressive" groups also care about policy results, they are motivated primarily by moral or ethical considerations rather than by material self-interest. Accordingly, the goal of political action by expressive groups is not to secure a particular policy result, but to act in support of some deeply held value or ideal.[28] Such expressions may have an immediate policy payoff, but that is not the primary motivation. Rather, according to Salisbury and Conklin, "at the core of expressive political action is the idea that political success is not a necessary condition. It is the moral declaration itself that is the essential justification of the effort, and making the effort creates its own rewards."[29]

Given these motivations, expressive and instrumental groups are said to engage in very different methods of political activity. Because they seek specific policy goals, for example, instrumental groups are more likely to value ready access to policymakers. Therefore, they are more likely to form political action committees, whose contributions to incumbent legislators are aimed at securing a sympathetic hearing for the group's policy wish list. They also prefer an inside lobbying strategy, which allows them to deal directly with legislators and their staffs and not attract unwanted attention to their efforts. Because instrumental groups want something from policymakers, they go to great lengths to avoid antagonizing them. Consequently, the language used by instrumental groups in their communications tends to avoid inflammatory words or symbols that might fan the flames of conflict.

Expressive groups, on the other hand, rely less on direct lobbying and bargaining and more on an outside strategy of indirect lobbying, which is consciously designed to attract the attention of the media and the general public. For expressive groups, protests, symbolic actions, and other confrontational tactics can be useful in publicizing their cause and in expanding the scope of conflicts. Similarly, in seeking to engage and mobilize a broad audience, expressive groups will often use emotional and ethical appeals in their public communications. They will often claim to be underdogs in battles against powerful and evil enemies, like corporate polluters, for example. According to Salisbury and Conklin, expressive politics is defined by expression—by what is said, by the language that is used, and by the symbols and values invoked in policy debates.[30]

Ronald Libby has argued that interest groups scholars have failed to recognize that expressive groups often have deep roots in broad-based social movements, which provides them with a major source of political support in their efforts to change public policy. For this reason, those expressive groups that are rooted in social movements, such as environmental organizations, function both as conventional interest groups and as organizers of citizen protest. In other words, expressive groups sometimes act as interest groups and seek to influence government policy, but at other times they try to mobilize citizen activity in social movements.[31] Their political strategies at any given moment, as a result, will vary with the particular role they are playing at the time.

Libby also contends that although expressive groups typically lack the money of corporate interests, they do have some valuable, noneconomic resources that enable them to wage effective political campaigns. Among those resources are networks of enthusiastic grassroots supporters, important political skills, media savvy, and a reputation for wielding political influence. These resources, he argues, can compensate for a lack of money.[32]

So where do environmental groups fit into this discussion? The best answer, I think, is that it depends. Some groups are primarily expressive, some are instrumental, while many others are a mixture. Most environmental groups, especially those active at the state and local level, do not engage in overtly political activity. Only a handful of organizations have PACs, for example, or even endorse candidates. Many organizations do not conduct large-scale campaigns to mobilize the public. Groups that primarily engage in research, such as the World Wildlife Fund or Resources for the Future, are known for providing detailed analyses of environmental problems. Those groups prefer to work behind the scenes, providing research and information to policymakers in order to make better policy.

Some of the membership organizations, on the other hand, exhibit both instrumental and expressive elements. The Sierra Club and the Wilderness Society, for example, conduct extensive public education campaigns aimed at generating letters, faxes, and emails to policymakers. Quite often, the language used in these campaigns, like that in their membership and fundraising appeals, can be dramatic and emotional. But both groups also conduct policy research and have full-time lobbyists in the nation's capital. The Sierra Club is also very active in elections.

Groups like the Nature Conservancy, which buys land to set aside for preservation, neither lobbies nor engages in electioneering. The environmental movement, in short, is too varied to fit into any one category.

LOBBYING AND ELECTIONEERING BY NONPROFIT ORGANIZATIONS

Although it is widely believed that the tax-exempt status of many expressive groups severely limits their ability to engage in political activity, the reality is quite different. To be sure, tax laws do constrain lobbying and electoral activity by nonprofits, but they also permit such groups to participate in a wide range of political actions. When discussing nonprofits, it is important to distinguish between 501(c)(3) and 501(c)(4) organizations. Both types face some restrictions on their political activities, but tax laws grant the latter much more leeway. For example, 501(c)(4) groups may not make direct contributions to candidates, parties, or political action committees, and they may not make independent expenditures. But they can do lots of other things. For example, 501(c)(4) groups can endorse candidates for elective office, they can encourage contributions to particular candidates, and they can publish comparative ratings of candidates. Such forms of expressive advocacy may be communicated to the group's members, but not to the general public. In practice, this means that 501(c)(4) groups can send direct mail or email messages to their members announcing the endorsements, but they would be prohibited from advertising the same information in newspapers, because that would be considered a communication with the general public. But there are ways around those provisions. For example, Internal Revenue Service rules allow groups to coordinate their messages with candidates and political parties. Moreover, 501(c)(4) groups are allowed to issue press releases announcing endorsements to the reporters on their regular press contact list, and can even hold press conferences to announce the endorsement. They cannot, however, coordinate the press release or press conference with the candidate's campaign. But the candidate's campaign may publicize the endorsement.

501(c)(3) groups, on the other hand, including most state and local environmental organizations, face greater limits on their lobbying and electoral efforts. For example, whereas the law allows 501(c)(4) organizations to engage in unlimited lobbying, 501(c)(3) groups are allowed to spend only up to 20 percent of their budgets on legislative lobbying. Grassroots lobbying is even more circumscribed—only 5 percent of a group's budget can be used for grassroots lobbying of legislators. There are no limits, however, on 501(c)(3) groups with respect to litigation or attempts to influence agency rule making. And although they cannot engage in express advocacy, 501(c)(3) groups may engage in a broad range of nonpartisan election activities. Local environmental groups can, for example, conduct voter registration and get-out-the-vote campaigns. With respect to the latter, the geographical areas selected must be chosen by neutral criteria and not to the advantage of a particular candidate or party. Similarly, in their get-out-the-vote campaigns environmental organizations can target members of affiliated groups, so long as the choice is made because of the group connection, and not with an eye toward deciding the election. As an example, environmental groups may target members of other conservation organizations. The assumption, of course, is that those folks share an interest in environmental issues. In addition, 501(c)(3) organizations are permitted to conduct candidate forums and to distribute candidate scorecards, so long as they do not endorse or oppose particular candidates. The release of the scorecards, moreover, must not be timed to coincide with an election. Candidate scorecards that indicate whether the group agrees with the candidates are acceptable if the scorecards are distributed to the group's members, and not to the general public. Groups may also distribute "voting guides," which discuss candidates' voting records on issues of importance to the group, so long as the guides do not exhibit a bias in favor of any candidate. As noted above, they can even air issue advocacy television ads explaining the group's position on key issues, as long as they avoid explicitly endorsing or supporting particular candidates.[33]

As Ronald Shaiko has noted, the organizational structure of some of the nation's larger environmental groups has evolved in recent years, in order to maneuver around the IRS rules regulating nonprofit organizations. For example, 501(c)(4) groups face no restrictions on their ability to lobby Congress and the executive branch. The problem, however, is that the group's donors are not allowed to deduct their contributions, which acts as a disincentive for giving to the group. To solve this problem, a number of groups structure their organization as two separate entities: a 501(c)(4) lobbying and influence organization, and a 501(c)(3) education wing, which is tax exempt. According to Shaiko, the 501(c)(3) organization acts as the "idea chamber," while the 501(c)(4) serves as the "money chamber" that puts the idea on the street. Under this arrangement, donors can be directed to the 501(c)(3) organization, where contributions are deductible. Under IRS rules, 501(c)(3)s may make grants to the 501(c)(4) groups, as long as the funds are used to pay for organizational costs, like overhead, salaries, and rent, and not for lobbying purposes. But disentangling the finances of such groups, and determining which money paid for lobbying and which paid for salaries is next to impossible. In any event, since the 501(c)(4) is not paying its organizational costs, it has more money to devote to its lobbying efforts, which, again, are not limited by IRS rules.[34]

Another important difference is that 501(c)(4) organizations can create connected political action committees, while 501(c)(3) groups may not. In fact, many expressive groups, such as the Sierra Club, have created connected PACs, simply by establishing a separate bank account, which is controlled by the connected organization. The affiliated 501(c)(4) is even allowed to pay all of the PAC's administrative and fundraising costs. Such PACs are allowed to solicit donations only from the group's members, and not the general public, which severely limits their fundraising options. For this reason, PACs connected to nonprofit groups often find they cannot raise the sort of money needed to compete with their political opponents.

Indeed, many assume that a chronic lack of resources prevents expressive groups from participating in the increasingly expensive and sophisticated public relations campaigns that characterize current elections and debates over policy. Richer groups, it is said, possess a distinct advantage in their ability to develop and market persuasive political messages. After all, they can hire pollsters, public affairs firms, media specialists, and other experts to inform and mobilize the public, and they can deliver their message in a myriad of ways. But thanks to grants from foundations and other donors, technological advances, and increasing professionalism, some expressive groups can afford to play the modern public relations game. Some groups routinely contract with public relations and media firms to help with issue campaigns, while others have developed their own in-house capabilities. In any event, expressive groups are no longer forced to rely on free media generated by press conferences or demonstrations.[35]

The Sierra Club and the League of Conservation Voters have exploited another loophole in the tax code by establishing 527 committees, which get their name from section 527 of the IRS tax code. Also known as "stealth PACs," 527 committees allow nonprofit, tax-exempt groups to conduct issue advocacy campaigns without disclosing their contributors or spending, as long as they refrain from explicit advocacy. Moreover, such committees face no limits on either their fundraising or spending. After spending by such groups skyrocketed in the 2000 election cycle, Congress enacted a law requiring the groups to register with the IRS and disclose their contributions and spending.[36]

Environmental organizations, like many other nonprofits, have reorganized themselves in order to be free to play a more aggressive role in elections, and to have greater leeway in their efforts to shape public opinion. Indeed, the creation of 527 committees, in conjunction with the increasing reliance on issue advocacy campaigns, has allowed the Sierra Club and the League of Conservation Voters to spend record amounts in recent election cycles. One of the goals of the increased spending was to enable the groups to introduce environmental issues into campaigns, whether or not the candidates wanted those issues addressed. This is the essence of agenda setting.

LOBBYING STRATEGIES

Political scientists generally agree that interest groups can choose from three lobbying strategies: an inside strategy, an outside strategy, or some combination of the two. Inside strategies, such as conventional direct lobbying, focus on the relationship between the group and policymakers, and are most often used by groups who seek ongoing access to those elected officials or administrators with jurisdiction over the programs that matter most to the group. Groups following an inside strategy often try to establish and maintain durable relationships with policymakers by being attentive to their internal legislative or political needs. For instance, groups that can offer credible policy information or useful political insights to policymakers may find it easier to obtain access. In contrast, an outside lobbying strategy seeks to influence policymaking indirectly, by shaping and mobilizing public opinion. Outside lobbying may be aimed at long-term agenda building or at encouraging the general public, or select segments of the public, to communicate their views on specific policy matters to policymakers.[37] Groups pursuing an outside strategy can use a variety of techniques, including mass media or more traditional grassroots campaigns, to attract attention to their cause and to promote their policy goals. These strategies are not exclusive, of course; some groups will utilize outside strategies in conjunction with inside lobbying campaigns.[38]

Although there are an almost infinite number of options, the choice of specific lobbying strategies is a function of several factors, including a group's resources, its goals, who is being lobbied, the specific issue at hand, and the current political context. As a general rule, group leaders also tend to rely on strategies and tactics that have been effective on prior occasions.[39] For example, groups that seek to raise public awareness of an issue or to shape the way the public thinks about an issue act differently than do those seeking to persuade members of a conference committee to offer an amendment to an appropriations bill. If the group's goal is to shape public opinion, then a mass appeal, such as a press conference, demonstration, or newspaper or television ad makes sense. Antinuclear activists sought to rally public opinion to their side in the 1970s by engaging in mass civil disobedience at a number of controversial reactor sites. The arrest of thousands of demonstrators at the Seabrook reactor in New Hampshire garnered headlines nationwide. If the group's goal is to generate letters and phone calls to elected officials, however, a narrower appeal targeted to the group's activist base may be more appropriate.

With respect to resources, organizations with little or no money will generally not advertise their positions on television, because the cost is prohibitive. The political environment matters a great deal as well. During the latter years of the Clinton administration, for example, progressive groups followed an inside strategy by seeking administrative actions from the White House rather than pushing for new legislation in the Republican-controlled Congress. When George W. Bush took up residence in the White House, that particular inside strategy no longer made much sense and those groups had to scramble to find new paths of influence. Indeed, until Senator Jim Jeffords of Vermont defected from the Republican Party and handed control in that chamber to the Democrats, progressive groups were in the unenviable position of having all three branches of the federal government controlled by their opponents. Many thus opted for indirect, grassroots approaches to highlight differences with the new administration and to generate pressure on moderate Republicans. Several of the mainstream environmental groups paid for newspaper, radio, and television ads to call attention to the Bush administration's decisions to revisit a number of environmental regulations issued in the final days of the Clinton White House.

According to Gais and Walker, the most important factors determining whether interest groups will engage in political action, as well as the type of tactics they will employ, are the degree of conflict in the group's political environment, the group's organizational resources, the character of the group's membership, and the principal sources of the group's financial support.[40] Generally speaking, increases in political conflict stimulate greater political activity by interest groups. Moreover, groups with large staffs are more likely to engage in inside lobbying. Groups with local or regional chapters, such as the Audubon Society or Sierra Club, will be more likely to pursue outside strategies, such as national campaigns of public education and grassroots mobilization, because they are better equipped to mobilize their memberships for political action.

A variety of resources are useful in politics, but it is widely understood that the most useful organizational resources for interest groups are money, membership size, policy expertise, political knowledge and skills, cohesion, and effective leadership. Money obviously has many important uses in politics, not the least of which is making contributions to elected officials. Money, however, also makes it possible for groups to purchase other valuable resources, such as legal, policy, or public relations expertise. On the other hand, group size can also be important, because groups with many members dispersed across a significant number of congressional districts are more credible when promising or threatening electoral retribution to legislators for their votes. Again, the Audubon Society is a good example—it has millions of educated, relatively affluent members across the nation, just the sort of people who write letters to public officials and vote regularly.

A variety of organizational traits can also be important political resources. Groups that are cohesive can speak with one voice, making them more effective than groups with internal schisms. Moreover, skilled leadership, which includes the ability to manage the group's other resources, to allocate them properly, and to determine priorities cannot be overlooked. A group with plenty of money may not achieve its goals if it spends its money unwisely. Similarly, knowledge of the political process is an important resource. As Ornstein and Elder note, knowing the stages of the legislative process, the relevant subcommittees, the key actors, and the best moments to act or to withdraw can make the difference between winning and losing.[41] As the next chapter demonstrates, it was only in the 1970s that the environmental movement acquired this knowledge.

With respect to membership traits, Gais and Walker found that citizen groups tend to prefer outside strategies, while for-profit organizations favor inside strategies. In explaining this difference, they contend that members of citizen groups often have limited ties to the group and minimal knowledge of its achievements, so their loyalties must be continually reinforced through an outside strategy of public persuasion and political mobilization designed to attract media attention.[42] In addition, groups that are organized around a cause or idea and that depend heavily on small financial contributions from large numbers of members scattered across the country are more likely to adopt an outside strategy based upon various forms of mass political persuasion.[43] This is because people who join citizen groups generally do so because of their attachment to a particular idea or cause, and they therefore expect their group to advance their concerns vigorously and publicly. Finally, Gais and Walker claim that citizen groups that depend on private patrons and foundations for much of their financial support show a pronounced affinity toward broad efforts to shape public attitudes and values.[44]

Environmental groups have a long history of outside lobbying, as we shall see in the next chapter. The reason is quite simple—as classic "outsiders," environmental activists had few real options. With few of the resources prized in politics, environmentalists had to rely on strategies that sought to shape and mobilize public opinion. Why such a strategy is essential is the focus of the next section.

ISSUE DEFINITION, AGENDA SETTING, AND POLITICAL MOBILIZATION

One of the more interesting trends in contemporary interest group politics is that organized groups have altered their political strategies by devoting more attention to the earlier stages of policymaking, especially issue definition and agenda setting. Agenda setting refers to which issues receive attention from policymakers and the public, while issue definition refers to which aspect of those issues receives attention.[45] Scholars have offered several explanations for why groups are paying more attention to this phenomenon. Bosso argues that one possible reason issue definition has become more important is that electronic mass media has penetrated all facets of policy formation, making rhetoric and symbolism "all the more critical to framing policy debates and policy directions."[46] Cigler and Loomis contend that problem definition and agenda setting have themselves become increasingly important elements of policymaking, and so groups have responded to this development by stepping up their attempts to expand, restrict, or redirect conflict on the issues that matter to them. Perhaps more relevant, though, is the declining distinction between the politics of elections and the politics of policymaking. Cigler and Loomis argue that, although there has always been a linkage, the links have become much stronger in recent decades, and that much contemporary lobbying resembles the "permanent campaign" that now characterizes presidential election politics. Today, many interest groups explicitly recognize that campaign-based strategies can be essential to securing their policy goals.[47] It is for this reason that environmental organizations are increasingly dedicating so much time and money to public education, independent expenditure, and issue advocacy campaigns. If they can succeed in framing issues for the public and policymakers, the groups will have a better chance of getting what they want.

Whatever the explanation, successfully defining societal "conditions" as "public problems" often represents the most important step in policymaking, because every attempt to define a problem entails a claim about responsibility, causality, or blame. How issues are defined influences the type of politics that surround it, the chances of reaching the agenda of a particular political institution, and the probability of a policy outcome favorable to advocates of the issue.[48] In this sense, problem definition is intimately linked to what E. E. Schattschneider famously called "the scope of the conflict." According to Schattschneider, "the outcome of every conflict is determined by the extent to which the audience becomes involved in it."[49] Political fights almost always involve struggles between those seeking to privatize conflict and those seeking to expand it. More often than not, those who are unhappy with the existing state of affairs, or more simply those who are losing, will try to enlist the help of the audience because conflicts, Schattschneider says, "are taken into the public arena precisely because someone wants to make certain that the power ratio among the private interests most immediately involved shall not prevail." While the weaker side tries to involve the audience by calling their attention to previously overlooked aspects of the issue, the stronger side strives to keep it on the sidelines, because when more actors become involved, "there is a great probability that the original contestants will lose control of the matter."[50] Problem definition is thus critical in the development of a conflict because the audience does not enter the fray randomly, or in equal proportion for the competing sides. Rather, they become engaged in response to the way participants portray their struggle. In political conflicts, in short, issue definition and redefinition are used as tools by opposing sides to gain an advantage.[51]

Experience shows that perceptions of public problems sometimes change dramatically. People who have been apathetic suddenly begin to pay attention to an issue and demand to be included in the debate. In 2001, for example, after years of little attention, media coverage and public interest in farm subsidies suddenly increased. Why does this change occur? What leads people to begin to think that a program affects them?

The answer lies in how policy issues are perceived or understood. Any given public policy issue or program can be understood in a variety of ways, some positive and some negative. Nuclear power, for example, may be perceived as either a cheap, plentiful source of electricity or as a significant threat to human health and safety. If people focus on its benefits and minimize or overlook its costs, nuclear power may enjoy widespread public and governmental support. On the other hand, support may wane if people perceive that the program's costs outweigh its benefits. The fate of public programs often hinges on which aspect or understanding is dominant among policymakers and the attentive public. Perceptions of issues can also change over time. Programs that were once quite popular may become the target of discontent if problems arise or if costs increase. Similarly, an issue that was once ignored may attract considerable attention if enough people come to believe that it affects them. In the case of farm subsidies, for example, the debate shifted when people began to focus on who benefited from the program. For years, the program was defended as aiding small family farms, but when evidence compiled by the Environmental Working Group showed that the bulk of the subsidies went to large, corporate-owned farms, perceptions of the program changed.

The key to attracting the attention of the previously apathetic or "creating a public," writes Christopher J. Bosso, "lies in shaping popular perceptions" about issues.[52] Issue definition is a critical part of politics, and political conflicts, we are told, are often characterized by struggles over issue definition.[53] Policy entrepreneurs seek to portray issues in ways that further their own policy goals; they thus have strong incentives to shape perceptions of issues. Actors in a policy monopoly, for example, try to promote apathy by showing that their issue, or their handling of the issue, has mostly beneficial results. Or they may try to define the issue narrowly, as a technical matter, for example, to limit public interest. Those seeking to change policy, on the other hand, must attract the attention of either the general public or policymakers. The attempt to mobilize new actors can be accomplished by highlighting a program's flaws or by showing others that the issue affects them. The definition and redefinition of policy issues, in short, is a political process that affects the mobilization of interests.[54]

Some types of issues are easier to redefine than others, and so issue definition and agenda setting often require a long-term commitment of group resources.[55] As Baumgartner and Jones note, "Those wishing to mobilize broad groups attempt to focus attention on highly emotional symbols or easily understood themes, while those with an interest in restricting the debate explain the same issues in other, more arcane and complicated, ways."[56] Broadly defined issues, especially those with an element of drama, admit a wide range of actors and often become the focus of widespread political debates, while those that are narrowly defined restrict participation to a small group, and often give rise to policy monopolies. When narrow issues become defined in broader terms, new groups of policymakers are attracted to them. The result can be dramatic policy change.

The amount and the type of information the public has about an issue or program are important determinants of political activity surrounding that issue. In fact, information is frequently used in an advocacy fashion. Bosso shows that one of the factors driving the expansion of the conflict over pesticides policy in the 1960s and 1970s was the spread of information suggesting a link between pesticide use and human health effects, notably cancer. The pesticides case also shows how policy entrepreneurs use information to shape people's understandings of public policy issues and to expand the range of actors in policy disputes.[57] Environmental activists set out to ensure that the media and the public were aware of studies documenting the potential health effects of pesticides, knowing that this information would spur people to demand action from policymakers. The more people who perceive a problem, Bosso says, "the more who wish to get involved."[58]

As James Q. Wilson has noted, it is the perceived distribution of costs and benefits rather than the actual distribution that shapes the way politics is conducted.[59] The amount of information the public has, then, is an important factor in shaping perceptions of an issue. In other instances, a "focusing event" such as a crisis or a revelation of misconduct or incompetence by policymakers may facilitate the flow of information, thus casting an issue in a new light.[60] The grounding of the Exxon *Valdez* off the Alaskan coast, for example, focused public attention on oil tankers, in the same way that medical waste washing ashore on the East Coast heightened awareness of ocean pollution. When enough information, or information of a certain type, becomes public, perceptions of an issue may change, redefining it in the process.

THE IMPORTANCE OF LANGUAGE AND STORIES

Clearly, then, interest groups need to pay attention to problem definition and agenda setting. Group communication strategies, for example, are designed with an eye toward shaping the way problems and proposed solutions are perceived. Critics of a policy or program want to highlight its flaws or costs, while its advocates stress its benefits. Most programs, of course, have both costs and benefits. What matters politically, then, are which outcomes or aspects of the issue people see when they look at it. That is why most interest group activity today is aimed at framing issues. When testifying at public hearings, meeting directly with public officials, mobilizing letter writing campaigns by group members or the public, airing television commercials, holding press conferences, issuing research studies, or talking to reporters, interest groups are engaged in problem definition. They are presenting policy information in a strategic manner.[61]

Every policy argument takes place in a particular context involving the speaker and the audience, and political actors frame their arguments in a language thought to be attractive to the intended audience. According to Rochefort and Cobb, the function of problem definition is at once to explain, to describe, to recommend, and, above all, to persuade. "It is," they suggest, "a distinctive form of public rhetoric made up of a habitual vocabulary."[62] Effective political actors know that language is a critical element of problem definition. Words, after all, influence attitudes and perceptions, which in turn shape the way people understand problems and, ultimately, the proposed solutions. The right language can evoke understandings and images that can bolster one definition and undermine others, thereby favoring one solution over others. It matters, for example, whether people believe that temperature fluctuations are "normal" or are the result of human actions. If they are "normal," then no remedial action is required. If, on the other hand, climate change is the result of fossil fuel use, then policies curtailing their use are open to consideration. Political rhetoric is, in short, the rhetoric of persuasion and advocacy.[63]

The importance of political communication in defining problems has been widely recognized. Problem definition, writes Deborah Stone, is the "strategic representation of situations." It is "a matter of representation because every description of a situation is a portrayal from only one of many points of view. Problem definition is strategic because groups, individuals, and government agencies deliberately and consciously fashion portrayals so as to promote their favored course of action. . . . Representations of a problem are therefore constructed to win the most people to one's side and the most leverage over one's opponents."[64] And since it is always the losing or weaker side who needs to call in help, strategic problem definition usually means portraying a problem so that one's favored course of action appears to be in the broad public interest. In this way, problem definition involves manipulating the scope of conflict by persuading some people that they are affected by it while others are not.[65]

Stone goes so far as to suggest that symbolic representation is the essence of problem definition. Political actors construct and use symbols to frame perceptions and interpretations of the meaning, significance, and consequences of problems, and to undermine the stories told by their opponents. Effective symbols, such as a good metaphor or story, capture our imagination and shape our perceptions by structuring our thinking on issues. In fact, Stone contends that definitions of policy problems usually have a narrative structure; that is, they are stories with a beginning, a middle, and an end, featuring heroes, villains, and victims.[66]

Some types of stories are common in political conflicts. Causal stories, for example, seek to explain the causes of problems, to attribute them to the actions of others and, in some cases, to assign responsibility for paying the costs of any solution.[67] In addition to assigning blame for the problem, causal stories have the added advantage of undermining the legitimacy of one's opponents. Environmentalists trace desertification in the American West to overgrazing by "welfare cowboys." Air pollution, toxic dumps, and contaminated drinking water supplies are attributed to greedy, self-interested "corporate polluters."

Also common are stories of decline, which often begin by describing how things have gotten worse over time and end with a prediction of a crisis and a specific recommendation for action.[68] Environmental groups frequently use stories of decline and crisis to describe particular problems, such as climate change, deforestation, or species loss.[69] Indeed, critics claim that environmental groups rely too heavily on predictions of imminent doom, and thus risk being perceived as shrill "Chicken Littles." Nevertheless, to be effective stories must persuade their intended audience that the problem under consideration is both severe and hits close to home. As we all know, people must believe that an issue affects them personally before they will take an interest in it.[70]

Some stories are, of course, better suited to certain audiences. As West and Loomis note, complicated or detailed narratives may work well with more specialized audiences, such as policymakers, but have little effect on the general public, which may not be familiar with policy details. For this reason, narratives tend to become less complex as the scope of conflict broadens. This means that communication patterns will vary from issue to issue, and over time as an issue moves through various stages of conflict expansion.[71] For this reason, interest groups may communicate one set of messages to members of Congress, their staff, regulators, and other organized interests, and offer another set of messages to the public via paid advertising, press conferences, or demonstrations. Consider, for example, drinking water. When discussing the issue with regulators and congressional staff, environmental groups are perfectly willing and able to talk intelligently about "parts per billion," "best available technology," and other technocratic terms. When communicating with the broader public, however, group leaders are much more likely to talk about threats to human health, which is a more accessible message.

Rarely is policymaking based entirely or even primarily on objective evidence or facts. Instead, it is affected by both the reality and perceptions of the evidence and facts. If people believe that nuclear reactors are unsafe, then no government study claiming to show otherwise will dissuade them. Similarly, despite overwhelming evidence that auto travel is considerably more dangerous than travel by air, fears of flying are far more common. In other words, facts do not speak for themselves—they are often contested and subject to interpretation and analysis. Moreover, there is considerable evidence that people's attitudes and assumptions, including any ideological biases, affect how they perceive and interpret information.[72] Take, for example, the oft-mentioned discrepancy between blacks and whites in reacting to the O. J. Simpson case, or the vastly different reactions offered by Democrats and Republicans to the Florida recount in the 2000 presidential election. Because facts do not speak for themselves, effective policymaking turns at least as much on the capacity of political actors to frame the terms of policy debate as it does on the facts themselves. Policy advocates, as a result, design communication strategies using language and rhetoric that is aimed at persuading the general public and key policymakers to adopt their interpretations of the facts, as well as their diagnosis of problems and their proposed solutions.[73] To do this effectively, policy actors need to know what factors influence perception, how people think, and how they process information.[74]

Although public acceptance of causal stories is certainly important, according to Stone the "real test of political success is whether it becomes the dominant belief and guiding assumption for policymakers. A causal story is more likely to be successful if its proponents have visibility, access to media, and prominent positions; if it accords with widespread and deeply held cultural values; and if its implicit prescription does not require a major redistribution of power and wealth."[75]

THE IMPORTANCE OF POLITICAL CULTURE

Problem definition, as Bosso notes, is contextual. A nation's political culture, including its dominant public values and its "topography of governance," significantly constrains the ability of political actors to portray issues and set political agendas. Because these factors are beyond their control, political actors do not have complete freedom to frame issues.[76] Bosso contends that in the United States, for example, the dominant political culture is built around core beliefs in individual liberty, limited government, private property, the Protestant work ethic, social mobility based on merit, and faith in progress and in the free market. Taken together, these beliefs make politics subordinate to the private sector and thus give business a privileged position in political debates.[77] Because many environmentalists seek goals that question or challenge these core beliefs, their efforts to define or redefine problems have a tough time finding fertile ground.[78]

Consider, for example, the debate in the United States Senate in early 2002 over a proposal to increase corporate average fuel efficiency (CAFE) standards. Advocates of the measure contended that higher fuel efficiency standards would make the nation less dependent on imported oil, reduce air pollution, and save enough oil to eliminate the need to drill in the Arctic National Wildlife Refuge. Automakers and their congressional allies, on the other hand, argued that higher standards would result in the loss of up to 100,000 jobs and force Americans to drive smaller, lighter, and less safe cars, resulting in more highway injuries and deaths. Speaking for the opposition, Missouri Senator Kit Bond said, "I don't pretend to know what's best for 15 million Americans purchasing a vehicle each year. I don't want to tell the mom in my home state that she should not get an SUV, because Congress decided that would be a bad choice."[79] To drive home the point, Senate Minority Leader Trent Lott held a photo-op featuring a tiny European car that he said Americans would be forced to buy if the measure passed. It did not pass, and part of the explanation is that opponents effectively framed the debate in terms of personal choice, jobs, and public safety, a powerful mix of images that fits neatly into the dominant political culture.

In the face of such constraints, many of the mainstream environmental groups have opted to limit their advocacy to "safe issues" that do not challenge fundamental tenets of our political culture. George Gonzalez, for example, argues that in the case of air pollution, environmental groups have chosen to focus on technological fixes rather than challenge the overarching political goal of economic growth, which many believe is the root cause of our environmental ills. Moreover, because environmental groups have lacked the resources needed to change the political agenda, most of their advocacy efforts are aimed at the less controversial goal of urging government to mandate clean technologies. The result is a restricted political debate that excludes serious consideration of central issues, such as the desirability of unfettered economic growth.[80] Given the dominant political culture, environmental groups have felt constrained to raise such issues indirectly, if at all.

Similarly, the nation's structures of governance affect problem definition and agenda setting. Consider the principle of federalism, which establishes and sustains a strong predisposition for local control of numerous policy matters, such as land use, that have important environmental implications. Traditionally, the preference for local control has worked in favor of developers, because debates over environmental issues are often framed in terms of property rights, economic growth, and progress, which are core elements of the dominant political culture, and thus give developers the upper hand. In this way, local control works to restrict political debate and keeps some issues favored by environmentalists off the political agenda.[81] Given the growth bias inherent in many municipal codes, environmentalists are thus forced to try to shift authority to the federal government, where local developers are typically less influential.[82] Although such venue shifting is possible, environmentalists are in the undesirable position of advocating something new, and the American political system is designed to frustrate departures from the status quo.

Culture, of course, is a social construct, and thus subject to change. And although the dominant culture exerts a powerful influence on issue framing, competing values do exist. Therefore, in addition to framing perceptions of particular problems or controversies, group communication strategies may also be intended to alter the larger political climate. Bosso, for example, notes the emergence of a "still nascent macrolevel debate between the norms of a traditionally individualist culture and a newer set of as yet subordinate 'green' values."[83] Other scholars have documented the ability of environmental groups to frame issues in ways that challenge the dominant culture with appeals rooted in other powerful societal values. Wilderness activists in the American West, for example, have crafted effective appeals based on a mix of nature, science, and economics. Some of the appeals draw attention to the role of wilderness in building character and contributing to a moral life.[84] Other appeals, which paint the West as a repository of the nation's wilderness treasures, tap into the widely held value of stewardship, in which humans have an obligation to protect what God has created. In the aforementioned case of debates over farm subsidies, the Environmental Working Group and others portrayed themselves as fighting to protect small family farmers from predatory behavior by corporate-owned factory farms. As Browne and others have shown, agrarian myths of the small, self-reliant family farmer have been and continue to be exceptionally powerful symbols in agricultural policy debates, even though few remain.[85]

CONCLUSION

This chapter has sought to document and explain some of the more important developments in contemporary interest group politics. The purpose of this discussion was to show that these developments have fundamentally altered the context in which environmental groups operate. For a variety of reasons, including the collapse of campaign finance rules, interest groups are more active in elections. Similarly, policymaking venues today are more open, crowded, and conflictual. Because politics and policymaking have changed in these ways, environmental groups have adapted by stepping up their electoral and lobbying activities. Consequently, environmental groups can now raise and spend more money, in new ways, in an effort to influence congressional elections. They also lobby in all directions and use tactics that were once discouraged, such as launching media attacks against unfriendly policymakers. Most importantly, changes in the nation's political institutions and processes have blurred the distinction between politics and policymaking.

The environmental movement has also changed quite a bit over the years, as it has matured, grown, and become more sophisticated. As a result, the lobbying strategies used by environmental groups have also changed over time. How and why that shift occurred is the focus of the next two chapters.

3

American Environmentalism through the Early 1990s

Diplomacy, perfection of techniques for getting along, will accomplish a great deal.
It will not, however, save what can only be saved by fighting.
—David Brower

In order to determine what environmental groups are doing new today, we need to know what they have done in the past. Compared to today, when several of the largest environmental organizations have more than one million dues-paying members, most groups were quite small until the late 1960s. Most also had meager budgets and none had a full-time lobbying staff or presence in Washington. What they did have, though, was a cadre of dedicated and creative activists who were committed to their cause, which was still unknown to most Americans. As other "outsider" groups faced with a similar lack of conventional political resources had done, these activists used every tool they could think of to call attention to environmental problems and to frame public perceptions of them. Accordingly, environmental advocacy in these early days relied heavily on outsider tactics, combined with some low-key but effective personal lobbying. Despite a chronic lack of resources, environmental activists managed to score some impressive policy victories, due in large part to their success in issue definition and agenda setting.

As the movement expanded, many of the older groups experienced dramatic increases in their memberships, budgets, and staffs. Once their organizational capacities increased, some of the larger and better known groups, such as the Sierra Club, the Wilderness Society, and the National Audubon Society, began to diversify their tactics, notably by engaging in more direct lobbying. At the same time, the influx of resources allowed the groups to experiment with new approaches to issue definition and agenda setting. The establishment of many new organizations in the 1970s, largely in response to growing concerns over pollution and its public health risks, reinforced this trend. Several of these groups, such as the Natural Resources Defense Council, chose to influence policy through litigation. High-profile court cases not only succeeded in capturing the attention of the media, the public, and policymakers; they had a profound effect on how policies were formulated and implemented. And in communities across the nation, thousands of grassroots groups sprang up to address specific local environmental ills. In many cases, these organizations relied on direct action and confrontational tactics. By the early 1990s, the environmental movement was characterized by an exceptional diversity in both goals and tactics, and many organizations had begun to redouble their issue-framing and agenda-setting efforts.

AN OVERVIEW OF AMERICAN ENVIRONMENTALISM

According to environmental writer Philip Shabecoff, there have been several waves of organizational environmental activity in the United States.[1] The first wave, dating back to the turn of the century, consisted of old-line conservation and sportsmen's groups like the Sierra Club, the Wilderness Society, the National Audubon Society, the Izaak Walton League, and several others. Their efforts were dedicated primarily to preserving resources for recreational as well as aesthetic purposes. With the notable exception of the Sierra Club's fight to preserve the Hetch Hetchy region of Yosemite in the early 1900s, environmental organizations avoided overt political activity throughout the first half of the century. Prior to that, the primary focus of many of the national groups was on public education.[2] The controversy over the proposed Echo Park dam transformed the actions of national environmental groups: the Sierra Club, the Wilderness Society, the National Audubon Society, and a few others became active in Washington, despite their lack of professional lobbyists. The key accomplishments of this first wave were the creation of the National Park, National Forest, and National Wildlife Refuge Systems.

Population growth and the tremendous economic expansion of the postwar years contributed to the birth of the second wave, whose focus was on dealing with the consequences of those changes. During the 1960s and 1970s, concerns mounted about air and water pollution, solid waste, and toxic contamination. One of the catalysts was the 1962 publication of Rachel Carson's book *Silent Spring,* which argued that pesticides posed a significant threat to animal and human health. Later in the decade, a series of environmental disasters, including a major oil spill off the coast of Santa Barbara, California, captured public and media attention.

Many new environmental organizations were established during this period, some with significant foundation support, including the Sierra Club Legal Defense Fund, the Natural Resources Defense Council, and the Environmental Defense Fund. These groups constituted the legal arm of the environmental movement and were responsible for establishing important courtroom precedents on behalf of the environment. Other new groups focused primarily on pollution and the accompanying threats to public health. At the same time, some of the existing groups concluded that a purely educational approach was unlikely to produce the results most of them sought. Consequently, many of the established organizations broadened their agenda to include pollution and other emerging environmental threats.[3] There was also a dramatic shift in the nature of environmental advocacy, with groups becoming more involved in explicit political action, including litigation and various forms of protest.

By all accounts, it was during this "Golden Age" of environmentalism, during the 1960s and 1970s, that Americans began to consider the effects of industrialization and modern living on the world. Membership in environmental groups began to mushroom. This era was also the high-water mark for governmental action on environmental issues. Support for environmental initiatives was never higher, as Congress adopted many of today's cornerstone environmental laws, including the National Environmental Policy Act (1969), significant amendments to both the Clean Air Act (1970) and the Clean Water Act (1972), and the Endangered Species Act (1973), among others.

During the third wave of environmentalism in the 1980s and 1990s, activists were forced to respond to significant shifts in the nation's political economy. An economic downturn and the ascendance of a conservative government pushed groups to become more professional, to develop new expertise in political and economic analysis, and to adopt more aggressive media and public outreach strategies. Moreover, with both the White House and the U.S. Senate in Republican hands, environmentalists had to look for new ways to achieve their goals without the help of either branch, or the courts. Some groups assembled large professional staffs of lobbyists, scientists, economists, lawyers, organizers, fundraisers, and public relations specialists. Some of the national groups began to conduct very sophisticated grassroots campaigns, using computerized membership lists in conjunction with direct mail and phone banks, to generate grassroots pressure on legislators. In the words of one group leader, the "process became almost routine."[4]

Writing in the 1990s, Jeffrey Berry argued that the environmental movement had evolved into three "wings" distinguished by their goals, attitudes, and tactics. The "mainstream" groups consisted of organizations like the Sierra Club, the Wilderness Society, the National Wildlife Federation, and others who preferred to work within the political system, relying for the most part on conventional political methods. The other two wings often criticized these groups for compromising too readily, on the one hand, and for not compromising enough on the other.[5] The "accommodationist" wing consisted of groups like the Environmental Defense Fund, the Conservation Foundation, Resources for the Future, and the World Wildlife Fund who were promoting a new era of cooperation in environmental politics. Many of these groups set out to work with business and advocated greater reliance on market incentives and regulatory negotiations. The "radical" wing consisted of groups like EarthFirst!, Greenpeace, and an increasingly large number of local grassroots groups organized around particular threats to their communities. The grassroots groups were generally smaller, more homogeneous, and poorer than the national organizations, and they were directly in the line of fire. Moreover, many of them distrusted the political process and thus opted instead for more confrontational tactics, including letter writing campaigns, attending town meetings, door-to-door canvassing, demonstrations, and even civil disobedience.[6]

Environmental organizations have, over the years, adapted to changing political and social conditions. More specifically, their electoral and lobbying activities and goals have evolved along with their available resources. As their resources increased, groups were able to do more than in previous years, and could engage in a broader range of political action.

THE GROWTH OF ORGANIZATIONAL CAPACITY

By 1971, with the federal government assuming greater responsibility over environmental problems, about seventy environmental groups had opened offices in the nation's capital. This marked the beginning of a period of rapid growth and change for the individual groups and the environmental movement as a whole. According to Berry, citizen group leaders consciously built their organizations in the 1970s so that they had substantial technical expertise and information capacities.[7] That decision, he suggests, was prompted by the recognition that a group's organizational capacity affected its ability to succeed in influencing policy. A group's organizational capacity, in turn, is largely a function of its physical, organizational, and political resources, as well as its effectiveness in using these resources. Among the most important group resources are the size and character of its membership, its total operating budget, the size and quality of its staff, and the quality and stability of its leadership. By almost every measure, the organizational capacity of environmental organizations increased dramatically between 1960 and 1990. The groups now have the resources to follow issues from initial proposals to legislative enactment to implementation.[8]

Consider, for example, the dramatic increase in the budgets of the nation's largest environmental organizations during the latter part of this period. In 1980, the Sierra Club had an operating budget of $9.5 million, but it had risen to $40 million just ten years later. During the same period, the National Wildlife Federation saw its budget increase from $34.5 million to just under $90 million. These groups were not aberrations. The average annual budget in 1991 for the ten environmental groups listed in the *Encyclopedia of Associations* was approximately $40 million.[9] Increasing budgets were made possible, in part, by a surge in donations to environmental groups, and by increased fundraising.[10]

The story is similar with group memberships, which began to take off in the 1960s and continued to grow through the 1970s and 1980s. As Table 3.1 shows, the combined membership totals for the ten largest environmental groups in 1970 was about one million. By 1980, the combined figure for the same groups had increased to 5 million, and by 1990 it had reached just under 9 million. This does not include membership totals for some of the newer organizations, like Greenpeace, which was founded in 1971 but claimed 2.35 million members in 1990.[11]

Table 3.1. Trends in Environmental Group Membership

Organization	1970	1980	1990	2001
National Audubon Society	148,000	400,000	600,000	600,000
Defenders of Wildlife	13,000	50,000	80,000	180,000
Environmental Defense	11,000	46,000	200,000	300,000
Greenpeace USA n/a		250,000	2,350,000	250,000
League of Conservation Voters n/a		35,000	25,000	60,000
National Parks Conservation Association	45,000	31,000	100,000	450,000
National Wildlife Federation	3,100,000	4,500,000	5,800,000	4,400,000
Natural Resources Defense Council n/a		40,000	150,000	400,000
Sierra Club	113,000	181,000	630,000	550,000
Wilderness Society	54,000	45,000	350,000	255,000

Sources: Christopher J. Bosso and Deborah Lynn Guber, "The Boundaries and Contours of American Environmental Activism," in Environmental Policy: New Directions for the Twenty-First Century, ed. Norman J. Vig and Michael E. Kraft (Washington, D.C. CQ Press, 2002), 93; 2001 totals from Encyclopedia of Associations (Detroit: Gale Research).

The growth in budgets and membership paved the way for an increase in the number of lobbyists and professional staffers the groups employed. The Sierra Club was fairly typical of this growth. It did not open its Washington, D.C., office until 1967, when it retained its first lobbyist. In the early 1970s, its lobbying staff had grown to six, and by 1986 it reached seventeen.[12] Similarly, there were only two full-time environmental lobbyists in 1969. By 1975, though, the twelve largest groups employed forty lobbyists, and by the 1986 the number was eighty-eight. In his study of some of the largest national environmental groups, Robert Lowry estimated that the average group was spending $17 million per year on lobbying and related activities in the early 1990s.[13]

There was similar growth in nonlobbying staff, as groups added fundraisers, lawyers, economists, scientists, policy analysts, and other professionals.[14] Undoubtedly, the growth in staff greatly enhanced the groups' expertise and sophistication as well as their ability to branch out into new areas.[15] In addition, Berry suggests that the creation of large professional staffs devoted to lobbying and research helped environmental groups generate attention and credibility, two valuable resources for any organization. First, staff with the ability to produce detailed reports and analyses will be of greater use to policymakers, who place a high value on timely and relevant policy data. Second, by investing so heavily in scientific and policy research, environmental groups enhanced their reputation for policy expertise, which in turn led to an increase in media coverage of their work. On a more practical level, in conducting their own studies environmental groups could counter arguments put forth by government agencies and business. Credibility and attention, in other words, were mutually reinforcing and both were enhanced by the increase in the groups' organizational capacity.

Kirkpatrick Sale claims that the growth of staff was an inevitable stage in the evolution of environmentalism from amateur protest to traditional interest group lobbying.[16] Although Sale admits this transformation did yield some important legislative, judicial, and administrative returns, he also notes some significant costs. Perhaps most notably, in his opinion, the decision to play the "Washington game" entailed an important shift in roles from adversary to potential ally, and in political tactics from confrontation to compromise.[17] The fear was that environmental leaders would moderate their demands in an attempt to retain their access to key policymakers and that, as a result, the environment would suffer. At least in the short term, though, the growth in staff and resources enabled groups to engage in a wider range of persuasion tactics. The traditional reliance on outside lobbying could be supplemented with inside tactics. In addition, some of the groups would now have the money and expertise to try new approaches to mass mobilization.

ENVIRONMENTAL GROUPS AND ELECTIONS

Elections can provide valuable opportunities for interest groups seeking to gain access to public officials. Campaign contributions, volunteers, and other forms of assistance can help groups establish and maintain cordial relationships with candidates and their staffs. Nevertheless, electoral activity by environmental groups was practically nonexistent until the late 1970s, and even then, involvement was generally limited to a handful of organizations like the Sierra Club, Friends of the Earth, and the League of Conservation Voters. Whether it was distrust of the political process, lack of resources, or IRS rules limiting political activity by nonprofit organizations, most environmental groups simply did not participate in elections.

That behavior began to change in the 1970s. In 1976 the Sierra Club established a Committee on Political Education to provide information on candidates' voting records to its members. Environmental Action (and later the League of Conservation Voters) began its "Dirty Dozen" campaigns aimed at publicizing the voting records of incumbents who had shown little support for environmental protection.[18] These campaigns generated a considerable amount of favorable media coverage, but it was not until 1980 that a number of the groups began issuing endorsements, forming political action committees, or making direct contributions to candidates. That year, after considerable internal debate, the Sierra Club endorsed five candidates for the California Legislature, and approved a plan to raise $80,000 for several close congressional races. Although the Club did not endorse candidates in the federal races, the donations were made in the Club's name.[19] It was in 1982, though, that environmental groups first formally endorsed candidates in congressional races and contributed significant money. The Sierra Club, for example, made more than $235,000 in direct and in-kind contributions to federal candidates. Those candidates, in turn, raised nearly twice that amount using Club mailing lists and Club-sponsored local fundraising events.[20] When thirty-four of the candidates won, *Business Week* suggested that the "environmental movement has established a beachhead in American electoral politics."[21] Throughout the remainder of the decade, group activity in elections steadily increased, with the Sierra Club and the League of Conservation Voters playing the most significant roles. Both organizations, as well as Friends of the Earth, formed PACs, as did a number of state League of Conservation Voters organizations.

In 1984, after much internal debate, the Sierra Club broke new ground by endorsing Walter Mondale, the first time the group had issued an endorsement for president. Club leaders were concerned that the endorsement risked making the election a referendum on the environment, and that if Mondale lost (as he did) it would undermine their claims that Americans cared about environmental issues. In a letter to Mondale, the Club's board of directors said that it reached its decision after being "confronted by a President whose first-term actions contain so blatant and tragically consistent a record of opposition to the environmental interests of the people of the United States."[22] In the end, Club leaders decided that Reagan's environmental record was so poor that they needed to oppose his reelection, even if their efforts were likely to be unsuccessful. Despite the endorsement, neither the Sierra Club nor other environmental groups devoted significant financial resources to the presidential contest.

That same year environmental groups stepped up their electoral activities, and were involved in at least one-third of congressional races as well as in many state and local elections. In addition, the Sierra Club and the National Audubon Society used computers to match their member lists to congressional districts in key races.[23] By the middle of the decade, the Sierra Club was endorsing about two hundred congressional candidates in each election and, as Table 3.2 indicates, it was making about $250,000 in direct contributions.[24] Indeed, the Sierra Club and the League of Conservation Voters were clearly the dominant players in electoral politics. In 1986, the two groups accounted for all but $7,000 of the $355,000 contributed by environmental organizations. A handful of other groups, like Friends

Table 3.2. Direct Federal Contributions by Selected Environmental PACs, 1986–1994 (in dollars)

	1986	1988	1990	1992	1994
Sierra Club	251,574	288,857	408,651	599,446	406,631
LCV	96,766	89,431	152,216	408,139	776,559
California LCV	6,247	12,770	0	17,837	20,490
Oregon LCV	0	91	5,968	2,522	1,000
NY LCV	0	0	0	0	2,000
Clean Water Action	0	0	21,179	21,172	8,308
Duc Pac	0	0	13,900	18,300	9,750
Friends of Earth	0	0	0	0	0
Greenvote	0	0	27,157	92,850	67,150
Totals	354,587	391,149	629,071	1,160,266	1,291,888

Sources: Center for Responsive Politics, FEC Reports COO135368, COO252940, COOO12401, COOO35154, COO278424, COO141044, COO243691, COO235564, COO251942: Larry Makinson and Joshua Goldstein, Open Secrets: The Cash Constituents of Congress (Washington, D.C.: CQ Press), various editions.

of the Earth or Clean Water/Vote Environment, also established PACs, but were active only sporadically and contributed little money.

For much of the 1980s the LCV's primary focus was the Dirty Dozen campaigns, but it gradually increased its involvement, and spending, in other races as well. In 1988, for example, sixty of seventy-six LCV-endorsed congressional candidates won their races. Despite spending much more money in 1990 and 1992, though, only 84 of 133 (63 percent) and 108 of 186 (58 percent) of LCV-endorsed candidates prevailed, respectively.[25] It was during this period as well that the LCV began to spend more heavily on radio and television advertising, but it was not until 1996 that such spending became the centerpiece of the group's electoral efforts.

Despite the steady rise in spending, environmental groups could not hope to match the contributions from their political opponents. It was only in 1992, for example, that spending by environmental groups topped the $1 million mark. While $1 million is not an insignificant sum of money to most people, it is not a lot of money in federal elections, even in the early 1990s. With campaign costs increasing in every election cycle, candidates for federal office needed to raise ever-larger sums of cash in order to compete. With a relatively paltry $1 million to give, environmental groups were hardly the candidate's first choice for cash, especially when compared to labor unions and corporate PACs. Moreover, with so little money available, environmental groups could only afford to make a limited number of the maximum $5,000 contributions per candidate per election allowed under federal law. Groups thus had to choose between making many small contributions, which would almost certainly have no bearing on the candidate's success or failure, or making a few large contributions. Even in the latter case, though, the group's $5,000 contribution would only be one of many received by congressional candidates, and would therefore have little effect on either the election or the candidate's voting record.

Finally, the increases in political spending seemed to be having little effect at the polls. Candidates rarely discussed environmental issues, and voters appeared not to care. In 1992, for example, exit polls showed that fewer than 10 percent of voters said that the environment was an important factor in their decision.[26] One might have expected that figure to be higher with Al Gore on the Democratic ticket, given that Gore had the "greenest" credentials of any major party candidate to seek such high office. But the Clinton campaign's now famous mantra of "It's the economy, stupid" more or less guaranteed that environmental issues would take a back seat in the election. Clearly, environmental groups would need to do something different if they hoped to have a more significant effect on elections.

ENVIRONMENTAL ADVOCACY: AN OVERVIEW

What exactly do environmental groups do when they seek to influence government decisions? The short answer is that they do what other interests groups do;

indeed, there is little that is unique about environmental group lobbying. Environmental groups are active throughout the policy process, in all branches and at all levels of government, and they engage in a wide range of advocacy techniques. Some environmental organizations specialize in particular advocacy techniques, such as litigation, while others do almost everything. Some, especially those with large professional staffs, tend to engage in more conventional inside lobbying, while others show a flair for unconventional tactics, such as protests, demonstrations, or consumer boycotts.[27] All in all, lobbying by the environmental movement, with its thousands of organized groups, is hard to categorize. No two groups, and no two lobbying campaigns, are exactly alike.

Nevertheless, when considered collectively the mainstream national groups—those whose names everybody knows, like the National Wildlife Federation, the Natural Resources Defense Council, and so on—engage in the full range of advocacy strategies and techniques found in American politics. Many state-based and regional groups do as well, although their primary focus is often on subnational issues and arenas. Some groups, though, do not lobby in the conventional sense of the term, focusing instead on other forms of action, such as litigation, direct action, policy research, public education, and, in the case of the Trust for the Public Land and the Nature Conservancy, land acquisition.

As we saw in Chapter 2, most advocacy strategies can be classified as either inside or outside lobbying, with the latter often playing a key role in supplementing direct appeals to policymakers. Inside, or direct, lobbying, as the name suggests, involves establishing personal contact with policymakers and their staffs. The specific tactics of inside lobbying vary, and include formal face-to-face appeals by a lobbyist or other group representative, testimony at legislative or regulatory proceedings, the provision of campaign support, and a host of information-providing activities, such as research and reports, the drafting of legislation, and serving on advisory committees. It can also include informal social contacts, such as conversations over lunch or during a game of golf. This form of lobbying is essentially "insider politics" and, in the words of William Browne, aims at durable relationships, sharing an understanding of process problems, credible information, trust among the participants, and the parties' keeping one another current.[28] Inside lobbying, in short, is what people usually think of when they hear the word "lobbying."

Outside, or indirect, lobbying, on the other hand, involves establishing contact with the policymaker through the group's membership, the media, or the general public. As with inside lobbying, groups employ a wide variety of tactics. Most notable, perhaps, are grassroots campaigns, which typically involve efforts by group leaders to mobilize their general membership, and sometimes others, to contact policymakers about some pending governmental decision. This can be done through direct mail, press conferences, or newspaper, radio, and television ads. The same communication sources can be used for public education campaigns, which may or may not be connected with any particular decision. Press conferences, staged media "events," protests, demonstrations, and boycotts are also employed in an effort to generate favorable media coverage of the group and its cause. On occasion, environmental groups have also sought to bypass policy-makers entirely through the use of initiatives and referenda, which allow the general public to make policy.[29] The precise mix of lobbying strategies used by environmental groups has varied over time, depending on the issue at hand, the resources available, and who the groups are lobbying. Lobbying a senator is different, after all, from lobbying an EPA official.

LOBBYING CONGRESS

Environmental groups have used a variety of inside and outside techniques when lobbying the United States Congress. During the 1950s, much of the inside lobbying was carried out by a small group of activists, such as David Brower and Ansel Adams of the Sierra Club, and Howard Zahnihser of the Wilderness Society. Much of the direct lobbying in these early days consisted of low-key personal appeals, congressional testimony, assistance with drafting legislation, and the provision of information about specific tracts of land that the advocates sought to protect. In 1956, for example, Senator Hubert Humphrey sponsored the nation's first wilderness bill. The Wilderness Society, the Izaak Walton League, the National Parks Association, and others had been consulted on the bill and had given their approval. In addition, the groups had worked together on the bill, a process made easier because of overlapping group membership among several of the key players.[30] Of course, environmental groups had few members in the 1950s and even fewer political resources, so the choice of lobbying tactics was quite limited. Moreover, for the vast majority of Americans and members of Congress, "the environment" was not yet a significant political issue. For these reasons, the handful of groups that were seeking to influence legislation relied heavily on outside tactics like public education and grassroots campaigns.

Perhaps this approach to influencing Congress is best illustrated by looking at actual lobbying campaigns. Consider, for example, the conflict in the early to mid-1950s over a Bureau of Reclamation proposal to build a dam at Echo Park in the Dinosaur National Monument in Colorado. One observer calls the Echo Park controversy "a key turning point in American environmental politics, both symbolically and practically."[31] At the time, the Bureau of Reclamation was one of the most powerful federal agencies, so the decision by some wilderness advocates to oppose the dam was not expected to yield much success. This was especially true given the Bureau's powerful congressional allies, and the army of pro-growth interests who supported the dam. And yet, the campaign to block construction of the dam, which united the Sierra Club, the Izaak Walton League, and the Wilderness Society, was a stunning success. Over the course of several long years, the assorted groups, working in concert in several coalitions including the Council of

Conservationists, the Emergency Committee on Natural Resources, and the Trustees for Conservation, worked behind the scenes and out in the open to highlight the project's flaws and the unique beauty of the land it threatened. To drum up knowledge of and interest in the area, dam opponents sponsored rafting trips through the national monument. Photographs taken on these trips were published and distributed widely, in an effort to increase visitation to the area as well as to make more people aware of its existence and its special nature.[32] In the same vein, the Council also printed and distributed pamphlets to members of Congress, newspaper editors, and state and local officials. Dam opponents even produced a motion picture, which was shown nationwide, and a book-length collection of essays and photographs.[33] In addition to their group's own magazines, opponents used the mass media to generate publicity for their cause and to encourage protest against the dam. Articles in *Life, Newsweek,* and other widely read magazines helped highlight the conflict and sway public opinion. These efforts were accompanied by what was then the largest mail campaign in conservation history. Some estimates claim that congressional mail ran an astonishing eighty to one against the dam.[34]

A key moment in the conflict occurred during congressional testimony, when dam opponents discovered errors in the Bureau's technical analyses and assumptions about the need for the dam. When Bureau representatives were forced to acknowledge these errors, its aura of infallibility was severely eroded and the momentum shifted. In retrospect, the battle over Echo Park marked the birth of modern environmental lobbying and the arrival of environmental groups as an effective political force. According to Richard Andrews, Echo Park taught environmental groups "new tactics for using the mass media to mobilize broad-based political opposition. From this experience they began to generate organizational momentum for more far-reaching campaigns."[35] Susan Zakin concurs, noting that lobbying tactics used in the Echo Park campaign would eventually become "standard issue" for environmental groups in the 1970s and 1980s, but that this was the first time they had been used on a mass scale.[36] Eventually, environmental groups would use radio, television, and the Internet toward the same end.

LOBBYING CONGRESS DURING THE "GOLDEN AGE"

Beginning in the late 1960s with the emergence of an "environmental movement" and the rise of environmental issues to prominence on the governmental agenda, Congress began to address a wider range of environmental problems. It was during this period when many of the nation's landmark environmental laws were adopted, with environmental groups playing a critical role in deliberations over the National Environmental Policy Act, the Clean Air and Water Acts, and the Endangered Species Act, to name just a few. Lobbying by the Natural Resources Defense Council and the National Wildlife Federation, moreover, was critical to the inclusion of environmental land use criteria in several public lands laws, such as the Federal Land Policy Management Act. The Wilderness Society and the National Parks Conservation Association, which have their own particular issue niches, were also quite effective in arguing for specific provisions in parks and wilderness legislation.[37] This is not to suggest that the laws were passed entirely because of environmental group lobbying. The groups were operating in a highly favorable political environment because, for most of the decade, there was widespread public support for action on environmental problems. After all, members of Congress find that it is relatively easy to reach agreement when there is public consensus on an issue.[38]

As their memberships and budgets increased, groups added staff and expanded the range of their congressional lobbying techniques. Several important changes within Congress in the 1970s and 1980s also increased the access and influence of environmental groups. As a case in point, the decision to decentralize power from committees to subcommittees and to increase the number and autonomy of subcommittees meant more freedom for junior members. Similarly, the dramatic increase in committee and personal staff and greater jurisdictional autonomy for subcommittees contributed to the rise of policy entrepreneurs in Congress. For those members of Congress who had been frustrated by the ability of committee barons to stifle new policies, the new environment was quite liberating. Members seeking to advance an issue, or their own career, were now free to delve into issues that had been beyond their reach. This also created an opportunity for interest groups that had been shut out under the old congressional rules and norms. By establishing alliances with entrepreneurial members of Congress, groups could advance their cause. As Kraft and Wuertz rightly note, lobbying is a two-way street, since group leaders need access to Congress and members of Congress need interest groups for the information and political support they can provide.[39] Of course, members of Congress have little use for interest groups that provide unreliable or misleading information. It was therefore imperative for groups to establish reputations as credible and trustworthy if they were to gain the confidence of potential allies.

With the increase in financial resources and professional staff, the mainstream national groups became legitimate and effective Washington lobbyists, engaging in all of the typical advocacy techniques. For example, it was not unusual for lobbyists to distribute policy papers to legislators, or to bring group members to Washington for face-to-face visits with policymakers, especially if those members happened to be influential constituents. Group lobbyists would work to alert members of Congress (or their staff) to the effects of a bill on their district. Many became adept at developing and coordinating legislative strategies with sympathetic legislators and other groups.[40] For strategic reasons, therefore, interest groups may want to take the initiative on proposals they dislike, because they recognize that action is likely. In these circumstances, group lobbyists may work with a friendly committee chair and try to persuade them to frame the hearings in such a way that the group's concerns take center stage.[41] Some groups developed reputations for doing quality research and for conducting effective lobbying campaigns. Representatives of environmental organizations were routinely invited to testify at congressional hearings, invitations they were happy to accept because testifying enhanced the group's legitimacy in the eyes of the public, the media, and the policymakers themselves. Moreover, media coverage of congressional hearings frequently meant that the group's message would reach a larger audience.[42] A number of group leaders also cultivated relationships with the media as they tried to drum up interest in their particular issues, and several made regular appearances on radio and television shows.[43]

A key question for any organized group is which members of Congress to lobby: friends, foes, or those in the middle. A considerable body of the interest group literature suggests that most groups waste little time and effort lobbying their opponents. Instead, groups concentrate on their friends and on undecided legislators.[44] Obviously, interest groups need legislators to lobby on their behalf, to sponsor or cosponsor legislation, and to help out in committee. Groups have an especially keen interest in maintaining good relationships with the key members of the committees and subcommittees with which they regularly interact. According to Melanie Griffin, a Sierra Club lobbyist, passing out position papers to friendly members serves an important purpose: "They're ammunition in a rhetoric war. We want to encourage our champions to go on the floor and represent the environmental position."[45]

It is difficult to gauge the effectiveness of environmental group lobbying.[46] There were some impressive victories in the 1970s, especially early in the decade. In the 1980s, furthermore, a campaign by community groups played a key role in adding right-to-know provisions about toxic chemical releases to the Superfund Amendments and Reauthorization Act (SARA).[47] Much of this success, though, is attributable to the bipartisan consensus on environmental issues that prevailed at the time. Gradually, as the costs and complexities of environmental programs became clearer, and as other issues displaced the environment from the top of the agenda, that consensus evaporated. Soon, very few issues would provoke stronger partisan disputes. Toward the end of the decade industry groups, who had been caught off guard by the rush of environmental legislation of the early 1970s, mounted a counteroffensive. Environmental groups would spend much of the next twenty years playing defense, rather than pushing through new legislative initiatives. Policy victories would be much harder to come by in the changed political environment.

Congress and the Clean Air Act

Consider, for example, the various battles over the Clean Air Act, which was first enacted in 1970, and then amended in 1977 and 1990. As noted above, environmental organizations were just beginning to assemble lobbying staffs in 1970, and did not play a major role in deliberations over the 1970 law. The groups did have a Washington presence by the middle of the decade, however, and were major players in the debates over the 1977 Clean Air Act Amendments.[48] Seeking to pool their resources, environmental groups joined forces with a number of labor, public health, and good government groups to form the National Clean Air Coalition.[49] Beginning with a list of activists from across the nation, the Coalition established a field organization. Each activist was asked to contact a dozen or more others, who would then do the same. The goal was to generate grassroots pressure on legislators through postcards, letters, and phone calls. The Coalition also distributed mimeographs to staff assistants on a daily basis in 1976 and 1977, detailing the latest medical research on clean air.[50]

By the time the Clean Air Act was up for renewal in the 1980s, the political and economic contexts were very different. First, Ronald Reagan had been elected president in 1980, and he was adamantly opposed to strengthening the law. Reagan believed that the excessive federal regulation was responsible for the nation's economic woes, driving prices up, profits down, and generally making American business uncompetitive. His appointments to key regulatory positions were carefully screened to ensure that they shared his antiregulatory views. Another complicating factor was that the Senate was in Republican hands from 1981 to January of 1987, and Senate Republicans were not enthusiastic about the Clean Air Act either. Despite their lack of enthusiasm, though, Republicans did not want to risk the political fallout that might follow from weakening the law. At the same time, those who wanted to strengthen the law did not have the votes to do so, so both sides opted to avoid a major showdown by postponing a major overhaul.

Confronted by this new and less hospitable political environment, the National Clean Air Coalition shifted to what Richard Cohen called the "guerrilla tactics of political opposition."[51] The Coalition, which was headed by Richard Ayres of the Natural Resources Defense Council, proved to be very effective at blocking changes that might have weakened the law. The organization had a staff of three and worked informally, serving as a forum for discussions among the groups and for the coordination of efforts, mostly outside of Congress. Once decisions were made, the various groups did the follow-up work. Lawyers from the Natural Resources Defense Council assumed a central role in analyzing proposed legislative and regulatory language, while Sierra Club lobbyists handled much of the congressional work. The America Lung Association, because of its credibility within the scientific community, gave the coalition an important boost by providing access to health data on pollution risks. By this time, the National Wildlife Federation and the National Audubon Society, who had not been politically active during earlier clean air fights, had joined the Coalition as well. The staff of the Audubon Society was especially good at packaging clean air stories and events that captured media attention.

Even though Democrats regained control of the Senate in 1987, there would be no deal on the Clean Air Act while Reagan was president. A deal seemed possible early in 1988, but it fell apart in election year politics. Senate Majority Leader George Mitchell had worked out some compromises with the White House behind closed doors, but environmentalists resisted, arguing that a better deal could be struck after the election, especially if a Democrat won the White House. Mitchell was quite angry about the rebuff, saying his environmental critics were rigid and unyielding. It would not be the last time he would express these sentiments.[52]

Prospects for an agreement brightened considerably in 1988, when George H. W. Bush, seeking to distance himself from Reagan, campaigned on a promise to be the "environmental president." After his victory, Bush promised to move on clean air legislation. A breakthrough came when two staffers from the Environmental Defense Fund proposed an innovative, but controversial, acid rain emissions trading system. Bush liked the idea, because of its reliance on market-type solutions, but many within the environmental community were opposed to it for precisely the same reason.[53] Eventually, a clean air bill passed Congress and was signed into law by the president in 1990.

Most observers have concluded that the mainstream environmental groups played a major role in shaping the 1990 Clean Air Act Amendments. According to Richard Cohen, the National Clean Air Coalition's views on specific provisions were "carefully considered" by others involved in the debate. Yet Cohen concludes that the Coalition's influence peaked when the Bush administration announced its support for a plan because, he says, interest groups generally begin to lose power when passage of a bill is seen as inevitable. In fact, Cohen argues that environmental groups made their most important contributions during the Reagan years, "first by helping to defeat weakening legislation and then by gradually building public support for a stronger law. By 1990, when the clean-air bill was at the top of the agenda for Washington power brokers, the environmentalists had been pushed toward the sidelines."[54]

The Coalition's influence was also limited by internal divisions, and by a lack of access during critical phases of congressional negotiations. On several crucial issues, environmental groups also believed they were let down by their congressional allies, such as Congressman Waxman's decision to abandon the quest for higher automotive fuel efficiency standards. With so many coalition partners, pleasing everyone was exceptionally difficult. For example, internal splits were revealed during debate over an amendment offered by Senator Robert Byrd. Byrd's amendment, which sought to compensate and retrain coal miners who might lose their jobs due to tougher clean air rules, drove a wedge between some of the environmental groups and their labor union allies. Most of the environmental groups supported the proposal, and were caught off guard when Jay Hair, president of the National Wildlife Federation, came out against it. Hair's opposition came as a complete surprise to the Wildlife Federation's senior lobbyist, who had worked for its adoption.[55] This internal disarray angered Senator Mitchell as well, who said of the groups, "They were not helpful in this process."[56]

The struggle to enact the 1990 amendments sparked tensions between Mitchell and the environmental groups, who thought Mitchell had compromised too much in his eagerness to get a bill. The groups were also angry because many important agreements were reached in closed-door sessions, from which they were excluded and where they had little influence. For a variety of reasons, the majority leader had also made a decision to reach an agreement with the White House on the entire bill before bringing it to the floor. As a result, a lot of compromises were struck along the way, angering environmentalists who believed they could have gotten a stronger bill on the Senate floor while scoring some political points by making Republicans cast some unpopular votes. In the end, environmental groups offered a number of strengthening amendments on the floor, not accepting Mitchell's view that the agreed upon measure was the best they could do. For his part, Mitchell had agreed to oppose all strengthening amendments. Most of the measures were defeated, including the two that were the focus of the most intense lobbying. One sought to establish more stringent tailpipe emission reductions, while the other tightened local smog control rules.[57]

As this discussion of congressional lobbying shows, the tactics of environmental groups have evolved over the years. As their budgets and staffs increased, environmental groups were able to engage in a broader range of lobbying activities. The discussion also shows, though, that their success was highly dependent on political circumstances. Not surprisingly, the groups tasted their greatest success when public opinion was supportive of their goals and when their friends controlled Congress and the White House. As we will see, that set of circumstances would not be permanent.

LOBBYING THE EXECUTIVE BRANCH

In addition to lobbying legislators, many environmental groups routinely lobby the White House and executive branch agencies as well. In their study of interest group lobbying, Schlozman and Tierney found that 89 percent of organized groups tried to influence the bureaucracy and 78 percent participated in drafting rules and agency guidelines.[58] With the rise of the modern presidency and administrative government, many important program details are inevitably resolved in the relatively less accessible administrative process. Interest group leaders know that presidents and bureaucrats can have a profound effect on policymaking. Moreover, group leaders also know that politics does not end after Congress has acted; indeed, "those vanquished in the legislative arena can, and often do, resort to the administrative forum where they successfully undercut the effectiveness of policy at the point where it is interpreted and applied."[59] In the words of Walter Rosenbaum, "vigilance over administration" is the "price of victory in the policy process."[60] In short, if environmental groups want to protect the environment, they need to try to influence the White House and bureaucracy.

This can be done in a variety of ways. With respect to the White House, groups seek to work through the Office of Public Liaison, which works with organized groups to exchange information about policy initiatives and decisions. Of course, different presidents are attentive to different interests, so group access tends to fluctuate depending on who resides in the White House. President Carter, for example, was much more receptive to environmental groups than was President Reagan.

Environmental groups also try to influence presidential appointments to key administrative positions, such as EPA administrator or Interior secretary. Some interest group scholars contend that appointments are generally made from among candidates who are acceptable to the major groups in that policy domain, but that has not always been the case with the environment.[61] In fact, the record here is quite mixed. While environmentalists were generally pleased with President Carter's nominees, at least in part because several of them actually came from environmental organizations, they were distraught over many of Ronald Reagan's choices. Indeed, most of the nation's environmental groups bitterly opposed James Watt, Reagan's first Interior secretary. President George H. W. Bush adopted a more moderate stance, and selected William Reilly, formerly head of the World Wildlife Fund and the Conservation Foundation, to head the EPA. Bush also chose Michael Deland, formerly director of the EPA's New England region, to chair the Council on Environmental Quality. EPA Director Russell E. Train, who had previously served in the same role and later as head of the World Wildlife Fund, was an informal Bush adviser as well. Although environmental groups did not universally embrace his appointments, President Clinton was considerably more sympathetic to environmental concerns than either Bush or Reagan. In addition to choosing Bruce Babbitt, former Arizona governor and head of the League of Conservation Voters to be Interior secretary, Clinton also appointed several representatives from the Wilderness Society and the Audubon Society to important policy positions in the Department of Interior.[62]

Participation in administrative hearings, regulatory workshops, and rule-making proceedings provide important pathways for interest groups seeking to influence federal and state bureaucracies. A number of the larger national groups, notably the Natural Resources Defense Council and the Wilderness Society, routinely testify in administrative proceedings, monitor rule making, and offer expert advice on drafting regulations. Under the Administrative Procedures Act, agencies must provide opportunities for public notice and comment for new rules as well as proposed changes to existing rules. Interested parties are afforded the opportunity to comment on the rules, either in person at a public hearing or in writing during an informal rule-making proceeding. Environmental groups have had some successes in this arena, such as the Environmental Defense Fund's efforts in the 1970s encouraging the EPA to ban the pesticide DDT. Other successes include the Forest Service's 1973 RARE I (Roadless Area Review and Evaluation), in which environmental groups generated more than eight thousand letters of support for increasing the wilderness study acreage. The campaign was announced after the Forest Service had announced its preliminary wilderness recommendations, calling for wilderness study status for about eleven million of the fifty-six million acres that had been reviewed.[63]

More recently, groups have had success in turning out large numbers of members at public hearings and in generating large numbers of public comments on proposed rules, at both the federal and state levels. For example, the Washington Wilderness Coalition, a relatively small group working to protect ancient forests in the state, claims that it turned out 1,200 people at two dozen public hearings on a proposed Forest Service rule limiting road building in the national forests. In all, the Forest Service received more than 60,000 public comments on the rule from residents of Washington, the fourth most of any state, with 96 percent of the comments calling for stronger wilderness protection. On the same issue, the Wilderness Society was part of a coordinated effort that helped generate more than 400,000 public comments in favor of the proposed rule. The group's Wild Alert email activist system was instrumental in that effort.

Despite these successes, some observers contend that industry interests, who typically have access to the best data and who can often generate more comments in support of their position, dominate the public notice and comment process.[64] The industry advantage is presumed to stem largely from its superior financial resources. For example, industry trade associations have generated large numbers of public comments on pending rules by paying for advertisements that direct people to call toll-free numbers. Once connected, the callers are asked for their names, telephone numbers, and addresses, and the group then sends a letter in the person's name to the agency official responsible for the issue.[65] The purpose of this "Astroturf" lobbying, of course, is to persuade the official that the group's position is widely shared by members of the public. Deep pockets also allow many businesses to employ staffers and analysts whose sole job is to track rule-making proceedings, hearings, and public comment opportunities. As Switzer points out, however, only a handful of the national environmental groups have a similar capacity to track and monitor the development and implementation of rules. Most groups, especially local grassroots organizations, do not have the budget or personnel to staff similar operations.[66]

Business interests, helped by their ability to make campaign contributions, are often invited to participate on federal advisory committees or boards and presidential task forces. Membership on such committees can provide access to valuable information about the agency's intentions and the opportunity to influence pending actions. Perhaps the best illustration of privileged access is the energy task force created by President George W. Bush in January of 2001. During its deliberations over a national energy policy, the task force met repeatedly with more than three dozen industry representatives, lobbyists, and executives, while virtually shutting environmental groups out of the process. In fact, environmental groups were consulted only at the last minute and, to compound the insult, were given just twenty-four hours to respond to inquiries from the task force. Many opted not to respond. According to the Center for Responsive Politics, twenty-nine of the thirty-six industry representatives who met with Energy Secretary Spencer Abraham, many of them in private, had contributed to the Bush campaign.[67] Abraham, who had been targeted for defeat in his 2000 Senate race by the League of Conservation Voters and the Sierra Club, held no meetings with environmentalists. In the end, the task force embraced many of the industry recommendations while giving short shrift to energy efficiency and renewable energy programs.

Environmentalists have long been skeptical of federal administrators, believing them to be beholden to industry and thus incapable of protecting the public interest. That is why environmental groups consistently tried to limit agency discretion in this period. Moreover, many also believed that they had limited influence over the agencies. This view was expressed by Michael McCloskey, executive director of the Sierra Club in the 1980s, who said that "although the bureaucracies are somewhat responsive to Presidential direction, they are not very responsive to outside lobbying and are subject to no self-correcting process if they fail to be productive."[68] Most groups, then, knew that lobbying the executive branch would not be enough to secure their policy goals.

LOBBYING THE PUBLIC

In addition to lobbying the various institutions of government, environmental groups frequently lobby the public. Such outside or indirect lobbying can take many forms, including direct mail, issue advertising on radio, television, or in newspapers, press conferences announcing the release of a new study, grassroots campaigns, and, in some cases, direct action and protests. Because environmental groups are often seeking to attract attention to their cause and to frame public perceptions of issues, obtaining media attention is often a key part of any attempt to lobby the public. As we have seen, environmental groups have long tried to influence the public. Over the years, though, technological developments have made communicating with the public easier and cheaper and many of the national groups have obtained the money to engage in more expensive forms of public outreach, such as radio and television advertising.

Groups can have several goals in lobbying the public, including public education, generating pressure on policymakers, legitimizing the arguments delivered by the groups' lobbyists, and increasing an issue's political salience. In some cases, the goal is to persuade the public to accept the group's position on an issue; in others, the goal is to mobilize people to take action, usually by contacting policymakers directly. Most grassroots campaigns are not spontaneous happenings; rather, they are carefully orchestrated by organized groups, which target their appeals to group members in particular legislative districts. The hope then is that constituents, who presumably have more sway with legislators, will help the group make its case. Perhaps most importantly, outside lobbying can also be used to shape people's attitudes about issues, in the belief that public attitudes are eventually reflected in public policy decisions.

Undoubtedly, the top priority for most interest groups is lobbying on what Jeffrey Berry calls "front-burner" concerns, such as legislation currently being debated in Congress or regulations pending before an administrative agency. As Berry argues, however, some interest groups also think strategically about long-term goals and about how they can convince the public, and the government, to pay attention to them. In fact, he contends that agenda building and the mobilization of public opinion are at the heart of the work of citizen groups.[69] As a result, if resources permit, leaders of such groups are highly active in trying to frame issues and define problems. That is, they work to persuade others to understand their issues in a way that is different from the prevailing conception.[70] As an example, during the debate over grazing reform in the early 1990s, the Wilderness Society and other reform advocates worked to link the issue of grazing reform to the then-popular theme of reducing economic waste, by depicting grazing rights as a form of corporate welfare. The groups noted that many permit holders were not family ranchers but rather large corporate behemoths with few ties to the land. The goal of such an argument, of course, was to alter the prevailing perception of the issue in the eyes of the public and key legislators.[71]

The process of agenda building, notes Berry, is a long-term undertaking, and entails several different tactics. At the most basic level, it is a process of educating policymakers, journalists, and the public about a problem they may not recognize or do not consider to be very important. Before any action can be taken, groups must convince the public, and ultimately key policymakers, that a serious problem exists, and that it deserves government action. Groups also must show why their recommended course of action is preferable to others.[72] John Kingdon contends that this process may require an extended "softening up" period while studies are issued, journalists are spun, forums are held, and committee staffers are lobbied. It can take years, he argues, from the time a group starts working to place its issue on the agenda to when policymakers actually start working on solutions.[73]

Grassroots campaigns have always been a popular tactic for environmentalists, in large part because a chronic lack of resources and prestige ruled out other forms of direct advocacy. Letter-writing campaigns and other outside tactics, such as protests and boycotts, are particularly common among local community groups, who typically have very little cash and depend on volunteers rather than paid staff. As noted above, groups that have been excluded from policymaking arenas often utilize grassroots campaigns. Moreover, in their study of Washington interest groups, Schlozman and Tierney document that 80 percent of all advocacy organizations conduct grassroots lobbying campaigns, while 84 percent encourage their members to contact public officials by mail or telephone.[74]

Environmental groups conduct grassroots campaigns for several reasons. One is to bring attention to their cause; another is to mobilize the public and key constituents to take some action designed to influence policymakers. In trying to educate and mobilize the general public, groups can "broadcast" their message through paid newspaper, radio, or television advertising. Group publications, like magazines and books, can also be used to great effect. In trying to mobilize their own members or activist base, on the other hand, groups may opt to "narrowcast" by communicating in the group's newsletter, or by direct mail, telephone, or fax. Both methods are costly, but over the years the advances in technology have made it easier for groups to communicate with the public, and they with policymakers, while reducing the cost. Environmental groups often use emotional, dramatic pleas in their grassroots communications. Kraft and Wuertz, for example, note the frequent use of "condensational symbols" or emotional appeals whose power, they claim, derives from the public's strong commitment to environmental values.[75] Until the 1960s and 1970s, environmental appeals relied on terms like "conservation," but they were replaced with powerful new symbols like clean air and water, public health and safety, and protections from toxic substances, which elicited "strong protective feelings among the public."[76]

A good illustration of this type of grassroots communication is provided by the Oregon Natural Resources Coalition's fight in the late 1980s and early 1990s to protect old-growth forests. The environmental community was divided, with the Sierra Club preferring to work with the region's congressional delegation while other groups wanted to be more aggressive. ORNC's strategy was to split the difference by using a national lobbying effort to persuade the delegation. Activists went to work to select a campaign slogan and, after some discussion, settled upon the phrase "ancient forests." "When we heard that phrase, 'ancient forests,' we knew we were dead," said a Forest Service public relations official to Brock Evans, an Audubon Society lobbyist who played a key role in the fight.[77] Perhaps the best example of the use of emotional appeals, however, is Greenpeace's famous and highly effective 1976 direct mail campaign depicting baby harp seals being clubbed to death. The copy read, "Kiss this baby goodbye." The ad campaign thrust Greenpeace into the spotlight, and within five years it would claim more than two million members.[78]

Some groups choose to conduct grassroots campaigns because they believe that constituents exert more influence over legislators than do paid lobbyists. In fact, many lobbyists encourage their groups to spend heavily to generate numerous constituent letters, not because they think the letters will work by themselves but because the lobbyists assume that the letters will give their own efforts legitimacy, and that congressional staffers and other public officials will thus be more responsive if they know that constituents are paying attention to the issue.[79] In its efforts to win greater protection for the Tongass National Forest, for example, representatives from the Southeast Alaska Conservation Council traveled around the nation, presenting a slide show at community meetings with environmental activists. These meetings succeeded in generating thousands of letters to Congress, and eventually forced Alaska's reluctant congressional delegation to the negotiating table. In 1990, Congress passed the Tongass Timber Reform Act.[80] According to Sierra Club lobbyist Melanie Griffin, it helps to have group members echoing her statements to policymakers. She adds, "The grassroots makes us different. When I go to the Hill, I know I have people behind me, that I'm speaking for them and their special places." Melinda Pierce, another Sierra Club lobbyist, says the letters and phone calls help because "when I go into a congressional office, they know that we have members who are constituents in their districts."[81]

Grassroots campaigns are not without their problems. They can be expensive; they are indirect, which risks confusing the group's message; and as they become more widely used, they may lose their effectiveness. This is especially true of orchestrated campaigns, where legislators may be inundated with preprinted postcards or faxes. Most importantly, though, grassroots campaigns typically come late in the political process, after the agenda has already been set. As Jeffrey Berry notes, letter-writing campaigns generally begin when the sides are fully mobilized, and when policymakers are thus apt to be less open to persuasion.[82]

Nonetheless, environmental groups learned early on that grassroots campaigns could be highly effective in promoting awareness of environmental issues in the public's mind. In the same vein, group leaders learned that effective grassroots campaigns provided a valuable opportunity to define issues for the public, the media, and, at least indirectly, policymakers.

Media Campaigns

Despite a chronic lack of money, environmental groups have long attempted to shape public opinion and attract attention to themselves and to their issues through the use of media campaigns. Until the 1980s, the media campaigns conducted by the national groups consisted primarily of magazines, books, films, paid advertising in magazines and newspapers, and a variety of tactics designed at generating free media coverage. Some groups could afford to hire public relations firms to help develop their campaigns and write their press releases, but most did the work in-house. Press conferences, press releases, staged media events, and demonstrations were also commonly used. As their budgets increased, groups were able to advertise more often, and several retained the services of professional public relations firms. Over the years, the groups' media campaigns became more sophisticated, and a handful of organizations now have the money to advertise on radio and television.

Environmental media campaigns are not new. Indeed, beginning in the 1930s the Wilderness Society used its magazine, *Living Wilderness,* to call attention to endangered areas and to mobilize public opinion in defense of those areas.[83] Similarly, under David Brower's direction, the Sierra Club began taking the organization's philosophical, educational, and scientific ideals directly to the public in the late 1950s and early 1960s. This was done even though the Club was a nonprofit organization and thus prohibited from lobbying by IRS rules. In anticipation of losing its tax-free status, the Club established a separate entity, the Sierra Club Foundation, in 1960, and began advocating letter-writing campaigns in its own name. In 1965, through publications like its Exhibit Format books, which featured photographs of endangered places, the Club sought to reinforce the "aesthetic of the monumental West." Brower believed that people could be moved to act to save a place if they knew about it, and the glossy, illustrated Exhibit Format books were designed to introduce a large audience to these special places.[84] One such book, *The Place No One Knew: Glen Canyon on the Colorado,* featured photos by Eliot Porter, with text from Aldo Leopold, Albert Einstein, and Henry David Thoreau.[85] When a proposed dam threatened the Grand Canyon, Brower announced plans for an Exhibit Format book, which included a budget to send copies to all members of Congress. The Club also produced two films and a special Grand Canyon newsletter alerting members to the threat.[86]

The Sierra Club films were important because they introduced people from across the country to places they might never have known existed. These films, and later television and videos, helped groups mobilize large numbers of people in support of wilderness. In the 1970s, for example, another Sierra Club film, *Alaska: Land in the Balance,* played a critical role in rousing public support for protecting Alaskan wilderness.[87] With the help of these visual aids, groups could generate national constituencies in support of local issues. In the words of Susan Zakin, "The emergence of nationwide mass media constituencies thus propelled several new kinds of environmental issues onto the national agenda." The primary beneficiaries, at least in the early years, were the old-line preservation groups, who seized on the new opportunities to dramatize their concerns to larger audiences, to mobilize public opinion, and to build larger, national memberships.[88]

The Sierra Club ran its first paid newspaper ad in December 1965—an open letter urging President Johnson to establish Redwood National Park in California. The ad, which appeared in papers across the United States, urged readers to "Write the President and Governor Brown yourself; support the organizations that support the real park." Then Secretary of the Interior Stewart Udall, who favored a somewhat smaller park, was angered by the ad, believing that the Club had crossed a line.[89]

Udall's anger paled in comparison to his response to the Club's famous series of Grand Canyon ads, which began running in June of 1966. The Club bought a series of four full-page ads in the *New York Times, Washington Post, San Francisco Chronicle,* and the *Los Angeles Times.* Each paper split its press run, with one featuring copy written by David Brower, the other written by an advertising agency. Both ads contained coupons readers could send to the Club, President Johnson, Secretary Udall, Congressman Wayne Aspinall, and the readers' own senators and congressional representatives. The second ad was more aggressive, and more effective, judging from the number of coupons returned to the Club. The ad copy read, "Now Only You Can Save Grand Canyon From Being Flooded—

For Profit." The very next day, the IRS hand-delivered a letter to Club officials stating that deductions to the Club could no longer be considered to be deductible, essentially revoking its tax-free status. The most famous ad ran later in the summer, and asked "Should we also flood the Sistine Chapel so tourists can get nearer the ceiling?" Despite the loss of its tax-free status, both the newspaper ads and the IRS response paid large dividends for the Club, generating considerable media attention, as well as thousands of telephone calls and telegrams to Congress.[90]

Despite a lack of money and a shortage of professional communications staff, some of the early media campaigns were quite successful. Still, group leaders had to learn through trial and error how to wage effective media campaigns. Quite clearly, before groups can educate or persuade the public, they must first attract the attention of media gatekeepers. Accordingly, that meant cultivating and maintaining relationships with reporters and editorial boards. Group leaders also devoted significant time and attention to designing stories that would attract media attention, and then "delivering" them to journalists. As many have noted, there is a symbiotic relationship between interest groups and the media: groups want maximum publicity for their stories, and journalists need "news" to report. In creating and planting news stories, then, groups were helping serve the needs of a production-oriented media.[91] Environmental groups soon learned that crises and disasters were effective ways of gaining media attention, and so issued press releases and held press conferences announcing scientific studies tracking signs of environmental decline. These would often receive prominent coverage, especially if the group was perceived as credible.[92]

Stories of gloom and doom are not by themselves enough to ensure media coverage, especially when thousands of other groups are striving to gain attention for their own issues. Competition among organized groups for media coverage is intense, and each group tries to ensure that its top issues gain attention.[93] Therefore, says William Browne, groups must design complex messages that, in his words, "stay in front of people, have a modestly lasting impact, and periodically recur." If a group can show, using examples over a period of time, that some problem persists, the chances of journalists paying attention are enhanced.[94] In 1988, for example, a record-breaking heat wave, combined with a series of large fires in the west, including one at Yellowstone National Park, seemed to many to herald the onset of global warming. That same summer, beaches across the nation were closed due to medical waste and dead marine life washing ashore. Each story built upon previous ones, reinforcing claims that the environment was deteriorating.

Stories like Love Canal, where toxic contamination sickened many families and rendered their homes worthless, received a tremendous amount of publicity in the late 1970s, at least in part because they reinforced prevailing images of corporate carelessness. In Deborah Stone's parlance, the Love Canal story was almost a classic example of a struggle between good and evil, with innocent citizens being victimized by corporate villains. Indeed, stories about threats to children's health were quite common, because they are so powerful. In the late

1980s, the Natural Resources Defense Council skillfully used television to prod the EPA to ban Alar, a chemical commonly used on apples. In actress Meryl Streep, the NRDC also had an effective celebrity spokesperson to make the case that Alar threatened the nation's children, who consumed large amounts of apple juice and apple sauce.[95]

Environmental groups often recruited celebrities to help publicize their causes and raise money. Beginning in the 1970s, popular musicians like the Eagles, Jackson Browne, and Bonnie Raitt held benefit concerts for a range of environmental causes and political candidates. A wide assortment of artists called Musicians United for Safe Energy (MUSE) held a series of concerts in New York to protest nuclear power and call attention to renewable energy sources. The concerts, which received a lot of media attention, were recorded and filmed as well, and later released in music stores and in theaters. Similarly, Don Henley, a member of the Eagles, created a nonprofit group called the Walden Woods Project in 1990 when he learned that developers were threatening the land made famous by Thoreau. Other musicians also donated a portion of their concert and recording proceeds to environmental causes and organizations.

As Kraft and Wuertz have suggested, media-based strategies have been appropriate and effective for groups outside of the mainstream, including many local grassroots organizations.[96] Generally speaking, both local groups and some of the more radical organizations have very little faith in the political process, and they thus tend to avoid the more conventional lobbying tactics. Some, like Greenpeace in the 1970s and EarthFirst! somewhat later, preferred direct action. Greenpeace's attempts to halt whaling and nuclear testing in the Pacific drew considerable media attention, as did alleged "monkeywrenching" by EarthFirst! The downside of direct action, of course, is that it is not perceived as a legitimate form of participation by many Americans, and despite all the media attention, groups that engage in it are often marginalized.[97]

COALITIONS AND ALLIANCES: WORKING WITH OTHER GROUPS

It was not always the case, but by the middle of the 1980s environmental groups were routinely building coalitions and alliances with one another and with a variety of labor, public health, and progressive organizations. Previously, coalitions were formed on an ad hoc basis around specific conservation battles, but once the battle was over, as in the fights over Echo Park and the Grand Canyon, the groups would go their separate ways. With so many groups opening Washington offices in the 1970s, however, the opportunities to coordinate strategies increased. Coalition building was an attractive option because it allowed risks and costs to be spread among the participating groups, so the groups could participate in more campaigns or could be more powerful in important efforts.[98]

In most instances, the coalitions formed by environmental groups tend to be rather loose configurations, focusing on some shared set of policy interests and goals.[99] Over the years, an informal division of labor has emerged, with different groups taking turns leading the coalitions. As David Howard Davis describes the process, leadership of a given coalition may depend on the issue at hand, or on the particular skills the groups can bring to bear, such as litigation, scientific research, grassroots organizing, Washington lobbying, or media campaigns.[100] More specifically, the Sierra Club, with its many regional and local chapters, has proven to be adept at mobilizing its grass roots, while the Wilderness Society has developed a reputation for credible research and effective public relations. Similarly, staffers at the Natural Resources Defense Council are often called upon to examine and decipher federal regulatory programs. The National Wildlife Federation has also filled a valuable niche because of its ability to communicate with sportsmen and the working class.[101]

Although groups had formed coalitions before, the Reagan administration was really the impetus for greater coordination and collaboration among environmentalists.[102] Leaders of the largest national organizations formed the "Group of Ten," which met quarterly to coordinate strategies. The conservation directors of these groups also met regularly to coordinate their campaign planning. Various ad hoc coalitions met as needed, with some, like the Clean Air Coalition, the National Campaign for Pesticide Policy Reform, and the Clean Water Network carrying on for years.[103]

One of the more effective coalitions centered on the decade-long 1970s campaign to set aside vast tracts of Alaska land as wilderness.[104] Preservationists had been studying the wilderness potential of Alaska since the formation of the Alaska Wilderness Council in 1967, and several groups began devoting significant resources to the issue. According to Craig Allin, preservation groups had the time to refine their proposals, "educate their memberships, and build the legislative machinery for an all-out drive" because the issue had germinated for a while.[105] Between 1973 and 1977 the groups worked to build grassroots support for a bill, with group magazines playing the primary role.

Environmentalists also used the time to build a potent lobbying institution to shepherd the legislation through Congress. Although the Alaska Coalition was actually created in 1971, it took on a major role in 1977, when staff from the National Audubon Society, the Wilderness Society, the Sierra Club, the National Parks and Conservation Association, and Defenders of Wildlife met and decided that Alaska was the most important conservation issue of the century.[106] By the end of the decade, the Alaska Coalition included almost every major environmental group.[107] As Craig Allin notes, the scope of cooperation was "unprecedented," with each group contributing money, office space, and support staff. In his opinion, "At the height of its activity, the Alaska Coalition mounted the best organized, best financed lobbying campaign in the history of conservation."[108]

With money obtained both from the groups and a highly successful direct mail campaign, the Alaska Coalition could engage in a host of advocacy tactics generally reserved for industry groups. The staff in Washington was large enough to achieve a degree of specialization unprecedented in environmental lobbying. The Coalition had ten full-time lobbyists working Congress. A separate staff worked the media.[109] Grassroots organizers had specific regional areas of influence. Indeed, a massive grassroots effort was a key part of the strategy. The Coalition sent out grassroots organizers to travel the country; they succeeded in building a network of an estimated ten thousand workers. Leaders communicated with the grassroots network through direct mail and a twenty-four-hour telephone hotline that offered daily updates. According to some sources, the volume of congressional mail generated by the Coalition was the greatest since the civil rights debates of the early 1960s.[110] In the end, the effort was successful, with President Carter signing the Alaska National Interest Lands Conservation Act into law just before he left office in 1981.

From time to time, and with mixed success, environmentalists tried to develop alliances with labor groups. In the early 1990s, for example, labor unions and some environmental groups opposed the North American Free Trade Agreement (NAFTA) because of a lack of protections for American workers and the environment. The environmental community was divided over NAFTA, with most grassroots organizations opposing the agreement and several of the national groups, such as the World Wildlife Fund and the National Wildlife Federation supporting it.[111] On other issues, though, such as the perennial attempts to open the Arctic National Wildlife Refuge to drilling, cooperation was more problematic, as some unions, notably the Teamsters, support drilling because of the potential for new union jobs.

When John Sweeney was elected AFL-CIO president in 1995, he set out to forge tighter links with environmental groups. Sweeney named Jane Perkins, a former Pennsylvania labor leader and president of Friends of the Earth to be the labor federation's first liaison to the environmental movement. He also created an environmental policy committee on the AFL-CIO executive council. These efforts have borne some fruit, as when a revived "green/labor" coalition worked in 1997 to defeat President Clinton's request for "fast-track" authority to negotiate global economic agreements.

Some labor unions have been especially supportive of environmental concerns, especially in the workplace. The Oil, Chemical, and Atomic Workers Union (OCAW) is an example of a union with a long history of working with environmental organizations. In 1973 OCAW, with support from the Sierra Club and others, called the nation's first strike over health and environmental issues. The union also worked with Greenpeace in support of banning organochlorines, an action that would ultimately result in union job losses. Finally, in the mid-1990s OCAW and a number of environmental justice groups began conducting encounters nationwide to foster cooperation and understanding between environmentalists, groups of the AFL-CIO, and community activists.[112]

Despite the obvious difficulties in forming and maintaining effective coalitions, environmental groups recognize that it is important to work together with allies to promote a common, coherent policy agenda. Groups stand a much better chance of pushing their issues onto the agenda if they can speak with one voice or, at the very least, with several voices speaking the same language.

LITIGATION

Over the last thirty-five years litigation has been, along with grassroots campaigns, the most effective weapon in the environmental group arsenal. Beginning in the late 1960s, environmental groups prevailed in a number of landmark court cases in the federal courts, which were generally sympathetic to their concerns. Although an increasingly conservative federal judiciary has more recently issued less favorable rulings, litigation continues to be an effective tactic for environmental activists. Indeed, in the eyes of many critics, environmentalists have been far too willing to use the courts, or the threat of legal action, to delay administrative decisions and drive up corporate costs. While there have surely been instances when environmental groups have filed frivolous or unwarranted lawsuits, in general the use of litigation has been justified.

As anyone who has ever taken a survey course in American government well knows, policy disputes of all stripes invariably wind up in the courts, and so it is not surprising that many environmental controversies do as well. In order to secure passage, Congress sometimes adopts vague or ambiguous laws, and leaves many important issues to be resolved by agency administrators. Bureaucrats sometimes issue confusing or complicated rules. Inevitably, the courts are asked to clarify matters. Because this litigation gives courts considerable policymaking power, the same organized groups that sought to influence legislative and executive decisions also try to influence the courts.

In American politics, it is typically the losing side, or the side that expects to lose, that appeals to the courts for help. After all, the winning side has no reason to change venues by seeking judicial relief—they are winning. But those interests who, for lack of money, size, or status, do not prevail in battles in the legislative or executive branches do have plenty of incentive to seek a more sympathetic hearing in the courts. Federal judges serve lifetime appointments, and, since they are not elected, do not answer to the citizens. Presumably, they are, therefore, less susceptible to majority pressures and have more leeway to do what is right, not what is merely popular. Litigation, in short, often represents the last, best hope for those segments of society that have been excluded, marginalized, or outspent in the more overtly political arenas. And so environmental groups have litigated in order to force neglected issues onto the policy agenda, and to defend their procedural rights to participate in the policy process.

That is why environmental groups, who were new arrivals on the Washington scene, opted to supplement their outside lobbying strategy with litigation. The late 1960s and early 1970s saw the creation of several new groups staffed with lawyers and scientists whose primary focus was on litigation.[113] The Environmental Defense Fund, which was established in 1967, grew out of a membership group of concerned scientists and lawyers who had sued the previous year to stop DDT spraying by local governments on Long Island. From its initial concern with pesticides, the group later took the lead in litigating on lead poisoning and a range of pollution issues.[114] EDF's early successes generated a considerable amount of publicity and favorable attention and helped pave the way for the creation of a variety of public interest environmental law groups. The Natural Resources Defense Council, like EDF the recipient of seed money from the Ford Foundation, was another of these groups. The Sierra Club Legal Defense Fund was a third. By the middle of the decade, these organizations had developed considerable legal and scientific expertise, which gave them the ability to participate effectively in both the legal and administrative arenas.[115]

According to Kirkpatrick Sale, the environmental law groups' emphasis on litigation was a major departure from the usual tactics of publicity campaigns and ad hoc lobbying. Their strategy was to use test-case litigation "to change federal policies through strategic legal challenges rather than merely to organize lobbying campaigns and represent the interests of national memberships." The goal was not just to win the particular case, but to force government agencies to defend themselves, and their enforcement of environmental laws, in court.[116] As noted earlier, many reformers of the period believed that the nation's regulatory agencies had been "captured" by the very interests they were supposed to regulate. As a result, regulated parties, like corporate polluters, could undercut the enforcement of even the most stringent statutes. The solution, then, was for environmental groups to act as counterweights to pressure government to do the right thing.

So the environmental law groups went to court to ensure that environmental laws were aggressively enforced. In some of the earliest cases, the groups brought suit under the National Environmental Policy Act to force federal agencies to prepare better environmental impact statements. Other suits were designed to compel agencies to carry out their congressional mandates. Throughout the 1970s and 1980s, environmentalists were aided by congressional Democrats who, suspicious of Republican presidents, adopted environmental laws containing citizen suit provisions. Laws like the Clean Air Act of 1990 opened the door to litigation by allowing private citizens or groups to act as private attorneys general and take legal action against polluters if the government failed to act. According to George Hoberg, these new legal arrangements "granted environmental groups institutional and legal foundations that to a large extent solidified their power status within the regime."[117]

By the 1980s, environmental groups were quite adept at going to court, but the strategy yielded fewer victories as the courts, staffed with conservative Reagan appointees, turned to the right. Groups began to find that courts in some regions tended to side more often with business and development interests.[118] A number of groups thus became more selective in the cases they chose to litigate, not wanting to risk setting a bad precedent. In any event, litigation provided environmental groups with an effective new tool of agenda setting. As such, it was part of larger strategy of promoting environmental perspectives in public debate, one that included both inside and outside lobbying techniques.

Interest group litigation has had a profound effect on several areas of environmental policy. In 1972, for example, a federal district court ruled in *Sierra Club v. Ruckelshaus* that the Clean Air Act required states to prevent the degradation of areas whose air quality exceeded national standards.[119] The courts have also played a crucial role in interpreting the Clean Water Act, the Toxic Substances Control Act, the Resource Conservation and Recovery Act, and many other environmental laws. Consider, for example, the 1980s controversy over logging on federal lands, notably in the Pacific Northwest. At the time, the issue was the most heated environmental dispute in the land, drawing considerable attention from the media and from policymakers. At the core of the dispute was whether the Fish and Wildlife Service should list the northern spotted owl as a threatened species under the Endangered Species Act.

Beginning in 1987, working with a coalition of local and state organizations, the Sierra Club Legal Defense Fund (SCLDF) launched a legal strategy that, in the words of one observer, "has to be considered one of the most successful legal campaigns in the history of American environmental law."[120] The first part of the strategy was aimed at getting the Fish and Wildlife Service (FWS) to list the spotted owl as "threatened" under the Endangered Species Act. Such a listing was deemed important by environmental groups because it would effectively place large tracts of forest off limits to commercial logging. The suit was prompted by a FWS ruling that listing the owl was not warranted, even though the agency's own scientists had previously concluded that it was. The agency's final report was, however, altered under the direction of Reagan appointees. The SCLDF challenged the FWS decision in federal district court, and in November 1988 the court vacated the agency's decision as "arbitrary and capricious." A year and a half later, the FWS relented and listed the owl as a threatened species.

The second prong of the legal strategy involved a series of challenges to the Forest Service's efforts to comply with the National Environmental Policy Act (NEPA). In December of 1988, the Forest Service prepared its final environmental impact statement (EIS) on the spotted owl and issued new regional guidelines for its protection. Environmental groups believed the EIS to be inadequate, so the SCLDF sued. In a landmark ruling in March of 1989, a federal judge agreed, and issued an injunction on timber sales in the states of Washington and Oregon. To many observers, the injunction was a pivotal event, because it shifted the balance of power in forest policy. Now, for timber sales to go forward, the Forest Service either had to comply with the judge's strict interpretation of the law, or Congress had to take specific action to change the law.

The battle then shifted to Congress, where the Northwest congressional delegation, which had been staunch supporters of logging on federal lands, worked to
attach riders to appropriations bills, which exempted the contested logging activities from lawsuits. The most prominent effort was known as section 318, which
exempted the Bureau of Land Management and Forest Service timber sales from
any ongoing litigation. Environmental groups then opted to challenge the consti-
tutionality of section 318, claiming that by trying to decide the outcome of particular cases, Congress had, in essence, violated the separation of powers.

At this point, the coalition of environmental groups also reconsidered their
political approach, recognizing that as long as the issue was perceived as a regional issue affecting only the Northwest, they would likely lose in Congress. The
decision was then made to nationalize the issue. The Sierra Club and others pur-
sued an aggressive media campaign and began to mobilize nationally. The goal
was to persuade lawmakers from outside the Northwest that they should take an
interest in the issue, and letters and phone calls from interested constituents were
designed to drive this message home. As part of this plan, the groups launched a
more targeted campaign to attack the legitimacy of the strategy of using riders to
exempt Northwest forests from environmental laws. In the end, their effort was
largely successful. The Ninth Circuit Court of Appeals struck down parts of section 318 as unconstitutional, on the grounds that Congress had directed a particular decision in pending lawsuits without amending the laws used as the basis for
litigation. In the words of George Hoberg, this was a "stunning blow to timber
interests and their congressional allies." But it was temporary setback: in March
1992, the Supreme Court unanimously overruled the Ninth Circuit. By this point,
however, the use of legislative riders had been delegitimized, and so logging supporters had to seek other methods of action.[121]

In assessing this case, Hoberg has argued that the decisions to litigate, and
then to nationalize the conflict, were critical to the environmentalists' success. As
long as the spotted owl controversy was perceived to be a regional issue, the Forest Service, the Bureau of Land Management, and the congressional delegation
from the Northwest would continue to make the key decisions. Since all were inclined to log rather than protect the owl, environmental groups could expect to
lose. Once the issue got into the courts, however, a different balance of power prevailed. The federal judges who were involved in the case were far more sympathetic to the arguments made by the Sierra Club Legal Defense Fund, as were
members of Congress from outside the Northwest. The lesson is that venue shopping can be an effective means of initiating policy change.[122]

THE REPUBLICAN TAKEOVER OF CONGRESS

From the standpoint of environmental activists, Election Day 1994 was a disaster.[123] Despite their spending record amounts in the midterm elections, many of

the candidates they had supported lost. To make matters worse, the political committees of the Sierra Club and LCV realized they had "wasted" much of their money on lopsided contests, backing candidates who won or lost by large margins. Worst of all, with Republicans gaining fifty-two seats in the House and eight in the Senate, both chambers of Congress would now be under Republican control. For the first time since the rise of environmentalism onto the national agenda, environmentalists would be forced to deal with an overtly hostile legislative branch. With most governorships and about half of the state legislatures in Republican hands, the entire political landscape had been turned upside down, and environmental groups were forced to rethink their political goals and strategies.[124]

Consider, for example, the shift in committee chairmanships that resulted from the partisan changeover. With their control of the formal agenda, Republican committee chairs could be expected to pursue very different legislative priorities. The new chair of the House Resources Committee was Alaskan Don Young, an avowed opponent of "environmental elitists" and their causes. Young was quite eager to let environmental groups know there was a "new sheriff" in town, and that the committee would pursue a very different agenda under his leadership. In the Senate, Alaskans Frank Murkowski and Ted Stevens assumed the chairmanships of the Environmental and Governmental Affairs committees, respectively. Stevens was also an influential member of the powerful Senate Appropriations Committee. To the great dismay of the nation's environmental groups, all three Alaskans devoted considerable attention to easing logging restrictions in the Tongass National Forest and facilitating drilling in the Arctic National Wildlife Refuge.[125]

Other members of the new majority had close ties to the increasingly vocal and influential property rights and wise use groups, such as People for the West! These groups had played an important role in several close congressional races in the western states, donating money and mobilizing significant numbers of voters. Five Republican members of the House Resources Committee were members of People for the West!, and another hired a former group official as a senior staff aide.[126] During the House Committee on Transportation and Infrastructure's markup of the Clean Water Act, industry lobbyists drafted much of the bill's language, and one even sat at the head table in the hearing room until Democrats complained. If they did not know it already, environmentalists soon learned that group access rises and falls with the election returns. With the change in partisan control, their political opponents had much greater access to the new majority.

In the months that followed, Republicans unleashed a torrent of direct and indirect assaults on many of the nation's key environmental laws.[127] Conservative senators placed "holds" on Clinton appointees to environmental agencies.[128] The administration's plans to reform the nation's mining and grazing laws were defeated, as were Interior Secretary Bruce Babbitt's plans to increase the grazing and mining fees paid by users of the public lands. The Endangered Species Act, the Clean Water Act, and many others were all up for grabs in the new Congress.

After minimal debate, and with considerable help from chemical industry lobbyists, the House adopted new amendments to the Clean Water Act. The bill, which
contained so many gifts to industry that environmentalists dubbed it the "Dirty
Water Act," never came to a vote in the more environmentally inclined Senate.

The new Republican leadership used any tool available to slash spending and
curtail enforcement of the nation's environmental laws, particularly in the House.
Within the first one hundred days, the House voted to cut the budgets of the EPA
and other regulatory agencies. The Concurrent Resolution on the Budget for FY
1996, which is nonbinding but does set spending guidelines, called for a 13 percent reduction in the Natural Resources and Environment category. The House appropriations bill for the EPA cut funding by a third, with enforcement programs
reduced by 22 percent, safe drinking water grants to the states by 45 percent, and
climate change programs by 40 percent. In addition, funding for the Council on
Environmental Quality was cut in half, while funding for the Department of
Interior's National Biological Service was eliminated entirely. Funding for solar,
renewable, and energy conservation programs were cut by more than one-third. In
the end, President Clinton vetoed the appropriations measure, part of the showdown with congressional Republicans that led to a government shutdown in December of 1995.[129]

In both the 105th and 106th Congresses, Republicans often opted to attach
legislative riders to spending bills. The riders, which were usually added with no
advance warning late in the legislative game, were aimed at significantly reducing environmental regulation. The tactic infuriated environmental groups because they saw it as a stealth attack on popular laws, allowing Republicans to gut
key laws without the public scrutiny that accompanied hearings or committee
votes. Because riders are often unnoticed and attract little media scrutiny, it gave
Republicans the opportunity to essentially rewrite environmental laws without
having a debate on the merits of the proposed changes. The unprecedented use of
riders threatened to overwhelm the ability of environmental groups to respond.
For example, the House appropriations bill for the EPA and other agencies alone
contained seventeen riders related to environmental policy; the Senate bill contained another seven. In all, the thirteen House appropriations bills for FY 1996
included fifteen riders involving the Clean Air Act, and eight each involving the
Endangered Species Act, wilderness protection, the Clean Water Act, and Superfund. Among the riders in the Interior appropriations bill was one placing a mor-
atorium on the listing of new species under the Endangered Species Act. There
were many others as well. Because Clinton vetoed many of the appropriations
bills, many of the riders never became law. Some did, though, such as a logging
salvage rider that allowed timber companies to log many areas under the guise of
"salvage" logging.[130]

Earthjustice, formerly the Sierra Club Legal Defense Fund, was one of the organizations that worked at monitoring and defeating riders to appropriations.
"Once Earthjustice takes a position on a rider," said Sarah Wilhoite, the group's

legislative assistant, "We reach out to congressional members and their staff, whether through personal meetings with members or their staff or phone calls to provide them with information. If the rider has yet to be included in a bill or report, we try to generate enough of a controversy over the language to keep it out. If we have time, or were expecting the "attack," we may have drafted a countering amendment and solicited a member of Congress to introduce our language. Also, depending on time limitations, we may seek opposition in the form of a letter from a supportive member or members to their colleagues informing them of the issue."[131] As it happens, time limitations were frequently an issue, as many riders were introduced less than twenty-four hours before they arrived on the floor for a vote. Without prior warning, Earthjustice and others had very little time to apply those strategies. Because secrecy was so critical to enacting the riders, Wilhoite claimed that "getting the word out about legislative proposals to not only our colleagues on the Hill but also to the media and the public is critically important. If we have time, we will send out releases to the media, to both reporters and editorial boards. The public, which strongly supports environmental protection, is a key ally in these battles. In all of these scenarios, we are typically working in coalition with other environmental groups. Some of these groups have large grassroots connections, and so they may contact constituents to speak out on a given issue and contact their legislators."[132]

A key element of Earthjustice's strategy focused on its friends in Congress. Depending on the issue, the group's lobbyists would look for members of Congress who had helped on the issue in the past. This could be determined by looking at letters the member had signed, legislation he or she had sponsored or cosponsored, and his or her voting record. The group's approach was also influenced by the nature of the attack. According to Wilhoite, "If the offensive language is added to the text of the bill itself, we can try to get an amendment in committee or on the floor to strike it. Often, however, the rider is in the form of a directive to an agency to do, or stop doing, something that is placed in the report language. Committee reports are not voted on at any stage of the process, so they provide more challenges."[133]

Sometimes the attacks came in the guise of seemingly innocuous and unrelated bills, such as the Job Creation and Wage Enhancement Act. Part of the "Contract with America," this appealing-sounding measure was actually an attempt to sharply curtail federal regulation. Under the measure, which passed the House but not the Senate, federal agencies were required to conduct elaborate cost-benefit and risk analyses before proposing new rules. In addition, the House created new "peer review panels" (often including industry representatives), which would be allowed to block proposed rules. Other reforms called for devolving greater authority to the states for devising and implementing regulatory policies.[134]

The Job Creation and Wage Enhancement Act also contained a provision that called for landowners to be compensated for any federal action that restricted the use of their property. Previously, compensation was awarded only when there was an actual physical taking of property. Under the House bill, however, property owners could demand compensation when the cost to comply with federal regulations exceeded 10 percent of their property or business value. In theory, a rancher could demand compensation for livestock losses from protected species or, according to critics, polluters could demand compensation for not polluting.[135]

The national environmental groups were initially caught off guard by the fury of the Republican assault on the environment, but within a few months they regrouped. The strategy was to launch a massive, coordinated grassroots lobbying campaign aimed at mobilizing their own members, as well as the general public. A crucial part of that effort involved rethinking their communication strategies. Groups began to pay greater attention to crafting effective conservation messages and to communicating them in new ways. To that end, in April of 1995 the Sierra Club and the Environmental Information Center announced a $2 million radio ad campaign warning that Congress was about to set environmentalism back by twenty-five years.[136] A number of the national groups put together "Breach of Faith," a report documenting the effects of the Contract with America on environmental laws. In addition to distributing the report through the usual channels, the groups also disseminated it by email to thousands of activists nationwide. Besides saving money on printing and postage, this tactic allowed the groups to disseminate their message more quickly. In addition to these new tools, most of the mainstream groups also made use of all the usual techniques of direct lobbying, including trying to persuade President Clinton to veto offending bills and riders.

Prior to 1994, environmental groups had operated in a predictable political landscape characterized by Republican control of the White House and Democratic control of Congress, most state legislatures, and most governorships. According to Christopher Bosso, environmental groups adapted their political strategies to these conditions, focusing their lobbying efforts on Congress, where they had ample access to legislators and key committee staff. The 1994 midterm elections fundamentally altered the political terrain, thus forcing environmental groups to work through the Clinton White House, urging the use of executive powers and agency rule making.[137]

The fight over the Contract with America illustrates the importance of language, and money, in politics. As noted above, many of the items in the Contract had warm and fuzzy, albeit misleading, names. This was not an accident, as the Contract was the end result of a lengthy and expensive series of polls and focus groups. According to West and Loomis, the Contract with America is an example of how powerful interest groups worked together to develop market-based narratives or stories in order to further specific policy changes. These groups spent considerable sums of money on polling, research, advertising, direct mail, and phone banks to build support for downsizing government in general and for Contract items in particular. The money allowed its backers to repeat their simple and consistent message repeatedly, until it dominated political discussion.[138] For example, one of the items in the Contract called for tort reform. In the weeks leading up to the Senate vote in June of 1995, backers of that provision spent $1.7 million on print and broadcast ads. The ads ran in twenty states whose senators had received campaign contributions from trial lawyers.[139] And because the public relations campaign went through a private individual, rather than the Republican Party or its congressional leadership offices, no disclosure of this spending was required.[140]

Faced with this impressive and well-financed public relations operation, environmental groups had little choice but to join the competition. If policymaking was becoming increasingly reliant on campaign-style tactics, environmental groups would have to develop the skills and resources to compete. The problem, of course, is that environmental groups do not have the deep pockets of industry.

In the end, the Republican effort to roll back environmental regulation in the 105th Congress largely failed. Environmental groups, relying heavily on President Clinton's veto pen, were able to beat back many of the attacks on environmental laws and regulations. A large part of the reason for the Republican failure rests with the outpouring of public outrage with what Congress was attempting to do. In the Northeast, in particular, moderate Republicans got an earful from angry constituents at town meetings, who wanted to know why clean water and air were suddenly unimportant. Congressional district offices were inundated with a flood of letters, phone calls, faxes, and emails from concerned citizens. Faced with this popular unrest, a small but critical number of Republican House members abandoned the more conservative leadership and began voting with most Democrats to maintain laws protecting the environment. Shortly thereafter, the Republican revolution, at least as it pertained to direct assaults on environmental laws, fizzled out.

In explaining this turn of events, Christopher Bosso suggests that the Republican leadership fell into a "salience trap" by misreading polling data and concluding that the public was unconcerned with environmental issues. More specifically, the leadership believed that the public's general support for less government and bureaucracy carried over to support for curtailing the federal role in protecting the environment. As the public response clearly indicated, however, they were wrong.[141] According to Riley Dunlap, overall public concern about the environment endures "to the point that support for environmental protection can be regarded as a 'consensual' issue which generates little opposition."[142]

CONCLUSION

As we have seen, by the late 1980s many of the national organizations had become established actors in the Washington interest group system. The aforementioned gains in organizational capacity had greatly enhanced their ability to engage in a broad range of advocacy activities. The growth in staff, for example, enabled a number of the national groups to establish ongoing and productive relationships with key policymakers. At the same time, staff increases gave the groups expertise and credibility, which are essential to the tasks of issue definition and agenda setting.

Despite these gains, however, environmental organizations lagged far behind their opponents in the resources they could bring to bear on the political process. Environmental lobbyists continued to be far outnumbered by the army of corporate representatives in Washington, and their skills, especially in the critical area of communications, paled in comparison. The imbalance in resources was even more lopsided with respect to campaign contributions, but that only became a problem in the 1980s, when environmental groups began to participate in elections. In the end, the disparity in organizational capacity meant that environmental groups would have to continue to rely heavily on the outside strategies commonly used by other citizen groups. Money was scarce, to be sure, but a large, cause-oriented grassroots base was still a valuable resource. Indeed, it is highly unlikely that environmental activists would have achieved many of their policy successes in the absence of effective grassroots and media campaigns. Group leaders used whatever tools they could to call attention to environmental problems and to frame issues for the media and the public. The problem was that for most of the period, they were simply overmatched.

By 1994, though, the environmental movement was larger, better funded, and more sophisticated than it had been thirty years earlier. But to what end? Most of the large national organizations had not only become more professional, using many of the same advocacy tactics as other Washington-based groups; they had also become more pragmatic.[143] Some argued that this transformation was both inevitable and necessary, but others lamented it. The critics, and there were many, argued that the mainstream groups were more effective at blocking their opponents' programs than at enacting their own, that they devoted most of their attention and resources to immediate issues rather than long-term agenda building, and, most importantly, that they were ineffective advocates. The national groups were also criticized for doing little to integrate the concerns of local grassroots groups into their decisionmaking, and for failing to mobilize at the community level. Robert Gottlieb argues that although a handful of individuals within the national groups did creative advocacy work, it "never became linked to the possibility of creating a new kind of social movement."[144]

Kirkpatrick Sale, one of the more outspoken and influential critics, faulted the mainstream groups for contenting themselves with "piecemeal reforms" rather than seeking to address the root structural causes of environmental problems. In his view, the national groups were more concerned with studying the location of toxic waste sites, for example, than with seeking to reduce the overall levels of toxics that were produced. To his credit, Sale acknowledges that "special interest lobbying" and what he calls "the lesser of two evils approach" are the way things happen in American politics. He also notes that Americans tend to see environmental problems as idiosyncratic and not as systemic in nature, and are thus wary of significant structural changes. He concludes, however, "This inevitably condemns the environmental movement to a kind of perpetual tinkerism and finger-in-the-dikeism, a never-ending record of defeats mixed with victories and of victories that are always provisional insofar as they do not alter the values of the prevailing system."[145]

On the other side of the equation, Michael McCloskey, executive director of the Sierra Club in the 1980s, explained that the Club was committed to working within the system, which had become increasingly legal and legislative. In response to the charge that the groups had become too accommodating and had lost their passion, McCloskey said, "Our business was not just to bear witness. Our business was to secure political change that would protect the environment."[146] Effective conservation, in his view, required more than staking out principled, but losing positions. It required lobbyists with political expertise, lawyers, policy experts, and money.

By any yardstick, the mainstream groups were struggling to balance the competing goals of being effective players in Washington with the idealism needed to motivate their more committed members. Group budgets were, for the most part, either flat or declining from 1990 through 1994, leading to downsizing, mergers, and in a few instances, elimination. Moreover, if the early 1990s demonstrated anything, it was that the "inside game" had inherent limits, especially with a hostile Republican Congress.[147] Environmental groups were about to embark on a difficult journey into uncharted waters, at a time when many seemed ill-prepared for the undertaking.

4

Environmental Advocacy in the Twenty-first Century

> Environmentalists cannot compete in the politics of interests. Fighting the moneyed
> lobbyists is a futile proposition. The future involves going directly to the people
> and changing the way they think and act. It involves the politics of values.
> —Christopher Bosso

Given the thousands of organizations active today, no single lobbying campaign can capture the full range of activities now employed by environmental groups. Moreover, lobbying strategies and tactics vary with the issue involved and the intended target, and whether organizations are acting alone or in a broader coalition. Nevertheless, contemporary environmental lobbying campaigns do have some common elements: they are more sophisticated than in the past, they rely more on grassroots mobilization, they make extensive use of technology, they are aimed at multiple audiences, and they are frequently collaborative efforts.

For example, message development workshops are now quite common, and many group leaders have attended at least one. At these workshops, participants discuss ideas for crafting effective conservation messages and groups are typically encouraged to use public opinion research in their ongoing advocacy and public education work. One such workshop, sponsored by the Biodiversity Project in 1996, consisted of twenty leaders throughout the United States with experience in water quality and wetlands issues. The discussion stressed the importance of linking biodiversity messages to local habitats and concerns. As one leader put it, "A picture of the Everglades is not going to persuade anyone in my neck of the woods about wetlands. I need to be able to show examples and tell stories about wetlands around here."[1]

Similarly, at a forest ecosystems message workshop in April of 1997, the participants realized that forest policy debates were taking place among the converted, but that the general public did not have a clear understanding of what natural forests were, why they were threatened, and how they might be valuable. Public opinion research, for example, revealed that most Americans knew very little about forest management and agency jurisdictions; that most did not believe that logging was allowed in national forests; and that most were surprised at how little forest land was permanently protected in parks or as wilderness. Moreover, forests were not an everyday concern for most Americans, although most did have an appreciation for forests based on their affection for particular trees or forested areas they had personally experienced. Therefore, workshop participants decided that their groups needed to develop educational messages that explained that a forest was more than just trees. The thinking was that once the public understood what a natural forest was, biodiversity groups would be able to engage more deeply in discussions of actual forestry practices. The discussion at this and similar workshops had a profound effect on the messages communicated by the Heritage Forest Campaign, which was discussed at the beginning of this book.

The groups seeking greater forest protection developed a communications strategy emphasizing several key concepts. The first was an educational message: that a forest is more than just trees—it is a complex ecosystem of trees, plants, wildlife, and soil. Forests provide food, shelter, and habitat for more species than any other ecosystem. They clean and restore fresh water, produce oxygen, and build soil. A second concept was to try to tap into the public's key values of concern for the future and the lives their children will lead, as well as to the desire to protect the recreational and spiritual values provided by nature. Their messages, therefore, stressed the notion of stewardship—that people should take care of the forests for future generations.

Survey data and focus groups also suggested that some messages were more persuasive than others. As a case in point, the Biodiversity Project recommended the following message for a general audience: "Healthy forest ecosystems are complex webs of life important to our own health and enjoyment. They provide clean drinking water, clean air, and places to play, swim, hike, fish, and hunt. They are habitat for countless plants and animals. Yet logging and development are destroying our forest ecosystems. We can protect our forests for the future and restore what we've lost for our children by acting now. (Specify an action here)." For those segments of the public who are religious, another message, one stressing God's connection to nature, was thought to be more appropriate: "Ancient forests can only be created by God, but they are being destroyed by humans. These special places are threatened with extinction by logging and development. When they are gone, they will be gone forever. We can protect these forests for future generations by acting now." Because effective messengers are those who are directly affected by the problem, the Biodiversity Project recommended children, whose world would be altered by our treatment of forests; forest workers; fish and game biologists; clergy; a family discussing with a grandparent how the forest used to be; or an angler.[2]

Clearly, there are some relatively new developments in environmental advocacy. As this chapter will show, the scale and intensity of lobbying has increased. More groups lobby, on more issues, and bring more resources to bear. As noted earlier, the sophistication of environmental advocacy continues to increase, and lobbying has become far more strategic. Among the national groups, there has also been a conscious effort to build the capacity of the environmental grass roots.

Technological advances have profoundly altered the methods of generating grass-roots campaigns, educating the public, and building coalitions. In addition, environmental groups of all sizes and at all levels are paying far more attention to issue definition and agenda setting, and this is shown by their heightened efforts to create and communicate more effective conservation messages.

CAPACITY-BUILDING PROGRAMS

One of the more important developments in environmental advocacy began in the late 1980s and early 1990s, when a number of foundations, national and state environmental organizations, as well as some intermediary nonprofit groups launched programs to increase the capacity of state and local groups to influence public policy. In large part, the emphasis on capacity building was a response to the national trend of delegating policy authority to state and local governments. At the time, "devolution" was a centerpiece of the Republican Contract with America, and many environmental groups were concerned about its ramifications for environmental policy. The capacity-building programs were designed to help state and local groups participate more effectively in policy debates at the state level, and to help them build and mobilize their memberships. These efforts also sought to strengthen conservation coalitions at the state level. As part of the programs, state and local organizations were trained on a variety of organizational mainte-nance tasks, such as fundraising, board development, and membership recruit-ment and retention. Other capacity-building programs were designed to increase citizen awareness of environmental issues and to boost turnout among environ-mentally minded voters. Many groups received grants to upgrade their technology and received training on how to use it effectively. Others received help with web-site development. Activists were also schooled on how to craft stronger messages and to communicate those messages more effectively to the media, the public, and to policymakers. In short, the capacity-building programs sought to help environ-mental groups become more strategic and effective advocates.[3]

An example of a nonprofit group providing such assistance is TREC, Train-ing Resources for the Environmental Community. TREC provides organizational development and technical assistance to environmental groups in an attempt to enhance their core capacities. As part of its organizational effectiveness pro-gram, for example, TREC performs on-site organizational assessment and devel-ops a capacity-building plan. It also offers on-site training and technical assis-tance. In addition, TREC has a fundraising assistance program and offers specialized consulting services on board development, financial management, and strategic planning.

Since 1995, the League of Conservation Voters Education Fund (LCVEF) has also been actively involved in building the grassroots power of the environmental movement. The group's primary focus has been on equipping state-based conservation coalitions with "cutting edge tools and leadership skills for strategic communication and organizing," in an effort to involve citizens in policy decisions at all levels of American governance. In pursuit of these goals, the LCVEF launched several programs for leadership development and citizenship training. One such example is the Environmental Leadership Institute (ELI). The Leadership Institute, considered the LCVEF's flagship training program, is a week-long workshop for state leaders whose purpose is to increase participants' efficacy in leading their organizations and community. The workshop includes role-playing, seminars, and simulation exercises revolving around a campaign case study. According to LCVEF literature, workshop participants are grouped into several teams according to their interest areas: legislative lobbying, candidate campaigns, grassroots organizing, and ballot initiative campaigns. The program emphasizes the specific product skills, such as strategy, message, and media training, needed to be an effective leader as well as the process skills of group dynamics, negotiation, and decisionmaking. In 1998–1999, LCVEF hosted Environmental Leadership Institutes in Alaska, Colorado, Georgia, Idaho, Michigan, North Carolina, Oregon, and Washington State. The following year, another two thousand activists were trained at seven regional ELIs across the nation. A national ELI for leaders from other states and national groups also took place in the summer of 2000.[4]

Along with the Center for Environmental Citizenship, the LCVEF also offers a Summer Training Academy for college students and other young activists. The Academy's curriculum is designed to train participants in the organizing skills they will need to work effectively in their communities. Participants in the Academy pledge to work later that same year on a community, issue, or electoral campaign of their choice in order to apply the training they receive. According to the LCVEF, over 80 percent of the students fulfill their pledge. The academies have been very popular. In 1998, the program generated so much interest that LCVEF could accept only one-third of the applicants. LCVEF opted to take the program on the road in 1999, training about three hundred students at seven regional training camps. The group also organized a special academy focused on students of color and on environmental justice issues.[5]

The LCVEF's capacity-building projects also include Strategic Planning Workshops, which are designed to help individual groups do strategic planning in the context of their own organizational development. These two-day workshops include representatives from a number of environmental organizations in the state to help participants develop "a shared strategy for elevating their issues and constituencies in the policy debate." The workshops are designed to walk participants through the strategic planning process.

Lastly, the LCVEF also trains activists on what sorts of activities are legally permissible for 501(c)(3) organizations. Many such organizations, especially small state-level groups, are confused by the IRS regulations, and this lack of knowledge has paralyzed some groups. To remedy this problem, the LCVEF invites both executive directors and designated board members to participate in 501(c)(3) workshops. It is hoped that once group leaders have attended the workshops, they will be able to use this information to help their groups become more effective advocates. Working with the Alliance for Justice and others, the LCVEF also organizes seminars on the laws governing political activities for tax-exempt groups.[6]

In underwriting capacity-building programs, the national groups and foundations are playing important roles within the environmental movement. Although local and statewide groups have passion and commitment, a lack of financial and organizational resources means that they are frequently unable to convert those attributes into tangible policy accomplishments. Without the assistance of the national groups and foundations, it is unlikely that many local and statewide organizations would have been able to develop the resources and skills they need to be effective advocates.

TECHNOLOGY AND ENVIRONMENTAL ADVOCACY

There is ample evidence that the introduction of more sophisticated communication technologies has changed the ways groups conduct their lobbying and outreach. One of the earliest and most important examples involved the development and use of computer databases, which have proven to be effective in helping groups understand and manage their members, their activist core, and their donor base. In its simplest terms, a database is essentially a computer file that organizes information. In the case of conservation groups, a typical database includes the names, street addresses, phone numbers, email addresses, donation amounts and frequency, and other data about members and donors. More sophisticated databases also make possible the use of sophisticated communications tools, such as the Internet and automated email and fax systems. In fact, one study of the use of such tools concluded that "a well-designed database may be the single most strategic information or communication technology available to conservation organizations."[7]

Some groups began building computer databases in the late 1980s, and although database management and technological capacity are still often quite limited in local groups, they have become increasingly accessible in recent years. That development is, in large part, a result of capacity-building efforts by foundations and intermediary nonprofit organizations seeking to enhance the effectiveness of environmental groups. Many environmental grant makers believe that computer databases offer a promising set of tools to help rebuild the grass roots and increase political activity among group members, and have thus provided significant funding, training, and other support for such projects.

List Enhancement Projects

List enhancement projects offer a clear example of the efforts to build capacity among state and local environmental organizations and to help them become more effective participants in policymaking. In part, the projects were motivated by the trend toward devolving responsibility for environmental regulation and enforcement to state and local governments. In response to this trend, groups such as the Washington Environmental Alliance for Voter Education (WEAVE) and the League of Conservation Voters Education Fund initiated a number of list enhancement projects nationwide, which were designed to increase the ability of state and local conservation organizations to boost public participation in these decisions. A typical list enhancement project combines the membership lists of several organizations, and then uses computer data matching programs to "enhance" them with additional information from outside data sources, such as statewide voter files and postal listings. Participating groups are then provided with enhanced membership lists, which include each individual member's voting frequency, party affiliation, congressional and state legislative jurisdictions, gender and age demographic data, and in some instances, responses to phone survey questions about issue priorities.

According to its proponents, list enhancements can help groups in a variety of ways. One is, of course, by providing groups with additional information about their individual members, their membership in aggregate, and how their membership compares to the public at large. For example, list enhancements make it easier for groups to target their communications to those members who are most likely to respond to a call for action. In addition, the messages can be tailored to reflect the issue concerns of individual members. In this way, list enhancements can supplement traditional methods of community organizing by enabling groups to develop one-on-one relationships with their members, and by increasing the likelihood that members will become more involved in the group, either as activists or donors. Armed with a better understanding of their membership, environmental organizations can thus increase their political clout by way of voter registration, voter education, and get-out-the-vote campaigns. Similarly, organizations can use the enhanced lists to identify and mobilize members to participate in administrative proceedings, such as in public comment periods on proposed regulations. List enhancements can also enable organizations to measure their appeal to certain demographic groups and, perhaps, to consider ways of recruiting members from new societal sectors.[8]

The first environmental list enhancement project was conducted in Washington State in 1995. WEAVE sponsored a collaborative project to develop a comprehensive, statewide environmental voter database in an effort to defeat Referendum 48, a "takings" ballot initiative that sought to require compensation for any regulatory action that affected a landowner's property value. Eighteen organizations participated in the project, which, using computer-matching techniques, combined their membership records into a single list of more than 233,000 registered voters. That list was then compared to the Washington State voter file. Each of the eighteen groups then received an enhanced membership list with additional information about each of their members. The environmental community then used this information to launch a get-out-the-vote campaign targeting those members with low to moderate voting rates. The targets of the campaign were contacted and encouraged to participate in the upcoming election. Each potential voter received a telephone call, a direct mail follow-up, and an absentee ballot form. The evidence suggests that the project was successful, as turnout among these voters increased by almost 13 percent. In the end, Referendum 48 was defeated by a margin of 60 percent to 40 percent.[9]

The success of the Washington project prompted similar efforts in other states, including one conducted in 1996 by the Northern Rockies Campaign and the Desktop Assistance for Idaho, Montana, and Wyoming conservation groups. That same year the LCVEF became actively involved in list enhancement projects in Colorado, Idaho, Maine, Michigan, North Carolina, Oregon, and Washington. The program was further expanded in 1998 to include Alaska and Georgia, and list enhancements were also undertaken by state LCV organizations in California and New York. In many of the states, the LCVEF would convene "summit meetings" of invited groups to explain the advantages of the project. In addition to coordinating the projects, the LCVEF also provided technical support, training, and financial assistance to the participating groups. Each group would receive its enhanced list with a written report from LCVEF highlighting the traits of their membership, along with a demographic comparison to members of other groups in their state. LCVEF field staff would then host communitywide training sessions, and would also provide one-on-one computer assistance for each group on how to technically and programmatically deploy their enhanced lists.[10]

Project costs, which include the data sources, computer consultants, computer equipment and software, supplies, legal assistance, and training, have varied from state to state. For example, the total cost of the 1996 list enhancement in North Carolina was $5,900, while in Colorado in 1997 the same services cost $14,500.[11] Without the organizational, financial, and technical support from LCVEF, it is highly unlikely that many of these list enhancements would have been undertaken.

To date, the LCVEF list enhancement projects have involved twenty-six state coalitions and over six hundred groups that collectively represent three million members. In 1999, based on the results of these efforts, the LCVEF also participated in the creation of a new "Partnership Project," a collaborative list enhancement project for national environmental organizations. The Partnership Project was designed to facilitate coordinated actions to mobilize environmentalists on national policy debates and other citizen education programs. The LCVEF is now matching the merged national lists, representing over six million names, with twenty-nine state voter files and other public records.[12]

The experience in these states shows that list enhancement projects can benefit a wide range of groups by increasing their understanding of their membership,
stimulating member involvement in the organization while saving money, and
providing new opportunities for collaborative projects. Once groups have learned
their members' voting history, they have used enhanced lists for education campaigns designed to increase participation by those members with spotty turnout
rates. In addition, groups have used enhanced lists to design fundraising appeals
to their most active members. The potential for cost sharing is in fact one of the
more significant benefits of cooperative list projects, allowing groups to enhance
their lists at a reasonable cost. For those groups who sell their membership lists to
other organizations, enhanced lists are potentially more lucrative as well. Cooperative list enhancement projects also build a foundation for future cooperation as
groups work with each other on a project that offers mutual benefits. With this experience, groups may find it easier to develop coordinated issue and advocacy
campaigns, allowing them to communicate consistent messages, an important element in issue framing and agenda setting.[13]

In using list enhancement projects for voter registration, political education,
and get-out-the-vote efforts, environmental groups are performing tasks that were
once the responsibility of political parties. Nor are they alone, as other organized
interests have also stepped into the breach created by weaker parties and the subsequent rise of candidate-centered politics. To make the most of these efforts,
though, it would make sense for the LCVEF and other sponsoring groups to develop a coordinated strategy and identify those areas of the country that can make
the best use of list enhancement projects. Some states and regions are more competitive politically, and environmental groups are stronger, more organized, and
more capable in some states. Given the close partisan divisions in Congress and in
many states, it makes sense to use list enhancement projects in those states that
promise the easiest and fastest rewards.[14]

List enhancement projects have become an important focus of recent
capacity-building programs. They represent, in many respects, a significant "first
step" on the path to a more sophisticated approach to lobbying. For example, before groups can lobby policymakers, they need to know who their members are,
where they live, and what they are concerned about. List enhancement projects
also make it possible for groups to experiment with a variety of new communication techniques in their continuing efforts to frame issues and define the political
agenda.

Email, Action Alerts, and Action Networks

In 1997, using the list enhancement project as the foundation, the LCVEF joined
with the Environmental Defense Fund, the Colorado Environmental Coalition,
and the Colorado Public Interest Research Group to create state-based email action alert systems in Colorado and Michigan. The enhanced list from Colorado,

which contained the names of 75,000 registered environmental voters, had been compiled from the membership lists of fifteen conservation groups. The LCVEF screened the list to identify highly active and motivated voters, who were then contacted by a telemarketing firm and included in the action network if they had email and were willing to participate. In a sign of the targeted campaign's effectiveness, over 65 percent of those contacted joined the Colorado Action Network (CAN). The Network, with over three thousand members, uses communications technologies developed by Environmental Defense's Action Network to send action alerts to its members. With just the activists' names, street addresses, and email addresses, the CAN database automatically assigns state legislative and congressional districts.[15] Action alerts are then sent to activists by email. Typically, the alerts include background facts on an issue and a sample letter pre-addressed to the targeted legislator or administrator. Members are encouraged to edit the letter and send it back via email to CAN, which automatically converts the email into a fax, which is then quickly forwarded to its target. The system also automatically records the member's response to the appeal in the CAN database, thus allowing the groups to track their members' actions. In Colorado, the Colorado Action Network generated so many messages with their first few alerts that the fax machine at the state capitol had to be to be turned off. CAN then hand-delivered the messages directly to the legislators' offices.[16] The LCVEF has since launched additional networks in Washington, Idaho, Oregon, and Ohio in 1999, and fourteen other states in 2001.

In the not-too-distant past, when group leaders wanted their membership to contact policymakers about some pressing legislative or administrative action, they would hold community meetings, publish newsletters, send "action alerts" to their members by regular mail, or, if time was of the essence, they would organize telephone trees. The advent of computer databases, email, and the Internet has changed all of that, though, as many environmental groups now distribute their action alerts via email because it is considerably quicker, cheaper, and cleaner. Typically, groups send action alerts by a listserv, an automated system that uses electronic mailing lists to send information to volunteers who have joined an activist network. The action alerts enable recipients to correspond directly with legislators and administrative officials either by replying to an email message from the group, or through a Web form that allows them to edit and "personalize" a pre-written letter. In many cases, the letters are then converted into faxes and delivered to the appropriate officials, usually within twenty-four hours.

Most activists agree that email has become the primary vehicle for disseminating information in the nonprofit community, and that it now rivals regular mail as means of encouraging grassroots involvement in policymaking. Some contend that the effects can be more profound, such as helping groups develop their current members into more informed and effective activists.

Many groups now use web technology that allows site visitors to customize their experience and their participation in online campaigns. The Wilderness Society hosts the Wild Alert Network, which allows visitors to address the issues that matter most to them. Through the "take action" option, which contains a legislative directory that allows visitors to search for their representative by zip code, visitors select which issues they want to follow. The group then sends action alerts on those issues. The site also allows visitors to follow issues using a legislative tracker that connects to THOMAS, Congress's website, and a profile center that allows the Wilderness Society to know who is writing letters. The profile center allows the group to collect information about which issues are most popular, and other data that may help it gauge its effectiveness. Wild Alert was part of a coordinated effort to generate 400,000 public comments in favor of the proposed National Forests roadless rule.

Most conservation groups use a system developed by the Environmental Defense Fund in the mid-1990s. EDF went online in early 1994, as did many other nonprofits, and has since considered email to be an essential part of its communication strategy. Initially, its website featured only "brochureware" about the group and its programs. However, as its Internet staff began to recognize the opportunities of the technology, the group began experimenting with recruiting new members online, servicing existing members with email newsletters, and attempting to build community through its discussion and bulletin boards. The next step was to create a more sophisticated and interactive communication tool. Bill Pease, then EDF's senior environmental health scientist and later its director of Internet projects, created an email-based activism service, which collected members' email addresses and then sent them alerts urging them to send messages to members of Congress. This system soon evolved into EDF's online activism service, under the name ActionNetwork.org. In addition to mobilizing EDF's members, ActionNetwork was designed to become a hub site for smaller environmental groups who were collaborating with EDF on specific issues. At the time, EDF was seeking to build more effective relationships with regional and local environmental organizations. To that end, EDF invited nonprofits that wanted to add email and web-based action alerts but did not have the financial or technical resources to do it by themselves to participate, for free, in the service's early online development. Most of the original participants in ActionNetwork are still involved in the project, although they are now paying customers of GetActive Software, an application service provider that was spun off from EDF in 2000.[17]

Action alerts delivered by email are significantly cheaper than direct mail or hard copies of newsletters. The printing and postage for the monthly newsletters of the New Jersey chapter of the Sierra Club, for example, cost about $6,000 annually. Putting the newsletter together was also labor-intensive. Its email alert system, operated by GetActive, is much less costly, which led the group to discontinue the printed version of the newsletter. It should be noted, however, that the Sierra Club, whose email list includes four thousand activists, pays GetActive forty-five cents for each fax delivered.[18] The lower costs are an important benefit for environmental organizations, particularly those classified as 501(c)(3) nonprofits. Under IRS rules, such groups are prohibited from devoting more than 20 percent of their budgets to legislative lobbying, and no more than 5 percent of the total can be classified as grassroots lobbying. Because groups can communicate their messages to more people, the low cost of e-advocacy thus allows 501(c)(3) organizations to engage in more lobbying within their expenditure limits.[19] This is an important consideration for groups that are seeking new, more effective ways to define issues and raise the prominence of the environment on the political agenda.

Another advantage of online advocacy is that it allows groups to contact members in minutes, rather than days, making participation easier. Recipients of action alerts can simply reply by email to targeted decisionmakers, or they can visit an online "Take Action Page" and participate with a single click of the mouse. The Take Action Pages provided by GetActive are really "mini-websites" that are integrated into a group's existing website. A typical Take Action Page provides the audience with opportunities to make their opinions known, to learn more about an issue, to "tell a friend" about the action alert, and, if they so desire, to participate in other campaigns the group is conducting. First-time visitors to the web page are asked to provide their contact information, and may then take action by sending their message. Current group members who click through the links to the Take Action Page from an email action alert will find the web form already filled in with their contact information, so that they can take action immediately. With the contact information, as well as the knowledge of which issues appeal to which people, groups can take steps to encourage continued participation by members. In fact, many of the groups using the web and email claim that they offer a "huge opportunity" to communicate more efficiently and effectively with their online membership "in order to develop them into more informed, active and effective activists."[20]

Still another advantage of online advocacy is that response rates to email action alerts tend to vary widely, but are often much higher than alerts delivered by direct mail. According to one mid-1990s estimate, less than 20 percent of the members of the Sierra Club, Environmental Defense Fund, Wilderness Society, National Wildlife Federation, and Environmental Action participated in issue alerts or had placed their names on special mailing or phone lists.[21] Most groups hope and expect that the new technologies will improve on that response rate. A big part of the reason is that email management tools allow groups to segment their membership based on interest and geographic region. As a result, the messages groups send by email can be tailored to reflect local concerns. According to Kathy Kilmer, manager of electronic communications for the Wilderness Society, this is crucial because "response rates are dramatically higher with localized issues. Residents of, say, Arizona are more likely to respond to an alert laying out specific information about Senator McCain's position on an issue than a more general 'The Senate will vote this week, please urge your senator to ———.'" While response rates to a direct mailing may be around 1 or 2 percent, Kilmer claims that the Wilderness Society has seen response rates to a personalized approach as high as 35 percent, although 5 to 15 percent is more typical. Other groups report similar results.[22]

Are Grassroots Communication Tools Effective?

There is some evidence that email action alerts have been instrumental in influencing environmental policymaking. The Washington Environmental Council, for example, claims that its online advocacy effort was able to generate over 350 public comments on a Washington Department of Ecology proposal for revising rules implementing the Washington Shoreline Management Act. Using an online comment tool developed for its website by One/Northwest, WEC emailed 950 members asking them to comment on the proposed rules. The tool consisted of a simple form that combined a prewritten statement from WEC with a space for the recipient to add a personalized message. Comments submitted by the online form were sent directly to the Department of Ecology for inclusion in the public record, and a copy of the comment, with the sender's contact information, was also sent to the Washington Environmental Coalition, allowing the group to track the response rate. Over 170 of those contacted responded to WEC's first email message and, a week before comment period ended, WEC sent a reminder message, which generated over 200 additional comments. Significantly, most of the comments were submitted by people who had not received WEC's emails directly; instead, the message had been forwarded to them by WEC members. According to WEC Environmental Organizer Amy Zarrett, the online activism was a good fit for the group for three reasons: "First, with one-click technology, an online comment tool made participating easy and quick. Secondly, marketing the online comment tool by email reached more people more quickly than we could have by calling or mailings, and made tracking and follow-up simple. Third, because email is paper and postage-free, online activism is congruent with WEC's conservation beliefs and saves money for the organization and its members."[23]

Environmental Defense also claims to have had some notable success with its own Action Network. In one recent case, information posted on the group's website, actionnetwork.org, described the practice of shark finning, in which fishermen remove shark fins and then toss the sharks back into the water. The site offered concerned citizens a means of faxing a prewritten protest letter to Hawaiian officials. According to Environmental Defense, hundreds of messages were sent, and the practice was ultimately banned in state waters. Following that initial success, Environmental Defense sought a nationwide ban. After the appeal appeared on the website, ten thousand faxes were sent to Congress, which passed legislation banning the practice. According to Daniel Freedman, Environmental Defense's chief Internet officer, "It's hard to say what tipped the balance, but [the site] had an impact." Environmental Defense also claims that, after President George W. Bush announced his administration's energy plans in May 2001, the Action Network prompted more than fifty thousand faxes to Congress.[24]

The common view among many group leaders is that the most effective methods for gaining the attention of elected officials are personal visits from constituents, handwritten letters, and faxes. Because time is short in many public comment proceedings and in pending legislative action, interest groups have decided that faxes are often the best option. That is why GetActive's alert system converts email messages into faxes that are then delivered to the target. In the case of local issues in particular, a few hundred thoughtful fax or email comments may be all that is needed to carry the day. But even then, most conservation groups recognize that emails alone carry little weight with legislators, especially since email has become so common. Indeed, with many members of Congress receiving thousands of emails each day, some have speculated that email activism has lost its novelty. Others say that the sheer volume of email has made getting noticed by policymakers much harder. Rep. James V. Hansen of Utah has been quoted as urging his colleagues to disregard email messages, saying, "I mean, you know, one guy writes it and 10,000 of them come in." Consequently, many groups also urge their members to follow up their message with a letter or telephone call. Mike Reberg, Media Coordinator for the Southern Utah Wilderness Alliance, has said that "At key times, we can send literally hundreds of phone calls into certain offices when we need to." In other words, it is not the quantity of communications that matters so much as the quality.[25]

The Wilderness Society's Kathy Kilmer echoes those sentiments in emphasizing the importance of the group's investment in an "online action tool that is fully editable. Now we are no longer locked into a single "form" letter, but can encourage activists to personalize their messages to decision makers, a more powerful vehicle for change." When asked what makes an effective advocacy campaign, Kilmer noted that "there is considerable skepticism on the Hill towards faxed or emailed 'form letters,' which have about as much impact as hard-copy petitions or postcard campaigns." Far better, most agree, are more personalized, targeted campaigns, referred to as "nuanced communications." As an example, if a member of Congress makes a floor statement about roadless area protection, that statement may not be picked up by the local news media. But through "nuanced" email communication, groups can be sure that some of that member's constituents receive the floor statement and respond to it. According to Kilmer, "That's the sort of communication that will get attention."[26]

When asked, several activists remarked that they believed emails were more effective in influencing administrative agencies than legislators, because email is relatively new to many federal agencies. Interest groups have always conducted public education campaigns to increase citizen input into agency public comment periods. Until recently, however, most agencies would not accept electronically delivered comments. More and more are, however, and so groups are now conducting grassroots campaigns aimed at agencies. Moreover, agency administrators are required to count each letter or email with the same weight, whereas elected officials put greater value on personal letters. For this reason, the NRDC, which has been working with the EPA on a rule involving arsenic in drinking water, has been asking its activists to send emails to the agency. According to Alan Metrick, the group's communications director, agency clerks pay more attention to their email than do members of Congress.[27]

It is not yet clear whether the use of email and websites helps groups expand their membership bases. The Natural Resources Defense Council, for example, opted to use email to reach out to a younger, more computer-oriented audience after realizing that efforts to recruit new members through direct mail had failed. Metrick believes that the group's email alert system has been very effective in increasing awareness of the group and in bringing new people to the group. In the last six months of 2001, the number of people subscribing to the system increased from 17,000 to 160,000.[28] Others claim, however, that email is more useful in servicing existing members than in recruiting new ones. ONE/Northwest, for example, claims to know of no organization that has significantly increased its membership via online tools. It may well be that national groups, with greater name recognition and resources, are better positioned to recruit new members with technology, while local groups will find more success with traditional methods of recruitment, such as community meetings and door-to-door canvassing. According to Devin Scherubel, listserv manager and webmaster of Heartwood, a regional group in the Midwest interested in hardwood forests, email "is quite useful in getting daily updates from the Hill out to all us field organizers, and for us to activate networks rapidly in response to moves to attach amendments to open the refuge to other bills, which can happen rather suddenly. Since the Internet seems better at moving information than facilitating real discussions, I think it serves this sort of 'top-down' organization better than it serves the grassroots collective of Heartwood."[29]

It may also be the case that email and the Internet are more effective in helping groups block actions they dislike than in initiating positive change. According to Ken Schneider, executive director of the Michigan Land Use Institute, a nonprofit concerned about sprawl, "We haven't been able to do much offense. Most of it is defensive."[30] This view is not universally shared, however, and some activists believe that email and other online tools can be used to take the initiative in pushing proenvironmental measures, as in the case of shark finning, as well as to engage in long-range efforts to shape agendas. This is the view expressed by Kathy Kilmer, manager of electronic communications for the Wilderness Society, who said, "Especially in today's climate, where the threats are coming fast and furious, it feels that longer-term attitude shaping might be unavailable to us. However, that is not the case. By sending out weekly emails to a community of online activists, we are, in fact, helping people new to the movement understand what is at risk, how the threats are evolving and the actions they may take to avert those threats. That's shaping attitudes and building more effective advocates."[31]

As Kilmer's words suggest, environmental groups are devoting more energy and attention to shaping public attitudes. The assumption behind these efforts, of course, is that public attitudes have an effect, albeit indirect, on policy outcomes. If groups can frame issues effectively, they stand a better chance of motivating their members, as well as the general public, to echo these concerns to policymakers. In the end, the expectation is that policymakers will thus be more likely to enact policies sought by the group.

Moreover, email action alerts can help groups spread their message exponentially, leading some to call it a form of "viral marketing." As a case in point consider the website for Save Our Environment Action Center, a collaborative effort of several national environmental advocacy groups, including Defenders of Wildlife, the Earth Justice Legal Defense Fund, Environmental Defense, Greenpeace, the League of Conservation Voters, and the National Environmental Trust. The website, which contains links to each of the participating groups, invites people to join an activist alert network by filling out a simple form. In this way, action alerts distributed by one group can be accessed by members of other groups, as well as by anyone visiting the website.

Despite its many advantages, technology is no cure-all. The challenge, according to some activists, is to use the tools strategically in order to advance the organization's mission.[32] If an organization is unable to establish clear goals, then better technology is of little use. What good are action alerts if they are sent to people who are unlikely to act, or if they communicate ineffective or contradictory messages?

Websites

In a relatively short period of time environmental group websites have proliferated to the point that it is almost impossible to count them. Today there are over 450 websites created by nonprofit conservation groups in the Pacific Northwest alone, and the number grows daily. Environmental groups use websites for a variety of purposes—electioneering, public education, community outreach, attracting new members, generating grassroots pressure on public officials, and raising money through donations or product sales. The best sites are part of a larger, long-term communications strategy designed to shape public opinion about environmental issues. Good websites provide viewers with accurate, current information about issues, invite them to take some action on behalf of an issue, and make it easy for them to act. As we have seen, environmental websites can come in a variety of forms. Environmental Defense, for example, pioneered the creation of both customizable action networks and Scorecard, an online database. Groups partnering on issues have also created campaign-specific websites, such as Saynotonorton.org, which was designed to build opposition to President Bush's nomination of Gayle Norton as Interior secretary. See page 97 for a list of environmental group websites.

Websites of Selected Environmental Organizations

National Organizations	Web Address
Defenders of Wildlife	www.defenders.org
Earthjustice	www.earthjustice.org
Environmental Defense	www.environmentaldefense.org
Environmental Working Group	www.ewg.org
Friends of the Earth	www.foe.org
Greenpeace USA	www.greenpeaceusa.org
Heritage Forest Campaign	www.ourforests.org
League of Conservation Voters	www.lcv.org
League of Conservation Voters Education Fund	www.lcvef.org
National Audubon Society	www.audubon.org
National BLM Wilderness Campaign	www.blmwilderness.org
National Environmental Trust	www.environet.policy.net
Natural Resources Defense Council	www.nrdc.org
Pew Wilderness Center	www.leaveitwild.org.org
Sierra Club	www.sierraclub.org
Wilderness Society	www.tws.org
WILD PAC	www.wildpac.org

Environmental Defense Websites

ActionNetwork	www.actionnetwork.org
Scorecard	www.scorecard.org
ActGlobal	www.actglobal.org

State and Regional Organizations

Colorado Environmental Coalition	www.ourcolorado.org
Greater Yellowstone Coalition	www.greateryellowstone.org
Heartwood	www.heartwood.org
Idaho Conservation League	www.wildidaho.org
Southern Utah Wilderness Alliance	www.suwa.org
WEAVE	www.weave.org
Washington Wilderness Coalition	www.wawild.org

Capacity-building Organizations

Biodiversity Project	www.biodiversityproject.org
Environmental Media Services	www.ems.org
Greenmedia Toolshed	www.greenmediatoolshed.org
Institute for Conservation Leadership	www.icl.org
ONE/Northwest	www.onenw.org
Safe Energy Communication Council	www.safeenergy.org
Strategic Press Information Network	www.spinproject.org
Sustain	www.sustainusa.org
TREC	www.trecnw.org

Although it is clear that conservation groups believe that websites are important, it is not yet clear whether the groups are using them effectively. Part of the problem is that some groups do not think carefully enough about what they want to do with their sites. For example, websites do make information available to a vast audience, but it does not do much good if no one visits the site—a real possibility given the explosive growth of websites. So although websites make information available, at least in theory, to millions, it does not mean that millions are actually accessing the site to view the information.

There is also some evidence to suggest that the environmental groups have not taken full advantage of their websites. Many of the grassroots applications of the Internet, like action alerts, require very little organizational support. Indeed, most groups use the system supported by Environmental Defense, and so do not have to devote extensive time or money to keeping them running. But that is not the case with community-building features, such as chat rooms or bulletin boards, which require considerable organizational resources. In their study of national environmental group websites, Bosso and Collins found that community-building tools were either underutilized or, in some cases, were absent entirely. Part of the problem, they suggest, is that group leaders are wary of the features because they have little control over them. Some nonprofit groups, for example, worry about losing their tax-exempt status if their members use bulletin boards or discussion lists to engage in political advocacy.[33]

Organizations like ONE/Northwest instruct their client groups to think strategically about their websites. Before creating a website, groups are encouraged to think about whom they are trying to reach, what information this audience may want, and how best to deliver this information to them. For example, a site designed for attracting new members will differ from one designed for people who are already familiar with the group and its activities. Since there is little evidence that websites are valuable tools for reaching *new* constituents, at least for regional or local groups, ONE/Northwest urges that such organizations' initial online efforts focus primarily on providing information to, and encouraging action from, existing members and activists. Moreover, according to ONE/Northwest, the goal of these early efforts "should be to *develop* your members into activists."[34] Only after a group has built a strong base among those most interested in its work should it seek to reach out to the general public.

In addition, because sharing information with members is one of the most practical applications for websites, many web consultants encourage groups to think of their sites as the organization's library, with separate sections for the most recent newsletters and action alerts, archives of past publications, general information about the group, and links to related sites and coalition partners. In addition to spreading knowledge about the groups and their key issues, the clear advantage of an online library is that interested parties can download and print reports and other information, thus saving groups money on printing and postage.

The Southern Utah Wilderness Alliance is an example of an organization that has used its website effectively. In addition to descriptive information about the group, the website contains information about pending legislation and existing laws, a newsletter, and other publications. The site also features a "What You Can Do" section, which offers potential activists a menu of options. Among the options are signing up for an Action Alert email list, writing a letter to the editor, and contacting senators and representatives to urge them to cosponsor legislation. The site also invites visitors to take photos of special places and submit them to the group's online photo archives for possible inclusion in the group's proposals for wilderness protection. Because of the ability to post pictures and other images, websites make it possible for groups to anger or inspire people in ways that printed messages cannot. In helping groups communicate their passion for the environment, websites can establish an emotional connection between a group and its members. More importantly, because they provide people with the opportunity to take immediate action on issues, good websites may be more effective in translating those emotions into grassroots action.[35]

Most of the large national organizations have extensive websites. The Natural Resources Defense Council's site, for example, features news, legislative updates, scientific research, policy analysis, an action center, and a gift shop. Few groups, however, have created more effective websites than the Environmental Defense Fund, now known as Environmental Defense. The organization was one of the first environmental groups to embrace Internet technology, going online in 1984. At the time, EDF's annual budget was approximately $25 million, a considerable sum in the environmental community. Most of the money for its technology investments came from the Heller Charitable Foundation, the Joyce Foundation, the New York Community Trust, and others. In addition to its own website, the organization's most noteworthy Internet accomplishments were Environmental Scorecard, a web-based project that integrated web and database technology to bring information on toxic pollutants to the general public, and ActionNetwork. Scorecard went online in April 1998, while ActionNetwork was launched in February of 1999. Both were built for less than $750,000.[36] In the case of Scorecard, EDF hoped to use information disclosure to create incentives for companies to improve their environmental performance; ActionNetwork, on the other hand, used email to generate immediate grassroots pressure in legislative debates. Both projects demonstrate that websites can do far more than provide services to members and educate the public about a group's activities.

Scorecard was an immediate success when it was launched in 1998, in response to numerous requests from grassroots groups seeking assistance on interpreting data about toxics in their communities. With money raised from the Clarence Heller Charitable Foundation, EDF began building an internal database to speed the flow of what it called "actionable information" to people concerned about toxins. To assist in the task, EDF also hired a team of environmental scientists and database consultants. The initial plan was to create a stand-alone program for interpreting toxics data—a CD-ROM, for example—but EDF abandoned that plan because its staff became convinced that the public would never use it.[37] The decision was then made to put Scorecard online. The site uses an online database to connect interested citizens to information specific to their areas. Users simply enter their zip codes to find out who is polluting in their community, the type and amount of pollutants being emitted, and information about the pollutants. Scorecard allows people to send free faxes directly to their community's largest polluters, and also provides updates on the actions taken. Finally, Scorecard allows visitors to customize the web page's appearance and includes a community home page connected to the viewer's zip code.

Although EDF had high hopes for the project, insiders were surprised at the extensive press coverage it received. The website was nominated for a Webby award, and large donors were ecstatic that EDF had broken new ground with its online experiment. EDF subsequently attracted a number of very large grants from foundations wanting to expand Scorecard to other pollution problems. EDF was also pleased that Scorecard resulted in a large number of online prospects and activists, at much more cost-effective rates than direct mail.

EDF leaders were also quite surprised by the number of people who visited the website, and by the thousands of faxes and emails those visitors subsequently sent to polluters and legislators. While it may be impossible to prove that Scorecard by itself was responsible for any changes in environmental policy, the sudden accessibility of data about what toxics were being released into communities, in what amounts, and by whom, fundamentally altered the debate over toxic pollution. Indeed, one of EDF's primary goals in making the information widely available was to shame companies with poor environmental records; the underlying theory was that companies would have a strong incentive to clean up their own messes in order to remove themselves from the list of top polluters.[38] The organization's biggest victory came in 1999, when the Chemical Manufacturer's Association agreed to a voluntary program to test high-production chemicals for toxicity. The industry had opposed such testing for decades, and the EPA had been unable to use the Toxic Substances Control Act to compel the industry to test on an expedited basis. Under the conditions at that time, testing of known chemicals was expected to take until 2110. In the end, though, the industry reached an agreement with EPA and EDF to complete an expedited testing program within three years.

In the spring of 2002, the organization launched a new global human rights and environmental network and activism service, called ActGlobal. The database website, designed for activists, journalists, and policymakers, provides a wealth of information and can be searched by country. The site includes a variety of interactive maps and detailed regional and statistical information about important global issues, such as water consumption, wetlands loss, agricultural land use, and deforestation. Another feature allows users to learn about the financing, structure, and policies of specific international financial institutions, like the World Bank, as well as about specific projects and activities they support around the world. With this data, interested citizens anywhere in the world can learn more about projects such as dams, pipelines, and highways that often have significant environmental consequences. Among its other possible uses, the site allows users to register at an International Action Center to read and send multilingual action alerts to policymakers around the world. The website offers the latest example of how technology can be used to develop and strengthen a burgeoning global network of environmental activists.[39]

ENVIRONMENTAL COMMUNICATION

In their oft-cited study *American Business and Public Policy,* Bauer, Pool, and Dexter claimed that communication of policy information was the essence of lobbying.[40] Baumgartner and Jones and others have documented the importance of ideas and policy images for defining issues and shaping popular and elite understandings of policies and programs. The language, symbols, and images used by policy entrepreneurs are essential in framing the debate over policy issues and in securing or blocking policy change.[41] For those seeking to shape environmental policy, effective communication is thus a crucial aspect of lobbying campaigns. If environmental organizations are to make progress in achieving their policy goals, they must be able to craft and deliver messages that both persuade and mobilize their targeted audiences. The chronic problem for many groups, though, has been a lack of access to the money, personnel, media tools, and skills needed to handle the work in-house. This is especially true of smaller grassroots organizations, which often rely on part-time staff or volunteers to handle their communications tasks.

In the last ten years, however, environmental groups have increasingly sought outside assistance with message development and communication. Although some groups now have the money to hire media and public relations firms to develop their communications strategies, most, especially those operating at the state and local level, do not. Instead, they seek the help of a loose network of nonprofit communications consultants and trainers that has been established in recent years, often with considerable foundation funding. Groups like the Citizens Clearing House for Hazardous Waste, for example, provided organizational and technical assistance to over five thousand local groups in the late 1980s.[42] In addition, some of the larger national groups, such as the Sierra Club and the League of Conservation Voters, provide media and communications training for other conservation organizations. As a result of these developments, even the smallest groups now have access to a range of communications resources and expertise that were simply unavailable a few years ago. There is considerable evidence that conservation groups, especially regional and state ones, are communicating more effectively than in decades past. They are better at determining who the key decision-makers are and which constituencies can be used to reach them, and then crafting messages that appeal to that constituency.[43]

With information so widely available, there has been a marked increase in the sophistication of the public education and advocacy campaigns conducted by environmental groups. There are, for example, an abundance of websites offering communications tips and how-to guides, as well as training and other forms of assistance. To take one case, the Biodiversity Project has posted its communications handbook on its website, where it can be downloaded for free by any interested party.[44] The group was established in 1995 as a public education initiative of the Consultative Group on Biological Diversity, an association of over forty grant makers that focus on such issues. The Biodiversity Project seeks to help environmental organizations craft and implement communications and education strategies on issues that promote smart growth, wilderness protection, endangered species, and habitat loss. Its goal is to help its partners develop a clearer understanding of people's attitudes about environmental issues in order to design more compelling and consistent messages. In its self-proclaimed role as a "nexus and catalyst" for collaboration on biodiversity outreach strategies, the Biodiversity Project has partnered with numerous organizations, including the Clean Water Network, Surfers Tired of Pollution, the Wilderness Society, and the World Wildlife Fund. In all, the group has trained more than one thousand group leaders in its workshops and working groups.

Most communications experts agree that the first step for any organization in creating a communications strategy is to determine its goals, whether it is broadbased public education, fundraising, or influencing administrative rule making. Messages that might be appropriate for one task are not necessarily appropriate for the others, in part because the audiences are different. Legislators, administrators, environmental activists, the media, and members of the general public have different concerns and may not respond to messages in the same way. Consequently, environmental groups must craft different messages for different audiences.

Although focus groups and public opinion research have become essential elements of modern "audience-driven" communication strategies, most environmental organizations have lacked the capacity to design and implement them until recently. Some of the larger national groups, however, do have the necessary resources. Groups such as the Nature Conservancy, the Wilderness Society, Earth Share, and the National Parks and Conservation Association have hired polling firms to conduct membership surveys, while the League of Conservation Voters Education Fund and the Biodiversity Project have commissioned state and nationwide public opinion surveys to gain insights into the knowledge, values, and concerns of various sectors of the public. Unfortunately, for many organizations, large and small, a chronic lack of resources makes these projects too expensive to use regularly. As a result, many groups have been hampered in their ability to know and understand their audience, a key component of effective communications.

Still, in the last five years, with money from grantmakers, organizations like the League of Conservation Voters Education Fund and the Biodiversity Project have been sharing the insights gained from their national and state polls with smaller groups. As part of their public education efforts, both groups posted the polling data on their websites, making it available to anyone who wants it.[45] In addition, both LCVEF and the Biodiversity Project use the information obtained from focus groups and polling for message training with leaders from state and local groups. The purpose of the training is to help them effectively frame issues in ways that engage the public. Such information and cost sharing means that smaller groups do not have to operate in the dark when developing advocacy or public education campaigns.

The most important aspect of increased collaboration in the environmental community involves the effort by grant makers and others to facilitate the acquisition and sharing of technology, information, and other important tools. Thanks to an abundance of workshops, training sessions, websites, handbooks, and other assorted capacity-building programs, groups no longer have to "reinvent the wheel." Nowhere is this more apparent than in the many workshops and training sessions to help groups develop more consistent and effective conservation messages. The LCVEF and other groups commission public opinion research on environmental issues and then conduct briefings to help activists from other organizations frame unified and effective messages. Numerous nonprofits provide message kits, talking points, and media skills training sessions to help activists get the message out. All of these activities are terribly important for the purpose of agenda setting. According to Kathy Kilmer of the Wilderness Society, "Agenda setting is essential because of the myriad of issues that decisionmakers must deal with today. That's one reason the conservation community has moved aggressively into coalition work within the past 5–8 years."[46] The chances of an issue rising on the agenda are greatly enhanced if its advocates are consistent in their rhetoric and argumentation.

Crafting Better Messages

Clearly, environmental groups now appreciate that focus groups and public opinion surveys can be valuable tools in developing effective communications plans. Although experience has undoubtedly provided many instructive examples of what works and what does not, public opinion research offers groups a more rigorous and less anecdotal means of testing messages as well as a chance to become better acquainted with their audiences. Focus groups, for example, examine the ways in which people process information and the values that underlie their attitudes. They can also help to uncover new themes to persuade people and test reactions to specific language and messages. Public opinion research, on the other hand, can help determine where the public stands on a group's issue, which segments of the public are most and least supportive of environmental protection, and what types of appeals are more likely to resonate with the public. Groups can then use that information to tailor their messages to specific constituencies. For example, LCVEF polling in 1996 and 1998 revealed the potency of appeals to clean air and clean water, and also showed that certain demographic groups, notably women with young children, were most likely to respond to those themes. The group then stressed those two issues in its public education campaigns, as did the LCV's political action committee in its independent expenditure campaigns in Dirty Dozen races.

Similarly, the Biodiversity Project has put considerable effort into designing and testing a public education strategy that is based on reaching people through messages that speak to their core values, defined as those deeply held beliefs that form the foundations of people's attitudes and behavior.[47] To that end, the group joined with the Communications Consortium Media Center in the spring of 1995 to commission focus groups to assess public concerns and perceptions about biodiversity. With funding from grant makers, they also hired two Washington, D.C., polling firms to conduct nationwide public opinion surveys to assess attitudes about biodiversity. More than sixty organizations reviewed and contributed to the questions for the survey of two thousand adults, which was conducted in early 1996. The focus groups and polls allowed the groups to learn about their audiences and their core values. Working with pollsters and communication experts, the Project then held national and regional briefings to share and interpret the findings and to help activists and educators craft more effective conservation messages.

The most important findings were that the public was most concerned about human health and well-being, including the loss of reproductive capacity and potential birth defects. Among environmental issues, the surveys revealed that Americans were most concerned about clean water and toxic pollution. When asked about their most important personal reason for caring about the environment, people cited three core values: responsibility to future generations, a belief that nature was God's creation, and a desire for one's family to enjoy a healthy environment. According to the Biodiversity Project, these findings illustrate that conservation messages based simply on the innate importance of protecting nature for nature's sake commanded much less public support than other messages. For the broadest audience, a more persuasive conservation message would link the values of responsibility to family and future generations to concerns about environmental quality and ecosystem services.[48]

Groups cannot, of course, sell any message to any audience at any time. Context matters. At the very least, an audience must be sympathetic to the idea being sold, or failing that, it must be educated so that it comes to accept the idea. This is true of both policymakers and the public. With respect to the former, Democratic and Republican members of Congress respond to different types of appeals and, with the change of partisan control in the early 1990s, environmental groups had to reevaluate their communication strategies. Many in the new Republican majority were hostile to environmental groups and their preferred policies, blaming them for the nation's economic slowdown. Groups thus had to adjust their communication strategies to reflect the new circumstances.

Interest groups can generate public support for their positions if they can link their issues to widely accepted values. Who, for example, is opposed to justice, fairness, or democracy? Over the last thirty years, support for the environment has become a consensual issue as well, with approximately three-quarters of Americans describing themselves as "environmentalists." Environmental groups thus begin with a reservoir of goodwill for the ideas they are selling. Nevertheless, public opinion research of the type conducted by the Biodiversity Project can enable groups to be more rigorous in linking their messages to broadly shared values, such as responsibility to future generations.[49] Public opinion research, in short, can enhance a group's ability to define issues.

Once groups have determined their goals and identified their audiences' values and concerns, the next step is to develop an appealing message or, given the multiple audiences of most advocacy campaigns, appealing messages. Once groups gain a better understanding of the audience, they have a much easier time knowing which words or images will move them to act. Some organizations have large professional communications staffs and do much of their message work in-house, while many others rely on the network of nonprofits that provide message workshops and training. A small but growing number of groups now hire public relations firms to conduct public affairs campaigns. In the late 1980s, for example, the Natural Resources Defense Council hired two public relations firms in its successful campaign to halt the spraying of the chemical Alar on apples. It is noteworthy that large national groups are not the only ones paying for communications help. Pyramid Communications, a Seattle-based public relations firm, works with many smaller nonprofits in the Northwest. Pyramid helps its clients identify the target audience for the campaign and, using focus groups, polling research, and in-depth interviews, will help groups develop a communications strategy.

Although there are many organizations providing communications skills and training, there is widespread agreement on what sort of messages will be effective. The Biodiversity Project handbook, for example, urges groups to use language that speaks to the targeted audience; to use anecdotes to illustrate the group's issue; to use images to dramatize the issue; to repeat the message frequently; and to choose messengers that complement the group's message and audience. Similar themes, which are apparent in the handbooks and tip-sheets published by other groups, help environmentalists become more effective in framing issues.[50]

Within the environmental community there is some sense that groups have relied too much on scientific and technical jargon in outreach efforts and have forgotten that what motivates the general public is what also motivated group members themselves. Most activists are interested in the environment for simpler, more personal reasons. For that reason, messages with simpler, more emotional appeals are very effective. With respect to language, it is best to avoid jargon and use language that the audience has heard before. When discussing rivers and watersheds, for example, messages that use words like "health," "drinking water," and "pollution" are more effective than those using words like "watershed" and "riparian"—terms that are unfamiliar to many Americans. The Biodiversity Project reminds groups that, in some regions, *environmentalist* is a dirty word, and thus urges them to use the less divisive "conservationist" instead.[51]

Effective messages, moreover, need to give people a reason to care about an issue. This can be done by emphasizing the issue's local angles and by linking the issue to the intended audience's core values. In the case of biodiversity, it is important to relate the concept to "ecosystems found in people's backyards—relating it to familiar or local landscapes, such as nearby forests, wetlands, prairies or particular river ecosystems. Local habitats provide tangible illustrations of living ecosystems."[52] According to Alan Metrick, communications director of the Natural Resources Defense Council, messages about public health and children's exposure to pesticides have proven to be very effective in print or broadcast appeals, while messages about wildlands and wild creatures, the so-called "charismatic megafauna," were more effective in direct mail.[53]

Most groups today also use visual images, such as pictures of children or cute animals, to help tell a story, evoke emotions, and appeal to people's core values. The power of such condensational symbols or images stems from their ability to arouse strong protective feelings from the public, which is already inclined to favor environmental protection.[54] Most consultants advise environmental groups that images should be at the heart of communications efforts aimed at the grass roots, and should thus be chosen very carefully. Moreover, visual images should be consistent with the story the group wants to tell. A typical "story" includes a description of a problem, an explanation of who is responsible for the problem, and an appeal to the audience to do something about it. Therefore, "winning" environmental messages will often include a mix of positive images about what is worth protecting combined with disturbing images of what threatens it. Television ads run by the Sierra Club and the League of Conservation Voters in recent elections clearly illustrate this approach. Both groups ran ads featuring images of children, juxtaposed with footage of raw sewage pouring into rivers or belching smokestacks. The soundtrack of the LCV ad also featured Louis Armstrong's rendition of "What a Wonderful World," an emotional staple in commercials hawking consumer products like perfume, but used here to sell an idea—that children deserve protection from the ravages of pollution.[55]

In addition to describing a compelling problem, effective messages should also offer a solution and give people something specific to do in pursuit of that solution, such as attending a public hearing or writing a letter to a public official. There is a growing recognition in the environmental community that groups in the past have been too shrill and pessimistic, leaving their members, and the general public, discouraged and overwhelmed. As a result, many groups are trying to overcome feelings of apathy by encouraging people to believe that they can make a difference. This usually takes the form of messages that offer possible solutions and that highlight local success stories. The rather remote and daunting issue of national and international biodiversity, for example, can seem overwhelming to many Americans. For this reason, groups are encouraged to speak of biodiversity in terms that are familiar to the everyday experiences of people, to stress the human connection by showing evidence that their own welfare is linked to threats affecting local ecosystems, and to give people something concrete to do.[56]

Communicating More Effectively

Once groups have crafted a message, they must still figure out how to communicate it to the intended audience. With advances in technology, groups today have a broader range of communication tools than in the past, and the environmental movement takes advantage of them all. Groups seeking to reach their own members publish newsletters and magazines and use email and websites. Others use direct mail. Groups seeking to spread their message more broadly work through the mass media, in either paid or earned forms. Some groups, such as the Washington Wilderness Coalition, have made a determined effort to reach out to newspaper editorial boards, as well as radio and television stations. At the same time, organizations looking to build broader coalitions may seek forums in community meetings or churches.[57]

A growing number of organizations now communicate their messages in paid issue advertising campaigns in newspapers, magazines, radio, and television. These ads, which have been called "genuine" issue ads because they address a substantive pending policy issue rather than seeking to influence elections, have become common in recent years. One of the largest spenders in 2000 was the National Environmental Trust (NET), a nonprofit, nonpartisan membership group established in 1994 to inform citizens about environmental problems and how they affect public health. Together with the Union of Concerned Scientists, the NET spent a reported $8 million on television ads in 1999–2000, highlighting global warming and urging viewers to "find out what we can do to fix it."[58]

Another group that turned to issue advocacy in 2000 was the Heritage Forest Campaign, an alliance of conservationists, scientists, and clergy working to protect wilderness forests. The group's public education campaign was designed to encourage citizens to inform legislators of their desire to protect wild forests. Members include the National Environmental Trust and the Natural Resources Defense Council. In the spring and summer of 2000 the group ran ads about forests and logging. It was reported that the group, which was consulting with leaders from the Sierra Club and Wilderness Society among others, was planning to spend $4 million during the year.[59]

In January of 2000 a group called Montanans for Common Sense Mining Laws spent $75,000 on three television ads demanding that Senator Conrad Burns remove his name from pending legislation on asbestos. The ads, which featured Montana residents suffering from asbestos illnesses, criticized Burns for supporting a law that would require people who wanted to sue a mining company over an asbestos-related illness to have their conditions verified and undergo mandatory mediation before filing the suit. A fourth ad, costing $50,000 ran in February. The organization also spent $82,000 on ads in the nation's capital saying that the Fairness in Asbestos Compensation Act of 1999 would "bail out" an industry that "lied" about asbestos rates to Libby, Montana, residents, where "over 100" are dead and "hundreds more" are "facing death."[60]

The Sierra Club took out a series of three full-page newspaper ads in March

2001 that were designed to dispel charges that environmental groups were responsible for California's energy shortages. The ads noted that environmental groups had supported the construction of new power plants in the state and that utilities and generating companies had blocked them. The ads ran in *Roll Call,* the *New York Times* West Coast Edition, the *Sacramento Bee,* and other weekly California papers. That same month, in reaction to a series of decisions by the Bush White House to suspend or delay a number of environmental rules issued in the waning days of the Clinton administration, the Club announced that it was launching a two-month advertising and organizing campaign designed to inform Americans about the need to make economically and environmentally wise choices about the nation's energy future.

In addition to paid advertising, some groups produce videotapes and films highlighting issues, often with the assistance of public relations firms or communications consultants. There are now radio and television programs with environmental themes, and some have even speculated about the possibility of creating an environmental television network.[61] Of course, not every group can afford to do all this. Even the Natural Resources Defense Council, a large and well-respected organization, did not buy television ads until the spring of 2001. The group's $500,000 cable ad buy, which focused on the Bush administration's plans to drill in the Arctic National Wildlife Refuge, was timed to coincide with a direct mailing. Both the television ad and the mail pieces were designed to signal its members that the organization was active on the issue.[62]

The choice of messenger is crucial as well. Moreover, it is important that the messenger complement both the message and the audience, because the most carefully crafted message will do very little if the audience does not perceive the person delivering the message as credible. In general, messages are typically most credible when they come from people directly affected by an issue or problem, and not necessarily by someone famous. Many groups believe that doctors and patients are the best messengers for stories about health threats to air and water.[63] As a case in point, the League of Conservation Voters ran television ads in the 2000 Michigan Senate race that featured a doctor from the state talking about health threats from local environmental problems. Children have also proven to be very effective messengers for environmental issues. The Sierra Club ran a series of ads in 2000 featuring a six-year-old Texas boy who suffered from asthma; the ad, which focused on then Governor George W. Bush's record on clean air issues, also used images of pollution spewing from smokestacks as a backdrop.

Cultivating the Media

Despite more money and the widespread recognition that effective communication is an essential element of comprehensive education and outreach plans, not all groups possess the necessary staff, skills, training resources, or other tools to do the job well. Some organizations, such as Clean Water Action, the Sierra Club

Training Academy, and the Western Organization of Resource Councils, conduct their own media training, though resource inequities mean that many others have not and cannot. Moreover, many environmental communications staffers lack access to the communications tools they have been trained to use. Without access to accurate media lists, public opinion research, and other media tools, improvements in staffing levels and training will have only a marginal effect on any group's ability to persuade policymakers and the public.

The significant decline in media coverage of environmental issues in recent years has been another barrier to effective communication. Environmental coverage in major news outlets is infrequent and superficial, tending to focus on unusual pollution episodes rather than the trends that produced them.[64] Although a number of factors are responsible for the decline in environmental news coverage, at least some of it can be traced to the fact that many groups have not devoted as much attention to cultivating and maintaining relationships with the media. For small groups in particular, the reliance on volunteer or part-time communications staff helps explain the failure to develop effective ties to reporters and editors. Today, however, an increasing number of activists recognize that working through the media is more than ever an essential way of reaching the public and improving its understanding of environmental issues. Consequently, more groups are seeking to establish relationships with print and broadcast journalists, editorial boards, assignment editors, or radio and television station news directors. A fortunate development for environmental groups is the number of organizations now working to help them design more effective media operations.

As an example, the Safe Energy Communication Council has offered an Environmental Media Training and Leadership Development Program since 1982. According to the group, the program has served over 4,500 activists, lawyers, grassroots and national leaders, and others since its inception. The program, which is coordinated by the SECC staff in conjunction with representatives of the sponsoring group, features workshops in which reporters explain how to develop and maintain good press relations. Among other skills taught are how to plan strategic and winning media campaigns, how to create and maintain an effective media outreach operation, how to write effective press releases, how to sharpen interview skills, and how to conduct press conferences and media events that receive favorable media coverage.

Several organizations focus on improving the communication skills of environmental groups through training and the provision of "message kits," communication handbooks, and other tools. One example is Environmental Media Services, a nonprofit communications clearinghouse dedicated to expanding media coverage of environmental issues. Former *Time* and *Newsweek* journalist Arlie Schardt, who headed EDF in 1970s, established the organization in 1994. Through media guides and newsletters, Environmental Media Services tries to provide journalists with reliable information about major environmental issues, which it tracks on a daily basis. In addition to its media guides, which are comprehensive summaries of environmental issues, the organization's newsletters offer journalists brief summaries of recent findings as well as contact information for experts from the academic, business, government, and the public interest communities. The organization, which is funded by donations from foundations and individuals, also assists journalists by compiling a list of the best websites for environmental issues. Since 1995 it has held a Washington Press Breakfast Series that brings together journalists and experts for briefings on environmental issues. On average, the breakfast series convenes about twenty-five times each year.

Although it is still too early to gauge its effectiveness, one of the more ambitious and intriguing organizations is Green Media Toolshed. Established by the Biodiversity Project and a number of other groups in 2000, Green Media is a cooperative communications service that seeks to improve the communications capacity of environmental groups by providing them with access to high-quality media tools, such as media lists, public opinion research, and photo and video stock. The organization's goal is to help environmental groups decide what to communicate and to increase their effectiveness in transmitting their messages to the public through the media. The underlying rationale for the Toolshed is that although very few groups can afford the staff and resources to obtain the tools on their own, together they can. As of the end of 2001, the Toolshed had about forty member groups, each of whom pays a flat yearly fee.

To date, the evidence on the effectiveness of such media projects is mixed. Environmental coverage in the national media is sporadic, superficial, and focuses on tradeoffs between jobs and environmental protection. Moreover, the national broadcast media has been cowed by conservative charges of "liberal bias" and thus bends over backward in an attempt to appear balanced. All too often, the result is a distorted picture of reality when it comes to environmental issues. Take, for example, the way the major networks have covered the issue of climate change. Despite nearly unanimous agreement among the world's climate experts that global warming is real and can be traced to human actions, the networks persist in giving equal time, and thus credibility, to a handful of skeptics, some of whom receive support from the fossil fuel industry. The viewing public is thus left with the inaccurate conclusion that "the experts can't decide," a view that leads to policy inaction, which is precisely the policy sought by the fossil fuel industry.

A FOCUS ON COALITION BUILDING

Many activists suggest that environmental groups are now working together more consistently and more effectively than in the past. Indeed, coalition building has become so widespread in the last five years that it may be the defining trait of contemporary environmental activism. Groups are joining forces to create joint websites, to produce and air television commercials about pending legislation and cabinet appointments, and to influence agency rule makings, among other things.

This is not to suggest that environmental groups are only now discovering the benefits of forming coalitions. Rather, there is now a conscious strategy among many activists to work together on a continuing basis. Coalitions form to oppose or support particular policies, but also to try to broaden the general appeal of environmentalism and to widen the base of political support.[65] Depending on the issue, coalitions today frequently include other public interest groups outside the environmental community, such as labor unions, businesses, and church groups.

Like other interests who have historically been disadvantaged in the American political process, environmental organizations have frequently joined forces in an attempt to expand the scope of the conflict. Coalitions, after all, enable groups to share their often meager resources, make use of a wider range of policy contacts, and win a measure of political credibility. Coalitions also allow diverse interests to speak with one voice, an advantage in any policy arena, especially for groups seeking to frame issues.[66] In the past, however, environmental coalitions were often formed for specific purposes and would disband once that purpose was either achieved or denied. That strategy started to change in the early 1980s with the formation of the "Group of Ten" by leaders from the large national organizations. Established as a means of responding more effectively to the immediate threats of the Reagan administration's environmental programs, the group gradually became a forum for greater communication and collaboration within the environmental community.

A division of labor characterizes environmental coalitions, with different groups taking the lead on different issues. For example, much of the research developed to advocate roadless area protection in the national forests was conducted by the Wilderness Society and then used by the many groups involved in the Heritage Forest Campaign. Organizations with different expertise, such as the Natural Resources Defense Council, often play a key role on issues like pesticides or toxic chemicals. There are many benefits to such a division of labor, not the least of which is that it allows a variety of groups to have their day in the sun, which can help with fundraising and membership drives.

In a study of coalition building by environmental groups, a team of market researchers found that two-thirds of its sample organizations had ongoing alliances with other environmental groups; just over half had alliances with government or regulatory agencies; and 30 percent had formal relationships with for-profit businesses. According to Ronald Shaiko, these alliances reflect a new pragmatism within the environmental movement, and recognition that the lines dividing "us" and "them" are not as clearly defined as in the past. These sentiments were echoed by David Yeaworth, a public relations associate with Pyramid Communications, who stated that half of the projects his firm worked on with environmental groups involve "win-win scenarios" in which the groups work with some business.[67]

In addition to foundations and some of the large national groups, Pyramid Communications is one of a number of public affairs firms that now help nonprofit organizations, including environmental groups, build coalitions. In the initial stages of public affairs campaigns, the firm's associates will ask group leaders to think about other organizations and interests that may have similar goals, with an eye toward building a coalition. If there are possible coalition partners, group leaders are asked on which issues they might contribute, who knows them, whether anyone listens to them, and how their involvement can be ensured.[68] The point of building coalitions is to take advantage of the synergies that might develop from having organizations with different skills and perspectives working on a common project. The hope, in short, is that the whole will be greater than the sum of its parts.

One of the more interesting recent examples of coalition building, albeit unsuccessful, was the campaign by a large collection of environmental groups to block George W. Bush's nomination of Gayle Norton as Interior secretary. The roster of groups who signed on to the effort included Defenders of Wildlife, the Sierra Club, the Natural Resources Defense Council, Friends of the Earth, the League of Conservation Voters, the National Environmental Trust, the Wilderness Society, and the Southern Utah Wilderness Alliance. After calling a Washington, D.C., press conference to announce the "Say No to Norton" campaign, the groups bought television and newspaper ads and even launched a website urging people to contact their senators to vote no on her nomination. The site included an editable "Dear Senator" letter, and an opportunity for writers to receive updates on other environmental issues.[69]

In March 2001, another coalition of environmental organizations launched a $650,000 television ad campaign to combat George W. Bush's battle proposals to open the Arctic National Wildlife Refuge to drilling. The ads, which ran in New York, Los Angeles, Indiana, Nebraska, Oregon, Arkansas, and Louisiana, urged viewers to write or call their members of Congress and ask them to defeat the plan. The ads were aired in those particular locations because of the influence of lawmakers from those regions and the activities of environmental groups in the area. According to Debbie Sease, legislative director of the Sierra Club, the ad campaign was not designed to influence individual votes in Congress; rather, the aim was to get Americans thinking about ANWR and, in turn, to influence the decision of lawmakers. The ad campaign was launched after a coalition of business and labor groups, known as the Energy Stewardship Alliance, spent $200,000 on radio and television ads in Washington, D.C., promoting "environmentally responsible exploration" of ANWR.[70]

These examples reflect a recognition that the environmental movement must broaden its appeal if it is to be more effective, especially in a hostile political environment. An important part of this trend involves reaching out to other groups and interests in an effort to build a larger and more effective political force. In the case of the Heritage Forests Campaign, for example, conservation groups in the Northwest made explicit appeals to churches, sportsmen's groups, and businesses involved in outdoor recreation. Accordingly, the Biodiversity Project launched a

"Spirituality Initiative," which brought environmentalists and religious communities together. That project was prompted by public opinion research that showed that more than two-thirds of Americans believed that the environment deserved protection because it was God's creation.[71]

Some environmental organizations have also worked closely over the years with organized labor, with mixed results. Coalitions have been formed to oppose the North American Free Trade Agreement (NAFTA) and permanent normal trade relations with China, as well as to protest policies of the World Trade Organization. In the case of China, the Sierra Club joined forces with the AFL-CIO in the spring of 2001 in an unsuccessful effort to persuade Congress to reject permanent normal trade relations. Despite these and other efforts, labor and environmentalists often do not see eye to eye and sometimes end up on different sides of issues, such as drilling in ANWR, raising the corporate average fuel economy standards, and, in the case of some environmental groups, the passage of NAFTA.[72]

Given the current political environment, in which Republicans control the presidency and both houses of Congress, environmental groups need any advantage they can get. Forming coalitions is important because it allows groups to take advantage of the different skills and resources of coalition partners. At the same time, given that groups have different goals and interests, it is difficult to form and maintain coalitions. There is always a temptation to cut the best deal for one's own group and leave the other coalition partners to fend for themselves.

THE IMPORTANCE OF FOUNDATIONS

As should be apparent by now, foundations are playing an increasingly important role in environmental advocacy, both as a source of funding for existing environmental organizations and in establishing new ones. With the bull market of the late 1990s, many foundations experienced a dramatic increase in their endowments and, to maintain their tax-exempt status, increased their grants. Environmental groups were one of the primary beneficiaries of this development, as foundations increased their support for a broad range of activities, including capacity building for local organizations. The largest donors to environmental organizations in recent years have been the David and Lucile Packard Foundation, the Pew Charitable Trusts, the Ford Foundation, the Robert W. Woodruff Foundation, and the W. Alton Jones Foundation. In December of 2001 the Gordon and Betty Moore Foundation announced plans to provide Conservation International with the largest gift ever given to a private conservation group, with a series of grants totaling up to $261 million over ten years. The previous year, the Packard Foundation awarded an astonishing $176,573,003 to conservation causes. Included in that total was a $2 million grant to Environmental Defense for the My-World Internet Project, which seeks to promote greater understanding of environmental issues through an interactive website. In all, private foundations spend more than $700 million each year on grants related to the environment and animals, a 350 percent increase since 1990, according to the Foundation Center of New York. It is too early to gauge the long-term effects of the terrorist attacks of September 11 and the sharp declines in the stock market, although early indications were that most groups experienced sharp declines in contributions. In 2002, for example, the Turner Foundation, which contributed $25 million to environmental causes the previous year, announced that it would not consider any grant proposals until 2004 at the earliest. Another large donor, the David and Lucille Packard Foundation, reduced its contributions to environmental causes from $96 million in 2001 to $33 million in 2002. These cutbacks had a significant effect on a number of small environmental groups, who often do not have large donor bases. At this writing, environmental groups were hoping that the 2002 elections, which placed Republicans in control of Congress, would stimulate giving by donors who feared environmental rollbacks.[73]

In recent years, the Pew Charitable Trusts have attracted the most attention, in part because of the amount of money they are spending and because, unlike many other foundations, they devote much of their budget to advocacy rather than to research. The Trusts are actually seven individual charitable funds established between 1948 and 1979 by the children of Sun Oil founder Joseph N. Pew and his wife Mary Underwood Pew. The seven trusts support activism in culture, education, the environment, human services, and religion. In its literature, Pew claims to make "strategic investments" that encourage and support citizen participation in addressing critical issues and effecting social change. Its grant-making activities are managed collectively and guided by a single set of programmatic priorities.

Pew's environment program awards grants in the general areas of marine resources, climate change, and old-growth forest and wilderness protection. It funds projects that seek to educate and mobilize the general public, the media, and policymakers about the causes and consequences of environmental problems. With respect to climate change, for example, Pew has encouraged the adoption of rules and policies that support the development of clean energy technologies and it conducts applied research aimed at informing policymakers and the public about the health effects of power plants. In addition, over the last three years the Pew Center on Global Climate Change has released more than twenty-five reports on climate change policy, impacts, and solutions. In the latter category, Pew claims that since 1991 it has helped promote $15.8 billion in energy-saving programs, which have reduced annual electricity sales by about 2 percent nationwide. It also claims that its Clean Air Task Force, created in 1996, and its "Clear the Air" initiative, a coordinated effort launched in 1999, encouraged the EPA to adopt two rules mandating significant reductions in power plant emissions in addition to bringing the largest enforcement action in history against aging power plants.[74] Pew's annual environmental grants have quintupled to more than $52 million since 1990, making it one of the largest donors to environmental causes. Some of the beneficiaries of Pew's largess include American Rivers Inc., Ducks Unlimited, and the

Wilderness Society. The largest recipients, however, are the new environmental organizations founded by Pew, such as the Pew Wilderness Center, the National Environmental Trust, the Heritage Forest Campaign, and the National BLM Wilderness Campaign. The National Environmental Trust was created in 1995 and received $6 million from Pew in 2000. The Pew Center on Global Climate Change received $5 million that same year.[75]

Consider the case of the Pew Wilderness Center. Established in 2000 by a grant from the Pew Charitable Trusts to the Earthjustice Legal Defense Fund, the organization has offices in Boulder, Colorado, Washington, D.C., and Seattle, Washington. The Pew Wilderness Center is not a membership-based organization and will exist for only ten years. The organization claims that it will spend no time or resources to establish a permanent infrastructure. Rather, its stated goal is to collaborate with local, state, and national environmental groups to protect publicly owned parks and wilderness. As such, the group claims that it seeks to complement rather than compete with other conservation organizations, working with them to involve more people in the democratic process by which policy decisions are made. More specifically, the organization provides educational programs so more people can learn about wilderness areas; it coordinates media efforts to bring increased attention to opportunities to protect wilderness; and it provides assistance to local, regional, and national citizens' groups to aid them in the protection of wild places. Accordingly, the Pew Wilderness Center will commission new research, conduct symposia, build public education campaigns, collaborate with federal agencies, academics, environmental organizations, and other organizations, and has plans to produce an annual publication entitled *The State of the Wild,* which will chart the nation's progress in securing wilderness protection.[76]

In May of 2001 the group launched its first ads as part of a ten-year campaign designed to educate the public about the need for increased wild lands protection. The television and newspaper ads, which ran in the spring and fall, were sandwiched around a door-to-door canvassing operation in metropolitan areas over the summer. The group's thirty-second television ads aired in Washington, D.C., Boise, Denver, Des Moines, Duluth, Fargo, Las Vegas, Lincoln, Little Rock, St. Louis, and Salt Lake City, areas where Pew determined that wilderness issues were, or should be, most prominent. The humorous commercial, which featured a brief narration by X-Files star David Duchovny, depicts a family camping on a highway median, the only undeveloped place left in a future America. The specific goal of the public education campaign is to increase the amount of land designated as wilderness by 2 to 3 percent over the next decade. Since the passage of the Wilderness Act of 1964, only 4.4 percent of the nation's land—some 100 million acres—has been protected as part of the National Wilderness Preservation System.

As a nonprofit, Pew does not lobby or support candidates for elective office. It does advocate specific causes, though, and its organizations have done so in many ways, including buying full-page newspaper ads and television ads as part of their public education initiatives. The Trusts view public education as one of their primary ways of encouraging a more inclusive process in environmental decisionmaking. Moreover, the Environment Program is "highly goal-oriented," and virtually all of the activities Pew supports "contain well-defined benchmarks that enable us to measure progress toward meeting explicit targets."[77]

Pew's money and aggressive environmental advocacy have generated resentment among foes and friends alike. Congresswoman Helen Chenoweth-Hage (R-Idaho), no friend of the environment, once cited Pew and its Heritage Forest Campaign as an example of how communities are "being crushed by an inaccessible and faceless movement wielding great power and influence." Similarly, Doug Crandall, staff director of the Republican-controlled House Subcommittee on Forests, called Pew "the 800-pound gorilla" on environmental issues "because they focus and target these issues quite effectively." Within the environmental community, Pew's actions have also rubbed some the wrong way. Some of the tension with established groups results simply from Pew's being the new kid on the block. Others may fear that Pew duplicates their own efforts and that there may not be enough room for everyone. Still others may resent it that Pew has not seen fit to fund their projects. Referring to the Pew groups' reputation for top-down management, the Sierra Club's Carl Pope said, "I don't think you make social change happen on the basis of paid staff in Washington and paid ads anywhere." Ironically, this same charge has often been leveled at the Sierra Club as well. As a large grassroots organization that is involved in many issues, the Sierra Club cannot match Pew's narrower programmatic focus. As noted above, Pew's Environment Program focuses on just three issues, which are chosen by its managers.[78]

Like Pew, the Bullitt Foundation, a Seattle-based nonprofit, has been active in supporting environmental causes. The Foundation awarded $843,000 in 2000, and another $525,000 in 2001 for public outreach, education, and capacity building. More specifically, it supports projects for technology improvements, media and marketing expertise, volunteer training, and board development for nonprofit, public interest conservation organizations. It also funds projects that seek to build the campaign skills of leaders within the environmental movement who are interested in running for public office. As a case in point, the Bullitt Foundation awarded a $35,000 grant to ONE/Northwest in 2001 for a project to provide digital presentation equipment, training, and resources to environmental groups in the region to enhance and amplify their messages. That same year, ONE/Northwest also received a $45,000 grant for overall operations. Bullitt awarded $75,000 grants to the Washington Environmental Alliance for Voter Education in both 2000 and 2001. Some of the money from the grants was dedicated to a project that assessed the needs of county-level conservation groups in Washington State. Bullitt also provides financial support for the Tides Center, which in turn supports Environmental Media Services, a national organization that offers media skill services to environmental activists and groups. The grant supports the overall work of the Tides Center's Northwest regional office.[79]

Although foundations have provided significant financial assistance to environmental groups since the early 1970s, they have come to play an even larger role in recent years. In particular, the recent emphasis on capacity-building has done much to enhance the effectiveness of groups at all levels, especially with respect to the essential task of political communication. Environmental groups now have much better access to the skills and tools they need to engage in issue definition and agenda setting. It is too early to say whether or not the capacity-building programs have been successful, but, as this chapter suggests, there are reasons to be optimistic.

CONCLUSION

Today most environmental organizations continue to do what they, and other groups, have always done. They make themselves available for publicity, research, and technical assistance; they offer help in drafting legislation and regulations; they testify at public hearings; they encourage members to contact public officials; and they seek to attract favorable media attention to their particular causes. What is different today, though, is the scale and intensity of these efforts. There are more groups lobbying, on more issues, and they have more tools to accomplish many of those tasks. In the end, this enables environmental groups to lobby more people in more focused, sophisticated, and strategic ways.

Compared to ten years ago, environmental groups conduct more frequent and more sophisticated grassroots campaigns. In addition to the obvious desire to generate public pressure for specific items on their legislative or administrative agendas, grassroots mobilization serves other goals. As Ronald Shaiko notes, group leaders use grassroots campaigns because constituent support supplements and reinforces the messages delivered by group lobbyists. In addition, grassroots campaigns can reenergize existing members, attract new members, generate media coverage, and even justify the group's technology expenditures.[80]

In some ways, the Internet has clearly changed community organizing. Because creating a website costs so little, almost anyone with access to a computer and the inclination to do so can launch an issue campaign. With negligible costs almost anyone, not just well-known groups with large memberships and superb fundraising skills, can be an advocate. This changed reality could someday allow new organizations to displace existing ones. Because the national groups, especially those with large grass roots, are typically involved in many issues, groups with more focused concerns may be better positioned to capture niches on particular environmental issues.

On the other hand, it seems just as possible that established groups would have a big advantage in online advocacy, at least for the foreseeable future. For one thing, established groups already have a large base of traditional and online supporters. That makes communication easier and faster for the larger groups, an important asset on issues where time is critical. Moreover, their greater name recognition gives them an edge in the overly crowded Internet. With millions of sites to choose from, curious browsers will be more likely to stumble across the websites of the better-known organizations. The larger national groups also have more avenues of communicating with people, such as magazines and paid advertising, and they also command the lion's share of free media.

Environmental groups have also taken some necessary steps toward building a grassroots presence in cyberspace and in rebuilding a grassroots presence on the ground. Of course, more can and should be done. As Bosso and Guber note, the environmental movement needs an effective ground force to back up the traditional lobbying the national groups do in Washington.[81] As the examples of the wise use and property rights groups attest, the arguments made by group lobbyists are much more effective when legislators hear the same things from constituents. Environmental activists can no longer afford to cede entire communities and regions to their opponents. In particular, environmental organizations must extend recent efforts on issue framing and agenda setting to the local level. As we have seen, most people's interest in the environment stems from an attachment to particular places, and groups need to tap into this phenomenon if they want to protect rivers, forests, or wetlands. A Washington presence is a necessary, but not sufficient, protection.

Finally, although the environmental movement has, on the whole, made impressive gains in recent years, it still cannot match the resources that corporate America can bring to bear on politics. With respect to communications and technology, most organizations trail business by at least a few years. Environmental groups do not have access to all of the communication outlets and tools utilized by their foes, nor can they expect it. No environmental group, for example, can afford to take out regular weekly ads in the *New York Times,* but ExxonMobil can, frequently touting the steps it has taken to protect the environment. In the end, environmental groups are doing a better job at crafting and communicating their messages, but their efforts are insufficient against the tide of resources available to the corporate world.

5
Environmental Groups in National Elections

Our kids depend on clean air and water laws.
But the politicians who make those laws are taking millions from polluters . . .
And protecting them . . .
Instead of our kids . . .
So remember, when you vote . . .
Our children will be drinking that vote . . .
And breathing that vote . . .
For a long time to come.
This fall, vote environment. Who we elect matters.
—League of Conservation Voters Education Fund television ad

Although most Americans say they care about the environment, the evidence suggests that environmental issues seldom shape individual voter preferences, especially in national elections. Environmental concerns rarely mobilize large numbers of voters; to the contrary, very few voters choose on the basis of a candidate's environmental record. In examining this apparent paradox, Deborah Guber argues that, in contrast to other concerns, environmental issues are relatively weak in national elections because of three factors. The first is low issue salience; that is, environmental issues rarely top voters' lists of important public issues. A second factor is that few voters perceive significant differences between major party presidential candidates on matters of environmental policy. A third explanation points to the tendency of environmental concerns to cut across traditional cleavages, such as partisan identification. Environmental preferences, it seems, are filtered through existing political values and attitudes, so ideology conditions which party voters perceive as better at handling environmental problems. Given current party platforms, voting "green" would thus require conservatives to cross party lines and vote Democratic, which they are reluctant to do.[1]

At the same time, though, there is evidence that environmental issues can, for certain voters under certain conditions, influence voting preferences and thus election results.[2] This is especially true for independents, who are less influenced by partisan ties. For these "swing" voters, environmental concerns may provide an important source of distinction between candidates, if those policy differences

119

are clearly articulated. The problem for environmental groups, however, is that independent voters are also the group least likely to perceive important differences between the parties on environmental policy. Moreover, because most independent voters are ideological moderates, "Green" candidates risk alienating this important slice of the electorate if they adopt positions that are too extreme.[3] Given the closely contested nature of elections today, though, even small shifts in voter preferences can be decisive in tilting elections. For that reason, says Guber, "in close races where victory is won at the margins, elite agenda setting by pro-environmental candidates might be successful in defining a unique environmental agenda and increasing the salience of environmental issues," both factors that should, in her opinion, shape the likelihood of an environmental vote.[4]

Of course, candidates are not the only ones seeking to shape electoral agendas. Increasingly, parties and organized groups are devoting time and money to the task as well. The League of Conservation Voters' "Dirty Dozen" list offers a classic example of a group seeking to hold elected officials accountable for their actions by publicizing their antienvironmental votes. And in close races, such actions by environmental groups offer the possibility of shaping the campaign debate and increasing the salience of environmental issues.

Despite the conventional wisdom, there is considerable evidence that environmental groups have become very active in recent elections, especially in closely contested races. In addition to endorsing candidates, environmental organizations are now raising and spending record amounts of money, and are communicating with more voters. Some groups are even taking sides in primary elections. In another departure, some of the groups have been spending their political money in new ways. In addition to contributing directly to candidates for federal office, as had been their usual practice, the Sierra Club and the League of Conservation Voters now use most of their money to mount less tightly regulated independent expenditure, issue advocacy, and voter education campaigns. This chapter seeks to document and explain this shift in strategy, and to speculate on its possible implications, including the important question of whether the increased electoral activity has been effective.

The Republican takeover of Congress in 1994 prompted environmental groups to alter their electoral strategies and political spending in an effort to play a larger role in national elections. Faced with the most serious threat to environmental laws and regulations in decades, environmental groups ratcheted up their fundraising, lobbying, and public education efforts. In large part, the unprecedented electioneering by environmental groups is best understood as an exercise in agenda setting. Rather than waiting for congressional candidates to raise environmental issues on their own, some environmental groups now wage their own paid media campaigns, which allows them to communicate with a much larger audience and enhances their chances of framing the issues in campaigns. In so doing, environmental groups hope to raise the prominence of environmental issues, to reenergize their grassroots, and thus to elect more people to Congress who support their policy goals. The electoral efforts are also aimed at enhancing the group's own profile in elections, creating relationships with the media, and building the organization by identifying and training activists and organizers.

The common understanding among students of American politics has been that political parties are in long-term decline and that candidates have supplanted parties as the leading forces in electoral politics. Recently, however, some have suggested that we may be entering a new phase of electoral politics, one in which organized interest groups play a more central role. Said to be among the distinguishing traits of this new era are a dramatic growth in the money that political parties and interest groups raise and spend to influence elections; the growth of creative money transfers among party committees, interest groups, and candidates; an increase in party and interest groups' independent expenditures and issue advocacy; and a greater overlap of the roles of political parties and interest groups in congressional elections. In recent years, for example, organized interest groups have begun to recruit candidates, organize congressional campaigns, mobilize voters, and sponsor their own electoral advertising campaigns. In addition, groups have supplied candidates with a range of campaign services that had previously been offered by either political consultants or political parties, including the provision of precinct-level targeting data, candidate training sessions, public opinion polls, absentee ballot programs, and fundraising assistance. Much of this has been done with the blessing and support of the national party committees.[5] Seen in this light, the increased activism by environmental groups is thus illustrative of an ongoing shift from candidate-centered campaigns to those in which candidates increasingly compete with groups and parties for control of the political agenda.

A GREEN PARTY?

Many environmentalists wonder whether it would be better to continue working within the two-party system or to form a separate "green" party. Advocates of a "green" party contend that it could challenge the two-party orthodoxy and force the major parties to pay more attention to environmental and other neglected issues. Such thinking was the rationale for Ralph Nader's presidential bids in 1996 and 2000. Unlike proportional representation systems, however, the winner-take-all electoral system in the United States does not yield any power to third parties. As most political observers have noted, greens are thus unlikely to win many seats in Congress unless they are able to displace one of the major parties.[6] That is unlikely to happen in the foreseeable future. In the interim, green party candidates will find their best prospects at the local level, where a number of them have already been victorious.

Ralph Nader's Green Party candidacy in the 2000 presidential election posed a dilemma for many environmentalists and, for a brief period, some of the mainstream national environmental groups. Friends of the Earth, for example, backed

Bill Bradley in the Democratic presidential primaries. After Bradley lost to Vice President Al Gore, the group's leader, Brent Blackwelder, suggested that the group would consider endorsing Ralph Nader. Voicing a common complaint, Blackwelder argued that both Gore and George W. Bush had too many ties to corporate interests. But in September, Blackwelder announced that the group was endorsing Gore, saying, "The vote in this presidential race is about governance. It is a decision about who is going to set budgets for the country, fill cabinet and agency posts, appoint members to the judiciary, and deal with national and global environmental problems. And this choice is between the two front runners."[7]

Many environmentalists were disappointed in Gore's record as vice president during the Clinton years, especially on greenhouse gases, and for breaking a promise to halt construction of an incinerator in Ohio. Candidate Gore's indecisiveness on the question of removing dams from the Snake River also disappointed environmentalists in the Pacific Northwest. Nader supported their removal, while Gore said he wanted to study the issue. His critics complained that although Gore talked a good game on the environment, his actions did not match his promises.[8]

The Gore versus Nader dilemma was particularly pronounced within the western environmental community. A number of grassroots activists founded Environmentalists Against Gore—a group of about one hundred people, including the iconic David Brower. The Oregon Wildlife Federation, one of the few local environmental groups with a PAC, endorsed the Green Party, noting that "business as usual" was unacceptable. In the end, although numerous environmental activists chose to support Nader, the mainstream groups threw their support behind Gore. Dan Weiss, the Sierra Club political director at the time, said that groups like Environmentalists Against Gore were not taking a responsible position, noting that the differences between Gore and Nader paled in comparison to the differences between Gore and Bush. Speaking at a news conference in Portland, Oregon, in the late stages of the race, Andy Kerr, an environmental activist working for Gore, said, "Ralph's greener and Ralph's better. Ralph has a better record on the environment. But the fact is a vote for Nader is a vote for Bush, and to protect the environment, one has to rise above principles."[9] The Sierra Club and the LCV devoted an enormous amount of money and energy in the final weeks of the campaign to persuading Nader voters in key battleground states to vote for Gore.

Although Gore did win most of those states, it was not enough to propel him to victory. In the postelection analysis, many observers concluded that although George W. Bush owed his victory to five Supreme Court Justices, he also owed a large debt to Ralph Nader, who pulled enough support in Florida and New Hampshire to cost Gore those state's Electoral College votes. Although it is surely the case that many Nader voters would not have voted at all if their choice had been limited to simply Gore or Bush, it is also likely that many other Nader voters would have cast their ballots for Gore in those same circumstances. In New Hampshire, Nader captured 4 percent of the vote, more than enough to throw the state to Bush. If Gore had carried New Hampshire and its four Electoral College votes, he would have had a total of 271 Electoral College votes and would not have needed Florida's twenty-five votes. Nader received more than 97,000 votes in Florida, a not insignificant figure given Bush's razor-thin margin in the state. After the election, many environmental leaders blamed Nader for Bush's victory. Among them was LCV President Deb Callahan, who also noted, however, that his candidacy did provide more attention to the environment. She said, "The environment played a bigger role in more campaigns and at higher level than it ever has before." Callahan also cited an LCV poll which showed that 50 percent of the public was unaware of the differences between Gore and Bush on the environment, leading her to claim that "Al Gore didn't talk about the environment clearly enough to distinguish himself from Bush."[10]

At the congressional level in 2000, there were forty Green Party candidates running for office. None of them won, but a few played a major role in determining the outcome. In Michigan's Eighth District, for example, the Green Party candidate received 3,400 votes, more than enough to provide the margin of victory to the Republican, who won by a mere 151 votes.[11] And in New Jersey's Twelfth District, where freshman Democrat Rush Holt won reelection by fewer than three hundred votes, a Green Party candidate was a significant factor. In that contest, one of the most expensive House races in the nation, Green Party candidate Carl Mayer received over five thousand votes, nearly throwing the election to Holt's Republican opponent, former Representative Dick Zimmer. Many of the state's environmental groups had worked hard for Holt's reelection.

Green Party candidates also played an important role in the 1998 elections. That year, 125 Green Party candidates ran for office at the state and local level, and 18 were elected.[12] They also were factors in several House races in 1997–1998, including a 1997 special election in New Mexico's Third Congressional District. In that race, Green Party candidate Carol Miller received 17 percent of the vote, allowing Republican Bill Redmond to capture the seat vacated by Democrat Bill Richardson, who had resigned to become U.N. ambassador. Redmond, who was quite conservative, won in the heavily Democratic district, despite receiving only 43 percent of the vote. It seems clear that Miller attracted votes that normally would have gone to the Democratic candidate, Eric Serna. Almost immediately, both parties, as well as a large number of interest groups, made the district a top priority in the 1998 elections. After defeating Serna in the Democratic primary, Tom Udall, the state's attorney general, set out to win back Democratic voters who in 1997 had supported Miller. The Sierra Club, the League of Conservation Voters, and many New Mexico environmental activists supported Udall, who in the end defeated Redmond 52 to 43 percent. Miller received just 5 percent of the vote. Among other things, the environmental groups spent heavily on television and newspaper advertising, direct mail, phone banks, and voter mobilization. The LCV also mailed out absentee ballots to voters and paid for half the salary of a staffer in the Udall campaign.[13]

The Green Party candidate also factored into the race in California's Thirty-sixth District, where Republican Steve Kuykendall defeated Janice Hahn by two points, which was the same percentage of the vote received by Green candidate Robin Barrett. Kuykendall was defeated in 2000 after being targeted by Democrats and progressive groups. That same year, in New Mexico's First District, Republican Heather Wilson beat Phil Maloof by six percentage points, while Green Party candidate Robert Anderson received 10 percent of the vote.

The examples noted above support the contention that although individual Green candidates may occasionally win local contests, the winner-take-all aspect of state and federal elections means that they are more likely to siphon votes from Democratic candidates and help elect Republicans. Against that backdrop, Christopher Bosso has argued that the threat of a Green Party candidacy can, under certain circumstances, give environmentalists some leverage with Democratic candidates to adopt stronger Green platforms. Even though a Green Party is unlikely to meet with much electoral success in the United States, Bosso suggests that Greens can still have an important influence by shaping the issue debate and by encouraging people to use environmental concerns as voting cues.[14]

It may be the case that Greens should adopt a page from conservative groups, such as the religious right, and begin by concentrating their energies on down-ticket races. Such an approach would have several advantages. First, many local offices actually have significant responsibility for environmental policy matters. If Greens can elect supporters to these positions, they can increase their influence over issues that matter to them, such as land use and growth. Second, positions on county commissions and other local bodies can be springboards for higher elective positions. Once Greens have experience in elective office, they will be more qualified to run for state legislative positions and, perhaps, Congress.

Christopher Bosso suggests that because the Green Party route offers little chance of success in the United States, at least in national elections, mainstream environmental groups have two viable options for influencing electoral politics. The first choice is to work more openly with the Democratic Party, which has been markedly more supportive of environmental policy goals than the Republican Party. Working within the framework of a larger coalition will require a balancing of environmental goals against others, to be sure. Environmental groups would have to be willing to compromise for the sake of party unity, at the risk of alienating many core activists. Working openly with Democrats also involves substantial political risks, with the Republicans in control of Congress and the White House. The second option is for environmental groups to seek allies in both parties. To date, this is the route chosen by the Sierra Club and the League of Conservation Voters, who have gone out of their way to provide support for Republican candidates with acceptable environmental records.[15] The second approach has its critics as well. Philip Shabecoff argues that environmental groups will have to shed "the fiction that environmental policy is bipartisan until it becomes so in reality once again. They need to get more deeply into the down-and-dirty political work of punishing their enemies and rewarding their friends where it counts most profoundly: in the electoral process. To do so, they will need more political clout, better strategies, and strong allies, and they will need to put far more effort into politics than they currently do."[16]

THE IMPACT OF THE 1994 ELECTIONS ON GROUP STRATEGY

As we have seen, twenty years ago, national environmental organizations did not pay much attention to federal elections. Some endorsed candidates, contributed money, or issued voting scorecards. Others made efforts to identify, register, and mobilize voters via phone banks and direct mail, but in general most environmental organizations did not devote significant resources to influencing election results. For example, it was not until 1984 that the Sierra Club even endorsed a presidential candidate, an action that was considered controversial at the time. Today, although it is still true that most environmental organizations do not play an active role in elections, some of the larger national groups, especially the League of Conservation Voters and the Sierra Club, have become quite involved in national elections, engaging in a broad range of activities and spending considerable sums of money. Environmental groups now conduct voter registration drives, collect and analyze polling and precinct data, and even help candidates with fundraising and media, tasks often associated with political consultants. Groups also help with district organizing, and provide candidates with expertise on policy issues. Some of the groups have also become very adept at using technology to identify and categorize voters, and have conducted extensive, and expensive, voter education campaigns to identify, inform, and mobilize key voting blocs. The use of phone banks and direct mail has become a major element of group tactics, as has the use of radio and television advertising, direct mail, and the Internet.

The paramount reason for the change was the Republican takeover of Congress in 1994. As discussed in Chapter 3, in that election, so-called wise use groups and extractive industries provided considerable financial support to Republican candidates, while issue advocacy campaigns by the NRA, term limits supporters, and the religious right helped many others.[17] With the new Republican Congress, the "rules of the game" in environmental policy changed dramatically. Hostile House members such as Don Young of Alaska now chaired key committees, while political allies were suddenly in the minority. Environmental groups lost much of the access and influence they had enjoyed. In the new context, environmental groups played a mostly defensive game, struggling to beat back the most onerous legislative proposals. Faced with such a direct threat to their policy interests, environmental groups responded by becoming more involved in electoral politics. The new political strategy, in short, was an adaptive response to a "disturbance" in the existing political order.[18]

Another factor explaining the heightened attention to elections is that since 1994 both chambers of the U.S. Congress have been closely divided along partisan lines. As a result, a shift of a few seats in either chamber could have profound implications for environmental policy, as the defection of Senator Jim Jeffords in 2001 demonstrated. A Democratic majority, with Democratic committee and subcommittee chairs, would be expected to take a very different approach to environmental legislation than a Republican one. Moreover, a Democratic majority, even if only in one chamber, would likely have a different agenda, and would conduct hearings on different environmental matters. Congressional oversight of the EPA and federal land management agencies would likely take on a different tone as well. That is why interest groups and parties have recently devoted so much attention to the handful of truly competitive races in each election cycle. Environmental groups are working much harder to inject their issues into campaigns and to increase the number of "green" officeholders.

CHANGES IN ENVIRONMENTAL PAC DECISIONMAKING

A mere handful of environmental organizations have active political action committees, and only a few of them have been active for an extended period of time. Most environmental PACs have a regional or state-level focus, have very small budgets, or contribute only to a limited number of candidates. To date, only two of the PACs—those affiliated with the Sierra Club and the League of Conservation Voters—raise and spend significant sums of money, despite legal constraints which restrict fundraising by membership organizations to group members only. In addition to endorsing candidates, both PACs contribute directly to candidates for federal office and make independent expenditures, which will be discussed below. WILD PAC, a nonmembership organization established in 2001, is free to solicit funds from the general public. As of this writing the organization, which plans to support a limited number of candidates who have demonstrated a commitment to wilderness protection, has a limited track record in federal elections.[19] For these reasons, much of the following discussion focuses on the actions of the Sierra Club and League of Conservation Voter PACs.

Since the Republican takeover of Congress, electoral activity by environmental groups has changed in several significant ways. First, both groups now place a greater emphasis on targeting close races and are much more selective in deciding when and where to expend their resources. Because it makes little sense to attempt to unseat Republican incumbents in heavily Republican districts or states, groups have decided to focus their energies on closely contested races in competitive areas. Environmental groups are also paying more attention to the ground war in campaigns, devoting considerable resources to voter targeting and mobilization. In low turnout elections, interest groups that energize their membership can play a decisive role in the outcome. Environmental groups are also doing more to target specific segments of voters, especially swing voters, in ways that won't alienate them. To this end, they now pay greater attention to the content of their political messages. Finally, as we have seen, the Sierra Club and LCV now spend their political money in new ways, shifting away from direct contributions to a greater reliance on independent expenditure, issue advocacy, and voter education campaigns.

While a number of factors influence PAC decisions on candidate contributions, the manner in which disbursements are made generally follows one of two strategies.[20] PACs may seek to cultivate or maintain access to officeholders who are in a position to advance the group's policy interests, or they may seek to maximize their legislative influence by increasing the number of sympathetic officeholders. The inevitable result of the first approach is a disproportionate allocation of funds to incumbents, particularly those members whose committee assignments affect the PAC's policy interests.[21] Conversely, the second, maximizing approach often entails replacing unfriendly incumbents or filling open seats with candidates who are supportive of the group's policy objectives. To that end, a higher proportion of the PAC's contributions would go to challengers or to candidates for open seats.

The bulk of the evidence on contribution patterns suggests that most PACs, especially corporate PACs, are focused on maintaining access to incumbents, not on maximizing their electoral influence.[22] Ideological PACs, on the other hand, are more likely to pursue a maximizing approach. Accordingly, these PACs follow a two-prong electoral strategy designed to elect the largest number of like-minded candidates: they only support candidates who share their policy goals, and they focus their contributions on closely contested races, where their financial support may affect the outcome. In addition to their financial support, ideological PACs tend to take on more of the characteristics of full-service electoral organizations: they rate and endorse candidates, register and educate voters, organize campaign events, and bring voters to the polls.[23]

Although environmental PACs have traditionally followed an electoral strategy, the evidence suggests that they became even more committed to this approach after the 1994 elections. The Republican victory prompted a number of environmental groups to rethink both their lobbying and electoral strategies, including their political spending. In general, environmental organizations decided to become more active in elections, supplementing their traditional efforts with a broader range of activities. Groups continue to provide campaign volunteers, as well as issue endorsements and "hit lists," although they now use new technologies to communicate that information to a larger audience. Environmental groups are also spending more to sway elections, and the spending has taken new forms. After the 1994 midterm elections, both the LCV and Sierra Club sharply curtailed their direct contributions to candidates and instead devoted most of their resources to massive voter education, independent expenditure, and issue advocacy campaigns.[24] Furthermore, both groups opted to become more selective in their electoral efforts, targeting their spending on close races in an attempt to maximize their influence.

In the case of the Sierra Club, endorsements originate at the local level, where candidates are screened and sometimes interviewed by volunteers. The state's political committee then decides whether to issue an endorsement, which requires a two-thirds vote. If an endorsement is approved, it is passed on to the Club's national Political Committee, which then takes its own vote. Among the criteria the Club uses to decide which candidates to support are the incumbent's voting record, whether there is a "clear difference" between the candidates, the presence of a salient local environmental issue and enthusiastic local activists, and whether the race will be close enough that the Club's efforts could make a difference.[25] In 1994, however, the Sierra Club contributed to many candidates who won or lost by wide margins, prompting Club officials to believe they had wasted a lot of money. They vowed to target their spending more carefully in future elections. In fact, the Sierra Club Political Action Committee's compliance guidelines now require the committee to target close races, noting that the "goal is to spend money where it has the greatest chance of having an impact, so more money will go to close races than to 'sure winners' or 'sure losers.'"[26] According to Dan Weiss, "We are not giving to people we love who have no chance of winning. In 1994, we gave to too many people who ended up with less than 40 percent of the vote. The goal is to only give to races that are within ten points at the end."[27]

As part of this new strategy, the political committee decided to hold their money until later in campaigns, hoping to better identify close races. In determining whether a race will be close, the Club's political staff consults with its local chapters and other progressive groups, and examines publicly available polling data, election reports, FEC contribution records, and district demographic and voting data. Among the factors considered are whether an incumbent is involved in the race and the status of the candidate's campaign, including the amount of money he or she has raised and whether he or she has any local support. In recent elections members of the Political Committee also relied on information provided by the Democratic Campaign Committees for the House and Senate, which provided polling data identifying close races. The political staff then makes its recommendations to the San Francisco office and volunteers on the political and voter education committees, which then modify and/or approve them. The new approach yielded immediate results in 1996, when 83 percent of the Club's contributions went to candidates in close races, compared to only 58 percent in 1994. By spending late, and primarily in close races, the Club clearly hopes to gain the attention—and appreciation—of legislators they have supported.[28] The Club was not as successful in identifying close races in 1998, however, when only nineteen of the forty-three races the Club targeted were decided by ten percentage points or less.

More recently, the Sierra Club has been spending money both early and late, as well as in areas with comparatively low advertising costs. In the 2000 election, for example, the Club took to the airwaves in April in the presidential race and in seventeen congressional contests. Spending early in the campaign allowed the

Club to take advantage of lower advertising costs, so its ads could be run more often in an effort to shape the agenda in the campaign. Because fewer political ads run in the spring, the ads were less likely to be drowned out by competing ads. The Club followed up its April ads by spending $3 million in October, focusing on the presidential race and on twelve closely contested congressional districts. Although advertising time is more expensive close to Election Day, in this instance the Club opted to buy the time because many of the races were so tight.

Unlike the Sierra Club, whose endorsement rules require it to support incumbents with good voting records even if they are not the "greenest," the League of Conservation Voters follows a more rigorous electoral maximizing strategy. After a careful evaluation of the candidate's environmental voting records, the League's board of directors determines the LCV Action Fund's general spending strategy, and the political advisory board (comprised of activists and representatives from other environmental organizations) selects the particular candidates to support or oppose.[29] The LCV Action Fund compiles three lists for use in making spending decisions. The "Dirty Dozen" list includes the twelve candidates with the worst environmental rating, while the "Environmental Champions" list notes the ten members with the best rating. The "Earth List" is a bundling program aimed at helping proenvironment candidates; the LCV solicits hard money contributions for these candidates and then passes the money along in a "bundle" to the candidates.

After 1994, the LCV made two major changes in its political spending. The first change, to be discussed in detail below, involved shifting most of its resources from direct contributions to independent expenditure campaigns. Direct contributions to proenvironment candidates thus dropped sharply. The second change was to focus on close races. In the case of the LCV Dirty Dozen races, over the last four election cycles forty-one of the forty-nine races have been decided by ten points or less. Twenty-five of the races have been decided by fewer than five points, and eleven have been decided by fewer than two points. This was particularly true in the 2000 elections, when nine of the twelve Dirty Dozen contests were decided by fewer than five points. Four of those races, including the Senate contests in which incumbents Slade Gorton and Spencer Abraham were defeated, were decided by two points or less.

In close, low-turnout elections, an interest group can play a decisive role if its members are mobilized. In recent years, environmental groups, along with labor unions and civil rights organizations, and numerous groups on the political right, have rediscovered the importance of organizing voters. Labor unions, in particular, have worked very hard at organizing. In 2000, for example, the AFL-CIO trained five hundred organizers, who then divided their states into geographic zones and met with local union leaders to identify a network of activists who would go out and talk to voters. The labor effort was based on the notion that workers would be more receptive to messages from other workers who understood their concerns. Labor activists aimed to reach workers through continual workplace contact, home visits, phone calls, and direct mail. In Pennsylvania, a battleground state that year, labor's goal was to contact each union member between eight and thirteen times by election day.[30]

Environmental organizations have adopted similar methods in their efforts to identify and organize voters. Like other organizations, environmental groups now use sophisticated tools such as GeoVoter and Voter Tracker to match their membership lists to voting records, census data, precinct maps, and other databases. With these tools, groups can now use multiple databases to create profiles of individual voters, and then plot them on political maps. Groups can see pockets of support and undecided voters, and can then figure out where to hold rallies, send volunteers, or hold meetings.[31] Armed with this information, groups can now go precinct by precinct, and even block by block, to identify voters who may be interested in environmental issues. The groups can then target those voters for direct mail, telephone calls, and personal visits. In the case of direct mail, the technology allows groups to send materials on specific issues of concern to particular voters. If a phone call reveals that a voter is interested in water quality, for example, groups can send that person mail addressing the issue. Groups do this because there is some evidence suggesting that the impact of direct mail, which is quite expensive, can be enhanced when it is combined with face-to-face contact or telephone calls.[32]

Environmental groups have also become quite sophisticated in the timing and nature of their electoral efforts. For example, in many cases the Sierra Club has run its radio and television ads early in campaigns, in an attempt to shape the campaign agenda, and then has shifted to direct mail, phone banks, and door-to-door canvassing in the campaign's final weeks. Those particular tactics allow groups to focus their efforts on likely voters. In House races in heavily populated metropolitan areas, groups have eschewed television advertising, which is costly and inefficient in such locations, in lieu of phone banks and direct mail, which can be more cost effective. Anticipating that every vote might count in the 2000 elections, environmental groups budgeted considerable money for extensive get-out-the-vote campaigns. In Washington State groups sent absentee ballots to targeted voters, while in Oregon, which allows voting by mail over a period of weeks, voters were contacted to see if they had mailed in their ballots. If people had already voted, the groups could then turn their attention to others who had not yet cast their ballots.

ENVIRONMENTAL GROUPS AND CAMPAIGN SPENDING

Beginning in 1996, environmental PACs raised record amounts of money, with slightly over $2.5 million raised in 1995–1996, a 20 percent increase over the previous election cycle. The League of Conservation Voters and the Sierra Club, the two largest environmental PACs, raised more than three-quarters of this money.

For its part, the LCV raised nearly $1.3 million, a 50 percent increase over 1994. The Sierra Club doubled its fundraising proceeds, to almost $750,000. Most of the remaining environmental PAC money was raised by Greenvote, a group based in Boston, and the California (CALCV) and Oregon (OLCV) chapters of the LCV. Ironically, the OLCV PAC actually experienced a $546,569 decline in receipts from the previous cycle largely attributable to the special Senate election in Oregon, in which environmental groups spent heavily in support of Democrat Ron Wyden, who won a very close election.[33] As Table 5.1 indicates, the handful of other environmental PACs have been minor players, with most raising and spending less than $20,000 per election cycle.

Despite these record fundraising amounts reported by environmental PACs, total direct contributions to federal candidates actually declined sharply over the next two elections cycles, before rebounding in 2000. Most of the reduction in 1996 is attributable to a staggering 91 percent decline in direct contributions from the LCV Action Fund, which contributed only $69,868, down from the record $774,559 it gave in 1994. In fact, among all PACs, only that of the United Parcel Service registered a larger decline in direct contributions to federal candidates.[34] The sharp reduction in LCV contributions means that the Sierra Club has regained its place as the largest contributor among environmental groups. And yet, the Sierra Club has also contributed less than in previous years. The approximately $370,000 the Club contributed in both 2000 and 2002 represents about 60 percent of its contributions in 1992. Indeed, as Table 5.2 indicates, the recent decline in direct contributions from the two largest environmental groups reverses a pattern of steadily increasing donations dating back to the early 1980s. In contrast to the LCV and the Sierra Club, many of the other environmental PACs actually stepped up their contributions in 1996. The third largest PAC, Greenvote, nearly doubled its contributions to $129,400 in 1996, while the Friends of the Earth PAC contributed nothing in 1994 but gave nearly $47,000 in 2000. Aside from the LCV and Sierra Club, though, other environmental PACs have been sporadic players. Greenvote, for example, disbanded its PAC in 1998 and has not been active in subsequent elections.

With respect to the recipients of environmental money, some patterns are clearly evident. Democrats, not surprisingly, fare better than Republicans, receiving 91 percent of environmental contributions since 1990, and 93 percent in the last two election cycles. Among the various groups, Greenvote was most supportive of Democratic candidates before it disbanded, and the LCV Action Fund the least supportive. All of Greenvote's contributions in the 1994 and 1996 election cycles went to Democrats. In addition to supporting individual candidates, Greenvote also contributed to various Democratic Party committees. In 1996, for example, the group contributed $2,500 to the Iowa Democratic Party, while in 1994 it donated $10,000, the legal maximum, to the Democratic National Campaign Committee. In a typical election cycle, 90 percent of the Sierra Club's direct contributions wind up in Democratic coffers. Given that the average Democratic candidate supported the Club's policy position 75 percent of the time, while the

Table 5.1. Fundraising by Selected Environmental PACs, 1994–2002 (in dollars)

	1994	1996	1998	2000	2002
Sierra Club	354,251	737,685	551,602	667,940	837,606
LCV	841,505	1,279,179	1,055,373	2,478,404	1,589,142
LCV-CA	69,235	114,856	42,200	25,530	32,065
LCV-OR	701,443	154,874	290	185	0
LCV-NY	0	19,304	22,894	6,235	1,136
American Forest Defense	0	0	0	0	7,708
Clean Water PAC	0	0	0	4,041	29,350
Clean Water Action	22,694	4,326	6,504	8,876	33,363
DUC	10,000	5,000	0	0	0
Friends of Earth	0	20,881	5,075	59,735	63,349
Forest & Nature Protection	0	15,801	58	0	0
Greenvote	117,200	197,125	8,000	0	0
Keep Tahoe Blue	0	0	0	16,388	7,065
Oregon Natural Resource Council	0	30,724	2,995	12,960	1,000
WILD PAC	0	0	0	0	207,440
Totals	2,116,328	2,579,755	1,694,991	3,280,294	2,808,224

Sources: Center for Responsive Politics, FEC Committee Reports COO135368, COO252940, COOO12401, COOO35154, COO278424, COO364695, COO347724, COO251942, COO235564, COO141044, COO320507, COO24369 1, COO311597, COO306613, COO364299.

Table 5.2. Direct Federal Contributions by Selected Environmental PACs, 1990–2002 (in dollars)

	1990	1992	1994	1996	1998	2000	2002
Sierra Club	408, 651	599,446	406,631	370, 459	235,708	369,134	514,583
LCV	152,216	408,139	776,559	68,590	70,926	88,682	219,987
LCV-CA	0	17,837	20,490	49,110	31,163	30,124	23,750
LCV-OR	5,968	2,522	1,000	3,000	1,496	100	100
LCV-NY	0	0	2,000	1,483	250	0	0
American Forest Defense	0	0	0	0	0	0	1,000
Clean Water PAC	0	0	0	0	0	1,000	16,000
Clean Water Action	21,179	21,172	8,308	0	5,000	73	0
Duc Pac	13,900	18,300	9,750	4,500	13,500	1,414	0
Friends of Earth	0	0	0	20,881	3,587	53,026	40,474
Forest & Nature Protection	0	0	0	6,725	2,025	0	0
Greenvote	27,157	92,850	67,150	129,400	4,000	0	0
Keep Tahoe Blue	0	0	0	6,000	2,750	2,000	500
Oregon Natural Resources Council	0	0	0	14,764	625	89	250
WILD PAC	0	0	0	0	0	0	20,242
Totals	629,071	1,160,266	1,291,888	674,912	371,030	545,642	836,886

Sources: Center for Responsive Politics, FEC Committee Reports COO135368, COO252940, COOO12401, COOO35154, COO278424, COO364695, COO347724, COO251942, COO235564, COO141044, COO320507, COO243691, COO311597, COO306613, COO364299; Larry Makinson and Joshua Goldstein, Open Secrets: The Cash Constituents of Congress (Washington, D.C.: CQ Press), various editions.

average Republican sided with the Club a mere 15 percent of the time, these results are to be expected.[35] What is surprising, given the Republican assault on environmental programs in the 104th Congress, is that Republicans fared slightly better in 1996 than in prior years. This slight increase can be attributed to contributions to the few Republican friends environmentalists have in Congress, notably Senator John Chafee (R.I.) and Representatives Sherwood Boehlert (N.Y.) and Connie Morella (Md.). In supporting these Republican incumbents, environmental groups were seeking to maintain some access to the new majority party, and to combat charges that they are merely surrogates for the Democratic Party.

The evidence indicates that, compared to other PACs, environmental groups have been quite supportive of challengers and candidates for open seats. In fact, although incumbents received two-thirds of all PAC direct contributions in 1996, just one-third of environmental PAC money went to incumbents. In other words, environmental PACs are twice as likely to contribute to challengers and open seats as the average PAC. Given that environmental PACs give heavily to Democrats and that Republican control of Congress means that most incumbents are Republicans, this fact is not surprising. Indeed, compared to previous elections, environmental PACs were more likely to favor challengers and open-seat candidates in 1996, the first election after the Republican takeover. For example, in both 1992 and 1994, the Sierra Club gave 45 percent of its money to incumbents, but only 36 percent in 1996. Fully 45 percent of the Club's direct contributions in 1996 went to challengers. The League of Conservation Voters, on the other hand, contributed half of its money to incumbents and only 25 percent to challengers. In this sense, the contribution patterns of environmental PACs are typical of other ideological groups, who tend to support mostly like-minded candidates. In an effort to protect those candidates elected in the previous two cycles, however, both groups directed about 60 percent of their money to incumbents in 2000.

As noted above, PACs seeking access tend to contribute heavily to members of those committees with jurisdiction over their areas of interest. A review of direct contributions to the Senate Environment and Public Works Committee, which has jurisdiction over many environmental programs, suggests that although members have received money from environmental PACs, they have received much more from industry groups. According to the Center for Responsive Politics, between 1996 and 2000, the League of Conservation Voters was the top contributor to members of the committee, but the next nineteen top contributors were all businesses, including over $1 million each from oil and gas concerns and miscellaneous manufacturing and distributing firms.[36]

As has been well documented, the 1996 elections witnessed the almost total collapse of the federal campaign finance rules and were marked by the rise of new forms of political spending. Candidates, parties, and contributors of all stripes discovered numerous ways to circumvent the Federal Election Campaign Act's contribution limits and disclosure requirements. In one such practice, donors who had already contributed the legal maximum to a candidate would then give money to a third party, who in turn would pass the money along to the same candidate. Because the money had, in essence, been laundered through a third party, it would be difficult to trace and contributors could thus give more than the law allows. There is some evidence that environmental groups played the role of a "third party" conduit in the 1996 elections. A review of the data reveals an upsurge in contributions to environmental groups from other ideologically compatible groups, notably organized labor. In the most extreme case, Friends of the Earth received almost 80 percent of its total receipts from labor PACs. In the final three months of the year, the group received $5,000 contributions from the American Federation of State, County, and Municipal Employees (AFSCME), the Democratic Republican Independent Voter Education Committee, the Committee for Good Government, the International Union of United Auto Workers, and the AFL-CIO Committee on Political Education. Without this money, Friends of the Earth would have been unable to make any direct contributions in 1996. Within two weeks of its FOE contribution, the AFL-CIO gave similar $5,000 contributions to the Sierra Club and the League of Conservation Voters. The Sierra Club was also the recipient of a $5,000 contribution from AFSCME. While there is nothing illegal about such contributions, it seems possible that the unions, having already contributed the legal maximum to some candidates, were funneling additional money to these candidates through environmental groups.[37]

INDEPENDENT EXPENDITURES

If environmental groups raised and spent more money after 1994 and yet their direct contributions to candidates declined, where did all the money go? At least some of it took the form of independent expenditures supporting or opposing particular candidates, an increasingly popular form of campaign spending. The term *independent expenditures* refers to spending on campaign activities, such as advertising, which expressly advocates the election or defeat of a specific candidate, but which is made without prior consultation with the candidates. Under the law, individuals and groups making independent expenditures may spend as much as they like, so long as the spending is not coordinated in any way with the candidate's campaigns. Although such spending faces no limits, it is subject to disclosure under FEC regulations.

Independent expenditures from all sources amounted to nearly $21 million in 1995–1996. According to the FEC, PACs made $10.6 million in independent expenditures in the same cycle, a $5.5 million increase over the previous cycle. By the year 2000, independent expenditures by PACs had increased to $21 million, with 125 PACs spending on behalf of candidates and 57 spending against.[38] Clearly, independent expenditures are increasing. In addition, close to 98 percent of independent expenditures were targeted to close House races in 1996, compared to only one-third of PAC direct contributions to candidates.[39]

Although the League of Conservation Voters had made some independent expenditures as early as 1982, most environmental groups did not follow suit until 1994, and then only in relatively small amounts. In 1994, the League of Conservation Voters and Greenvote each made about $25,000 in independent expenditures, a fraction of their direct contributions. That was only the beginning, however. In January of 1996 the LCV Action Fund and the Sierra Club combined to spend $200,000 in a special Oregon Senate race, helping Democrat Ron Wyden defeat Gordon Smith. Most of the money went for radio and television commercials attacking Smith's environmental record. Although there were certainly numerous factors involved, many observers attributed Wyden's narrow victory to the independent spending by environmental groups and others.[40]

Because of this success, independent expenditures by the two groups skyrocketed beginning in the 1996 election:[41]

	1994	1996	1998	2000	2002
LCV	$25,000	$1,500,000	$2,300,000	$3,400,000	$4,500,000
Sierra Club	$ 0	$ 300,000	$ 166,000	$ 300,000	$ 300,000

In fact, in a major shift in strategy, the LCV Action Fund opted to use the vast majority of the money it raised for independent expenditures rather than direct contributions to candidates. As a result, in 1996 the LCV contributed less than $70,000 to candidates but made nearly $1.5 million in independent expenditures, almost 80 percent of all such spending by environmental groups. In explaining the unprecedented spending, the League's political director, Betty Loyless, said that the 104th Congress's environmental record was "the worst ever." In the 1996 elections, she said, "We're not counting on somebody else to raise the visibility of the environment as an issue."[42]

All of the LCV's independent spending was directed against the "Dirty Dozen," those congressional candidates with the worst environmental voting records. According to an LCV press release, the Dirty Dozen campaigns used a combination of strategic grassroots organizing, polling, earned media, and advertising to inform voters about the environmental records of such candidates.[43] In the months leading up to the election, the LCV paid for more than nine thousand television and radio ads in the districts of the targeted Republicans, sent over 250,000 pieces of mail, and hired seven field organizers. In some instances, the issues mentioned in the LCV's direct mail reflected those in the candidate's own campaign materials. The group also held numerous conferences, issued press releases, and used its website and email alerts to publicize the Dirty Dozen campaigns. In preparing its advertising campaign, the LCV carefully tailored its ads to young married women who had not attended college, since opinion surveys had shown that this group was especially concerned about the future of their families, and thus would likely be very receptive to environmental appeals. In most races, the LCV ran its ads in two waves, with the first focusing on two major issues: clean water and public notification of toxic releases, the environmental issues that polling revealed to be of most concern to potential voters. A second, smaller wave of ads ran two weeks before the election, documenting the targeted candidates' receipt of campaign money from polluters.[44] Seven of the twelve targets were defeated, a success rate of nearly 60 percent. Whereas the seven defeated candidates had a lifetime average LCV environmental score of 13 percent, their replacements have since averaged 87 percent.[45]

The success of the independent expenditure campaign in that election prompted the LCV to make an even more intensive effort in 1998, when the group spent over $2.3 million in thirteen targeted races. Although all of the ads emphasized the same two issues, clean water and the public's right to know about toxics in their communities, each campaign was tailored to the particular district, the nature of the race, and the environmental voting records of the candidates. LCV-backed candidates won nine of the thirteen races, including all five Senate contests.[46]

A brief review of some of the LCV Action Fund's activities in some of the 1998 Dirty Dozen campaigns illustrates the newly aggressive tactics used by environmental groups. Perhaps nowhere was the LCV effort more noteworthy than in the Nevada Senate race between Harry Reid and Republican challenger John Ensign, which Reid ultimately won by a mere 481 votes. With its budget of $356,000, the LCV Action Fund ran 661 television ads in Las Vegas and Reno from late September through late October. Separate versions of the ads were prepared for each television market, focusing on Ensign's votes to weaken clean water protections for Lake Mead and the Truckee River. The LCV also hired four organizers in the state, coordinated a number of visibility events, including a kayak flotilla on the Truckee River, and did literature drops. Although environmentalism is not generally popular in the state, the issue of high-level nuclear waste disposal is a hot-button issue in Nevada. Senator Reid's campaign highlighted the issue in its own campaign materials, as did the LCV. A source in the Reid campaign later remarked that the group's "heavy-lifting" on the issue allowed Reid to take the high road. Because turnout in the race was only 46 percent of registered voters, it seems likely that the efforts of environmental groups to mobilize voters was crucial to Reid's victory. A media consultant for Ensign's campaign later cited attacks on Ensign's environmental record as one of the pivotal factors in the election's outcome. According to one set of observers, "in terms of interest group support, Reid likely owes his victory to the mobilization of two traditional Democratic constituencies: organized labor and environmentalists."[47]

Not all of the LCV's Dirty Dozen campaigns were successful, however. The group spent $220,000 in its effort to unseat Helen Chenoweth of Idaho. As in other states, the LCV sent a full-time campaign manager to the district and focused on turning out "green" voters. The LCV compiled a list of such voters, and contacted them with 24,000 pieces of mail, 12,000 paid telephone calls, 7,000 volunteer telephone calls, and 5,000 leaflets. The LCV also aired 109 television ads criticizing Chenoweth for selling public lands to mining companies for a mere $5 an acre, and for accepting over $200,000 from polluter PACs. In the end, though, Chenoweth won reelection with 55 percent of the vote.[48]

The LCV Action Fund had an even more ambitious campaign effort in the 2000 elections. Nationwide, the LCV distributed almost two million pieces of direct mail, made more than 400,000 get-out-the-vote telephone calls and placed nine campaign organizers in the field. In addition to its $3.4 million "Dirty Dozen" campaign, the group spent another $700,000 on a newly established "Environmental Champions" campaign. The latter effort was designed to promote the environmental records—and reelection prospects—of elected officials with strong environmental records. All six of the Environmental Champions, three Democrats and three Republicans, won their races. According to the LCV's Deb Callahan, "The 100 percent success rate of the Environmental Champions program proves that both Republican and Democratic candidates benefit when voters learn of their strong environmental credentials. The environment is a winning issue for candidates, and our goal is to make sure that pro-environment issues win in Congress."[49] Only one of the candidates, however, was involved in a close contest. Despite Callahan's claim that environmental issues were the determining factor in those races, it is important to note that all of the Environmental Champions had the advantages of incumbency, and only one faced a credible challenger.

In the race that was its highest priority in 2000, the group spent an astonishing $705,000 to defeat incumbent Michigan Senator Spencer Abraham. In Michigan, the LCV paid for a full-time campaign manager, made more than forty thousand telephone calls to voters, and ran thousands of TV ads attacking Abraham's votes on clean water and toxics. Polling conducted just before the election showed that voters who saw the group's ads ranked the charges against Abraham's environmental record as the first or second strongest reason to vote against him—even more than his positions on prescription drug benefits and his opposition to a patient's bill of rights. In all, 85 percent of likely voters said that clean air and water issues played an important role in their voting decisions.[50]

In its unsuccessful Dirty Dozen race in Michigan's Eighth Congressional District, the LCVAF conducted a four-piece direct mail campaign aimed at Republican state senator Mike Rogers. The direct mail campaign, which charged Rogers with voting against stronger drinking water standards and with allowing the discharge of untreated wastewater into the Great Lakes, totaled 392,000 pieces sent to 98,000 homes. In addition, the LCVAF conducted a "Letter to the Editor" campaign and a large GOTV effort, which included 40,000 phone calls to voters likely to support Rogers's opponent, Diane Byrum.

In other races, the LCVAF timed its television ads to run prior to televised debates, placed newspaper ads, and conducted "earned media" campaigns. As an example of the latter, the group would contact reporters to keep them informed on candidates' environmental records, to see that environmental questions were raised during debates. In addition, there were "rapid response" programs in which the group would alert media of inaccurate environmental claims made by candidates in speeches or campaign materials.

As in 1996, seven of the twelve Dirty Dozen targets were defeated, many in exceptionally close contests. In fact, eight of the twelve elections were decided by fewer than five points, and in four races the margin was less than two points. Among those defeated were three incumbent Republican senators—Spencer Abraham of Michigan, Rod Grams of Minnesota, and Slade Gorton of Washington, leading to a fifty–fifty split in the U.S. Senate. All three of the races were decided by fewer than two points, with Gorton losing to former Representative Maria Cantwell by five thousand votes.

In 2002 LCV spending on its independent expenditure campaigns amounted to $4.5 million, and it "won" only five of the Dirty Dozen races, which were all decided by fewer than ten percentage points. The year was not a total disaster, though, as thirteen of sixteen Environmental Champions won their races. Compared to previous years, the LCV spent less on television and more on direct mail and, because of the exceedingly close division in the Senate, focused on more Senate races.[51] In most other respects, the LCV campaign in 2002 was similar to its earlier efforts.

Since 1994, the LCV Action Fund has also assisted candidates through its "Earth List" program, whereby the LCV solicits contributions from its members written directly to the candidate's campaign. The organization then bundles the checks and forwards them to the candidate. The LCV claims to have raised over $1.2 million for candidates since the program's inception.

After making no independent expenditures in 1994, the Sierra Club contributed approximately $140,000 in 1996 to the joint effort with LCV to assist Ron Wyden in Oregon. In that election cycle, the Club's independent spending more than doubled, to over $300,000. Although this is not a lot of money in the grand scheme of campaign finance, the Club sought to maximize its effect by focusing the independent spending on a few races. Certainly the biggest targets of the Club's independent spending were two vulnerable Republican freshmen, Andrea Seastrand (Calif.) and Dick Chrysler (Mich.). Both were defeated. According to Chuck McGrady, then the Sierra Club's vice president for political affairs, "Educating voters about these two incumbents' records played a major role in their defeat. In our election-eve polling in Seastrand's district, voters said her dismal environmental record was the number one reason to vote against her."[52] In the opinion of Dan Weiss, then the Sierra Club's political director, independent expenditure campaigns "are very effective at defeating anti-environmental candidates."[53] Although independent spending by the Sierra Club and other environmental groups clearly played a role, it would be inaccurate to attribute these electoral results solely to their actions. Both Seastrand and Chrysler had drawn the ire of a number of progressive groups, many of whom also ran independent expenditure and issue advocacy campaigns against them. It is worth noting, however, that environmental groups often worked, at least informally, in alliance with women's, consumer, and labor groups in the 1996 elections. Progressive groups targeted a number of the same seats, especially those held by vulnerable Republican freshmen.

The Sierra Club waged three successful independent expenditure campaigns in each of the next two election cycles, spending $166,000 in 1998 and $300,000 in 2000.[54] The group's PAC also spent approximately $300,000 on two independent expenditure campaigns in 2002. One of its 1998 campaigns was conducted on behalf of Democratic challenger Dennis Moore in the Third District of Kansas. The Club aired radio ads attacking the environmental record of the incumbent, Vince Snowbarger, who had a LCV rating of 7 percent. In addition, Sierra Club volunteers distributed literature, sent direct mail, and telephoned voters. According to Moore, the Sierra Club ads were a "defining moment" of the campaign: "It was like a whole new campaign had started out of some sort of spontaneous combustion." What makes this race notable is that Moore is the first Democrat to represent the district in fifty years.[55] All three of the Club's campaigns in the 2000 elections were waged in House districts with open seats and, as in 1998, all of the Club-backed candidates won. Moreover, because the districts in Washington, Utah, and Ohio had relatively low campaign costs, the Club's money went further than it would have in more costly regions.[56]

ENVIRONMENTAL VOTER EDUCATION CAMPAIGNS

As noted above, organized groups are now performing many of the tasks formerly done by political parties. In addition, interest groups are increasingly providing campaign services to candidates, and because some groups can produce the services at below market rates, they can save candidates money. Examples include donating public opinion polls, as well as the training and provision of campaign staff. Many interest groups now conduct training seminars for volunteers, who are then "lent" to campaigns. In 1996, for example, the League of Conservation Voters sent eighty volunteers and paid staffers to work in targeted congressional districts. For the groups, the provision of campaign staff has obvious advantages. If the candidates supported by the groups win, they will presumably be more likely to support the group's agenda, and because successful candidates often hire their campaign workers to work for them in Congress, the group also gains valuable access to policymaking.[57] Groups also benefit from recruiting and training a stronger pool of political organizers, who can then work on future campaigns.

As we have seen, some of the larger national environmental organizations such as the Sierra Club and League of Conservation Voters have become quite active in federal elections. At the same time, though, IRS regulations severely limit explicitly political action by nonprofit organizations, which include many local and regional environmental groups. For this reason, many of those groups are not actively involved in federal elections, although many of their members may be involved in campaigns on an individual basis. Only a handful of groups have national political action committees that spend money on federal elections. Much of the following discussion thus focuses on the Sierra Club and the League of Conservation Voters, who, in an unprecedented attempt to influence federal elections, have raised and spent record amounts of money in the last three campaign cycles. In the two years preceding the 1996 election, for example, the Sierra Club spent a self-reported $7.5 million on its voter education, issue advocacy, and get-out-the-vote efforts, including more than $1 million on TV, radio, and print ads.[58] The Club followed that record effort by spending $6 million in 1998, and another $8.5 million in 2000.[59] The League of Conservation Voters also spent heavily. In large part, these expanded political activities were made possible because contributions to the groups increased dramatically as the public became aware of the actions of the Republican-controlled Congress.[60]

The influx of money is only part of the story—the Republican Congress's legislative assault on the environment prompted environmental groups to overhaul their electoral strategies and to devote much more of their available resources to influencing federal elections. Although typically short of money, environmental groups do possess other valuable resources, such as politically savvy national organizations and dedicated grassroots activists that can educate the public about issues, provide staff for campaigns, and get out the vote. Increasingly, both the League of Conservation Voters and the Sierra Club have used these resources, along with their new money, to conduct ambitious public outreach and education campaigns in recent elections. Although these campaigns are relatively new, they are not unique to environmental organizations; many other interest groups are now doing the same thing, in part because so-called voter education campaigns, which are ostensibly nonpartisan, are not subject to campaign finance restrictions. In fact, the lines between voter education campaigns and issue advocacy campaigns, which will be discussed below, are very blurry, making it almost impossible to determine where one activity ends and the other begins.

Typically, an environmental voter education campaign, known as an EVEC, will include radio and television advertising, broadcast and printed voter guides, direct mail, rallies or demonstrations, literature drops, telephone banks, and creative "political theater" designed to highlight environmental issues. Since 1996, both the Sierra Club and the League of Conservation Voters have waged elaborate EVECs, utilizing the services of pollsters, media consultants, direct mail firms, and other specialized services. In addition, both have formed nonprofit organizations, separate from their PACs, to pay for these campaigns. The Sierra Club, for example, funds its EVEC from its 527 group. The campaigns serve several purposes, not the least of which is to build the organization by energizing and strengthening the group's grass roots, which many believed had been neglected in recent years. Other goals include publicizing the candidates' environmental records, raising the prominence of environmental issues (and groups) in campaigns, and advancing their substantive agenda on the issue on each district.[61] Other groups use the campaigns to grow. WILD PAC, for example, set out to recruit one thousand new members during the 2002 election cycle; they actually exceeded the goal by five hundred.[62] Rightly or wrongly, group leaders concluded that, to succeed politically, they needed large numbers of volunteers, as well as paid political organizers, to educate and mobilize their grass roots and ultimately to elect sympathetic legislators.

The League of Conservation Voters

The League of Conservation Voters established its 501(c)(3) Voter Education Fund (LCVEF) in 1985. The LCVEF is a nonpartisan public education organization, whose avowed goals are to raise awareness of environmental issues, to build the capacity and effectiveness of state and local environmental organizations, and to encourage citizens to become involved in policy decisions at all levels of government. Although the LCVEF has been in existence since 1985, it did not spend a lot of money until 2000. That year, with a reported budget of $7.4 million, the LCVEF conducted a national polling, advertising, and grassroots public education campaign. Working with twelve polling firms with different political allegiances, the LCVEF conducted twenty-two polls covering twenty-six states, and one national poll. The polling project had two main goals: to research public attitudes about the relationship between environmental issues and voting, and to educate state-based environmental advocates, legislators, media, and the public about the findings. The LCVEF also conducted "message training seminars" with state and local groups to ensure that the findings were used effectively.[63] Finally, the LCVEF created its own website (www.voteenvironment.org), which featured its television ads and results from the nationwide polling effort, and asked visitors to take an on-line pledge to ask candidates where they stood on environmental issues.[64]

The LCVEF polling revealed some interesting results. When asked to rate their level of concern about a variety of issues, 71 percent of voters indicated "extreme" concern about clean air and water issues, placing these issues on a par with education (73 percent), crime and drugs (71 percent), and health care (70 percent). When asked about "clean air and water," voters responded with much more intensity than when asked about "the environment" in general. Regardless of party affiliation, the specific environmental issues that most concerned voters were those that affect everyday life and health, such as clean drinking water (81 percent) and clean air (80 percent). Nearly two-thirds of voters characterized environmental and clean air and water issues as important to their voting decisions, and 28 percent of voters saw those issues as "very important." It is for this reason that the LCV Action Fund ads typically focused on candidates' votes on clean air and water, rather than other issues.

In every state where the LCV polled, a strong majority of voters said that clean air, clean water, and open spaces were important factors in their voting decisions. This was particularly true of voters in New England (92 percent), New York and Michigan (91 percent), and Ohio and Wisconsin (90 percent). In the national poll, 77 percent of voters supported increased government involvement in environmental matters, either in the form of stricter regulation or stronger enforcement of current laws. The LCVEF also claims that the poll results demonstrate that the environment has a direct link to people's lives and, when it is connected to their health and well-being, can be a powerful voting issue.

As noted above, the LCVEF polling showed that concern about the environment cuts across party lines, with three-quarters of Democrats and independents and nearly two-thirds of Republicans expressing high levels of concern about clean air and water issues. Each of the groups placed these issues in their top tier of concerns. While Democrats were most likely to consider clean air and water issues when making a voting decision (72 percent), nearly two-thirds of independents (66 percent) and 55 percent of Republicans said those issues were important factors in their decision. Clean water was the issue most likely to generate support or raise doubts about a candidate, both in terms of enforcement of current laws and the passage of new ones. Moreover, a large majority of voters said they were more likely to support candidates who favored stricter enforcement of clean water laws (82 percent), while 71 percent reported serious doubts about candidates who oppose stricter enforcement. Additionally, 78 percent of voters reported that they were more likely to support candidates who favor passage of tougher clean water laws. Open space and wilderness preservation were also important issues to voters. More than three-quarters of voters said they were more likely to support a candidate who favored these types of measures, while 61 percent expressed very serious doubts about a candidate who opposed them.[65]

The Sierra Club

For its part, the Sierra Club's EVEC activities really began in 1996. In response to Republican efforts to weaken the Safe Drinking Water Act in the 104th Congress, for example, the Sierra Club drafted radio and television ads and organized community clean water events.[66] During Earth Week, the Club launched a public education campaign with thousands of volunteers distributing door hangers to 2.3 million homes in one hundred cities. The materials urged citizens to write the president and other public officials to protect the environment by vetoing antienvironmental riders to key appropriations bills. And in the weeks leading up to the election, Club volunteers distributed 500,000 voter guides detailing the candidates' positions; another 700,000 were mailed to what the Club called "crucial swing voters." According to one observer, "Some of these activities were expressly political, unapologetically aimed at changing the makeup of Congress, state legislatures, and city councils. But others had a subtler, more far-reaching goal: to raise the visibility of environmental issues across the nation and, in the process, reinvigorate the Club's grassroots presence in local communities."[67]

Sierra Club volunteers were also active in dozens of congressional races across the country. In the Minnesota Senate race, for example, the Sierra Club distributed

80,000 pieces of voter education information and provided hundreds of volunteers for Paul Wellstone, who won a close race for reelection. In New Hampshire, the Club produced and paid for radio ads attacking incumbent Senator Bob Smith as a mouthpiece for industrial polluters.[68] Walter Capps (D-Calif.) was also the beneficiary of active Club support. A coalition of labor unions, consumer, women's, and other environmental groups worked to defeat his opponent, incumbent Andrea Seastrand, who had angered many progressive groups during her freshmen term. In that race, the groups used an impressive array of tools to communicate with voters, including television, the Internet, faxes, congressional score cards, phone banks, training schools, and direct mail. When Capps later died of a heart attack, environmental groups played a key role in helping his widow, Lois, win a special election for the seat. In Oregon, the Sierra Club joined the LCV and other groups in identifying more than 100,000 voters with environmental sympathies in Portland and its suburbs, and then bombarded them with postcards, phone calls, and paid media urging them to vote.[69] According to Burt Glass, a spokesman for the LCV, the new tactics were designed to send a message to members of Congress: "It is making those targets pay for their anti-environment votes."[70]

The criteria for selecting the Club's EVEC sites include a strong contrast in the environmental records of the candidates, a competitive race, the presence of a locally salient environmental issue, and the capacity within the chapter, group, or staff to run what is a fairly complicated program. Each site was organized with a committee of volunteers and professional staff, who developed a campaign plan focusing on a local issue, which was then approved by the Club's steering committee. Typical components of EVEC programs are paid and free media, outreach to grassroots organizers, a full-time campaign organizer, postcards, voter guides and charts, and other written materials. Depending on the location, these materials were delivered door to door or at tables in malls and state or county fairs.[71] This increased activism continued in 1998, with the Sierra Club actively involved in over forty federal campaigns. As part of its efforts, the Club's PAC conducted a large-scale get-out-the-vote program that contacted 250,000 of its members, close to half its total membership. In addition, the Sierra Club mailed and distributed one million voter guides detailing candidates' positions on important environmental issues. The Club's political committee also broadcast television and radio issue advocacy ads in forty markets detailing the environmental records of twenty-five incumbents.[72]

The Sierra Club's $8 million EVEC in 2000 differed from prior campaigns in one crucial respect. That year, the Club broke from tradition by devoting significant attention and resources to the presidential race. Among other things, the Club launched an EVEC home page on its website, which included information about the presidential election, such as a presidential voter guide that compared the candidates' records. The site also featured information about many congressional races, and included versions of the Club's television and radio ads, voting charts showing how elected officials had voted on environmental issues, and contact information for each EVEC organizer in the various locations.

The EVEC actually began in New Hampshire in November of 1999, when the Club began airing radio and television ads criticizing George Bush's record on air pollution. A second round of radio and television ads, focusing on toxic chemicals in Texas, began airing in January of 2000. The ads personalized the issue by focusing on how pollution affected William Tinker, an eleven year old with asthma from Desoto, Texas. Tinker lived downwind from a cement kiln, whose emissions aggravated his breathing problem.[73] The Club ran similar ads in California and Michigan during the presidential primaries.

In April of 2000, the Club formally launched its EVEC campaigns in seventeen states and congressional districts. Local Sierra Club chapters ran television and radio ads to "inform their communities about the environmental positions taken by their public officials, and to urge the public to ask their officials to take specific actions to support the environment." In announcing the campaign, Club officials said they wanted to focus on close races where their efforts could make a difference. The campaign began in April to take advantage of low advertising rates, and because the Club wanted to draw attention to environmental issues early in the campaign year, at a time when few other groups were advertising.

After conducting polls to determine the level of interest in environmental issues, the Club focused each of its ads on a local environmental issue. In explaining this decision, pollster Celinda Lake, who helped the Club develop its ad campaign, said, "All politics is local when it comes to the environment."[74] As a case in point, the Michigan ads featured pictures of children jumping into one of the Great Lakes, and informed viewers that Senator Spencer Abraham voted against a bill to clean up water pollution. The ad then urged viewers to call Abraham and ask him to vote in future bills to clean up the Great Lakes. In Connecticut, radio ads told listeners that Representative Christopher Shays was leading the fight to help the Long Island Sound recover from pollution that contaminated shellfish beds. Listeners were asked to call Shays to ask him to continue his leadership on the issue.[75]

The EVEC culminated in October with a $3 million spending effort in the presidential race and in twelve congressional races. Of that total, $2 million went for broadcast voter guides, with the remainder for printed voter guides with side-by-side comparisons of the candidates. In addition to comparing the candidates, the voter guides, which were aimed at likely voters, also provided information about local issues. In Washington, for example, voters learned about salmon and wild forests, while in Michigan the guides focused on efforts to clean up the Great Lakes. The television ads in the presidential race were tailored to local issues as well. The ads ran in Philadelphia, St. Louis, Detroit, and Madison, Wisconsin, which were key markets in some of the most closely contested states.[76]

In yet another departure, the Club used its EVEC to reach new audiences. In September, for example, the Club broadcast Spanish-language versions of its voter education television ads. The ads, which aired on Univision in California, Florida, Illinois, and New Mexico, were designed to inform Latino voters about

George Bush's environmental positions. Alejandro Queral, an associate representative of the Club, said of the ads, "The Sierra Club recognizes the growing involvement of Latinos in environmental protection. We want Latinos and others to know about Governor Bush's pollution policies and to urge him to oppose efforts in Congress to weaken clean air standards."[77]

The Sierra Club also joined forces with the NAACP National Voter Fund, a 501(c)(3) education organization established by the NAACP, on a $100,000 radio ad campaign in Michigan, Kentucky, and Virginia. The ads were designed to inform citizens about the environmental records of local congressional candidates, and urged people to call their officials to take specific actions on upcoming legislation. As was the case with the Spanish-language ads, these ads were aimed at minority voters, who had not been targeted in prior environmental voter education campaigns.

The budget for the Club's 2002 EVEC was $3.7 million, a significant drop from previous election cycles. Contributing to the decline were the economic recession, frantic fundraising by the parties in advance of the soft money ban adopted by Congress earlier in the year, and new rules barring anonymous donations to 527 groups, all of which reduced donations to environmental groups.[78] Many Sierra Club donors, for example, also contribute to the Democratic Party, which aggressively raised as much soft money as possible before the ban went into effect. The competition from the Party sharply limited fundraising. Similarly, a significant portion of the Sierra Club's EVEC activities in previous years had been financed by a few large anonymous donations, which were no longer allowed in 2002.

The sharp drop in revenues meant that the Club could be involved in fewer races than in the prior years. The EVEC staff also opted to focus on a larger number of statewide races and fewer House races than in the past. This decision was prompted, in part, by congressional redistricting, which made it difficult to figure out the electoral "lay of the land" in a number of districts, especially because some states did not finalize their districts until late in the year. The problem with that decision is that it is harder and more expensive to educate the larger number of voters statewide than in House districts.

About half of the overall EVEC budget in 2002 went to paid advertising, and about one-quarter went to staffing, travel, and training. In a new twist, the remainder went to paid phone contacts and direct mail, a result of the EVEC committee's decision to do more direct voter contact in 2002.[79] Beginning in July, which was about two months earlier than in prior years, the Club began its ground campaign. This time, the EVEC used voter files and polling data to identify and target persuadable voters with paid phone calls, direct mail, and, in Colorado, New Hampshire, and Minnesota, door-to-door canvassing. The Club opted to begin its voter contact earlier because there would be less competition from other groups for voter's attention. Also in contrast to previous years, when Club volunteers did literature drops but did not actually speak with voters, in these three states the Club made more of an effort to engage voters in discussions of environmental issues and encourage them to vote. The assumption was that personal contact would be more effective than written material in delivering the group's message.[80]

The final new development in the Club's EVEC efforts was a decision to feature local people discussing local issues in its paid media. The typical ad focused on a local doctor or parent explaining why he or she was concerned about protecting the environment. The ads in New Hampshire, for example, featured a Dover man speaking of his worries about his daughter's safety and whether toxins from local Superfund sites could make her ill.[81] The decision was prompted by the belief that local citizens would have more credibility than outsiders or anonymous narrators.

ISSUE ADVOCACY

Environmental groups also broke new ground in 1996 with the use of issue advocacy advertising. Although these ads are often indistinguishable from the ads aired by candidates, the term *issue advocacy* refers to communications to the public whose primary purpose is to promote a set of ideas or policies. Unlike independent expenditures, issue advocacy ads cannot explicitly advocate the defeat or election of a particular candidate.

In the late 1990s many of the groups engaging in issue campaigns were aligned with one of four loose alliances. Most relevant here is the Progressive Network, an alliance of environmental, feminist, gay and lesbian, and peace groups. Because campaign laws forbid such groups from formally joining forces to conduct orchestrated campaigns, the Progressive Network nevertheless shared information and plans in a way that often resulted in its members targeting the same races. The Sierra Club's Dan Weiss describes the Network as "a progressive coffee klatch where we exchange information, gossip, hearsay, and innuendo." He added, "By law we are prevented from coordinated action, but it's helpful to know which organizations and individuals are doing what in which districts."[82]

Citizen Action, which has since disbanded, was among the groups that conducted issue advocacy campaigns in 1996. A nonprofit and tax-exempt grassroots consumer and environmental group that had offices in thirty states, Citizen Action took a lead role in organizing for the 1996 elections. In 1995, the executive director of the group convened a meeting in New York of representatives from a number of women's, environmental, consumer, and gun control groups for the purpose of bringing the groups together with pollsters and donors to fund an issue advocacy campaign against Republican freshmen. Citizen Action intended to use the issue ads to define the issues early in the campaign, thus putting the Republicans on the defensive. Citizen Action and its state affiliates subsequently spent $7 million on its "Campaign for a Responsible Congress," using paid media, direct mail, and phone banks to target Republican incumbents in thirty-five districts. In addition to the environment, the group's ads focused on Medicare and education.[83] Beginning in July in fifteen of the districts, Citizen Action worked with the Sierra Club and the League of Conservation Voters to conduct a joint media campaign.[84] Of the fifteen targeted incumbents, seven lost their bids for reelection.

Although it is not entirely clear how it spent its money in 1994 and 1996, it is likely that the Oregon League of Conservation Voters also engaged in issue advocacy campaigns. In both years, the group spent heavily, but not on direct contributions to candidates or on independent expenditure campaigns. In 1994, for example, the OLCV spent nearly $700,000, but only $1,000 is accounted for. Similarly, in 1996 the group spent $159,000, but only contributed $3,000 to candidates for federal office. Again, the remainder of the spending is unexplained in the group's FEC filings.

As discussed above, in addition to its other political spending in 1996, the Sierra Club used nearly $7 million from its general treasury for its voter education campaign, a significant portion of which went to issue advocacy advertising. Although it is impossible to determine exactly how the EVEC budget has been apportioned over the years, it seems that about half of the money has been used for issue advocacy, with most of the money going for broadcast ads and voter guides. After spending $100,000 in 1994, the Club spent $3 million on its voter education effort, which included approximately $1 million for radio, television, and print issue ads in some two dozen districts. The remainder of the funds paid for staff, grassroots organizing, direct mail, and phone banks.[85]

According to Dan Weiss, the Club's use of issue ads "enables us to take our message to a broader group of people because we'll be able to use resources we wouldn't otherwise be able to use."[86] Weiss further asserted that the Sierra Club uses "issue advocacy as a tool to affect environmental policy and to increase congressional accountability—not to affect the outcome of elections."[87] Of course, Weiss also said that the Club was "going to work to defeat those members of the 104th Congress who tried to roll back environmental laws. There is no question that the new leadership of the 104th Congress is at the heart of the effort to weaken environmental laws."[88]

Despite the unprecedented issue campaigns by Citizen Action, the Sierra Club, and others that year, the environment was the topic of only 3.7 percent of all broadcast issue ads, ranking eighth among the most frequently mentioned topics. Medicare was the issue mentioned most often, followed by government spending, taxes, abortion, and education.

In the 1997–1998 election cycle, however, the environment was the focus of 15 percent of all issue ads. Only taxes were mentioned more often.[89] Of course, environmental groups were not the only ones sponsoring such ads; opponents of the Kyoto global warming treaty also ran major issue ad campaigns. Still, the increased prominence of environmental issues in such ads suggests that environmental groups, notably the Sierra Club, have made such spending a priority. In the 1998 campaign, the Club spent a reported $6 million on its EVEC and issue ad campaigns, although it is not known how the funds were allocated. Work on the ads had actually begun in December of 1997, when the Club commissioned focus groups in five states to develop and test messages for the upcoming campaign.[90] The Club's political committee began researching the records of potential candidates in early 1998, scouring voting records, the Internet, newspapers, and speeches for information on environmental issues. The goal for each Environmental Voter Education Campaign site was for one hundred volunteers to distribute ten thousand voter guides.[91]

The Club also aired ads attacking North Carolina Senator Lauch Faircloth, who lost his race to Democrat John Edwards. The Club's ads focused on Faircloth's voting record on clean water issues, and highlighted his ownership of a large hog farm. In Washington's Senate race, the Club launched its ad campaign before Labor Day, targeting challenger Linda Smith, who was seeking to move up from the House. The focus of the ads was Smith's support for a bill limiting the ability of local governments to protect salmon populations. Starting early helped the Club in two ways: it could take advantage of cheaper advertising rates and, because there were few other political ads airing at the time, the anti-Smith ads received considerable attention. In the end, incumbent Patty Murray won reelection by a wide margin.[92]

The Sierra Club continued its voter education and issue advocacy campaigns in 2000, spending more than $8 million nationwide. During the general election for president, the Club ran numerous television ads, which aired in the important Philadelphia, Detroit, St. Louis, and Madison markets. Each ad was tailored to a local environmental issue. In addition to the presidential race, the Club also ran ads in seventeen congressional districts. Many of the races involved first- or second-term Democratic incumbents who had won their seats in narrow elections. Each of the ads, which began airing in April, was targeted at a potent local issue. In the state of Washington, for example, the ads featured wild forests and efforts to protect salmon populations. In Michigan, the focus was on the Great Lakes.

The Sierra Club's ad campaign continued through election day, with the group spending a reported $3 million in October alone, including $2 million for broadcast voter guides and an additional $1 million for printed voter guides featuring side-by-side candidate comparisons. By October, the Club was focusing its issue campaign on the presidential race and twelve contested congressional races. In addition to its broadcast ads, the Club used the Internet, direct mail, and door-to-door canvassing, and distributed more than two million printed voter guides. Banner ads on the Internet sites lycos.com and voter.com directed users to the voter guides at the Club's own website.

In Washington state, the Club spent a reported $250,000 on the "Slade Gorton Accountability Project," using five hundred volunteers, paid advertising, and direct mail to contact residents in the Spokane and Puget Sound areas with nearly 250,000 voter guides. Gorton also attracted the ire of some groups who were not traditionally active in politics, most notably the First American Education Project,

Table 5.3. Estimated Issue Advocacy/Voter Education Spending, 1996–2002 (in dollars)

Organization	1996	1998	2000	2002
LCV Education Fund			7,400,000	
Sierra Club EVEC	7,000,000	6,000,000	8,000,000	3,700,000
Citizen Action	6,000,000			
National Environmental Trust			8,000,000	
Friends of the Earth			300,000	
Heritage Forest			4,000,000	
Washington Conservation Voters			500,000	
Clean Air Trust			30,000	
Montanans for Common Sense Mining			130,000	
First American Education Project			400,000	
Oregon LCV	700,000			
Totals	13,700,000	6,000,000	28,500,000	3,700,000

Note: 2002 totals are incomplete, based on self-reported spending by groups as of November 22, 2002.
Sources: Annenberg Public Policy Center, Issue Advocacy Advertising During the 1997–1998 Election Cycle (Philadelphia: Annenberg Public Policy Center, 1999); Craig B. Holman and Luke P. McLoughlin, Buying Time 2000: Television Advertising in the 2000 Federal Elections (New York: Brennan Center for Justice, 2001); www.sierraclub.org; www.lcvef.org.

the first nationwide political campaign funded entirely by Native Americans. The Project, which attracted contributions from twenty-nine tribes in Washington and more than twenty others nationwide, spent a reported $400,000 on a television advertising campaign attacking Gorton's environmental record, as well as his record on health care and tribal sovereignty.[93]

As Table 5.3 indicates, the number of organizations, including environmental groups, that are engaged in issue advocacy advertising grows every election cycle. The Clean Air Trust, a nonprofit environmental group that monitors implementation of the Clean Air Act, spent a reported $127,000 in the final months of the campaign on an ad criticizing George W. Bush's environmental record.[94] In addition to the spending by environmental groups, the various campaign committees of the Democratic Party ran millions of dollars of issue ads in the campaign, covering a broad range of issues, including the environment. One of the ads noted that "back in Texas, George W. Bush appointed a chemical company lobbyist to enforce the environmental laws" and that Houston is now "the smog capital of the U.S." because "as governor, George W. Bush made key air pollution rules in Texas voluntary."[95]

In perhaps the most notorious issue ad featuring environmental themes, a mysterious group called Republicans for Clean Air spent an estimated $25 million during the Republican presidential primaries in California, Ohio, and New York.[96]

The television ads harshly criticized John McCain's record on clean air and praised George W. Bush. After a media firestorm erupted in New York as to the group's identity, Texas energy billionaire Sam Wyly stepped forward to claim responsibility for the ads. Wyly, an avid Bush supporter and contributor, owned Green Mountain Energy, a firm that sought changes in the regulations governing power generation and distribution. Although Bush disavowed the ads, Senator McCain's campaign filed an official complaint with the FEC, arguing that Wyly, who had contributed the legal maximum to Bush during the primary, was an "authorized fund-raiser" for the Bush campaign. The complaint further alleged that the ads violated an FEC regulation that treats expenditures by an authorized campaign fund-raiser as contributions to the campaign.

The controversy over the Republicans for Clean Air issue advocacy campaign illustrates many of the potential problems inherent in such spending. First, the group's name was misleading because it conveyed the impression that it was a grassroots organization speaking for many, when in fact it was an energy company seeking favorable regulatory policies that could greatly enhance its profit margins. Second, the size of the ad purchases enabled the group to air its ads repeatedly, drowning out McCain's efforts to communicate with Republican primary voters. Issue advocacy advertising thus gives well-funded groups the potential to dominate the discourse during campaigns, relegating interests with less money, and perhaps even candidates themselves, to the sidelines. Third, the ads contained several misleading characterizations of McCain's record, but because of the ads' anonymous source, viewers had no point of reference for evaluating the accuracy of the claims. For better or worse, if a viewer knows that a television ad has been paid for by the Sierra Club, he or she has a frame of reference by which to judge the information in the ad. If the viewer generally agrees with the Sierra Club, he or she may be inclined to accept the claims made in the ad. Conversely, if the viewer generally disagrees with the Club, he or she may be inclined to be skeptical. In either case, the viewer can place the ad's claims in some context. When viewers do not know who is paying for an ad, though, they may have a more difficult time judging its reliability.

ENVIRONMENTAL GROUPS AND THE NEW FORMS OF POLITICAL SPENDING

Campaigns in the 1990s were increasingly marked by the involvement of individuals and groups not formally affiliated with either the candidates or the parties, since federal election laws limit direct contributions by both individuals and groups. In a dramatic departure from previous practice, the largest environmental groups are now playing this game by relying less on direct contributions to candidates and more on the newer forms of political spending. The explanation for this shift in tactics is quite simple: environmental groups have never been able to match direct contributions from corporate interests, so they have decided to spend their scarce resources in ways that leverage their political influence. The virtue of independent expenditures, issue advocacy, and voter education efforts is that they allow the groups to inject environmental issues into campaigns, rather than waiting passively for the candidates to raise them. In short, the new forms of spending increase the ability of environmental groups to define the issues in campaigns and drive the debate.

All forms of political spending, including the newly popular varieties, should be viewed in this light. Environmental groups, like other political actors, struggle to define the nature of political issues, lest others define them first. "The art of politics," notes Christopher Bosso, "is not practiced in a vacuum. The very rules of the game themselves shift and mutate endlessly—at times imperceptibly—and those who seek to participate must adapt to each new bundle of conditions if they are to remain relevant."[97] The increased use of issue advocacy and independent expenditures demonstrates that environmental groups are trying to adapt their behavior to two significant changes in the "rules of the game." The first was the collapse of the campaign finance regime, which opened the door even wider to wealthy donors, while the second was the Republican takeover of Congress. In conjunction, these two developments fundamentally altered the political landscape and forced environmental groups to adapt their political behavior. Moreover, as Dan Weiss, director of the Sierra Club's political action committee, said, "We increased our advocacy effort because of the increased threat to the environment."[98]

In short, environmental groups have turned to the new forms of political spending at least in part because of their greater utility in agenda setting in campaigns. Rather than waiting for candidates to raise environmental issues on their own, more groups now wage their own paid media campaigns to frame the issues for debate, seeking to force candidates to assess environmental issues. This is not to suggest that environmental groups have only recently discovered the importance of agenda setting. Rather, the point is that the groups are now experimenting with new methods of agenda setting, and are now employing new communication technologies and techniques in their effort to define issues. In so doing, environmental groups hope to raise the prominence of environmental issues, to attract attention to themselves, to reenergize their grass roots, and elect more people who support their policy goals. In this sense, the groups clearly recognize that electoral politics and environmental policymaking are inextricably connected.

In a study of the new forms of political spending, David Magleby has suggested that independent spending by interest groups is most likely to occur in close election contests. According to Magleby, their involvement serves two related goals. If the group is successful, it elects a friendly member to Congress, while also sending a cautionary message to other members to vote as the group desires, or else they may be the target of an interest group campaign in the next election cycle.[99] If they are successful, the groups also gain credibility with the media and candidates as important players in electoral politics.

Similarly, a review of the independent expenditure and issue advocacy campaigns waged in recent years by the LCV and Sierra Club confirms another of Magleby's findings. Such spending, he contends, is more likely in locations with lower media and campaign costs, because interest group money buys more advertising per voter in such districts. And because environmental groups typically lack money, such a strategy makes abundant sense. Indeed, low advertising and campaign costs help explain the LCV's decision in 2000 to focus on races in Michigan, Nevada, Montana, and other states with relatively low advertising costs. The same is true of many of the Sierra Club's "priority races" in recent years.

Magleby also argues that outside spending by interest groups is most effective when it raises questions about the target of the campaign, when it is aimed at specific groups of voters, and when the frequency of voter contact is high. As already noted, the LCV's broadcast ads were designed to target young mothers with children, and both groups made explicit appeals to suburban voters concerned about clean air and water issues. And by running the ads in less expensive media markets, the groups were able to run the ads more frequently. Perhaps most importantly, the groups' volunteers in their large-scale voter education campaigns reinforced the message of the ads. Utilizing phone banks and door-to-door canvassing, environmental activists made frequent contact with targeted voters, stressing the importance of voting "green" on election day. The "ground war" can be vitally important in low-turnout races. Interest groups, even small ones, can have an impact on elections if they can mobilize their membership.[100]

It also seems clear that group campaigns are most effective when there are clear differences between the candidates. This is especially true for independent voters, who are less influenced by party cues. When voters perceive significant policy distinctions between the candidates on environmental issues, it generally works in the favor of the candidate backed by environmental groups. Candidates have learned this lesson over the years, and thus virtually every candidate now at least claims to be "good" on the environment. Indeed, in 2002 a number of candidates with poor environmental records, such as Colorado Senator Wayne Allard, managed to blur the distinction with their own ads claiming environmental achievements. The dilemma now facing environmental groups is how to overcome such "green-scamming" by candidates seeking to hide their actual environmental records.

THE EFFECTIVENESS OF ELECTORAL POLITICS

Bosso and Guber argue that most gains cited by environmental groups in recent congressional elections have come in districts or states in which moderate Republicans were unseated by constituencies that tended to lean Democratic.[101] Although there is a good deal of truth in their argument, it's not quite that simple. The Environmental groups have not been very successful in unseating conservative Republicans in heavily Republican districts or states, but then again, neither has anybody else, including the Democratic Party. More importantly, though, those environmental groups who do get involved in elections no longer tilt at those windmills. As we have seen, since 1994 the Sierra Club and LCV have chosen to avoid these symbolic fights, which they almost always lost, and focus instead on races they can actually win. That means concentrating their efforts and resources on competitive districts and states that, by definition, are riskier. And in those races, candidates backed by environmental groups have often fared well. Some of those races have involved open seats in Democratic-leaning districts, but environmental groups have also contributed to the defeat of incumbent Republicans in a variety of electoral settings.

That was clearly not the case in 2002, which was a very bad year for candidates supported by environmental groups, and for Democrats overall. The LCV was successful in only five of its Dirty Dozen races, its worst showing ever, while the Sierra Club lost all but two of its seventeen priority races. All of the races were close, but that counts for little in the zero-sum game of U.S. elections. About the only bright spots for environmental groups in 2002 were in South Dakota, where Senator Tim Johnson won reelection by the narrowest of margins, and in Arkansas, where David Pryor unseated incumbent Senator Tim Hutchinson, who was plagued by a personal scandal. In virtually all of the other high-profile contests, the candidates backed by the LCV and the Sierra Club lost. It does not seem to be the case, though, that voters were repudiating environmental candidates. Indeed, in many of these contests, the successful candidates campaigned as protectors of the environment. So although environmental groups did not succeed in electing their preferred candidates, in some places they did succeed in forcing the candidates to discuss environmental issues.

Although 2002 was a bad year for environmental groups, the environment worked as an issue in some places. Polling conducted by the LCV and others shows that the environment continues to be a key voting issue for some segments of the public, notably independents, women, and Republican swing voters. This is especially true for the specific issues of clean air and clean water. What was different in 2002 was that the environment was not an effective wedge issue in as many locations, at least in part because the candidates on either side of the issue did not emphasize the distinctions. In states like Colorado, New Hampshire, Minnesota, and Missouri, the Republican candidates blurred the issue by running ads claiming some green positions or accomplishments, which made it harder for Republican swing voters to defect on the issue. At the same time, Democratic candidates, like Tom Strickland in Colorado, were content to allow the environmental groups to carry the weight on the issue. Contrast that with the 2000 Senate race in Michigan, in which incumbent Republican Spencer Abraham, targeted by both the LCV and

Sierra Club, did not raise environmental issues in his campaign, and spent no money of his own on paid media to rebut the claims of environmental groups. Debbie Stabenow, the eventual winner, did address environmental issues in her campaign, and the issue was very popular with women and other targeted voters.[102]

In the 2000 Senate elections, on the other hand, environmental groups had more success. They devoted significant financial and organizational resources to defeating Republican incumbents in Washington, Michigan, and Minnesota. All three states were hotly contested in 2000, and the difficulty of unseating incumbents, even in the more competitive Senate, cannot be minimized. Although the state of Washington has been trending Democratic in recent years, it was a toss-up in 2000, and Slade Gorton had won there before, so by no means was it an easy win for Democrat Maria Cantwell. Michigan leans Democratic as well, but it has a Republican governor and is competitive at the state level. Minnesota, which elected former wrestler Jesse Ventura governor, is, to say the least, somewhat unpredictable and has a recent history of closely contested Senate elections. In Montana, environmental groups tried unsuccessfully to unseat incumbent Conrad Burns. The race, however, was very close, with Burns winning by three percentage points in a state that is increasingly Republican and voted for George W. Bush by a two-to-one margin.

Environmental groups also spent a lot of money supporting the winning Democrat in a race for an open seat in Florida, hardly known as a Democratic bastion. Republican Connie Mack had vacated the seat, and the state's governor was, after all, the brother of the Republican presidential candidate. Even before the 2000 presidential contest, Florida voters had been involved in a number of hotly contested statewide races. According to political analysts, polls in the state consistently demonstrate that environmental issues matter to voters, especially to swing voters. That is why, since the election, the Bush administration has supported a Park Service plan to restrict access to motorized vehicles to the Everglades and backed off proposals to drill for oil and gas off the Florida coast. Both decisions were quite popular in the state, and seem to have been made with Jeb Bush's re-election prospects in mind. According to one observer, "Jeb Bush was shocked by the political damage caused by the president's plans for offshore drilling. In this state, offshore drilling is a no-compromise political issue."[103]

In taking a closer look at the 2000 congressional results, the Sierra Club concentrated its efforts on thirteen Senate and forty-one House races. In the Senate, candidates helped by the Sierra Club won ten of the races, including four of the five challengers and four of the five candidates for open seats. In the House races, twenty-two of the twenty-three incumbents the Club supported won. As might be expected, challengers and candidates for open seats were less successful, with only three of the eight challengers winning and five of the ten candidates for open seats.

There is some evidence that environmental issues helped Al Gore in the 2000 presidential race, although not in every state, and not enough to win the election.

According to polling conducted by the Sierra Club, nationwide, 61 percent of voters thought Gore was better on the environment, compared with 23 percent who favored George W. Bush. Gore did even better among voters from both coasts and in the upper Midwest. In all, Gore won seven of the eight states (all but Missouri) where the Club concentrated its election efforts. Nationally, however, the environment ranked only fifth as a reason to vote for Gore, and seventh as a reason to vote against Bush. According to Carl Pope, the Club's executive director, "This was partly because the Club did not have the resources to focus on the culturally conservative states that make up half the Electoral College, allowing Bush to pay no price for his anti-environmental record there." Indeed, environmental issues took a backseat to other concerns among social conservatives, particularly in the Southeast. According to Pope, "The Club's future success lies in forming winning alliances across regional and ideological lines—something we simply don't do effectively today, even with those who share our environmental values and goals. We don't need to change those goals, but we do need to change our language, our style, and our tactics. Above all, we need to start listening better to folks who may speak with different vocabularies about our common dreams."[104]

Environmental groups also supported winning candidates in some tough districts in 1998. In California's Twenty-second District, where voter registration was evenly split between Democrats and Republicans, environmental groups were very active in helping Democrat Lois Capps hold on to the seat previously held by her late husband. That same year, the League of Conservation Voters spent heavily to elect Democrats in very close Senate races in Wisconsin, Nevada, and North Carolina. Wisconsin and Nevada are both competitive at the state level, although Nevada increasingly leans Republican. In Nevada, as noted above, Democrat Harry Reid won reelection by a mere 481 votes. North Carolina, on the other hand, is considered to be a Republican state. Nevertheless, Democrat John Edwards, who received considerable support from the Sierra Club and the League of Conservation Voters, unseated incumbent Lauch Faircloth.

Similarly, in South Dakota in 1996 the LCV worked to elect Democrat Tim Johnson, who defeated incumbent Larry Pressler. South Dakota is a state that is trending Republican, and that voted for Bob Dole over Bill Clinton that same year. Clearly, then, environmental groups have had some success in a variety of states and districts, not just in those that lean Democratic. Many of these victories were razor thin, to be sure, but environmental groups were significant factors in all of them.

Of course, a host of other factors could explain these results as well. Democrats, for example, fared pretty well in three election cycles preceding 2002, winning the presidency outright in 1996 and the popular vote in 2000. Democrats also gained House seats in all three elections, and in 2000 they picked up four Senate seats to gain a fifty-fifty tie in that chamber. In a highly unusual electoral environment in 1998, Democrats did far better than expected in the midterm elections for the House. Typically, the president's party loses seats in midterm elections, but

Democrats actually gained five seats—quite a feat considering that President Clinton was about to be impeached by the House. In the inevitable backlash among Republicans after the election, House Speaker Newt Gingrich was blamed for the loss and opted to resign from the House rather than face another challenge to his leadership. The 1998 elections were, however, also marked by an exceptionally strong get-out-the-vote effort by interest groups supportive of Democratic candidates. In a number of races around the country, the ground campaigns waged by labor unions, civil rights, and environmental organizations were decisive in electing Democrats.[105] It seems, though, that the Republican Party learned from these defeats and made a concerted effort to turn out its voters in 2002. In fact, the Republican get-out-the-vote effort was so successful in some locations that it more than compensated for the increased turnout produced by progressive groups.

Although very few voters base their election-day decision solely on environmental issues, candidates endorsed by environmental groups generally do quite well. In both 1998 and 2000, for example, 80 percent of the candidates endorsed by the Sierra Club won their races, while 90 percent of candidates endorsed by the LCV prevailed. Even in the bad year of 2002, more than 70 percent of LCV-endorsed candidates won their races. Of course, many of these candidates were heavily favored to win their races, so the won-loss ratio of endorsed candidates is not the best measure of environmental group influence.

As Table 5.4 illustrates, candidates in priority races, those in which the two groups invested heavily in time, money, or both, also won most of their contests. Candidates backed by the Sierra Club won thirty-nine of fifty-four priority races in 2000, a success rate of 72.2 percent. As noted above, seven of the twelve Dirty Dozen candidates were defeated on election day, many in very close races. In 1998, candidates backed by the Sierra Club won thirty-eight of forty-three priority races, while candidates supported by the LCV won nine of thirteen Dirty Dozen contests and all ten "Earth List" races. Candidates endorsed by the two groups enjoyed a similar success rate in 1996, when more than 70 percent won their races. In priority races that year, candidates backed by the Sierra Club won thirty-three of fifty-three House contests and seven of eleven in the Senate.[106]

In assessing the 1996 elections, Pope claimed, "The Sierra Club and the

Table 5.4. Sierra Club and LCV Election Results, 1996–2002

	1996	1998	2000	2002
Sierra Club's Success Rate in "Priority Races"				
No. of races	64	43	54	17
Win-Loss (%)	62.5	88.3	72.2	11.8
LCV "Dirty Dozen" Success Rate				
No. of races	12	13	12	12
Win-Loss (%)	58.3	69.2	58.3	44.2

Sources: www.sierraclub.org, www.lcv.org.

environmental movement played a central role in the unmaking of this Congress."[107] Although Pope clearly had reasons to exaggerate the environmental community's role in thinning the ranks of antienvironmental forces in Congress, there is some truth in his claim. In a survey conducted in January 1996 by Republican pollster Linda Divall, voters had more confidence in Democrats than Republicans as the party most likely to protect the environment, by a greater than two-to-one margin. Even more striking was the finding that 55 percent of Republicans did not trust their own party when it came to protecting the environment.[108] Moreover, claimed Pope, "An exit poll commissioned by the Republican Party showed that the environmental issue had cost the Republicans twice as many votes as any other, even Social Security and Medicare."[109] Polls commissioned by the LCV after the 1996 elections also indicated that voters were very concerned about environmental issues. More specifically, clean water was the issue mentioned most often by voters, followed by the public's right to know about toxic pollution. These were the two issues highlighted by the LCV in its television and radio ads, which suggests that the ads made an impression on voters.[110] Polling in subsequent years reveals similar results.[111]

ENVIRONMENTAL GROUPS AND THE CAMPAIGN AGENDA

Assessing the effectiveness of environmental group political activity is a difficult task. The most obvious measure is whether the candidates they support win or lose, but assigning responsibility to any one group is clearly problematic. In addition, the groups' political efforts have multiple goals beyond electing "green" candidates. In the case of the Sierra Club, the organization uses its EVEC campaigns to strengthen its chapters, grow its membership, and energize its activist base. The political season also provides a good opportunity to raise the group's profile with the public and to establish relationships with the media. And perhaps most importantly, the campaigns seek to alter the campaign agenda by getting environmental issues into the debate. Even if their preferred candidates lose, the groups can still accomplish one of their goals if the candidates talk about environmental issues. After all, you can't win a debate that never occurs.

Determining whether the new forms of political spending by environmental groups actually shape the campaign agenda is a difficult question, though. Anecdotal evidence abounds, but large-scale, systematic studies of the question do not exist. In 2002, polls and newspaper accounts suggested that the environment was one of the two most important issues to voters in Colorado and Missouri, two states where the Sierra Club conducted EVEC activities.[112] That same year, polling suggests that the LCV's Dirty Dozen campaign was a significant factor in raising environmental issues in a Maryland House race and in changing people's perceptions of the targeted candidate's position on environmental issues. Pre-election polling by the LCV revealed that by a 3 percent margin the voters said the targeted Dirty Dozen candidate, Helen Bentley, "takes the right position on the environment." The LCV campaign, which was critical of Bentley, focused on pollution in the Chesapeake Bay and stressed the bay's importance to the local economy. When the ads finished airing, polls showed that there had been an eighteen-point swing in voters' perceptions of whether Bentley took the right position on the environment. Dutch Ruppersberger, the Democratic candidate, stressed similar themes in his campaign. It seems clear that something caused the shift in voters' perceptions, and it was almost certainly the ads run by the LCV and Ruppersberger. According to Betsy Loyless, the LCV's political director, this race shows that it is important for candidates to reinforce the proenvironment message of groups like the LCV.[113]

In an attempt to find an answer to whether or not group campaigns are shaping the campaign agenda, one could compare districts in which environmental groups waged issue campaigns to those where they did not. If the ads were effective in framing the debate, we would expect to see the issues discussed in those ads playing a greater role in voters' decisions in the districts where the ads were aired. Fortunately, a number of pre- and post-election public opinion surveys were conducted in races in which the groups mounted their campaigns. In 2000, for example, the League of Conservation Voters Education Fund launched a $7.4 million voter education and polling program. Working with Democratic and Republican polling firms, the LCV conducted polls throughout the year—at the front end of races and again just before and after the election—to gauge the influence and effectiveness of environmental messages in numerous races. According to the LCV, the polling showed that even in those races in which the LCV-backed candidate lost, environmental issues were frequently important issues for voters. In many of the races, the specific environmental charges levied by the LCV in its ad campaigns became the first or second most powerful reason to vote against the Dirty Dozen candidate or for the Environmental Champion.[114]

Similarly, the Sierra Club conducted election-eve polling in New Hampshire and Colorado in 2002. These polls indicated that people recalled seeing their television ads and had a favorable impression of them. In New Hampshire, polling suggested that people in the Manchester area, where the ads ran, expressed a higher level of concern about environmental issues than did voters in other parts of the state. Pollster Celinda Lake, who was working for a House candidate in the state, conducted a focus group using the Sierra Club's ads for Democratic Senate candidate Jeanne Shaheen. In characterizing the focus group results, the Club's political director said that the ads were well received, and that the participants knew and trusted the Club. One respondent remarked of the Club, "They're fanatics, but they tell the truth."[115]

Polling conducted in 1998 by a variety of organizations also found that the environment could be a potent and sometimes decisive electoral issue. A series of polls conducted for the LCV just before election day found that in eight of nine races in which the LCV actively informed voters about a candidate's environmental record, the environment became the first or second reason people voted against the Dirty Dozen candidate. These findings prompted Deb Callahan to claim that "people will vote the environment when they know the facts."[116] According to pollster Alan Quinlan, in 1996 "environmental issues played a large role in swinging close elections throughout the country in which these issues were spotlighted and became part of the debate." One of the lessons of 1996, he noted, was that voters now consider a clean environment a norm and will punish politicians who do not support efforts to protect the environment. "The power of the environment," said Quinlan, "continues to be in its use as a negative positioning against politicians with poor environmental records. It serves to position those candidates outside the mainstream in an important way."[117]

A brief review of the 1998 polling data from seven Dirty Dozen races illustrates both the importance of the environment as an issue and the role of the LCV in highlighting it. According to Quinlan, environmental attacks against candidates ranked in the top three of all issues tested in four races: the North Carolina and Nevada Senate races, and the House contests in New Mexico's Third District and Washington's First. Environmental issues were fourth in the remaining races. In the Nevada and New Mexico campaigns, environmental issues were the most important to voters. When asked how important the environment was in making their voting decision, the strongest responses came from voters in North Carolina (45 percent said very important), New Mexico (45 percent), and Nevada (43 percent). Interestingly, environmental concerns cut across partisan and ideological lines and are now important to the vast majority of voters. Overall, in the seven races surveyed, 84 percent of voters said the environment was either a very important factor in their voting decisions (40 percent), or that it was somewhat important (44 percent).[118]

In the Wisconsin Senate race between Russ Feingold and Mark Neumann, polling showed that advertising by the LCV and other groups had a dramatic effect on Neumann's image by increasing voters' negative impressions of him. The LCV's ads focused on Neumann's votes against cleaning up toxins in waterways, against wetlands protection, and in support of weakening laws to protect drinking water. These charges were then cited by 40 percent of voters, more than any other single charge, and by 53 percent of Feingold voters.[119]

In the Washington Senate race between Patty Murray and Linda Smith, 83 percent of voters viewed the environment as a very important or somewhat important issue affecting their decision. Again, the LCV claimed success in making the environment a reason to vote against Smith. The group's ads highlighted her votes "to weaken clean water laws" even though "more cancer-causing toxins are dumped into Washington's waterways than in any other state." The ads also focused on Smith's vote to limit the public's right to know about toxics in their communities. Nearly half of the state's voters said they had seen environmental ads targeting

Smith, and her votes against clean water and the public's right to know on toxics emerged as the number two reason Murray voters cited in opposing Smith.[120]

In the Nevada Senate race between Harry Reid and John Ensign, 85 percent of voters cited environmental issues as very or somewhat important in their voting decision. As in other races, support for the environment cut across party lines, with 56 percent of Democrats, 42 percent of independents, and 46 percent of Republicans saying the environment was very important in making their decisions. The issue of nuclear waste was very effective as the single strongest negative against Ensign (27 percent) and the second most compelling argument for Reid (38 percent). Close behind were Ensign's efforts to weaken clean water laws (22 percent). Three out of four voters recalled seeing television ads detailing Ensign's environmental record.[121]

CONCLUSION

In recent elections environmental groups have tried to maximize their electoral influence by mobilizing their grass roots, forging alliances with other progressive organizations, and by raising and spending more than ever before. In an important development, much of the spending took new forms as environmental groups aggressively tried to set the agenda in numerous campaigns nationwide. Rather than wait passively for candidates to raise the environment as a campaign issue, the groups spent large sums on radio, television, and print ads in order to thrust the issue into the campaign. These new tactics demonstrate that environmental groups are adapting to the new "rules of the game" in campaign finance, which allow virtually unlimited and unregulated spending by those seeking to influence elections. Under current law, the most any PAC can contribute directly to a given candidate in an election cycle is $10,000. But, as Ellen Miller of the Center for Responsive Politics put it, "a $10,000 contribution to a political campaign doesn't buy much" today.[122] For groups seeking to get the most from their political spending, independent expenditures and issue advocacy are clearly more attractive options. For environmental groups, who typically have little money, the new forms of political spending allow them to concentrate their energies and money on carefully selected races. Nor are they alone, as more and more groups adopt similar tactics. For this reason, Deborah Callahan of the League of Conservation Voters argued in 1997 that "everybody will start earlier, and be louder" in the 1998 elections.[123] She was right.

Although political spending by environmental groups can be successful, one should not overlook the fact that these groups typically cannot match the financial resources of corporations or conservative groups. Any success that environmental groups have had with the new forms of political spending may be short-lived, as other groups discover the loopholes and flood the airwaves with antienvironmental or, more likely, probusiness ads. It is for this reason that many activists believe that the best long-term approach for environmental groups is to rely on an enthusiastic and energetic grass roots to raise the prominence of environmental issues, to convince voters to focus on these issues, and to get out the vote.

It also remains to be seen whether environmental groups can sustain their recent fundraising and spending levels. With Republicans in control of Congress and the White House, it seems likely that they can, at least for the next two election cycles. Still, one has to wonder how many times environmental groups can go to the well before donors become weary of the latest plea for money. Much of the $7.5 million spent by the Sierra Club in 1996, in fact, was rumored to be from a single anonymous donor. The group's EVEC fundraising declined sharply after Congress banned such donations.

With the memory of the 2000 and 2002 elections still fresh, and with Congress so closely divided, environmental groups are likely to be particularly aggressive in defending their supporters in Congress and in targeting those members who have been most hostile to the environment. It is also likely that environmental PACs will also be more generous to challengers and to candidates for open seats than most other PACs. This pattern of support for those candidates who embrace a green platform suggests that environmental groups will continue to try to increase the number of friendly members in Congress, rather than merely seeking to maintain the access they already have.

At the beginning of the 1990s the environmental movement was at a crossroads, suffering from stagnant memberships and declining revenues, which forced staff layoffs, salary freezes, and other cost-cutting measures. Mainstream groups like the Sierra Club were increasingly attacked for being too willing to compromise on issues and tactics in order to remain respectable. As is often the case, these problems sparked an intramural dispute within many organizations over goals and tactics. The dilemma facing environmental groups, as articulated by Christopher Bosso, was how to remain active players in national politics without blunting the enthusiasm of local activists.[124]

The more recent efforts of many of these groups to raise the visibility of environmental issues in congressional campaigns suggest a possible solution to that dilemma. Environmental groups have used independent expenditure, issue advocacy, and voter education campaigns to rebuild and mobilize their grassroots constituencies. In carefully selected contests, environmentalists have helped define the issues and forced candidates to address their policy concerns. They have not always been successful, but green candidates and causes have won often enough to show that political spending by environmental groups is not necessarily wasted.

6
Environmentalism in the States

Successful environmental policy implementation is best accomplished through balanced, open, and inclusive approaches at the ground level, where interested stakeholders work together to formulate critical issue statements and develop locally based solutions to those issues. Collaborative approaches often result in greater satisfaction with outcomes and broader public support, and can increase the chances of involved parties staying committed over time to the solution and its implementation.
—Western Governors' Association

As we have seen, the conventional wisdom that environmental groups and issues are minor factors in national elections is not entirely true. To be sure, other organized interests have more money and can spend more heavily in their efforts to sway elections. Despite record fundraising, the few environmental PACs that are active in congressional elections can only afford to play in selective races, which limits their overall effectiveness. But in those races, which are increasingly important given the close partisan divisions in Congress, environmental groups have made a difference. There is also some evidence that their independent expenditure and issue advocacy campaigns have been successful in raising the prominence of environmental issues in targeted races.

In this chapter, the focus shifts to what environmental groups are doing to influence elections and policymaking in the states. This topic is increasingly important, given the 1990s trend toward decentralization, which called for transferring authority from Washington to state and local governments. More and more, states are assuming greater responsibility for monitoring and implementing environmental programs. Moreover, local and county officials continue to make many decisions regarding solid waste, land use, and zoning, all of which have considerable environmental consequences. This chapter seeks to explain what state and local environmental organizations are doing, and whether their actions are comparable to those of the large national groups, particularly with respect to their issue definition and agenda-setting efforts.

Given the thousands of groups that are active at the state and local level, however, as well as the exceptional diversity in their goals and tactics, this discussion must be rather impressionistic. It would be an enormous undertaking to systematically evaluate or discuss the many groups now in existence, never mind those that have already come and gone. This is particularly true with respect to local environmental organizations, which vary widely in their capabilities, goals, and modes of action. At the same time, the task is not as daunting when it comes to analyzing electoral activities. Simply put, there have not been that many environmental groups active in state and local elections, at least until recently.

That said, it should soon be clear that many state and local environmental organizations have been profoundly affected by the capacity-building efforts discussed in the previous chapter. With assistance from foundations and several national groups, a growing number of statewide, regional, and county environmental organizations have upgraded their technology, as well as their political and advocacy skills, and have become more adept at lobbying and electioneering. With respect to the latter, a small but steadily growing number of groups evaluate and endorse candidates, make campaign contributions, wage independent expenditure campaigns, and provide other means of campaign support, such as volunteers and polling data. Similarly, technology has facilitated greater coordination and information sharing, which has enabled more groups to monitor state agencies and legislatures. State and local groups have also greatly enhanced their public education efforts, using media events, public forums, publications, websites, and other outreach efforts to spread their message as they seek to frame issues and shape the political agenda.

ELECTORAL ACTIVITY IN THE STATES

Until quite recently, state and local environmental organizations had been minor players in elections. To be sure, there were some exceptions, notably the League of Conservation Voter affiliates in California, Oregon, and New York. The California League of Conservation Voters (CLCV), for example, is the largest and oldest state political action organization for the environment. It was founded in 1972 and has been, for the most, involved in elections ever since, especially from the 1980s on.[1] But historically, most state and local groups have shied away from explicit electioneering because IRS rules impose severe limits on such activity by 501(c)(4) nonprofit organizations. With the exception of those already mentioned, electoral activity by state and local environmental groups tended to be sporadic, amateurish, and woefully underfunded.

That began to change, however, in the late 1990s, when the number of organizations seeking to influence state and local elections skyrocketed. There are now more groups active in more states, and they have more money, which allows them to be involved in more races. In fact, some are quite sophisticated in their approach to political campaigns, and now rely on an array of professional pollsters, consultants, and fundraisers. Some have begun sponsoring their own independent expenditure campaigns as well. Moreover, there is often considerable coordination among the state groups and between the state and national organizations. It is not unusual, for example, for the state groups to target county and state legislative races in those congressional districts chosen as "priorities" by the national groups. In this way, environmentalists hope to create a dynamic in which their campaigns overlap and generate additional votes for proenvironment candidates at all levels. Clearly, state and local environmental groups have come a long way in a very short period of time.

The state-based groups have become more professional for a variety of reasons. First, campaigns at all levels are more professional than in the 1980s. Even in down ticket races, campaigns are increasingly run by professionals, and it is not uncommon for candidates for county-level office to employ campaign managers, media consultants, direct mail specialists, and so on. Interest groups had to adapt in order to compete in the new campaign environment. A second factor was the growing recognition of the connection between issue work and political work. As the groups' issues staff became more professional, they recognized a need to upgrade the political operations as well.

The Washington Environmental Alliance for Voter Education (WEAVE) was one of the first organizations to focus on promoting voter participation among environmentally minded citizens in the states. Established in 1993, WEAVE designs programs for strengthening the local chapters of environmental groups. The organization specializes in list development for voter education, voter identification and targeting, campaign plans and strategy, and electoral skills training. Although WEAVE is based in Washington State and works primarily with groups from that state, its services are available to organizations and activists across the country.

The increased political activism and sophistication of state and local groups is also a product of the capacity-building efforts of foundations and national groups discussed above. Beginning in the late 1990s, both the Sierra Club and the League of Conservation Voters, through its 501(c)(3) education fund, decided to significantly enhance the electoral capacity of their state affiliates and other environmental groups. Both organizations subsequently set out to provide money, training, and other forms of assistance, including political and legal advice. Mirroring the national groups, many of the LCV and Sierra Club state chapters rationalized their organizations, creating affiliated political action committees and 501(c)(3) educational arms to carry out activities that are prohibited to the parent 501(c)(4) organization. In 2000, for example, the national Sierra Club launched a new program of nonfederal environmental voter education campaigns, or EVECs. As with the federal EVECs discussed in Chapter 3, the state programs enable environmentalists to engage in a broad range of political activities, including issue advertising and the distribution of voter guides.[2]

The League of Conservation Voters' drive to upgrade the environmental movement's state-level political capacity began in early 1996, when the directors of the California and New York League of Conservation Voters organizations decided to bring together the leaders of similar groups from across the nation. The first meeting, which was held in San Francisco later that year, was largely devoted to finding out what aspects of running a state LCV group they had in common. At the next meeting, held in New Orleans in 1997, the twelve state LCV directors who were present adopted a resolution calling for the establishment and incorporation of a formal group called the Federation of State Conservation Voter Leagues. They also decided to form a board of executive directors and to hold at least an annual conference. Tensie Whelan, then director of the New York League of Conservation Voters, later met with key national environmental donors on helping fund a staff position and defraying the costs of running the annual conference.[3]

Several of the state LCV directors began working to establish similar organizations in other states. With the assistance of some anonymous donors, they created a grant program to raise seed money for the project. The plan was to establish 501(c)(3) and (c)(4) organizations in each state to conduct various kinds of election activities. The first grant was for the groups to buy computers, and the second offered matching money for groups to hire full-time executive directors, which was a requirement for membership in the Federation, and a crucial step in establishing stability and expertise. The idea proved to be very popular. By early 2002, the number of state League of Conservation Voters organizations grew to thirty, with plans for others in the works.

The Federation of State Conservation Voter Leagues now acts as a trade association for the various state groups, providing grants, training, technical support, and other resources. The Federation also works with the national League of Conservation Voters to offer the state directors training on a variety of organizational and campaign-related matters. The Federation continues to hold annual meetings, and has established a listserv to allow the directors to communicate regularly. According to Ed Zuckerman, the Federation's executive director, the organization's key contribution is its focus on state and local electoral politics and issues. Previously, says Zuckerman, the Sierra Club was "the only real national environmental group putting a national strategy together around local and state legislative environmental issues."[4]

Voter Identification and Mobilization

Beginning in the early 1990s, environmental groups began to turn their attention to another task formerly performed by political parties—targeting and mobilizing voters. In 1993, for example, the New York League of Conservation Voters established a 501(c)(3) organization to educate New Yorkers about environmental issues and environmental decisionmaking procedures at local, regional, and state government levels. Subsequently, the New York Conservation Education Fund compiled an "Eco-Voter" file of 170,000 activists from twenty groups around the state. The list details their voting frequency, age, gender, political and jurisdictional information, and allows groups and selected political campaigns to target their outreach efforts.[5] Finally, the Oregon League of Conservation Voters sponsors a "Green Voter Captain" program, in which volunteers sign up to spend two hours every election cycle calling up to fifty other environmentalists to remind them of the need to vote for proenvironment candidates. As part of the program, the group holds training sessions to teach volunteers about the candidates and how to make effective get-out-the-vote phone calls. The group also has a political action committee to issue endorsements, contribute money, and provide volunteers to proenvironment candidates.[6]

In 1996, in an effort to identify and understand environmentally minded voters, the League of Conservation Voters Education Fund (LCVEF) matched state voter files with the membership lists of conservation groups in several states, and learned that many group members demonstrated the same low turnout rates as the general public. They also learned that the primary causes of nonvoting among group members were the lack of time, information, and direct encouragement for voting. At the time, most of the local groups were unaware of their members' voting patterns and had not systematically encouraged them to vote as a means of advancing the group's policy goals. The LCVEF subsequently decided to work with local groups to find ways of overcoming the obstacles to voting and increasing turnout among their membership.[7]

The first project, begun in the state of Washington in 1998, was a three-year investigation into whether a systematic absentee voter enrollment program would help citizens overcome the time barriers to voting and increase turnout. The primary goal of the program was to improve voter participation among conservation-minded citizens by enrolling them as permanent absentee voters. The targets of the program included infrequent voters who were members of conservation organizations and people who had previously signed a conservation-related initiative petition. Working with the LCVEF, the Washington Environmental Alliance for Voter Education (WEAVE) used focus group and polling research to design a brochure that promoted the convenience of voting by mail. The mailing was designed to appeal to all voters, but especially to women aged thirty-five to fifty-four, a key demographic group known to have many conservation-minded citizens in the state. Sixteen thousand packages, which included absentee ballot application forms, were sent to occasional voters in three Washington counties. The response rates to the mailing were quite good—18 percent of those contacted enrolled as absentee voters, compared to only 1.7 percent of a control group. In addition, the voting rate of enrollees was 33 percent higher than the general electorate in the primary, and 11 percent higher in the general election. In Washington, where the conversion to absentee status is permanent, LCVEF and WEAVE set a goal of enrolling twenty thousand mail voters for the next election. Pleased with the results, the League replicated the procedure in Colorado, mailing nearly forty-four thousand forms to members of eighteen conservation groups. The response rate there was 17 percent. Postelection analysis conducted by LCV revealed that 93 percent of absentee voters cast their ballots in the state's three most populous counties, compared to 36 percent of the general electorate. The two groups expanded the vote-by-mail program in 2000, and also provided technical and financial assistance to 501(c)(3) groups in other states who had expressed an interest in launching similar programs.[8]

Recent developments in Colorado illustrate the emerging role of environmental groups in state and local elections. Environmental lobbyists in the state, frustrated by their dealings with an unresponsive state legislature, had been making the case that environmental groups needed to become more explicitly involved in electoral politics if they wanted to enact better environmental policies. In their view, it was easier to change legislators than it was to change legislators' minds. To fill this void, a new PAC, Colorado Conservation Voters, was created in 1999.[9]

The nonpartisan organization contributed to seventeen candidates and ran three independent expenditure campaigns in 2000, spending a total of $65,000 in its first election cycle.[10] Two of the candidates supported by the CCV in its independent expenditure campaigns prevailed, and thought that the group's actions had helped their candidacies. One lost, and later claimed that independent expenditure campaigns run by CCV and other groups had cost him control of his own campaign. In 2002, the CCV contributed to twenty-one candidates and raised more than $150,000. Candidates supported by the PAC won only three of seven priority races in 2002, and one of two key state Senate races, but all of the contests were close, including several that were decided by fewer than two hundred votes.[11] According to Tony Massaro, the group's executive director, the CCV must conduct independent expenditure campaigns to educate voters about candidates' actual environmental records. Because the environment is now a consensual issue in the state, candidates of all stripes claim to be in favor of environmental protection. In election years, this means that candidates with poor environmental voting records try to blur the differences on the issue. Massaro argues that because media coverage of environmental issues is often infrequent and superficial, groups like the CCV must undertake independent spending campaigns to combat this problem.[12]

In deciding which candidates to support, Massaro considers several factors, beginning with the need to "protect your friends," by which he means those incumbents who have a record of supporting the environment. But CCV is quite strategic in its decisionmaking, helping only those friends who actually need it. The group does not want to squander its limited resources in helping safe incumbents. Massaro also believes it is important for environmental PACs to beat their enemies and "send a message" that there will be a price to pay for voting against the environment. Again, though, the group is strategic and does not tilt at windmills. Massaro, who had extensive campaign experience before joining CCV, studies district profiles, voter registration figures, and previous election results to identify vulnerable incumbents and promising open seats. CCV then works with the state's other two environmental PACs to select the targeted races and develop a strategy, including a compelling conservation message.[13]

Although the fact that candidates were discussing environmental issues suggests that CCV and other groups have managed to raise the profile of such issues in Colorado elections, the 2002 results were disappointing. Part of the explanation is that 2002 was an unusual election year in that it featured a number of high-profile contests, including a U.S. Senate race and two open House contests. These races attracted a lot of national attention, and money, which meant that voters in targeted districts were inundated with campaign materials. That made it much harder for groups like CCV to break through the clutter and have voters pay attention to their message. In addition, 2002 was a congressional midterm election, in which turnout is generally quite low, especially among unaffiliated voters. A number of environmental groups devoted significant resources to contacting and persuading these voters, to little avail. In retrospect, it probably would have made more sense for the groups to target their own activists and other environmentally minded voters and urge them to go to the polls. In future elections, state conservation groups will likely devote even more resources and energy to email, telephone calls, and door-to-door canvassing in an effort to identify and mobilize environmental voters, and they are more likely to start earlier in the electoral cycle. The hope is that by starting early, the groups will have an easier time getting their message out, while assembling an army of volunteers who can be counted on to organize precincts.

The conservation community in Colorado also coordinates its efforts with labor groups, NARAL, the Colorado Education Association, and other progressive organizations. Moreover, the state's AFL-CIO director is on the CCV board. Leaders of the various groups meet regularly to talk about issues and selecting races. They also talk about the division of labor, such as which groups will run phone banks, and when, which groups will do direct mail, and so on. In several races in the Colorado Springs area in 2002, for example, the groups decided to target swing voters, primarily women between the ages of twenty-five and fifty-five, and conducted polls to determine which group's message would be most effective in swaying those voters. When the polling showed that education and environmental messages moved swing voters best, the decision was made to highlight those issues in the primary.

Given its still limited resources, Colorado Conservation Voters cannot afford to do much polling on its own. It has, however, collaborated with groups in New Mexico and Arizona to poll Latino voters, and also receives poll briefings from the League of Conservation Voters. Those polls are used to help focus the group's campaign messages. To date, the organization cannot afford to poll to ascertain to what extent its efforts have influenced voters. Instead, the group relies on its won-loss tally and informal conversations with candidates to gauge its effectiveness. The group also selectively checks voting records to gauge turnout among those who were targeted during the campaign—in the 2002 elections, turnout rates among voters who appeared on environmental voting lists approached 80 percent, a very strong number.[14]

In an effort to maximize both their electoral influence and their ability to obtain policy results, a number of environmental groups are beginning to "play in primaries." As an example, the CCV is nonpartisan and looks to support candidates from both parties. As in many other mountain states, however, the state's Republican Party made a hard turn to the right in the 1990s, and often expressed hostility to environmental laws and programs. Consequently, environmental groups have to look far and wide to find Republican candidates to support. In Massaro's view, with so many safe legislative districts in the state, especially after the 2002 redistricting increased the number even further, about the only way his group could support Republicans was to get involved in Republican primaries in largely Republican districts and support moderates over conservatives. Otherwise, CCV would be "forced" into the undesirable option of supporting the Democratic candidate in a safe Republican district in the general election. While supporting the "greener" candidate might please movement activists, it would do little to change the legislature that makes the state's environmental laws. In explaining his rationale, Massaro said, "If you can replace a conservative Republican with a zero score with one with a better score, you've helped in the legislature."[15]

In addition to the League of Conservation Voters, the Sierra Club has also begun to devote more attention to state and local elections. The national Sierra Club, in conjunction with its chapters, now conducts campaign-training sessions for local activists. Featuring staffers from the Club's Political Committee as well as local politicians, lobbyists, and political experts, the training sessions familiarize activists with relevant campaign finance laws, and offer insights into how to run effective campaigns. Among the topics covered are voter targeting, preparing an effective conservation message, and cultivating the local media.

Since 2000, the Minnesota chapter of the Sierra Club has been conducting a "Toxic Twelve" campaign, a state-level equivalent of the LCV's national "Dirty Dozen" campaign. The "Toxic Twelve" campaign identifies legislators with poor environmental voting records and then sets out to educate the voters in the legislator's district of his or her votes. The chapter, which had limited resources but a desire to influence environmental policymaking by the state legislature, used a number of factors in compiling its list of targeted candidates. The first factor was the candidate's environmental voting record. The group chose to focus on candidates with a Sierra Club environmental voting record of less than 10 percent, which, according to the chapter, candidates could have achieved merely by voting for the environment just once each year. Second, the chapter evaluated the state's legislative district to determine how many Club members each contained and to identify which districts might provide enough activists who could be organized in the effort. Next, the chapter looked at district characteristics and the legislator's margin of victory in the previous election to see if any incumbents were vulnerable. For example, a conservative Republican representing a district that usually votes Democratic in presidential elections would be an appealing target. Because they are generally easier to defeat, the group gave special consideration to freshman incumbents. Finally, the group made its final selection based upon geographic considerations, specifically to ensure that the races covered all parts of the state.[16]

Ten of the original thirteen targeted candidates were Republicans, including all eight of the candidates for the Minnesota House. According to the group, the average Republican House member had a 5 percent Sierra Club voting record in the 1990–2000 legislative session. In the state senate races, the Club targeted two Democrats, two Republicans, and one Independent. In carrying out the campaign, the Club issued press releases, ran a series of newspaper ads, participated in a number of parades during the summer, and encouraged a "letters to the editor" campaign among its members. The campaign appears to have been marginally successful. Of the thirteen legislators on the original Toxic Twelve List, three were defeated in the election and three were removed from the list after the 2000 legislative session ended because their voting records had improved, in some cases quite dramatically. In assessing its own efforts, the chapter claims to have "dramatically improved the profile of the environment as an issue throughout Minnesota" and to have succeeded in "changing Legislators' minds and influencing voting patterns." To support these contentions, the group cites poll numbers revealing a 6 percent shift against Toxic Twelve candidates in districts where the Club campaigned.[17]

In addition to the groups already discussed, there are a variety of other organizations active in state and local elections. One is WILD PAC, a political action committee established in 2001 to assist candidates who are supportive of wilderness protection. As noted in Chapter 3, WILD PAC will focus on a limited number of congressional races, as well as selected state offices. Decisions about which races to target are made by its regional advisory committees, which sends questionnaires to candidates, and interviews them as well. In its first round of campaigns in 2002, WILD PAC focused on get-out-the-vote campaigns and provided candidates with assistance with fundraising, media, organizing, and public lands expertise. As part of its long-range plans to protect wild places, WILD PAC intends to be involved in identifying and cultivating local leaders.[18]

Participation in Down-Ticket Races

As groups like the CCV raise more money, they will almost certainly opt to become involved in more races, including those "down ticket." Indeed, the effort to increase their political presence at the local level is an intriguing and potentially important new path for environmental groups, who have for too long neglected the importance of local politics. Local or county governments make many important environmental policies involving land use and sprawl, for example. And as the religious right demonstrated so well in the 1980s, experience in local government can be a springboard to higher office. In many parts of the country, religious and other conservative groups recruited and trained members to run for school boards and planning commissions, as part of an overall strategy to develop a "farm system" of experienced candidates, who could then run for higher office. Eventually, many of those recruits were elected to the House of Representatives in 1992 and 1994, giving the Republicans control of the chamber. So if environmentalists hope to increase their voice in state legislatures or in Congress, it makes abundant sense to try to encourage activists to first seek local political office.

There are signs that some environmental groups are beginning to do just that. In Montana, for example, the nonprofit Center for Environmental Politics has been working to identify and recruit individuals to serve in key governmental offices that affect environmental decisions. The group focuses on elected positions, like city council and conservation district boards, as well as on appointed offices, such as zoning and open-space boards, and water quality advisory committees. After identifying interested individuals, the Center supports and trains them on how to organize a campaign for elective office, and how to apply for appointed offices.[19] Similarly, the Oregon League of Conservation Voters Education Fund is working to increase participation by environmentalists in local policy boards and commissions. To aid in that task, the group monitors openings on boards across the state and provides a list of those openings on its website, as well as information on how to seek that office.

If they are to be successful in framing issues and in raising the profile of environmental issues, conservation groups will need to get more involved in local campaigns. In these smaller arenas, resource disparities are often less pronounced, and citizens can readily perceive the link between the environment and their everyday lives. In the long run, this strategy may yield big dividends should environmentally minded candidates seek higher office.

ENVIRONMENTAL BALLOT INITIATIVES AND REFERENDA

One of the major differences between policymaking at the state and at the federal levels is that many states allow voters to use the initiative and referendum process to make policy. Indeed, thirty-one states have some form of direct democracy for approving legislation, and all states but Delaware require voters to approve constitutional amendments by referendum.[20] Moreover, with the move to devolve greater responsibility to the states in the 1980s and 1990s, these tools have been used with increasing frequency, especially with respect to environmental policy.[21] In recent years, voters across the nation have considered a wide array of environmental proposals, such as recycling programs, environmental bond issues, open space preservation, and growth control. This section examines what environmental groups are doing to influence these direct democracy measures.

Initiatives, in particular, have some clear advantages for environmental groups. Most importantly, because groups often draft the proposals themselves, they get to choose the issue, the time, and the decisionmaking arena. The initiative process can thus be an important tool in framing public perceptions of issues and in exerting some control over the agenda. Raising topics early increases the chances that issues will be debated in favorable terms and on favorable terrain. Direct democracy provisions also allow groups to bypass state legislatures, where, conventional wisdom holds, they are no match for their wealthier, better-connected opponents. Moreover, groups can take their issues right to the public, which tends to be more supportive of environmental protection than are elected officials. Deborah Lynn Guber explains, "We would more fairly judge the environment's 'bottom line' by looking to other political arenas, such as ballot initiatives and referendums at the state and local level where environmental issues seem to enjoy greater salience and less competition for room on a crowded political agenda."[22] In many states, moreover, a lack of money does not prevent groups from placing their proposals before the voters; indeed, qualifying for the ballot is often possible with the signatures of only a small portion of the electorate, a relatively easy task for citizen groups with committed volunteers.[23] In short, initiatives and referenda offer the potential for environmental groups to assume a lead role in state policy development.[24]

Although many state constitutions contain provisions allowing voters to make policy decisions, only in the last two decades have environmental initiatives and referenda become ballot box staples. From the early 1970s to 1986, voters approved only eighteen environmental ballot measures in the entire United States. It was in 1986, for example, that California voters approved Proposition 65, a very controversial measure that banned chemicals known to pose a significant risk of cancer or birth defects. Also known as the Safe Drinking Water and Toxic Enforcement Act, Proposition 65 was the product of a coalition of environmental, labor, and consumer groups, including the Environmental Defense Fund, the Natural Resources Defense Council, the Sierra Club, the AFL-CIO, and a host of California-based organizations.[25] Proposition 65 passed easily, despite a $5 million spending campaign by opponents. Buoyed by that success, environmental groups began to employ initiatives more often, and in 1988 voters approved seventeen environmentally related measures.[26]

In the early 1990s environmental groups, in alliance with consumer groups and many municipalities, also derailed several notable antienvironmental ballot measures, including a number of "takings" initiatives. In several state legislatures, mainly in the West, property rights advocates had won passage of bills requiring compensation to landowners whose property was adversely affected by governmental action. Following those victories, property rights activists decided to take their issue directly to the voters through the initiative process.[27] In some respects, the battles over these initiatives convinced many within the environmental mainstream of the need to rebuild their grass roots, because it was only through the hard work of community organizing that the offending measures were defeated.

In the following years, environmental ballot victories were accompanied by some notable defeats as well, none more noteworthy than the 1990 California vote on Proposition 128, popularly known as "Big Green."[28] The measure, which was drafted in large part by individuals from the Natural Resources Defense Council, was breathtaking in its scope. If enacted, Big Green would have phased out many pesticides, banned logging in old-growth forests, eliminated chlorofluorocarbons

(CFCs), curtailed carbon dioxide emissions, and prevented drilling off the California coast. After a long and expensive campaign, Big Green was soundly defeated, at least in part because it was so ambitious and affected many powerful business interests.

More recently, there has been an explosion of ballot measures with environmental overtones, and most of them have fared quite well at the polls. The sheer number and diversity of these measures, however, precludes easy description. For example, on election day 2000 voters in thirty-eight states and hundreds of localities were asked to vote on 553 growth-related measures alone.[29] Moreover, the laws and regulations governing the use of initiative and referendum procedures vary from state to state, making exact comparisons almost impossible. Similarly, issues change over the years, as do economic conditions and political tides. Nevertheless, a review of environmental ballot measures in recent election cycles does reveal some significant insights.

In both 1996 and 1998, for example, voters approved nearly three-quarters of all state and local initiatives and referenda.[30] On election day 1998, voters in thirty-one states voted on 240 state and local measures related to conservation, parkland, and smarter growth, a 50 percent increase from 1996. The approved measures supported a wide range of conservation and community enhancement activities, including brownfield restoration, watershed protection, conservation easements, and farmland preservation, and they entailed $7.5 billion in additional state and local conservation spending.[31]

The most noteworthy of the 1998 measures included New Jersey's constitutional amendment to set aside $98 million per year for the next thirty years to protect half of the state's open space.[32] Arizona voters approved a controversial growth proposal, labeled "Growing Smarter," which protected some state-owned open space while at the same time enacting statewide restrictions on antigrowth measures. Supporters of the measure, who included developers, some open space groups, and the Nature Conservancy, spent $700,000 on their campaign. The Sierra Club and the Southwest Center for Biological Diversity, which supported a competing initiative, opposed the proposal.[33]

That same year, Oregon voters overwhelmingly rejected a ban on clearcutting forests on public and private land. The proposal was pushed by Oregonians for Labor Intensive Forest Economics, and opposed by the state's Democratic governor, some mainstream environmental groups, and the timber industry's Healthy Forest Alliance. In assessing the outcome, Healthy Forest Alliance representative Bill Wynkoop said, "The voters were quite clear. The initiative process is not the place to write forest management rules. It's too complex."[34]

It was also in 1998 that the League of Conservation Voters Education Fund began working with state and local environmental groups to influence ballot questions. The LCVEF initiated the program after its polling and focus group research showed that citizens often did not understand the relationship between voting and environmental protection. The goal was to help local groups develop a strategy and message to encourage citizen participation and voting among their members. The LCVEF believed that the initiative and referendum process, where the "substance of environmental policy-making is squarely on the shoulders of citizens," provided a good vehicle for experimentation. Accordingly, in 1998 the LCVEF began working with its state partners to develop and implement citizen participation strategies in the context of significant environmental ballot questions. The groups participated in a number of initiative campaigns that year, including efforts to halt billboard construction along scenic highways in Alaska and measures to protect land and wildlife habitat in Michigan and Georgia.[35] In many of the states, supporters conducted both air and ground campaigns, following up radio and television advertising with intensive on-ground organizing. LCVEF field staff worked with grassroots activists to develop a set of state-specific policy questions, and involved them in a range of traditional activities, including writing op-eds, attending candidate events, and organizing candidate debates.[36]

In Colorado, environmental groups also played a role passing Amendment 14, a measure to regulate waste from commercial hog farms. The initiative required hog factories to get permits, control the smell, and monitor waste to prevent groundwater contamination. The battle in Colorado was complicated by a tactical move from the commercial hog industry, which placed a competing measure on the ballot as well, which made it unconstitutional to regulate hog operations without simultaneously regulating other livestock. According to Dave Carter of the Rocky Mountain Farmer's Union, which campaigned for the measure, the ballot proposal was a last resort. Convinced that further lobbying of the state legislature was "fruitless," activists decided to "gamble" and let the voters decide. Carter said that although there were concerns that voters would not understand the details of the debate, "we came to the conclusion that voters actually read these issues and make serious decisions."[37]

In Colorado, the LCVEF worked with Environmental Defense, the Clean Water Fund, and the state's Public Interest Research Group to convene a series of meetings to organize and coordinate the environmental community's response. In addition to holding get-out-the-vote training and strategy discussions, proposal supporters mailed out forty-four thousand absentee ballot applications to members of eighteen conservation groups that had participated in a list enhancement project, and brochures to more than fifty thousand voters. They also recruited two hundred phone bank volunteers to call over ten thousand voters to explain the ballot initiatives and encourage them to vote. Supporters also took to the airwaves, running ads on radio and television. Denver businessman Phil Anschutz, whose own land was threatened by an industrial hog farm, was a key supporter, and he put over $400,000 into the race. In the end, Amendment 14 won with 64 percent of the vote, while Amendment 13, the industry-backed measure, lost by almost the same margin.[38]

Montana voters were confronted with Initiative 137, a measure to phase out cyanide heap–leach mining in the state. The ballot measure, which had been drafted by Jim Jensen, executive director of the Montana Environmental Information Center (MEIC), passed by a margin of fifty-three to forty-seven. The measure was a response to the poor environmental record of open-pit cyanide leach mining in the state, and the Montana Department of Environmental Quality's failure to adequately regulate such mines. As required under state law, supporters of the measure formed a principal campaign committee, Montanans for Common Sense Mining Laws, to promote the measure and shepherd it through the certification process. Under Jensen's direction, the campaign committee used a variety of techniques to collect signatures. In conjunction with U.S. Term Limits, the group hired a professional firm to gather signatures. In addition, petitions were mailed to MEIC members to gather signatures from family and friends, and MEIC staff collected signatures in targeted cities. The group also hired the Montana Public Interest Research Group's canvas program to collect signatures door to door in targeted districts.[39]

Montanans for Common Sense Mining Laws asked other Montana environmental groups to endorse the initiative and to urge their members to support it. Several groups joined the effort, including Trout Unlimited, the Clark Fork Coalition, the Montana Wilderness Association, and the Northern Plains Resource Council. The last group also provided local support and volunteers for a benefit concert by Jackson Browne in Billings on the Saturday before the election.[40] During the campaign, most of the coalition's money went to television advertising in the state's major media markets. Supporters also printed a few hundred bumper stickers and placed several half-page newspaper ads the day before the election. Jensen also traveled to major cites to debate the measure with opponents before civic organizations and press groups. Ranchers and other private property owners who had been negatively affected by heap–leach mines spoke at similar gatherings in the state's rural communities.[41]

Initiative backers cited three arguments in their campaign. First, they argued that open-pit cyanide leach mines threatened the property rights of neighboring landowners, and cited examples of landowners downstream of mines who were forced to sell their property after their wells were contaminated with cyanide. Second, they argued that the mines exposed Montana taxpayers to the costs of reclamation and imposed enormous financial liabilities for future generations. The Montana Environmental Information Center noted that one company declared bankruptcy in 1997, leaving the state with insufficient funds to reclaim what had once been the state's largest gold mine. Finally, MEIC published a study documenting contamination of the state's lakes, rivers, and streams with cyanide and other pollutants from gold and silver mines, and argued that it placed public health at significant risk. As evidence, they pointed to the fifty cyanide releases at the state's mines since 1982, which released millions of gallons of cyanide solution into the state's oil, surface, and groundwater resources.[42]

There were a total of 553 state and local growth-related measures on the ballot in November 2000; 518 were local and 35 were statewide. As in earlier years, more than 72 percent of them passed, although because business groups sponsored several of the measures, not every "yes" vote indicated a proenvironment position. Over half of the ballot measures appeared in just five states: California, Ohio, Colorado, Illinois, and New Jersey.[43] As one might expect, the measures dealt with various aspects of the growth debate. According to a Brookings Institution study, approximately 45 percent of the proposals involved open space preservation; 26 percent were related to infrastructure such as water quality, recreation facilities, and affordable housing in states and towns; and 16 percent were designed to manage growth.[44]

The proposals to regulate growth were by far the most contentious. Consider, for example, the debate over a Colorado growth control amendment to the state constitution, which was soundly rejected by the state's voters. Amendment 24, also known as the Responsible Growth Initiative, was the product of several years of work by a coalition of the state's environmental, consumer, and planning organizations, headed by the Colorado Environmental Coalition. The measure was prompted by the region's explosive growth (the population of the Denver metropolitan area had increased from 1.8 million in 1990 to 2.3 million in 2000) and by the state legislature's inability to enact a growth control measure in the prior years. In many ways, Amendment 24 was one of the most stringent statewide growth control measures to come up for voter consideration. The measure would have required counties and cities to prepare master plans showing maps of future growth areas, along with an explanation of how growth would affect schools, traffic, city finances, and the environment. The plans would then be submitted to voters for approval. Although most Colorado cities and counties already had master plans, they were not subject to voter approval, and they could be altered or even ignored by elected officials. If it had been approved, Colorado would have been the only state to require voter approval of city plans.

Amendment 24 required counties with more than twenty-five thousand residents to prepare the master plans; those with fewer than ten thousand residents would be exempt; while those in between could vote to exempt themselves. Under the initiative, new development would be limited to "committed areas," those areas that were already partially developed or that had been approved for development, or to "growth areas," which have been defined on growth maps approved in general elections.[45]

In drafting the initiative, supporters purposely avoided centralized growth controls. In the words of Elise Jones, head of the Colorado Environmental Coalition and one of the proposal's authors, "More government would never fly [in Colorado]. What Coloradans want is local control."[46] Supporters also stressed the importance of citizen participation in stemming sprawl, noting that all too often, local planning boards and city councils hear from citizens only after a project has been proposed in their neighborhoods. According to proponents, having the opportunity to vote on citywide plans would lead citizens to think in bigger terms than how their own neighborhoods were affected. According to Jeannette Hillery of the League of Women Voters, which supported the measure, "It would defi- nitely draw more people into it and hopefully make people aware of how their community is trying to address their growth issues."[47]

In addition to putting citizens in charge of development, supporters of the in- itiative argued, it would curtail the influence of developers, reduce congestion in the streets and in schools, and curtail pollution. Additionally, supporters claimed the measure would force cities to channel new homes and businesses to sites near existing development, thereby reducing the amount of open space lost to growth. Finally, in anticipation of attacks from the measure's opponents, backers argued that uncontrolled growth threatened Colorado's unique qualities that had made it so attractive in the first place. Amendment 24, they said, would actually protect and strengthen the state's economy.

Although it ultimately was defeated by a seventy to thirty margin, the Re- sponsible Growth Initiative enjoyed widespread voter support in the months pre- ceding the vote. Statewide polls in June showed that 78 percent of voters sup- ported the measure, while an early October poll reflected a 62 percent favorable rating.[48] But those polls were conducted before opponents began a massive adver- tising blitz. In fact, the fight over Amendment 24 was the most expensive ballot measure in state history, with both sides combining to spend more than $7 million. Supporters of the measure raised about $1 million, with the National Wildlife Federation contributing $50,000, the Colorado Environmental Coalition $25,000, and Colorado Public Interest Research Group $25,000. Despite raising such large sums of money, supporters of the measure were outspent by a margin of more than six to one. Their opponents, who called themselves Coloradoans for Responsible Reform, raised over $6 million, fully three-quarters of which came from develop- ers, including $100,000 contributions from Castle Rock Development Company, the Colorado Association of Realtors, Colorado Realtors I-PAC, Home Lumber, and Shea Homes.[49] In discussing the "Vote No on 24" campaign's television, radio, and newspaper ads, spokeswoman Jan Rigg said, "Education is part of our job."[50] In addition to the state's development and real estate interests, Amendment 24 was opposed by a coalition of about fifty groups, including the state's cham- bers of commerce, the Colorado Municipal League, supporters of affordable housing, and the Colorado AFL-CIO. The state's Republican governor, William Owens, was also opposed. In opposing the measure, critics argued primarily that it would restrict personal property rights, cost jobs, and drive up housing costs. Higher housing prices would, in turn, price middle-income people out of the mar- ket, which would make it harder for businesses to attract and maintain workers, so they would be forced look elsewhere to relocate or expand.[51] In the words of Greg Downs, senior regional director of First Industrial Realty Trust, "Basically, this amendment would be putting a 'Closed for Business' sign on Colorado."[52]

It seems fair to say that the opponents' attacks on Amendment 24 were effec- tive. As noted earlier, the proposal had a 62 percent favorability rating just one month before the election, but then the "Vote No on 24" coalition unleashed their ad campaign. In the end, the proposal gathered a majority of votes in only one of Colorado's sixty-three counties. The $6 million spent by opponents surely had something to do with that. Actually, the expensive fight over Amendment 24 is not that unusual. To be sure, the initiative did attract a lot of attention nationwide, but spending on statewide ballot measures is steadily increasing, and since there are no limits on such spending, it will continue to increase. Opponents of a similar ballot measure in Arizona that same year, for example, spent $4 million, with much the same result. That proposal, Proposition 202, was also defeated by a seventy-to-thirty margin, after enjoying a 68 percent favorability rating in earlier polls.[53] Steve Weichert, a consultant who works on ballot initiatives in Colorado, said in 1998, "I think Colorado is moving from a candidate-driven process to an initiative-driven process. . . . We're going to begin to manage our state through initiative and not legislative action."[54] If true, that observation raises some interesting and important questions. Because if spending on such measures continues to rise, then citizen groups will need to raise much more money than they have been able to so far. They will also have to do a much better job of framing perceptions of ballot measures and in communicating with voters, especially in the rural West and in the South, which are not as supportive of environmental initiatives.

The evidence shows that environmental ballot measures fare just as well in off-year elections. In 1999, voters approved 90 percent of the 102 measures on ballots. According to the Trust for Public Land and the Land Trust Alliance, 70 percent of 196 local ballot measures in two dozen states won voter approval.[55]

In reviewing the returns from recent election cycles, some general trends are clear. First, most environmental proposals pass, especially those at the local level. Whereas the approval rate for statewide measures in 2000 was just under 50 percent, voters approved three-quarters of local proposals. Measures designed to preserve open space have proven to be very popular on election day. In 2000, for example, measures designed to preserve open space or build and maintain parks and recreation facilities continued to be very popular. Of the 257 open space measures on the ballot in 2000, almost 78 percent were adopted. According to a Brookings Institution study, the number of open space proposals was a 15 percent increase over 1998. By far the largest number of open space measures were on ballots in the Northeast, and a whopping 97.8 percent of them were approved.[56]

With the passage of so many open space measures in recent years, state and local spending on open space land purchases and conservation easements has increased greatly.[57] According to some observers, the increased spending demonstrates the willingness of communities throughout the nation to finance green infrastructure with locally raised revenues. Voters, it seems, are willing to spend money locally, and to raise taxes, for local needs and to protect places they know, even though they remain averse to federal taxes. A recent poll by Smart Growth America seems to confirm this, as it found that citizens have more confidence in decisions by state and local, rather than federal, officials on land use issues affecting their communities.[58] Moreover, the proliferation of such open space measures shows that towns are learning from one another. Media coverage and enhanced communication through the Internet appear to stimulate similar ballot measures in neighboring jurisdictions.[59]

This trend is particularly apparent in America's suburbs. Of the local ballot measures in 2000, nearly three-quarters were in suburban jurisdictions, leading Myers and Puentes to conclude that the increase in "growth-related measures is primarily—but not exclusively—a suburban phenomenon."[60] In addition, nearly 90 percent of citizen-led ballot initiatives occurred in the suburbs, lending further credence to the notion that political activism is a middle-class phenomenon. Suburban voters in 2000 approved 77 percent of growth proposals, which was similar to the urban approval rate of 80 percent but much higher than the 60 percent approval rate in rural areas. One explanation for the difference is that residents of rural areas are far more likely to own farms and other agricultural land, and are thus apt to be leery of ballot proposals that may restrict their ability to sell or subdivide their land. Suburban and urban voters, on the other hand, have different concerns, such as traffic congestion, pollution, and access to recreational facilities, and thus are more inclined to see value in preserving open space and limiting development. Clearly, then, environmental organizations need to do a better job of addressing the concerns of people outside of metropolitan regions if they are to enhance their success in passing statewide measures.

While open space measures are very popular with voters, those designed to regulate growth are often contentious and thus much less likely to pass on election day. Given the lack of consensus on how to deal effectively with growth, these results are not surprising. There were ninety-four measures aimed at regulating growth on the ballot in 2000, but only 54 percent were approved. Campaigns over growth proposals, especially statewide measures like the one in Colorado, tended to be more expensive and were marked by considerably higher levels of group activity and media coverage.[61] Again, that makes sense because statewide votes affect more voters and can thus be expected to garner more attention than local proposals.

The number and outcomes of ballot proposals also vary by region. In general, all categories of environmentally related measures tended to have the highest approval rates in the Northeast, with more than 90 percent of the measures there passing. In contrast, southern voters gave their approval to 79 percent of proposals, while in the Midwest and West the approval rates were 66.4 percent and 62.4 percent, respectively.[62] Typically, voters in the Northeast also have the most ballot measures to consider. Although the West has lagged behind, since 1996 voters in the region have had more proposals to consider and have been more favorably disposed toward them.[63] Most notably, there has been a significant increase in open space measures proposed and approved in the West, a trend that is likely to continue, given the region's explosive population growth. In 1998, western states were experiencing the nation's highest growth rates, and voters approved the second-highest number of open space measures, with a 67.8 percent approval rate.

That trend continued into 2000, when voters in the West approved forty-four open space measures, a rate of 64.7 percent. The West also leads the rest of the nation in the number of growth-related measures, with 197, or 34.2 percent of the total.

The vast majority of the provisions before voters in recent years have been referenda, while less than 10 percent have been citizen-sponsored initiatives.[64] The high proportion of referenda suggests that state legislators have clearly discovered the importance of environmental issues. Whether state legislatures are responding to citizen demands or trying to preempt interest-group-sponsored initiatives is hard to say, although preemption does seem to have been the intent in certain instances. Citizen-sponsored initiatives tend to be the most controversial of all ballot measures, and thus attract considerable media attention, which legislators do not always cherish. Almost one-third of the statewide growth-related measures in 2000 were citizen initiatives, although not necessarily the product of volunteer grassroots efforts. In fact, many of them were the products of either wealthy individuals or organized groups that relied on private firms to collect the signatures needed to qualify for the ballot.[65] At the very least, the increasing number of environmental ballot measures clearly indicates that environmental issues are on the state and local policy agenda, which suggests that group efforts to shape policy agendas are yielding some dividends.

Finally, how do we explain the popularity of environmental initiatives and referenda? Leaders of environmental groups would attribute the success to the innate popularity of environmental protection among ordinary Americans and, perhaps, to their own campaign efforts on behalf of many of these measures. "The issues are on our side" is a constant refrain among environmentalists, who are convinced that they begin these campaigns with an inherent advantage, albeit one that can be overcome with lots of money and persuasive advertising. In her study of environmental ballot measures, Myers claims that the high success rate reflects "astute crafting of measures and campaigns." This is especially true of some of the statewide measures, which are often drafted and supported by or with the help of professionals working with national organizations like the Natural Resources Defense Council, the Trust for the Public Land, the Nature Conservancy, and the American Farmland Trust. Myers also argues that "successful measures typically are quite specific about purpose, projects, funding, and process—how the measures will be implemented, where, how much they will cost, and what the decision process will be."[66] Indeed, it is the most ambitious proposals, such as Amendment 24 in Colorado or "Big Green" in California, that generate the most controversy and garner the fewest votes on election day. Of course, it is precisely because those measures are so ambitious that they attract such opposition from industry groups, who typically raise large sums of money and fill the airwaves with critical ads. In the end, it is hard to say whether the measures fail because of their broad scope or because of the intensity of the opposition they generate.

Although it is too early to say for certain, there is anecdotal evidence to suggest that state and local groups are taking advantage of the capacity-building programs discussed in Chapter 4. In particular, groups now have access to a broader array of communication skills and tools, which can be very useful in the effort to adopt environmental initiatives. Politics is not static, however, and opponents will certainly learn from previous campaigns and adjust their tactics accordingly. Conservation messages that work at one time may not work in the future, so environmental groups will have to continually adjust their campaign rhetoric and strategies.

ENVIRONMENTAL ADVOCACY IN STATES AND LOCALITIES

Environmental referenda and initiatives tell only part of the nonfederal story, as state legislatures, county commissions, and city councils are increasingly involved in debates over measures designed to limit growth, control sprawl, and address a wide range of other environmental matters.[67] States and communities have always played an important role in environmental policy, but the transfer of policy authority from Washington to the states and localities in the 1990s has certainly heightened their importance and thrust regional, state, and local environmental organizations into the middle of the political action.

In some states, and in some regions, environmental groups are numerous, well organized, and actively involved in trying to influence policymaking. As discussed above, many environmental groups at the state and local level have benefited greatly from the capacity-building efforts of foundations and national groups. Compared to five or ten years ago, many organizations have more money, staff, and members. It is no longer uncommon to find more than one full-time environmental lobbyist walking the halls of state capitols. In addition, technology has facilitated greater coordination and information sharing, which has enabled more groups to monitor state agencies and legislatures. A number of state and local groups have also greatly enhanced their public education efforts, using media events, public forums, publications, websites, and other outreach efforts to spread their message and set the political agenda.

The environmental movement in the Pacific Northwest, for example, has been very active on state and local issues. In addition to its electoral programs, which were discussed earlier, the Washington Environmental Alliance for Voter Education (WEAVE) has been working since 1993 to strengthen the organizational and the campaign skills of local environmental groups. WEAVE offers training in a wide variety of organizational skills, including strategic planning, lobbying, fundraising, media, campaign plans and strategy, list development, and building grassroots movements, as well as membership research, development, and targeting. The group also offers training on legal issues for nonprofits.

Also in the Northwest, the Oregon Conservation Network is a statewide coalition of more than environmental groups that tracks environmental issues in the state legislature. The Oregon Conservation Network, which is coordinated by the

Oregon League of Conservation Voters (OCLV), works to inform conservationists about environmental issues being considered by the state legislature and to improve coordination and information sharing among its member organizations. Like WEAVE, it also offers programs to increase the grassroots advocacy skills of conservationists and conservation groups.[68]

For its part, the Oregon League of Conservation Voters has been working for more than twenty-five years to educate the state's voters about environmental issues. OCLV publishes a legislative scorecard to help voters distinguish real pro-environmental candidates from those who merely claim to be. Like many other state LCV chapters, it has established an affiliated voters education fund, whose mission is "to provide education and training to increase the effective participation of environmentalists in the political arena and to educate legislators, the media and the public about environmental issues."[69] Every year the Oregon League of Conservation Voters Education Fund produces its *Environmental Handbook* for the Oregon Legislature. The *Handbook,* which is available online to maximize is distribution, is designed for elected officials, candidates for public office, and citizens, and claims to offers a detailed overview of environmental issues in Oregon.[70] This publication, and others like it, is clearly an attempt to frame perceptions of environmental issues and highlight their importance to both policy-makers and the public.

Although they are typically overmatched, environmental groups have won some impressive victories at the state level. As an example, in July of 2002 the California Assembly approved a bill requiring cuts in tailpipe emissions of carbon dioxide and other greenhouse gases from cars and light trucks. The bill's passage marked a major victory for the Bluewater Network and the coalition of municipalities and environmental and public health groups that had worked for its passage. Professionals at Bluewater drafted the initial bill in 2000 as part of their global warming campaign. The San Francisco–based group opted to focus its efforts on California because they thought the odds of passage were better than in the U.S. Congress. To aid in their efforts, Bluewater sought assistance from a variety of national environmental groups. Most of them, however, opposed the idea and tried to talk Bluewater out of it, arguing that a state bill stood little chance of success and also risked a backlash against other environmental measures.[71] The group then turned to other state and local groups, including the Coalition for Clean Air Los Angeles, and started "shopping" their idea to state legislators. Eventually, Bluewater found a willing sponsor in Democratic Assemblywoman Fran Pavley, and began to work the halls in Sacramento's legislature. When the bill made it through the first stages of committee votes, several of the national groups changed their minds about its prospects and decided to pitch in.

According to Elisa Lynch, campaign director for Bluewater Network, the coalition's lobbying and public relations strategy had two key parts. First, believing that all politics is local, they stressed global warming's effects on California. This part of the strategy was helped by the fortuitous release of several reports documenting the environmental consequences of climate change for the state. One was a June National Academy of Sciences report confirming the reality of global warming and outlining its potentially serious consequences. At roughly the same time, a University of California–Santa Cruz study linked global warming to serious threats to the state's water supplies and coastal areas.[72] The second piece of the strategy was what Lynch colorfully described as the "man bites dog" aspect—that something unusual has to happen. Legislators had to hear from a wide range of supporters, not just the usual environmental groups, if they were to pay attention to the issue. So Bluewater set out to assemble a broad coalition of groups, including the American Lung Association of California, the California Teacher's Association, the California Nurses Association, and California Professional Firefighters. Crucial support also came from the city councils of Los Angeles, San Francisco, San Diego, and San Jose, the water management authorities in Marin and Santa Clara Counties, and endorsements from most of the state's major newspapers. At the height of the lobbying effort, about a dozen groups were actively involved, with another two dozen groups helping from time to time. Among the national groups that eventually took an interest in the issue, the Natural Resources Defense Council and Environmental Defense contributed in various ways, including financially.

With so many partners, the coalition was a bit disorganized at first, but it eventually settled upon certain "point people" to speak with the media and others to handle organizing. To coordinate strategy and decide upon the "weekly spin," the key coalition partners held weekly conference calls. Each group used its own resources and contacts to move the bill through the legislature. Bluewater Network took the lead in contacting the various city councils and in educating them about the bill. Supporters also did some free talk radio, they talked to newspapers in the hopes of obtaining positive editorials, and undertook a classic grassroots lobbying effort to persuade their members to write letters to their legislators. Because many of the groups, including Bluewater Network, were nonprofits, their fundraising was severely limited by IRS rules. Many groups relied on member dues and special fundraising appeals. The California League of Conservation Voters paid for several ads, including one newspaper ad in Spanish. Other groups enlisted the support of celebrities, including Robert Redford, Barbra Streisand, and Paul Newman. According to Elisa Lynch, "every vote counts," and because some state legislators were influenced by these celebrity appeals, it was an effective tactic.[73] In the days and weeks leading to the final vote, notable politicians such as Senators John Kerry, John McCain, and Joseph Lieberman, as well as former president Bill Clinton, weighed in with letters and phone calls to California legislators.

Under federal law, California is allowed to enact more stringent air pollution rules than those set by the EPA. Because California accounts for one out of every ten vehicles sold in the United States, and because other states can and often do choose to adopt California's standards, the law, if enacted, would almost certainly have national ramifications for the auto industry. As one might expect, then, the auto industry, through the Alliance of Automobile Manufacturers, opposed the measure, and devoted considerable resources to defeating it. Other opponents included the state's Chamber of Commerce, the state association of car dealers, and the United Auto Workers. Together, these groups waged a multimillion-dollar ad blitz against the measure. Some of the television ads featured legendary California car salesman Cal Worthington, who argued that the bill would result in large tax increases and the loss of freedom to choose what to drive. One of the opponents' newspaper ads claimed that the bill would give the California Air Resources Board, which would have the responsibility of making the new rules, "a blank check to decide . . . how many miles you drive." Another ad in the *Sacramento Bee* said, "They're even talking about charging two cents for every mile you drive and 50 cents per gallon more in gas taxes."[74] Shortly after the opponents launched their counterattack, which prompted thousands of calls and emails to legislators' offices, several lawmakers changed their positions.[75]

Commenting upon the lobbying surrounding the bill, John Burton, president pro tem of the California Senate, said, "The enviros weighed in like professionals." His views were echoed by Phillip L. Isenberg, former state assemblyman and a lobbyist representing opponents of the bill, who said, "It was a terrific lobbying campaign. If you create enough commotion in the states to get Bush and Congress to change their minds about mileage standards, that might be a good strategy."[76] Indeed, since Congress failed to approve a similar measure earlier in 2002, taking the fight to the states may be the only real option at this point. Of course, few states are as innovative as California when it comes to environmental programs, and even fewer have the political will to take on the auto industry and its allies. At the same time, though, since a large number of Northeastern states opted in the 1990s to adopt California's emission standards, there may be a critical mass in support of more stringent measures. Taken together, the automobile markets in New York, New Jersey, Massachusetts, and the others do add up.

Interest group activity might change if devolution of environmental policy-making to the states continues. A power structure more characteristic of issue networks may result, in which loose affiliations of interests dominate the policy process. These coalitions would probably have a bottom-up orientation, allowing previously excluded interests to have a say. This is especially true in the West, because of the small size and limited expertise of state legislatures and their staffs, many of which are part-time.[77]

Still, there is a wide range in the capacities of state and local environmental groups, and environmental lobbyists continue to be far outnumbered by those representing corporate interests. Moreover, the environmental movement in certain states and regions is small, unorganized, or on the defensive. Perhaps most importantly, the political environment in which groups operate has also changed dramatically over the years, with other issues occupying more prominent positions on the political agenda.

Consider the South, which has never been the most hospitable terrain for environmental activists. Although there were more than one hundred environmental groups in Alabama, and public opinion polls showed that the state's voters put a high priority on environmental issues, they often went their own way on issues and had no political or lobbying arm. It was not until the winter of 1998 that a number of environmental leaders, with support from several large environmental groups and a handful of "anchor donations" from other sources, decided to establish the Alabama League of Environment Action Voters (AlaLEAVs) to fill that role. The new organization went to work immediately, and its three registered lobbyists, including former congressional candidate Joe Turnham, monitored legislation and pushed several "green" bills during the 1999 legislative session. It recently announced plans to establish a political action committee as well. During its short existence, AlaLEAVs has received a considerable amount of positive publicity in the state, and has generated enthusiasm from others in the environmental community. Dick Bronson, president of a small group named Lake Watch of Lake Martin, said, "This is a great outlet for groups like ours. It gives us a stronger voice. . . . [Turnham] can devote a major part of his funding to actual lobbying. That gives an opportunity to groups like Lake Watch to affect policy."[78] Actual accomplishments are at this point hard to document. The governor did appoint a representative of the group to a fifty-six-member Commission on Environmental Initiatives, but it remains to be seen whether he will have any discernible effect on decisions made by that body. It also remains to be seen what the state's three registered environmental lobbyists can accomplish in a conservative state with a business-friendly state legislature.

There is also the example of the mountain West, which has a large and very active environmental movement but whose politics have become much more conservative in recent decades. Thirty years ago, for example, there was one professional full-time environmental activist working in the state of Montana. Today, there are several hundred, employed by the approximately thirty-five conservation groups in the state. Public opinion polls show that Montana residents are very supportive of environmental protection, and yet Montana's environmental groups now have far less clout in the state, which has turned its back on many of the programs enacted in the earlier era. One hotly contested explanation for this puzzling turn of events places the blame squarely on environmentalists themselves. According to this view, too many conservation groups today are interested only in pursuing their own narrow agendas and have not done enough to create a broader, more potent political coalition. In the 1970s, in contrast, environmentalists were part of a larger citizen movement that included labor unions, cattle ranchers, grain farmers, and groups representing women, senior citizens, Native Americans, and the poor.[79]

There are, of course, alternative explanations for Montana's retreat from environmental protection, including the long economic decline that has ravaged the region's logging, ranching, and mining sectors. The state's stagnant economy has

provided fertile ground for the antigovernment attacks of corporate and conservative interests, who have blamed much of the decline on overly strict environmental protections. Whatever the explanation, however, the reality is that the state's
environmental movement does not have as much influence as it did in the 1970s,
though one could say the same thing about the national environmental movement.
For better or worse, the 1970s was a high-water mark for congressional action on
environmental legislation. Congress today is clearly much less receptive to new
environmental initiatives.

Although empirical data is lacking, it may be the case that environmental
groups have more influence with legislators from competitive two-party states and
districts, because they face pressure from constituents to deliver on popular issues,
such as the environment.[80] Compared to the early 1970s, when the environment
first reached the political agenda, state governments have greater financial and
regulatory capacity. Furthermore, in ranking the environmental "performance" of
states, several studies have suggested that states with high levels of wealth and
economic activity perform better, and many of these states have a vibrant environmental community that is active in seeking to influence state legislatures.[81]

COLLABORATIVE CONSERVATION: A NEW PARADIGM?

Much has been written in recent years about the emergence of cooperative, place-
based conservation movements. Although different people call it different things,
there is general agreement that it developed in the late 1980s and early 1990s and
has become increasingly popular. There is also general agreement on the defining
traits of this new movement, which typically involves efforts by an inclusive assortment of "stakeholders" to seek common ground on how to manage particular
local ecosystems. Stakeholders are generally defined as anyone with an interest in
the issue, and usually includes local environmentalists, ranchers, loggers, miners,
state and federal agencies, and others from the affected community or region.
These collaborative efforts have frequently been described as "pragmatic," "decentralized," "results-oriented," "integrated," and "consensual." To cite but one
example, Edward Weber says that the new movement's defining elements are "its
focus on local community as the primary management unit, its definition of community as comprising those within a specific ecologically defined geographical
space, its location in rural economies dependent on nature's bounty, the direct involvement of citizens as partners in the policy process, and the sharing of authority among public and private participants."[82]

In fact, Weber argues that the emergence of so many of what he calls grassroots ecosystem management (GREM) efforts across the United States constitutes
"a new environmental movement that challenges the fundamental premises of existing natural resource and public lands institutions." He goes on to suggest that
GREM is "qualitatively different" from prior environmental movements and

offers a "fundamentally different approach . . . which relies on decentralization, collaboration, citizen participation, and a holistic worldview that seeks to simultaneously promote environment, economy, and community." Weber acknowledges that not all aspects of the collaborative approach are new, calling it a "grand synthesis" that "borrows from past movements, adds new ideas and approaches to environmental management, and transforms the whole into a distinctive new movement worthy of study."[83] Advocates argue that the new approach developed in response to deep dissatisfactions with prevailing environmental decisionmaking procedures, which were widely perceived to be ineffective, excessively adversarial, and inflexible. More specifically, existing processes were criticized for their reliance on top-down, command and control regulation, for rigid decisionmaking arrangements that left industry and government with very little flexibility, and for neglecting sustainable development concerns.[84]

In contrast, supporters of the more decentralized and collaborative community-based efforts believe that it produces more creative, flexible and more popular long-term solutions than the one-size-fits-all approach that now dominates. Some of these results are attributed to the notion that local stakeholder participants have a better understanding of local conditions and will work with one another to produce "win-win" solutions.[85] Indeed, community-based efforts are said to reject traditional "conflict style" politics and to encourage a new style of decisionmaking, one that is more cooperative, deliberative, and consensual, as stakeholders search for common ground. Rather than view other participants as opponents to be defeated, stakeholders instead work with rather than against each other.[86] In the process of working together, naked self-interest will be transformed into enlightened self-interest.[87] What matters most is the long-term well-being of the community. Because citizens are involved at every stage of the process, from agenda setting through monitoring and enforcement, community-based processes offer a compelling vision of self-government.

Indeed, Weber notes that from the grassroots perspective, the sense of "place" becomes a catalyst for self-governance. It mobilizes citizens to care enough to participate in the act of "governing" their place by reminding community members of what they share in common, which is a reliance on the natural landscape. "As a result," writes Weber, "the movement takes an inclusive, pluralistic approach grounded in local participation. Meetings are open to all (even to those who live outside a given "place"), decisions are made collectively, consensus is emphasized," and "leadership and responsibility are shared equally among participants."[88] All stakeholders are equal in this view, with business leaders or government officials enjoying no special privilege or status. Everyone has input, at all phases, and the process continues until agreements are reached. According to Daniel Kemmis, "This cooperative or collaborative phenomenon has spread so fast because people who encounter it in one situation like both the results and the way the experience feels to them, and they take the first opportunity to replicate it in other settings."[89]

According to some accounts, more than two hundred rural communities, mostly in the West, have experimented with collaborative grassroots ecosystem management processes.[90] The first collaborative agreements developed around watershed protection and water management problems and then spread to other issues. Today, as a result, there are a large number of similar efforts in other regions of the country, dealing with a wide range of environmental issues.[91] The Henry's Fork Watershed Council in Idaho, the Malpai Borderlands Group in New Mexico and Arizona, the Quincy Library Group in Northern California, and the Applegate Partnership in southern Oregon are among the most commonly cited examples of community-based projects. Many of these efforts have been undertaken with financial support from foundations and private donors, including the Ford Foundation, the Bullitt Foundation, and the Northwest Area Foundation.[92] The Environmental Protection Agency has also been encouraging community level activities through its Sustainable Development Challenge Grant Program, a component of its Community-Based Environmental Protection program (CBEP). According to EPA rules, "CBEP requires an open, inclusive decision-making process and emphasizes a shared responsibility among all stakeholders for implementing all decisions."[93]

In many of these collaborative projects environmental organizations have been actively involved in implementing and monitoring programs, including habitat restoration and wildlife censuses. In their study of natural resource policymaking in the states, Mutter, Virden, and Cayer suggest that the move to devolve authority to the states may lead environmental groups to move beyond their traditional roles in agenda setting and policy development. Instead, national groups might shift resources to their state chapters and begin to play a larger role as policy implementers or coproducers.[94]

One current example of this is provided by a small Seattle-based group called Long Live the Kings, which is working to restore wild salmon stocks in the Puget Sound area. The group focuses on reforming the state's nearly one hundred hatcheries, the largest concentration in the world. Hatcheries are controversial because many believe they spread disease and weaken the genetic strength of wild salmon. Long Live the Kings works with scientists, tribal leaders, and representatives from federal and state agencies to find a middle ground that has room for both hatcheries and wild salmon. According to Barbara Cairns, the group's director, "We wanted to escape the religious debate of whether hatcheries are good or evil. With the [human] population expected to double in the next twenty-five years, we recognize that hatcheries will be here. As desperate pragmatists, we wanted to ask a different question—could we use hatcheries to recover natural populations?"[95]

More specifically, Long Live the Kings leads a multiagency effort to improve the region's hatcheries. The goal is to reduce the impact of hatchery fish on wild salmon runs, while creating more efficient and cost-effective hatcheries. Long Live the Kings also seeks to make hatchery fish as much like the wild fish as possible. The group itself manages three hatcheries and has spent more than a decade researching how hatchery fish can help wild salmon stocks recover. Since 2000,

Long Live the Kings has provided a panel of nine independent scientists with information on the history and goal of each hatchery, as well as the status of the stocks and habitat in each. The scientists then evaluate the hatchery to see if it meets its goals without jeopardizing wild salmon recovery. The group then works with the hatchery managers to discuss how to implement the scientific recommendations. In describing the group's approach, Cairns says, "We let the scientists be scientists and the managers be managers. We create crosswalks between the two." To date, the project has worked on forty-six of the region's hatcheries.[96]

As is often the case with collaborative projects, though, observers disagree on its achievements. Rowan Gould, deputy assistant director for fisheries in the U.S. Fish and Wildlife Service, says "I think what they're doing is absolutely the right way to do business." On the other hand, a number of fish biologists and environmental activists are more skeptical and suggest that the reforms are merely window-dressing for an unacceptable status quo, which allows overfishing and does little to restore habitat. In the words of Joe Whitworth, executive director of Oregon Trout, "We're just putting a smiley face on what we want to do [which is use hatcheries], the way we've always done it." By most accounts, full-scale implementation of the hatchery experiment will require considerable money. To date, most of the funding for hatchery reform has come from the federal government, but more will be needed and it is unclear if the states and tribal governments will come through.[97]

Although collaborative processes are increasingly common, not everybody embraces their use. Critics of the emerging approach, including a number of national environmental groups, worry that the emphasis on "local involvement" is really shorthand for "local control," which in much of the West means continued dominance by extractive interests and traditional resource users. Concerns abound about unequal representation, in which environmental interests would be far outnumbered by industry and prodevelopment forces. Critics also suggest that collaborative processes invite co-optation of local environmentalists and that peer pressure to reach agreements will lead them to give in so as not to be called obstructionists.[98] Perhaps the most important concern, though, is that "successful local partnerships may be used in the future to argue that national environmental laws should be curtailed or eliminated."[99]

This view was forcefully expressed by Michael McCloskey, then chairman of the Sierra Club, in a 1995 memo to the Club's board of directors. In the memo, which was subsequently published in the *High Country News,* McCloskey refers to the increasingly popular collaborative approach as a "new dogma."[100] In explaining why national groups like the Sierra Club shun the partnerships, he explained, "Industry thinks its odds are better in these forums. It is ready to train its experts in mastering this process. It believes it can dominate them over time and relieve itself of the burden of tough national rules." He also argues that shifts in decisionmaking venues usually have policy consequences, and worries that the move to local venues would have the effect "of transferring influence to the very communities where we are least organized and potent." The membership of many of the national groups, after all, is heavily urban and coastal, and would not likely be recognized as legitimate "stakeholders" in the largely rural communities where collaborative experiments are taking place. Moreover, because collaborative procedures tend to be time intensive, paid industry participants could wear down local activists, who might not be able to devote the time and attention needed to defend environmental goals. McCloskey also notes that even in places where local environmentalists exist, "they are not always equipped to play competitively with industry professionals. There may be no parity in experience, training, skills, or financial resources; parity is important both during negotiations and in follow-on phases on watchdogging agreements."[101] David Pellow seconds this view, arguing that local environmental activists, unlike industry participants, frequently need help in interpreting legal, scientific, and technical information. He concludes that although collaborative decisionmaking in environmental policy "hinges strongly upon the availability of technical assistance for grass-roots organizations," such assistance is often unavailable.[102]

In response to these concerns and criticisms, supporters of collaborative processes correctly note that well-organized political and economic interests can dominate decisionmaking at the national level as well as the local. From their perspective, that is all the more reason for measures that invite broad participation and citizen oversight at all levels in order to safeguard the public interest.[103] In an open letter to the environmental community in 1996, representatives of the Applegate Partnership wrote, "We feel that the danger is not in going back, but failing to go forward. One of the unfortunate consequences of the preoccupation with the risks of partnerships is that the national groups have missed an enormous opportunity for improving stewardship on both public and private land. A combination of national environmental policy and local oversight and implementation can work to improve lawful resource use on all lands."[104]

There can be no question that community-based collaborative processes have been widely embraced, and that there is considerable enthusiasm for them, especially among academics studying the matter. What is less clear is whether the enthusiasm is warranted. Given that many of the partnerships are still in their infancy, even supporters like Dan Kemmis acknowledge that "it is still too early to quantify results and present conclusive evidence" about their effectiveness.[105] There is, as Kemmis notes, plenty of anecdotal evidence suggesting success, but in the context of issues like forest and rangeland health or endangered species preservation, some systematic, long-term studies would be desirable. Policies that look successful today may prove not to be in twenty or thirty years.

For example, some of the enthusiasm for the Applegate Partnership dimmed after a timber industry lawsuit led the Forest Service, one of the central stakeholders, to withdraw from subsequent meetings.[106] Similarly, the much-touted Comprehensive Everglades Restoration Plan, initiated during the Clinton administration, shows signs of unraveling amid an internal dispute among conservation groups. Although representatives of the National Audubon Society continue to defend the plan, others believe it to be fatally flawed. Citing the plan's shortcomings, Alan Farago, a Sierra Club representative from southern Florida, said, "Audubon sold out—completely, unnecessarily, irresponsibly." Critics claim that Audubon is willing to tolerate a bad plan in order to maintain its seat "at a stacked negotiating table." In response, Audubon leaders say they have a better chance of fixing the plan from the inside than by criticizing other participants.[107] Regardless of who is correct in this particular case, the reality is that it is often easier to talk about "inclusiveness," "collaboration," and "win-win" solutions than to accomplish them.

In another instance, the Forest Service's efforts to establish a collaborative process to develop a management plan for winter use in Wyoming's Medicine Bow National Forest fell apart almost immediately. In the summer of 2001, an assortment of local business owners, snowmobilers, environmentalists, and cross-country skiers began work on the plan, but by fall, the two environmental stakeholders had left the group. According to William L. Baker, a University of Wyoming professor and one of the environmental stakeholders, the Forest Service established the process without giving the stakeholders an opportunity to comment upon either the makeup or balance of the group, or on the group's facilitator.[108] Problems were evident at the very first meeting, when the group decided not to address environmental concerns, notably the impact of increased snowmobile traffic on ptarmigan habitat. Instead, the group would limit its discussion to resolving conflicts between snowmobilers and cross-country skiers. After the two environmentalists complained, environmental issues were added to the agenda for the next meeting. The facilitator, however, refused to include "protection of the environment" as a phrase in the group's overall mission statement, leading the environmental stakeholders to call for her replacement. The Forest Service refused that request, as well as one for additional environmental representation in the group. Approximately a dozen of the thirty stakeholders were presumed to favor increased snowmobile access to the forest. One of the sponsors of the collaborative process, the University of Wyoming's Institute for Environment and Natural Resources, tried unsuccessfully to convince the Forest Service to replace the facilitator with someone who was acceptable to all of the stakeholders.[109] These events led one of the activists, Eric Bonds of Biodiversity Associates, to say, "They never really attempted to evaluate the environmental impacts of snowmobiles. The Forest Service continues to be an ostrich with its head in the sand and ignore these contentious issues that have polarized this community." In response, a Forest Service representative said that the group "decided not take on bigger issues; they were trying to find successes."[110] As this case suggests, the problem is not with collaboration itself, but in creating a truly inclusive and collaborative effort. With passions running high, as they often do on environmental issues, one should not minimize the difficulties inherent in getting collaborative efforts off the ground.

Context also matters. Many of the collaborative groups were established during the Clinton administration, which many accused of embracing a top-down approach to regulation. Today, however, logging, mining, ranching, and developers may have less incentive to devote time and resources to collaborative efforts now that they have a more sympathetic White House to negotiate with. Given the Bush administration's statements and actions on the environment, those interests may believe that they can get a better deal through administrative action or the federal courts. This is especially true given the Bush administration's penchant for not defending Clinton-era environmental rules in court. At a press conference called to highlight this trend, Earthjustice executive director Vawter Parker said, "There is a disturbing pattern where industry sues to overturn environmental regulations and the Justice Department puts up only the feeblest of defenses and refuses to appeal adverse rulings." Parker added, "The judicial process in our country depends on two parties making the strongest case [they] can. When the administration purposely makes a weak argument, it subverts the entire democratic process."[111] As evidence of this subversion, Parker cited the Bush administration's refusal to defend several environmental rules that had been issued in the waning days of the Clinton White House, including the Forest Service's rule that would have prohibited road building in 58.5 million acres of national forest. The Bush administration also refused to defend a Park Service rule that proposed banning snowmobiles in Yellowstone National Park. The snowmobile industry promptly sued to block the rule, but instead of defending it, the Bush administration decided to negotiate with the industry and work on devising a new plan. In the end, the Park Service reversed its earlier decision and opted to allowed snowmobiles into Yellowstone.[112]

It is too early to judge the effects of recent rulings by the federal courts on collaborative decisionmaking efforts. Yet, if the reaction to a September 2001 federal district court ruling on protecting wild salmon habitat is any indication, the future does not bode well. In that case, District Judge Michael R. Hogan overturned a Fish and Wildlife Service decision that had protected Oregon wild coho salmon under the Endangered Species Act. Hogan's decision effectively lifted prohibitions on logging and road building in the salmon's habitat. Property rights groups throughout the Northwest promptly announced plans for additional lawsuits designed to remove protection for salmon and steelhead from a number of the region's other river basins.[113] These court rulings, coupled with the Bush administration's clear signal that it will not defend environmental rules, threaten to unravel many collaborative processes in the region. Why, after all, would property rights groups, miners, or timber companies negotiate with environmentalists when the courts and the White House have been so helpful? Under these circumstances, even conservation-minded business owners, farmers, and ranchers may be unwilling to devote time and money to community-based restoration projects. Who, then, would be left for environmentalists to collaborate with?

CONCLUSION

Many environmental organizations at the regional, state, and local levels have become more capable in recent years. Thanks to considerable support and encouragement from foundations and several of the national groups, they now have more money, staff, and expertise. Today, an increasing number of state groups are mimicking the organizational structure of the largest national groups by establishing affiliated 501(c)(3) voter education arms and political action committees. Furthermore, in many locations environmentalists have formed effective statewide coalitions to fight for their policy concerns. Consequently, their ability to participate in elections and policymaking has been greatly enhanced, as have their tools for issue definition and agenda setting.

After two decades of intermittent and largely ineffective efforts, a growing number of state and local groups are now focusing on elections. There are now more groups active in more states, and many conduct sophisticated campaigns. As a result, electoral activity by these groups promises to be sustained, better funded, and more professional than in prior years. Despite these gains, however, environmental groups will need to raise much more money and participate in more campaigns than they have to date. They will also have to follow through on plans to recruit and train candidates for local offices as a prelude to campaigns for higher office. Moreover, environmental groups will need to work hard to push environmental issues first onto the campaign agenda, and ultimately onto the policy agenda. This will undoubtedly require considerable investments of money and time. Money will buy radio, television, and newspaper ads, but, as at the national level, the so-called "air war" will be insufficient. Environmentalists will also need to do the hard work of community organizing and voter outreach. An effective "ground war" is needed to educate, target, and mobilize voters, and get them to the polls. With the lower turnouts that are so common in state and local elections, the ability to turn out voters with a solid ground campaign is vitally important.

The recent explosion in electoral work by groups and the much-heralded rise of so many grassroots collaborative decisionmaking ventures illustrate that environmentalists across the nation are searching for new answers. There is clearly much going on today at the subnational level, but many of the developments are so recent that it is too early to tell if they will succeed. It may be that the trends discussed here will falter and fade, and that ten years from now others will be discussing some new fad. It could also be the case, though, that these trends will continue to gather momentum. With elections, for example, many of the recently established state LCV groups have participated in only one or two election cycles. There is very little evidence, at this point, to support any sort of judgment as to their effectiveness. Within the next two election cycles, however, we should have more examples to determine if the efforts have been worthwhile. Similarly, few if any of the collaborative community-based projects have been in existence long enough to say with any certainty that they have produced lasting policy change. When it comes to managing rivers, forests, and other complex ecosystems, it can take decades or longer to gauge success or failure. In the end, it is one thing to say that collaborative processes are more likely to result in an agreement; it is another thing entirely to say that the agreement resulted in an effective environmental policy.

7
Conclusion

Natural gas is hemispheric. I like to call it hemispheric in nature because it is a product that we can find in our neighborhoods.
—George W. Bush, December 20, 2000

In November of 2001, the Environmental Working Group, a small Washington-based organization of about twenty researchers, computer experts, and writers posted the names of the recipients of federal farm subsidies on its website. What happened next was truly profound. The website, which showed that nearly 60 percent of subsidies went to the largest 10 percent of farms, quickly captured the attention of farmers, journalists, and lawmakers, and received thirty million hits in the next five months. In the process, the information posted on the website helped transform the relatively obscure annual debate over farm subsidies into a headline-grabbing controversy about the fairness of corporate handouts and the survival of the family farm. In an effort to reverse years of farm policy, the Senate voted sixty-six to thirty-one to cap annual subsidies at $275,000 per farm, a 40 percent cut from previous levels. In the words of Ken Cook, the Environmental Working Group's director, "We figured that the power of information alone would do more than we could accomplish lobbying or writing elaborate reports. The data show what farmers already knew—the big farms are getting bigger and driving out the smaller farms, thanks to big government subsidies."[1]

That such a small group could play such a profound role in shaping a public policy debate is truly impressive. Perhaps even more impressive, though, is that the farm subsidy database was its first major project. The group, which was established only in 1993, worked on the project for almost six years; it took four years to obtain the data from the government and two years to compile and post it on the website. The group's interest in the subsidy program stemmed from the belief that it encouraged large, corporate-owned farms to overplant in order to receive even larger subsidies. Overplanting, in turn, entailed heavy use of fertilizers and pesticides, and contributed significantly to agricultural runoff and groundwater contamination. It also resulted in crop surpluses, which lowered prices and squeezed many smaller farmers, who could not pay their bills.[2]

In the end, though, the House-Senate conference committee backed away from the proposed changes, leaving the subsidy program largely intact. Despite pushing the issue onto the agenda and attracting a great deal of attention to itself

196

in the process, the Environmental Working Group was unable to secure the policy changes they sought. Because the farm bill comes up for renewal on a regular basis, it is too early to determine if the 2002 defeat was the beginning or end of the story. It is tempting to conclude that the farm bill is yet another example of big business overpowering environmental interests in the halls of Congress. It would not be the first time, nor will it be the last. At the same time, though, it is important to remember that agenda building is a long-term process. When it comes to policy change in the United States, there are very few overnight sensations. It may well be that this defeat was merely a momentary setback, and that it paved the way for Congress to enact more dramatic change in the years ahead.

It is not too early to determine, though, that the case of the farm bill and the Environmental Working Group illustrates much of the promise and disappointment that mark modern environmental activism. Who, after all, had ever heard of the group before these developments? That such a small group, with virtually no record of accomplishment, could use modern technology and savvy communications strategies to push an obscure issue onto the agenda and come so close to victory on its first major campaign should offer great hope to environmental activists. And yet, the bottom line is that all of the skillful application of technology, all of the positive publicity, and the "power of information" were not enough to carry the day. Although issue definition and agenda setting are important parts of the policy process, they are not the only parts. It is one thing to get your issue talked about, but it is another thing to get your policies adopted and faithfully implemented. Environmental groups have clearly come a long way in the past two decades. Just as clearly, they still have a long way to go.

AGENDA SETTING

As we have seen, environmental groups are devoting significant attention and resources to issue definition and agenda setting. Their task is complicated by intense competition from other interests seeking to define issues in different, often contradictory ways. Furthermore, those interests are also paying more attention to issue definition, and they typically have more money and other valuable resources at their disposal. In recent congressional debates over automobile fuel efficiency standards, for example, environmental arguments about greater efficiency standards were effectively countered by the auto industry's claims that such standards would come at the expense of jobs, individual choice, and personal safety. These claims were effective because they tapped into deeply held American values such as individualism, support for free markets, and distrust of government. The auto industry and its allies were also helped by their army of professional lobbyists and by years of campaign contributions to members of Congress.

William Browne has argued that the selection of issues is often crucial to successful lobbying, because marketable issues can make an interest successful. As an example, Browne notes that environmentalists in the 1960s and early 1970s skillfully tied their policy concerns to existing and often mythic public beliefs or symbols, such as the idea of responsible stewardship and related American myths about the frontier and agrarian countryside. Through an effective long-term strategy of public education that targeted teachers and schoolchildren, environmental interests were slowly able to convert these public myths into more specific public support for environmental programs. Groups provided schools with free educational materials and helped educate teachers about environmental problems. Gradually, knowledge and concern about environmental issues moved from the elementary schools to secondary schools, then to parents, colleges, and eventually to the general public. Policymakers then found it hard to keep the issue off the agenda. In Browne's opinion, environmentalists also succeeded because they identified themselves as outsiders in order to win sympathy from the public and the media, while labeling their opponents as villains.[3]

Environmental groups today continue to tell the same sorts of stories and invoke many of the same symbols outlined by Browne.[4] Sometimes they are successful, but sometimes they are not. Stories of environmental decline, with many of the same set of heroes and villains, are still commonplace. References to "corporate polluters" are standard fare, as are appeals to deeply held American beliefs about the special importance of wild places and the threats facing cuddly animals—so called "charismatic megafauna." In the never ending debates over logging on public lands, the villains are always greedy corporations seeking to extract every last penny from the public domain, leaving forests and forest communities devastated in their wake. The reason these appeals are often so effective is that they tap into the long-standing American distrust of "big business." This distrust, which was manifest in the 1960s and 1970s before receding in the deregulatory mania that dominated the following two decades, may reemerge in the aftermath of the recent corporate scandals involving Enron, Harken Energy, Haliburton, Worldcom, and others. If that happens, environmentalists should find more fertile ground for their critique of society and for their policy recommendations. There are no signs yet of that happening—the issue did not resonate with voters in the 2002 midterm elections and vulnerable Republican candidates escaped unscathed.

In describing how policy issues tend to rise and fall on the agenda in a regular pattern or cycle, Anthony Downs notes that the environment had certain traits that seemed to ensure its periodic reemergence. First, like poverty, racism, and crime, the environment was an issue that affected a numerical minority, albeit a substantial one. Over time, as public understanding of the scope and severity of environmental problems has increased, and as new problems have been discovered, more people have come to believe that one environmental issue or another personally affects them. Second, the suffering caused by the problem is attributable to social arrangements that provide significant benefits to much of the population.[5] Air pollution, for example, is in large part a consequence of Americans' love affair with the car. In the same way, the trash problem can be traced to our high-consumption lifestyle. In both cases, the search for solutions is complicated because most of them seem to require major changes in things we need and/or cherish.

Echoing Downs, Kirkpatrick Sale argues that environmentalism has been vulnerable because "it sought protection for long-term non-market values that were inevitably in conflict with short-term self-interests," and because "it required sustained support for collective action, rather than individual choice, to achieve its goals."[6] Sale is undoubtedly correct, and the antigovernment, deregulatory ethos that marked much of the last two decades has complicated matters even further. It has been exceedingly difficult to muster support for collective action of any sort, as the fight to defend Social Security from the privatization movement clearly illustrates. Proponents of collective action have had to swim upstream against a very powerful tide, and, frankly, they have not gotten very far at all. Environmentalists, who have depended on governmental action for nearly three decades, are no exception to this general rule. Knowing that they have plenty of company is little solace.

MONEY AND COMMUNICATION

The dilemma, of course, is that with more interests seeking to define problems and push their own issues onto the agenda, policymakers, the media, and the public are deluged with a flood of communications from organized groups. On any given day in Washington, and in state capitals throughout the land, dozens of interest groups hold press conferences, issue news releases, and engage in other means of issue framing. But as more groups try to define issues and capture the public's attention, it becomes more difficult for any one group to break through the clutter and get its message heard.[7]

In fact, some contend that the changes in contemporary interest group lobbying have made it easier for wealthier interests to dominate political communication on both the electoral and policymaking sides of American politics. Increasingly, argue Cigler and Loomis, politics is an offshoot of marketing, and richer groups develop and market their ideas more effectively than others.[8] Today, for example, it is not uncommon for interest groups to commission public opinion polls in order to learn about public values and beliefs. Using focus groups and other techniques, groups can then experiment with messages that seek to link those values to their preferred policy goals. They can even develop different messages for different target audiences. Other, less privileged interests may have to muddle through in their efforts to develop persuasive messages.

Well-funded groups may also be advantaged in the new environment because they can communicate more often and in more powerful ways. West and Loomis, for example, contend that groups with resources can afford to repeat their stories, and they can use a variety of vehicles, such as direct mail, radio and television advertising, or the Internet, to deliver them to the public. More and more, interest groups that can afford it conduct large-scale public education, issue advocacy, and grassroots campaigns to advance their positions in policy debates. Policy information, in short, is increasingly shaped by expensive campaigns, with groups competing to sell their versions of public policy problems and solutions. And today, the ability to deliver a message to a broad audience has become increasingly dependent on the ability to pay for that delivery. Only a fraction of the interest group universe, for example, can afford to air televised issue ads, and not every interest can afford to hire professional lobbyists, public relations firms, or media consultants. These trends, argue West and Loomis, have made the voices of the disadvantaged and unorganized even less a part of the policy debate.[9]

Why does any of this matter? That groups with greater resources can market their ideas more effectively and thus crowd out the voices of other, less privileged interests hardly seems compatible with notions of pluralism or representative democracy.[10] Government of, by, and for the people implies a more inclusive vision of citizen participation than does the "cash and carry" model of government described above. The notion that the rich and privileged have more influence than others should not come as a great surprise—but if that influence gap is growing wider today, we may wish to consider our options. This is especially so because prevailing federal election laws allow individuals and groups to spend unlimited amounts in independent expenditure and issue advocacy campaigns, and because that spending has been so difficult to track. Such groups have provided an ideal vehicle for those seeking to influence elections while leaving no trace of their actions, and the outcome is hardly consistent with notions of representative democracy. How can citizens make informed decisions when they do not know who is paying for the ads and messages coming into their homes?[11]

The potential problems are magnified by the increasingly inequitable distribution of wealth and income in the United States. If one assumes that economic wealth somehow translates into political power, then the thirty-year trend of rising economic inequality suggests that the old pluralist claim that all legitimate interests can get heard at some point in the decisionmaking process becomes even more unrealistic. The reality is that if politics is increasingly dependent on money, which is not distributed equally throughout society, then the interests of business and wealthy individuals will continue to be overrepresented in politics.

ENVIRONMENTAL SPENDING IN PERSPECTIVE

Although political spending by environmental groups reached unprecedented levels in recent years, it is merely a drop in the ocean of money that floods federal campaigns. To put things in perspective, candidates for the U.S. Congress spent over $1 billion in 2000, a figure that does not include the hundreds of millions of dollars in independent expenditures and issue advocacy by parties and groups.[12] Assuming that overall spending by environmental groups amounted to $20 million, it would still be less than 1 percent of the total spent by congressional candidates, hardly enough to sway many elections.

With respect to direct contributions from PACs, the picture is even more telling. According to the Federal Election Commission, financial activity by political action committees increased during recent election cycles. PACs spent $579.4 million in the 2000 elections, an increase of 23 percent from the previous cycle. For the same period, PACs contributed $259.8 million to federal candidates, a 17 percent increase from the previous cycle.[13] That year, environmental PACs gave just $546,000 to candidates, which is less than one-half of one percent of all PAC direct contributions.

As is well documented, business interests are by far the biggest source of campaign money. Including contributions to candidates and soft money contributions to the political parties, business contributions swamp those from environmental groups.[14] In fact, in the three years leading up to the 1996 elections, businesses and PACs intent on rolling back environmental regulations contributed more to congressional campaigns than any other cluster of interest groups.[15] Going back to the 1990 election cycle, contributions from the energy and natural resources sector alone totaled more than $225 million. In that same period, electric utilities gave almost $55 million, mining firms contributed $19 million, the forestry sector gave $26.5 million, and contributions from the chemical sector amounted to $38 million. In comparison, environmental PACs contributed just $7.6 million, ranking seventy-fifth out of eighty contributor groups tracked by the Center for Responsive Politics.[16] Although environmental groups have been raising and spending record amounts, they cannot match the torrent of cash flowing from corporate coffers.

The corporate money appears to have been well spent, as business lobbyists enjoy unparalleled access to congressional decisionmakers. In the energy field, for example, studies suggest that top contributors to Republican candidates in the 2000 elections were rewarded for their support in the form of numerous legislative and administrative actions. In May of 2000, the Bush administration included in its energy plan a proposal from the Southern Company for a reconsideration of the Clean Air Act's new source review program, something the firm had long sought.[17] The energy plan also included a number of giveaways sought by the nuclear industry, which had contributed nearly $9 million to members of Congress. Among them were an extension of the Price-Anderson Act, which limited industry liability in the event of a reactor accident, a reversal of a prohibition on the reprocessing of spent nuclear fuel, and a resolution of the controversy over a high-level nuclear waste repository at Yucca Mountain, Nevada.[18] Moreover, in the 104th Congress, it was widely reported that industry lobbyists actually wrote the Republican bill revising the Clean Water Act, a bill dubbed the "Dirty Water" bill by critics. In a 1997 study investigating the link between campaign contributions and Senate voting records, the Sierra Club and the Environmental Working Group examined votes on regulatory reform. According to the study, more than four hundred PACs associated with an industry coalition pushing for regulatory relief contributed more than $26 million between January 1991 and November 1996, about two-thirds of which went to senators who cast votes in favor of regulatory relief legislation. Senators who voted for regulatory relief in the 104th Congress received an average of two and one-half times the industry PAC contributions that senators who opposed the bills received.[19] Said Carl Pope, executive director of the Sierra Club, "As long as money is allowed to talk in the form of millions of dollars in campaign contributions, the saga of the 104th Congress will be told over and over again."[20]

Although environmental groups have limited financial resources, especially compared to their corporate foes, their contributions may still affect certain campaigns. First, by concentrating their resources on specific races, environmental groups may be able to tip the balance in very close elections. This was the case in Oregon's special Senate election in 1996, and in several others in 1998 and 2000. And as environmental groups begin to participate more often in primaries and in elections for state and local office, where turnout is typically lower, their impact may grow.

Certainly, that was not the case in the 2002 midterm elections, which yielded the worst showing for environmental groups, and their candidates, in a decade. Despite the millions spent on its Dirty Dozen races, candidates supported by the League of Conservation Voters won only five of the contests. The Sierra Club was also disappointed with the results of its campaigns. There are several reasons that the group's efforts were not as effective as in earlier years. First, many of the candidates targeted by the groups tried to blunt the effectiveness of the issue by portraying themselves as friendly to the environment. As noted earlier, the environment is now a consensual issue, so the vast majority of candidates now claim to be "green" in their campaign materials. Apparently, the LCV and the Sierra Club, and the candidates they supported, could not educate voters as to the reality of those claims. Secondly, other issues, such as the economy, terrorism, and a possible war with Iraq were clearly more important to voters. Third, and perhaps most importantly, Republican candidates benefited from an unprecedented get-out-the-vote effort waged on their behalf by the party and by affiliated organizations. The unexpected turnout more than offset the efforts by Democrats and progressive groups, with predictable results. Finally, Republican candidates also had a tremendous financial advantage over their Democratic counterparts. The Republican Party outspent the Democratic Party by a two-to-one margin.

THE PROMISE AND PERIL OF INDEPENDENT EXPENDITURES AND ISSUE ADVOCACY

The advent of widespread independent expenditures and issue advocacy by environmental and other groups raises many important questions. Never before have so many interest groups become so involved in so many races. This involvement has created longer, more expensive, and more confusing campaigns in which the candidates themselves now worry about controlling the agenda. Moreover, by injecting national issues into congressional and state campaigns, interest groups may transform the nature of those races. House contests traditionally have been local in focus, for example, but the use of independent expenditures and issue advocacy by interest groups has the potential to "nationalize" House campaigns, resulting in races across the county being contested on the same set of issues.[21] In the case of the League of Conservation Voters' Dirty Dozen independent expenditure campaigns since 1996, the group's ads have highlighted the same two issues nationwide, although each ad was tailored to emphasize the issue's local implications.

Some worry that with the airwaves full of group advertisements about national issues such as abortion, term limits, and gun control, there may be little room for discussions of local matters. Indeed, many worry that the new forms of political spending may nationalize local elections and, in the process, transform them into "ideological battlegrounds for forces much bigger than individual candidates."[22] For example, members of the AFL-CIO voted a special assessment on themselves in 1996 in order to launch a well-publicized $35 million issue advocacy campaign. The union insisted that its motives were legislative, not electoral, and that it wanted to change public opinion on key issues rather than sway the outcome of particular elections. The unions sent organizers into 102 House districts and spent a total of $25 million advertising in an estimated 44 districts. One result of the issue campaign was to force candidates to take a position on the minimum wage, which was featured prominently in many of the ads. Although Congress ultimately approved an increase in the minimum wage, the larger point is that the union was able to make the minimum wage an issue in many congressional campaigns across the nation.[23]

One could make a case, of course, that nationalizing congressional campaigns would be a good thing, because it would introduce a measure of coherence to an otherwise fragmented and decentralized political system. Presumably, the winners of such a campaign would have some sort of public mandate to carry out the programs they had campaigned on. The real danger, it seems, is not with nationalizing elections per se. Rather, the danger lies in the greater ability of wealthier interests to mount and coordinate such campaigns. Simply put, not everyone can afford to run independent expenditure and issue advocacy campaigns, especially not nationwide. As a result, if campaigns were to be nationalized around a small set of issues, the likelihood is that they would be issues chosen by the wealthy, which should give the rest of us pause.

Another possible result of the growing use of these new forms of spending is that candidates may lose the ability to frame the issues and set the agenda in their own campaigns. This is particularly true of House elections. According to data compiled by the Brennan Center for Justice, interest groups accounted for 15.6 percent of the spending and 16.9 percent of the television ads in the 2000 primary and general House elections. That compares to just 5.1 percent of the spending in

Senate elections and 8 percent in the presidential contest. In House elections, moreover, there are signs that although candidates still dominate the airwaves, other actors are rapidly closing the gap. House candidates paid for 57.3 percent of ad spending in their districts, and were responsible for 60.7 percent of the ads aired, a significant decrease from just two years earlier, when House candidates accounted for 69 percent of the ad spending in their races and 72 percent of the airings. More and more, it seems clear that office seekers are forced to share the stage with other actors who face no spending limits or disclosure requirements. In certain circumstances, candidates have been outspent by outside groups, making it difficult for the candidates to be heard above the fray. In the 2000 race for California's Forty-ninth Congressional District, for example, interest groups spent $3.7 million, while the two major candidates spent just $1.9 million.[24] Some candidates have been unable to purchase airtime because groups waging issue campaigns had already bought all of the available time slots. In many respects, agenda setting in a growing number of congressional districts resembles a free-for-all, with the candidates themselves playing smaller roles. The campaign manager for Jim Maloney, a Connecticut Democrat ostensibly helped by a Sierra Club ad campaign in 1998, complained to a reporter for *CQ Weekly* that "you have a message you're working on and an independent group comes in and their message is the message."[25]

In addition to interest groups and individuals, political parties are also spending millions on issue campaigns, although their spending and contributors must be disclosed. According to the Annenberg Public Policy Center, more than 70 percent of all issue ads aired in the final two months of the 1997–1998 election cycle were sponsored by the parties.[26] The parties, however, have been paying for their issue campaigns with soft money, which also allows contributions from corporations, labor unions, and wealthy individuals to play an important role in campaign finance. Moreover, the parties have been using issue campaigns to evade the spending limits in presidential elections. After Bob Dole secured the Republican nomination in the spring of 1996, his campaign was out of money. The Republican National Committee (RNC) stepped into the breach, running a $20 million issue campaign until the Republican convention, when Dole received his share of the public financing for the general election. There is also mounting evidence that the political parties have been funneling money to interest groups so they can run their own issue campaigns. The RNC, for example, gave $4.6 million to the nonprofit Americans for Tax Reform, which then launched a direct mail attack on numerous Democratic candidates.[27]

Given the prevailing state of campaign finance law, it is no wonder that such an imbalance exists between candidates and other actors. Candidates face strict contribution and disclosure requirements while issue advocacy is essentially unregulated. Regardless of their stated goals, interest groups and wealthy individuals will increasingly channel their political spending into the unregulated forms of political spending. As these new forms of spending increase, more and more po-

litical money will be unregulated and undisclosed, thereby diminishing accountability in the electoral process and possibly promoting misinformation. Concluded a report by the Annenberg Public Policy Center, "If you were a wealthy
donor interested in affecting the outcome of a campaign, but not interested in leaving any fingerprints, it is pretty clear where you would put your money."[28]

At the same time, though, proponents of such spending claim that groups fill
an important role in the electoral process. Russ Lehman, of the First American
Education Project, has argued that groups like his "are absolutely essential to the
electoral process and democracy itself. We not only have a right, but an obligation, to provide information to the public about issues important to Indian people
including the record of our elected leaders." He added that "to rely merely on the
candidates, in the existing money-distorted system, would be to conduct campaigns and elections on the narrowest terms as dictated by pollsters and consultants. Clearly, the losers in that process would be exactly the type of already dis-
connected citizens, like Native Americans, we have been created to assure regain
standing in the political process."[29]

Although Lehman's concerns are valid, in the long run it seems likely that the
shift toward independent expenditures and issue advocacy will disproportionately
benefit wealthy interests. Again, not every interest has the money to wage these
sorts of campaigns. And as the campaigns become more common, those who can
afford them will be able to dominate campaign discourse even more than they do
now. In the short run, though, environmental groups have found success with the
new forms of spending, especially in close races, and will continue their use until
they are no longer effective. This may be shortsighted, though. Given the environmental movement's inability to compete with business interests in electoral
spending, it will not be a major factor in the elections unless and until the campaign finance system is overhauled.

Although campaign finance reform is clearly in the best interests of the environmental community, only the Sierra Club made it a legislative priority. Many
environmental activists argued that the issue was outside of their area of expertise
and interest. But by failing to enthusiastically support an overhaul of the nation's
campaign finance laws, argues Philip Shabecoff, environmentalists undercut their
own chances of significant progress on the policies that matter most to them.[30] In
the end, as concerns about unregulated spending by outside interests began to
mount in the late 1990s, it was left to reform groups like Common Cause and the
Center for Public Integrity to do the heavy lifting on campaign finance reform.
Their efforts received a big boost when Senator John McCain made campaign finance reform the centerpiece of his 2000 presidential bid. Although McCain did
not gain the Republican nomination, his candidacy propelled concerns about
money's corrosive effect on elections and public policy to new heights. Shortly
thereafter, questions about the role of campaign contributions in former President
Clinton's pardon of fugitive financier Marc Rich led the Senate, after years of Republican filibusters, to adopt campaign finance legislation. The McCain-Feingold

bill languished in the House for several months until a new scandal, this one involving the collapse of the Enron Corporation, which had exceedingly intimate ties with President George W. Bush and many others in his administration, forced that body to act.

LIFE AFTER THE BIPARTISAN CAMPAIGN REFORM ACT

Signed into law by President Bush on March 27, 2002, the Bipartisan Campaign Reform Act (Public Law 107-155) made several significant changes to federal election campaign law. In addition to banning soft money contributions to the national parties, the measure also restricted election-oriented issue advocacy ads in the final sixty days of general elections for Congress, and in the final thirty days of primary elections. The law also addressed questions of accountability by requiring that spending in excess of $10,000 on such ads in any year must be disclosed within twenty-four hours.

More specifically, the new law bans corporate- and union-funded broadcast "electoral communications," which are defined as any broadcast, cable, or satellite communication that refers to a clearly identified candidate for federal office. It remains to be seen whether this portion of the law will withstand judicial scrutiny, as the Supreme Court has long held that campaign spending is a form of "free speech" and therefore cannot be restricted. In anticipation of such a ruling, the law also states that if the Court struck down the aforementioned definition, then "electoral communication" would mean "any broadcast, cable, or satellite communication which promotes or supports a candidate, regardless of whether the communication expressly advocates a vote for or against a candidate, or which is suggestive of no plausible meaning other than an encouragement to vote for or against a specific candidate."[31]

Speculating about future events is always a dangerous proposition. This is especially true with respect to campaign finance reform, which has a long history of spawning unintended consequences. Presumably, the Bipartisan Campaign Reform Act of 2002 will be no different. Early indications are that the law will both constrain environmental groups and create new opportunities for them. First, the new law doubles the maximum individual hard money contribution to $2,000 per candidate, per election. This change will likely enhance the already disproportionate importance of wealthy contributors and help Republican candidates, who rely far more heavily on hard money contributions in their campaigns. Second, although the law bans the flow of soft money from narrow interests to the national party committees, it does allow such contributions to state and local party entities. Much of the money that had gone to the Republican and Democratic National Committees will instead now flow to their state and local counterparts. Third, the new law may encourage groups to "bundle" contributions from individual donors, and then pass them along to candidates. In 2002, the LCV

PAC passed on more than $540,000 in bundled contributions to candidates.[32] Bundling is popular with contributors because the recipients know that they have contributed, and groups like it because it magnifies their role in funneling money to candidates.

Moreover, because the law does not place any restrictions on them, independent expenditure campaigns will undoubtedly increase dramatically in future election cycles. With more groups running more ads about more issues, the League of Conservation Voters and other environmental groups will have to raise much more if they want to be heard above the competition. It seems clear that the LCV's independent expenditure campaigns have been effective in forcing environmental issues into campaigns and, to a lesser extent, in influencing election results. A good measure of their effectiveness is the extent to which candidates do not want to be included in the Dirty Dozen list. Candidates know that the environment enjoys wide support among voters, and so they will at least claim to be supportive of the environment during their campaigns. Environmentalists will have to find a way to hold them accountable for their campaign rhetoric.

Furthermore, the Bipartisan Campaign Finance Reform Act restricts *broadcast* issue ads only. As a result, we can expect that groups like the Sierra Club that have been waging broadcast issue ad campaigns will shift their money to direct mail, phone banks, and other "ground war" activities. This shift may actually help environmental groups by encouraging them to devote more time and resources to voter contact and to building (or rebuilding) the grass roots, an important consideration in elections where low turnout is typical. Indeed, the Sierra Club's recent voter education campaigns have relied on both broadcast ads and on the ground activities, with an increasing emphasis on the latter. Critics like Phil Shabecoff have long argued that environmental groups need to do much more in terms of building an "army" of campaign organizers and volunteers. This law may finally push the national groups to do just that and devote even more resources to establishing personal contacts with voters and to building the electoral capacity of state and local organizations. Similarly, with the airwaves free of issue ads (but not independent expenditure ads), the candidates may opt to spend more on television advertising, while relying on the party committees and supportive interest groups to do more with respect to voter mobilization.[33]

Moreover, the new campaign finance law restricts issue ads only in the final weeks of campaigns. This may induce parties and groups to begin their electoral efforts earlier in the campaign cycle. By getting involved earlier, environmental groups may have greater flexibility in tactics and strategies. In assessing the 2002 elections, for example, some in the League of Conservation Voters concluded that they may have entered some races too late, which "forced" them to rely on broadcast ads and direct mail. The problem was that in some locations, like Colorado, New Hampshire, and South Dakota, the airwaves and mailboxes were filled with campaign appeals from the candidates, the parties, and other groups, which made it hard for the environmental message to break through the clutter. If groups get involved earlier, though, they have more of an opportunity to establish personal contacts with voters, build their organizational base, and assemble an effective presence in communities.

One of the clear lessons from recent elections is that turnout matters. In recent years many races, especially those at the state and local level, have been decided by an agonizingly small number of votes. Although members of environmental groups tend to have high turnout rates, it is imperative that environmental groups continue to build and expand on their efforts to identify, educate, and mobilize voters. The national groups can play a crucial role in this effort, beginning with an emphasis on establishing an ongoing dialogue with their members and voters throughout the year, not just in the final months of campaigns. Voter education is a long-term process, with voters needing frequent updates on policies and candidates. Voters, after all, are more likely to be responsive to a group's message if there is a relationship of familiarity and trust. Environmental groups should thus devote more attention and resources to not only connecting more often with their own members, but to connecting with more people by encouraging and training their members to reach out to their friends and families. In this way, the groups can enlarge the pool of voters with environmental interests.

Similarly, the groups should continue to train political organizers and place them in campaigns. Not only do candidates appreciate the help, but by increasing their political skills, the groups build their organizations as well and increase their chances of electing sympathetic candidates. In fact, according to WILD PAC's Vicki Simirano, the best use of her group's resources in 2002 was putting staff on campaigns and getting them some political training.[34] Until recently, though, many environmental activists did not recognize its importance. Perhaps the exceptionally high number of close races in recent years will lead even more to recognize that a little bit of organization can make a big difference on election day.

It would also make sense for environmental groups at all levels to dedicate significant resources to campaigns for local offices. Not only are these offices responsible for many important environmental issues, but they can also be stepping-stones to higher office. Before environmentalists can be elected to Congress or statewide positions, they must first have some political experience. A number of the state groups have already embraced this long-term approach, and are even beginning to recruit and train individuals for a variety of appointed and elected positions. The hope is that these individuals will develop the experience and expertise needed to someday run for state legislature or even Congress. Additionally, the combination of smaller districts and low turnout afford environmental groups tremendous opportunities for influencing election results. In Colorado alone in 2002, a half dozen state legislative races were decided by fewer than two hundred votes. In those locations, and others like them across the nation, groups that can mobilize their members can make the difference between winning and losing.

Finally, environmentalists should continue to be strategic in their electoral calculations. For too long, environmental PACs squandered their scarce resources backing safe incumbents or "pure" but doomed challengers. Until groups have much more money, they must pick their battles carefully. With Congress and many state legislatures so closely divided along partisan lines, this means focusing on the handful of races where they can make a difference. Environmentalists must thus defend friendly but vulnerable incumbents, target unfriendly incumbents in close races, and be opportunistic in seeking winnable open seat contests. Focusing on close races is risky because their candidates cannot be assured of victory and the group's "won-loss" ratio may suffer as a result, but the rewards today are potentially high, with the swing of a few seats determining which party is in the majority, and thus controls committee and subcommittee chairmanships and, ultimately, the legislative agenda.

Because money is and will continue to be vitally important in elections, environmental groups must continue to raise as much as possible and, ideally, much more than they have to date. Despite raising record amounts in recent years, environmental groups continue to be outspent by their political foes, who are now reaping the legislative and administrative benefits of their largesse. Although environmentalists will never be able to match corporate spending, additional money would enable the groups to become involved in more races, which is critically important if they want to have a voice in shaping the makeup of Congress and state legislatures. For now, though, the remarks of George W. Bush that open this chapter illustrate that environmentalists will have to rededicate themselves to playing defense in an overtly hostile political environment. Although the groups are by now familiar with the underdog role, they have never been faced with the prospect of all three branches under simultaneous Republican control. The best hope for environmentalists may be to remember that, as George Harrison once wrote, "all things must pass."

Notes

1. ENVIRONMENTAL ACTIVISM IN THE UNITED STATES

1. The suspension of the roadless rule essentially gave its opponents ninety days to challenge it in court. The governors of Idaho and Alaska did so, and when the Bush administration put forth a halfhearted defense, a federal judge enjoined the rule. *State of Idaho v. United States Forest Service*, U.S. District Court, District of Idaho, Case No. CV01-11-N-EJL, Order by Judge Edward Lodge, May 10, 2001.

2. According to Jon Owen, outreach and advocacy director of the Washington Wilderness Coalition, although the Heritage Forest Campaign was a national organization and included many of the largest environmental groups, it was not a case of the national groups imposing their views on the grassroots organizations. Rather, the campaign helped the local groups coordinate their actions and develop a consistent message. Telephone interview conducted November 8, 2001.

3. Leech et al. note that the effort to recast the forest issue can be traced back at least as far as the Carter administration. After years of working to convince officials that the key issue was not finding a way to harvest more trees, but the environmental problems caused by extensive road building in the forests, environmental groups took advantage of the access created by the election of Bill Clinton, who appointed more sympathetic forest officials. See Beth L. Leech et al. "Organized Interests and Issue Definition in Policy Debates," in *Interest Group Politics*, 6th ed., ed. Allen J. Cigler and Burdett A. Loomis (Washington, D.C.: CQ Press, 2002), 284.

4. In addition to Pew, other foundations that contributed to the Heritage Forest Campaign included the W. Alton Jones Foundation, which gave $200,000 in 1999 to the Southern Environmental Law Center to fight for permanent protection of southeastern forest tracts. Other foundations awarded a total of $1.9 million to groups specifically promoting the protection of Alaska's Tongass and other forests. For a discussion of the funding effort, see Michelle Cole, "Wealthy Environmental Groups Help Crusade to Protect Forests," *The Oregonian*, January 3, 2001. For Pew's role in funding environmental causes, see Douglas Jehl, "Charity Is New Force in Environmental Fight," *New York Times*, June 28, 2001, A1.

5. See Cole, "Wealthy Environmental Groups."

6. The "ONE" in ONE/Northwest is an acronym for Online Networking for the Environment.

7. For a discussion of ONE.Northwest and the services it offers, see its website www.onenw.org.

8. Sierra Club News Release, April 4, 2001.

9. Ibid.

10. Mark Dowie, *Losing Ground: American Environmentalism at the Close of the Twentieth Century* (Cambridge, Mass.: MIT Press, 1995), 192–95.

11. See, for example, the controversial articles by Tom Knudson in the *Sacramento Bee*. The series, entitled "Environment, Inc," began on April 12, 2001.

12. A number of scholars have commented upon the importance of issue definition and agenda setting to environmental activism. See, for example, Sheldon Kamieniecki, "Political Mobilization, Agenda Building, and International Environmental Policy," *Journal of International Affairs* 44 (Winter 1991): 339–58; Denise Scheberle, "Radon and Asbestos: A Study of Agenda-Setting and Causal Stories," *Policy Studies Journal* 22, no. 1 (1994): 74–86; Kathryn Harrison and George Hoberg, "Setting the Environmental Agenda in Canada and the United States: The Cases of Dioxin and Radon," *Canadian Journal of Political Science* 24 (1991): 3–27; and John C. Pierce, Mary Ann E. Steger, Brent S. Steel, and Nicholas P. Lovrich, *Citizens, Political Communication, and Interest Groups: Environmental Organizations in Canada and the United States* (New York: Praeger, 1992).

13. For issue framing in wilderness debates, see R. McGreggor Cawley, *Federal Land, Western Anger: The Sagebrush Rebellion and Environmental Politics* (Lawrence: University Press of Kansas, 1993), 112; for a discussion of the political art of framing alternatives, see Deborah Stone, *Policy Paradox: The Art of Political Decision Making*, rev. ed. (New York: W. W. Norton, 2002), 246–48.

14. Michael E. Kraft and Norman J. Vig, "Environmental Policy from the 1970s to 2000: An Overview," in *Environmental Policy*, 4th ed., ed. Norman J. Vig and Michael E. Kraft (Washington, D.C.: CQ Press, 2000), 1–31.

15. Philip Shabecoff, *Earth Rising: American Environmentalism in the Twenty-first Century* (Washington, D.C.: Island Press, 2000), 22–24.

16. Christopher J. Bosso and Deborah Lynn Guber, "The Boundaries and Contours of American Environmental Activism," in *Environmental Policy*, 5th ed., ed. Norman J. Vig and Michael E. Kraft (Washington, D.C.: CQ Press, 2002), 94.

17. For a chronicle of congressional attempts to redirect environmental policy, see Bob Benenson, "GOP Sets 104th Congress on New Regulatory Course," *Congressional Quarterly Weekly Report*, June 17, 1995:1693; see also Natural Resources Defense Council, "The Year of Living Dangerously: Congress and the Environment in 1995," December 1995.

18. Jacqueline Vaughn Switzer, *Green Backlash: The History and Politics of Environmental Opposition in the U.S.* (Boulder, Colo.: Lynne Rienner Publishers, 1997), 293.

19. Shabecoff, 41–42.

20. Shabecoff, 11.

21. Many environmental groups were established with foundation money, and foundations continue to be an important source of funds for many groups. Ford Foundation grants established the Natural Resources Defense Council, for example, and more recently Pew has created the Heritage Forest Campaign. According to published reports, foundations provide about one-fifth of environmental group money. See Tom Knudson, "Fat of the Land," *Sacramento Bee*, April 22, 2001.

22. Shabecoff, 37–38. In addition to those groups already mentioned, the Pew Wilderness Center was established in April 2000 to combat the public's lack of knowledge about wilderness. The group, which conducts education initiatives on television, radio, and in newspapers, is designed to complement the efforts of other wilderness organizations in raising public awareness. The group works closely with other groups: the American Wilderness Coalition, which was created in 2001 to show citizens how they can contact members of Congress and lobby for preservation, and WILD PAC, a political action committee established in 2001 to aid congressional supporters of wilderness. See Mike Matz, "The

Politics of Protecting Wild Places," in *Return of the Wild: The Future of Our Wild Lands,* ed. Ted Kerasote (Washington, D.C.: Island Press, 2001), 98.

23. Shabecoff, 121.

24. Knudson, "Fat of the Land."

25. Quoted in Knudson, "Fat of the Land."

26. Ronald T. Libby, *Eco-Wars: Political Campaigns and Social Movements* (New York: Columbia University Press, 1998), 12.

27. See, for example, Shabecoff, 113.

28. Bosso and Guber, 85–86, cite V. O. Key's *Public Opinion and American Democracy* (New York: Knopf, 1961) on this point.

29. Shabecoff, 116.

30. Shabecoff suggests that the Internet may allow groups to bypass the "media gatekeepers" who have ignored the environment.

31. Shabecoff, 126; see also Ray Ring, "Bad Moon Rising: The Waning of Montana's Once-Mighty Progressive Coalition," *High Country News,* December 17, 2001, 1.

32. Shabecoff, 128.

33. Shabecoff, 126–28.

34. For a discussion of recent ground war campaigns by environmentalists and other progressive groups, see David Magleby, ed., *Outside Money: Soft Money and Issue Advocacy in the 1998 Midterm Congressional Elections* (New York: Rowman and Littlefield, 2000).

35. Robert C. Mitchell, Angela G. Mertig, and Riley E. Dunlap, "Twenty Years of Environmental Mobilization: Trends among National Environmental Organizations," in *American Environmentalism: The U.S. Environmental Movement, 1970–1990* (Philadelphia: Taylor and Francis, 1992), 21.

36. Michael E. Kraft and Diana Wuertz, "Environmental Advocacy in the Corridors of Government," in *The Symbolic Earth: Discourse and Our Creation of the Environment,* ed. James G. Cantrill and Christine L. Oravec (Louisville: University Press of Kentucky, 1999), 112.

37. Ronald Shaiko, *Voices and Echoes for the Environment* (New York: Columbia University Press, 1999), 144. See also William P. Browne, "Lobbying the Public: All-Directional Advocacy," 347 in *Interest Group Politics,* 5th ed., ed. Allan J. Cigler and Burdett A. Loomis (Washington, D.C.: CQ Press, 1998), 347.

38. Christopher J. Bosso and Michael T. Collins, "Just Another Tool? Environmental Groups Use the Internet," in *Interest Group Politics,* 6th ed., ed. Allan J. Cigler and Burdett A. Loomis (Washington, D.C.: CQ Press, 2002), 100–101.

39. Email interview with Andy Schultheiss, November 26, 2001.

40. Browne, "Lobbying the Public," 355–57. But, as Browne cautions, because of their cost these tools are not available to every interest, and these differences in group resources can profoundly affect their ability to generate narratives that help them in policy debates.

41. Others have made similar arguments, of course. See George A. Gonzalez, *Corporate Power and the Environment* (New York: Rowman and Littlefield, 2001).

42. Email interview with Kathy Kilmer, November 21, 2001.

43. Quoted in Shaiko, 66.

44. In 1996, for example, the Washington Wilderness Coalition launched a successful door-to-door canvassing campaign that increased its membership from eight hundred to

more than thirteen thousand. In explaining the decision, Jon Owen, the Coalition's outreach and advocacy director, said, "When you don't have door-to-door canvassing, people have to find you." For that reason, the group went out to engage and educate the public. More importantly, Owen claims that the group also began talking to the public in a new way, to raise public awareness of wilderness issues and to stimulate public action. In the end, the Coalition claims, these efforts were responsible for generating "thousands" of comments to administrative agencies and other public officials. Information obtained during a telephone interview with Jon Owen, November 8, 2001. For a discussion of some capacity-building efforts, see Marshall Mayer, "Conservation Database Report: A White Paper Prepared for the Rockefeller Family Fund" (October 1997), 7.

2. INTEREST GROUPS, ISSUE DEFINITION, AND AGENDA SETTING

1. For a discussion of all-directional lobbying see William P. Browne, *Groups, Interests, and U.S. Public Policy* (Washington, D.C.: Georgetown University Press, 1998).

2. See Robert J. Duffy, *Nuclear Politics in America: A History and Theory of Government Regulation* (Lawrence: University Press of Kansas, 1997), esp. chap. 6.

3. For some of the earliest, and best, discussions of subgovernments, see J. Leiper Freeman, *The Political Process: Executive Bureau—Legislative Committee Relations* (New York: Random House, 1955); Douglas Cater, *Power in Washington* (New York: Random House, 1964); and Emmette S. Redford, *Democracy in the Administrative State* (New York: Oxford University Press, 1969).

4. On the variable influence of subgovernments, see Jeffrey M. Berry, "Subgovernments, Issue Networks, and Political Conflict," in *Remaking American Politics,* ed. Richard A. Harris and Sidney M. Milkis (Boulder, Colo.: Westview Press, 1989), 253–55.

5. See Hugh Heclo, "Issue Networks and the Executive Establishment," in *The New American Political System,* ed. Anthony King (Washington, D.C.: American Enterprise Institute, 1980); Berry, "Subgovernments"; Paul Sabatier and Hank C. Jenkins-Smith, *Policy Change and Learning: An Advocacy Coalition Approach* (Boulder, Colo.: Westview Press, 1993); and Christopher J. Bosso, *Pesticides and Politics: The Life Cycle of a Public Issue* (Pittsburgh, Pa.: University of Pittsburgh Press, 1987).

6. William P. Browne, "Lobbying the Public: All-Directional Advocacy," in *Interest Groups Politics,* 5th ed., ed. Allan J. Cigler and Burdett A. Loomis (Washington, D.C.: CQ Press, 1998), 344.

7. Browne, *Groups,* 131–33.

8. Browne, *Groups,* 97–101.

9. *New York Times,* July 6, 1991, cited in Walter A. Rosenbaum, *Environmental Politics and Policy,* 4th ed. (Washington, D.C.: CQ Press, 1998), 123–24.

10. Paul S. Herrnson, "Parties and Interest Groups in Postreform Congressional Elections," in *Interest Group Politics,* 5th ed., ed. Allan J. Cigler and Burdett A. Loomis (Washington, D.C.: CQ Press, 1998), 145–46; Mark Rozell and Clyde Wilcox, *Interest Groups in American Campaigns: the New Faces of Electioneering* (Washington, D.C.: CQ Press, 1999), 1. See also Allan J. Cigler and Burdett A. Loomis, "From Big Bird to Bill Gates: Organized Interests and the Emergence of Hyperpolitics," in *Interest Groups Politics,* 5th ed., ed. Allan J. Cigler and Burdett A. Loomis (Washington, D.C.: CQ Press, 1998), 391–99.

11. Cigler and Loomis, "Big Bird," 391–93.

12. Herrnson, 150–51; see also Cigler and Loomis, "Big Bird," 391.

13. M. Margaret Conway and Joanne Connor Green, "Political Action Committees and Campaign Finance," in *Interest Groups Politics,* 5th ed., ed. Allan J. Cigler and Burdett A. Loomis (Washington, D.C.: CQ Press, 1998), 200.

14. Herrnson, 155–57; see also Rozell and Wilcox, 15.

15. For a discussion of the importance of interest groups to parties' electoral efforts, see Robert Dreyfuss, "Rousing the Democratic Base," *American Prospect,* November 6, 2000, 20–23.

16. Burdett A. Loomis, "Interests, Lobbying, and the U.S. Congress: Past as Prologue," in *Interest Groups Politics,* 6th ed., ed. Allen J. Cigler and Burdett A. Loomis (Washington, D.C.: CQ Press, 2002), 198.

17. Craig B. Holman and Luke P. McLoughlin, *Buying Time 2000: Television Advertising in the 2000 Federal Elections* (New York: Brennan Center for Justice, 2002), 31–33.

18. Holman and McLoughlin, 29. Similarly, a 1998 study found that only 4 percent of candidate ads used the "magic words."

19. Larry Sabato and Glenn Simpson, *Dirty Little Secrets* (New York: Random House, 1996).

20. *Federal Election Commission v. Christian Action Network,* 92 F.3d 1178 (4th Circ. 1996).

21. Louis Jacobson, "Are Advocates Sidestepping Federal Code?" *National Journal,* January 7, 1995, 27.

22. Jacobson, 27–28.

23. http://www.appcpenn.org/issueads/estimate.htm.

24. Holman and McLoughlin, 29–31.

25. Rozell and Wilcox, 5.

26. Cigler and Loomis, "Big Bird," 394.

27. Herrnson, 164.

28. Ronald T. Libby, *Eco-Wars: Political Campaigns and Social Movements* (New York: Columbia University Press, 1998), 10.

29. Robert H. Salisbury and Lauretta Conklin, "Instrumental Versus Expressive Group Politics: The National Endowment for the Arts," in *Interest Group Politics,* 5th ed., ed. Allan J. Cigler and Burdett A. Loomis (Washington, D.C.: CQ Press, 1998), 286–87.

30. Salisbury and Conklin, 287–88.

31. Libby, esp. chaps. 1 and 7.

32. Libby, 208.

33. For a discussion of tax laws and their effects on nonprofits, see Libby, 208–10; see also Elizabeth Kingsley et al., *E-Advocacy for Nonprofits: The Law of Lobbying and Election-Related Activity on the Net* (Washington, D.C.: Alliance for Justice, 2000).

34. According to Shaiko, the transfer of funds from 501(c)(3) groups to 501(c)(4)s are not unusual. In 1985, for example, 15 percent of Environmental Action's funds were tax deductible, but then transferred to the group's 501(c)(4) organization. During the latter half of the 1990s, moreover, the Sierra Club annually received grants of $3 to 4 million from its 501(c)(3) foundation. Shaiko describes the Sierra Club as a full-service group, consisting of the parent 501(c)(4) organization, the 501(c)(3) Earth Justice Legal Defense Fund, the Sierra Club Political Action Committee, the Sierra Student Coalition, and Sierra Club Books. See Ronald B. Shaiko, *Voices and Echoes for the Environment: Public Interest Representation in the 1990s and Beyond* (New York: Columbia University Press, 1999), 44.

35. Libby, 12.

36. Diana Dwyre, "Campaigning outside the Law: Interest Group Issue Advocacy," in *Interest Group Politics*, 6th ed., ed. Allan J. Cigler and Burdett A. Loomis (Washington, D.C.: CQ Press, 2002), 153–55.

37. For a discussion of group strategies, see Thomas L. Gais and Jack L. Walker Jr., "Pathways to Influence in American Politics," in *Mobilizing Interest Groups in America: Patrons, Professions, and Social Movements*, ed. Jack L. Walker Jr. (Ann Arbor: University of Michigan Press, 1991), 103–21.

38. Norman Ornstein and Shirley Elder, *Interest Groups, Lobbying, and Policymaking* (Washington, D.C.: CQ Press, 1978), 83–85.

39. Kay Lehman Schlozman and John T. Tierney, *Organized Interests and American Democracy* (New York: Harper and Row, 1986), 160. Kraft and Wuertz state that strategies are general plans for using political resources in support of selected policies, while tactics are the specific methods used to carry out the general strategies. See Michael E. Kraft and Diana Wurtz, "Environmental Advocacy in the Corridors of Government," in *The Symbolic Earth: Discourse and the Creation of Our Environment* (Louisville: University Press of Kentucky, 1999), 105.

40. Gais and Walker, 111–14.

41. Ornstein and Elder, 69–70.

42. Gais and Walker, 105–6.

43. Gais and Walker, 120.

44. Gais and Walker, 107.

45. See Beth L. Leech et al., "Organized Interests and Issue Definition in Policy Debates," in *Interest Group Politics*, 6th ed., ed. Allen J. Cigler and Burdett A. Loomis (Washington, D.C.: CQ Press, 2002), 280.

46. Christopher J. Bosso, "The Contextual Bases of Problem Definition," in *The Politics of Problem Definition: Shaping the Policy Agenda*, ed. David A. Rochefort and Roger W. Cobb (Lawrence: University Press of Kansas, 1994), 183.

47. See Darrell M. West and Burdett A. Loomis, *The Sound of Money: How Political Interests Get What They Want* (New York: W.W. Norton, 1998), 20; for a similar argument, see Cigler and Loomis, "Big Bird," 395–99.

48. Mark P. Petracca, "Issue Definitions, Agenda-Building, and Policymaking," *Policy Currents* 2 (1992): 1, 4, cited in David A. Rochefort and Roger W. Cobb, "Problem Definition: An Emerging Perspective," in *The Politics of Problem Definition: Shaping the Policy Agenda*, ed. David A. Rochefort and Roger W. Cobb (Lawrence: University Press of Kansas, 1994), 9.

49. E. E. Schattschneider, *The Semi-Sovereign People: A Realist's View of Democracy in America* (Hinsdale, Ill.: Dryden Press, 1960), 2.

50. Schattschneider, 2, 7, 11, 38.

51. Rochefort and Cobb, 5.

52. Bosso, *Pesticides,* 80.

53. Deborah A. Stone, "Causal Stories and the Formation of Policy Agendas," *Political Science Quarterly* 104 (1989), 281–300; see also Frank R. Baumgartner and Bryan D. Jones, *Agendas and Instability in American Politics* (Chicago: University of Chicago Press, 1993), 25–38.

54. Baumgartner and Jones, 239.

55. Jeffrey Berry, *The New Liberalism: The Rising Power of Citizen Groups* (Washington, D.C.: Brookings Institution Press, 1999), 70. Leech et al. make a similar point in their study of issue definition; see 284.

56. Berry, 30.

57. Sabatier and Jenkins-Smith, 24, 45.

58. Bosso, *Pesticides,* 256. For a detailed discussion of this issue, see especially 237–56.

59. James Q. Wilson, *American Government: Institutions and Policies,* 2d ed. (Englewood Cliffs, N.J.: Prentice-Hall, 1982), 418–19.

60. John W. Kingdon, *Agendas, Alternatives, and Public Policies* (Boston: Little, Brown, 1984), 100. For another view of agenda setting, see Roger W. Cobb and Charles D. Elder, *Participation in American Politics: The Dynamics of Agenda-Building* (Boston: Allyn and Bacon, 1972).

61. John Tierney and William Frasure, "Culture Wars on the Frontier: Interests, Values, and Policy Narratives in Public Lands Politics," in *Interest Group Politics,* 5th ed., ed. Allan J. Cigler and Burdett A. Loomis (Washington, D.C.: CQ Press, 2000), 312.

62. Rochefort and Cobb, 15.

63. Rochefort and Cobb, 9.

64. Stone, 133.

65. Stone, 155–56.

66. Stone, 137–38; see also Tierney and Frasure, 304.

67. Stone, 209.

68. Stone, 137–38.

69. A particularly good example of an environmental story of decline is offered by Ross Gelbspan in *The Heat Is On: The Climate Crisis, the Cover Up, the Prescription* (Cambridge, Mass.: Perseus Books, 1998); see especially 11–13.

70. Rochefort and Cobb, 21.

71. West and Loomis, 40–41.

72. James G. Cantrill, "Perceiving Environmental Discourse: The Cognitive Playground," in *The Symbolic Earth: Discourse and Our Creation of the Environment,* ed. James G. Cantrill and Christine L. Oravec (Louisville: University Press of Kentucky, 1999), 76.

73. Kraft and Wuertz, 96.

74. Cantrill, p. 76.

75. Stone, 203.

76. Bosso, "Contextual Bases," 198.

77. Bosso, "Contextual Bases," 184.

78. Bosso, "Contextual Bases," 184; emphasis in the original.

79. Tom Doggett, "Senate Rejects Huge Hike in Vehicle Fuel Standards," Reuters, March 14, 2002, http://enn.om/extras/storyid=46666.

80. George A. Gonzalez, "Local Growth Coalitions, Environmental Groups, and Air Pollution," paper presented at the Annual Meeting of the Southern Political Science Association, November 6–9, 2002, Savannah, Georgia.

81. For the classic treatment of how the agenda is managed to exclude certain issues, see Peter Bachrach and Morton Baratz, "Two Faces of Power," *American Political Science Review* 56 (1962): 947–52.

82. Bosso, "Contextual Bases," 195.

83. Bosso, "Contextual Bases," 189–90.

84. Tierney and Frasure, 313.

85. William P. Browne et al., *Sacred Cows and Hot Potatoes: Agrarian Myths in Agricultural Policy* (Boulder, Colo.: Westview Press, 1992).

3. AMERICAN ENVIRONMENTALISM THROUGH THE EARLY 1990S

1. Philip Shabecoff, *Earth Rising: American Environmentalism in the Twenty-first Century* (Washington, D.C.: Island Press, 2000), 3–9.

2. Robert C. Mitchell, Angela G. Mertig, and Riley E. Dunlap, "Twenty Years of Environmental Mobilization: Trends among National Environmental Organizations," in *American Environmentalism: The U.S. Environmental Movement, 1970–1990*, ed. Riley E. Dunlap and Angela E. Mertig (Philadelphia: Taylor and Francis, 1992), 19.

3. See Kirkpatrick Sale, *The Green Revolution: The American Environmental Movement, 1962–1992* (New York: Hill and Wang, 1993), 19. According to Mike McCloskey, former president of the Sierra Club, the decision to add pollution issues to the group's agenda was essentially pushed by the group's national leadership "as an exercise in intellectual commitment," but there was no passion for the issue among the Club's rank and file membership. In his opinion, the issues were simply too complex and technical. Eventually, he says, concerns about toxic chemicals emerged, and people began to notice, but those people tended to join local groups fighting to protect their communities from specific toxic threats. At the national level, though, the issue was too remote. In the end, the best issues for the national mainstream groups, in terms of attracting and retaining members, were, as before, public lands and nature protection. See also Michael McCloskey, "Twenty Years of Change in the Environmental Movement: An Insider's View," in *American Environmentalism: The U.S. Environmental Movement, 1970–1990*, ed. Riley E. Dunlap and Angela E. Mertig (Philadelphia: Taylor and Francis, 1992), 80.

4. McCloskey, 82.

5. David Brower gave voice to these sentiments when he wrote in a letter, "My thesis is that compromise is often necessary but that it ought not to originate with the Sierra Club. We are to hold fast to what we believe is right, fight for it, and find allies and adduce all possible arguments for our cause. If we cannot find enough vigor in us or them to win, then let someone else propose the compromise. We thereupon work hard to coax it our way. We become a nucleus around which the strongest force can build and function." Cited in Michael P. Cohen, *The History of the Sierra Club, 1892–1970* (San Francisco: Sierra Club Books, 1988), 403.

6. See Sale, 59–60.

7. Jeffrey M. Berry, *The New Liberalism: The Rising Power of Citizen Groups* (Washington, D.C.: Brookings Institution Press, 1999), 30.

8. Mitchell, Mertig, and Dunlap, 21.

9. William P. Browne, *Groups, Interests, and U.S. Public Policy* (Washington, D.C.: Georgetown University Press, 1998), 147. See also Christopher J. Bosso, "Environmental Groups and the New Political Landscape," in *Environmental Policy in the 1990s*, 4th ed., ed. Norman J. Vig and Michael E. Kraft (Washington, D.C.: CQ Press, 2000), table 3.2, p. 69.

10. According to Browne, 147, the entire environmental movement generated more than $4 billion in revenues in 1996, with donations increasing 91 percent from the prior decade.

11. Membership totals from Bosso, "New Political Landscape," table 3.1, p. 64.

12. Cohen, 446.

13. Cited in Browne, *Groups,* 147.

14. Lowry notes that in 1991 the Sierra Club and the National Wildlife Federation employed three hundred and eight hundred staffers, respectively. Cited in Ronald G. Shaiko, *Voices and Echoes for the Environment: Public Interest Representation in the 1990s and Beyond* (New York: Columbia University Press, 1999), 148.

15. Berry, 157, argues that this is a luxury for small groups, who are forced to use their limited resources to fight on immediate policy concerns.

16. For example, Sale claims that the intense influence of mass protest was "channeled into longer-term representation by environmental interest groups, which in turn hired permanent staffs to research and publicize issues, lobby for tougher legislation, monitor and challenge the administrative agencies, and mobilize new public protests against proposals" that threatened the environment (239).

17. Sale, 54–56.

18. Berry, 97.

19. Marlene J. Fluharty, "The Sierra Club's Electoral Program," in *Sierra Club: A Guide,* ed. Patrick Carr (San Francisco: Sierra Club, 1988), 49–50.

20. Fluharty, 49–50.

21. R. McGreggor Cawley, *Federal Land, Western Anger: The Sagebrush Rebellion and Environmental Politics* (Lawrence: University Press of Kansas, 1993), 48.

22. Berry, 150.

23. Sale, 53.

24. McCloskey, 82.

25. Sale, 90–91.

26. Sale, 90–91.

27. Thomas L. Gais and Jack L. Walker Jr., "Pathways to Influence in American Politics," in *Mobilizing Interest Groups in America: Patrons, Professions, and Social Movements,* ed. Jack L. Walker Jr. (Ann Arbor: University of Michigan Press, 1991), 112.

28. Browne, 66.

29. For a good overview of lobbying tactics, see Ronald J. Hrebenar and Ruth K. Scott, *Interest Group Politics in America* (New York: Prentice-Hall, 1982).

30. Craig Allin, *The Politics of Wilderness Preservation* (Westport, Conn.: Greenwood Press, 1982), 105–6. According to the Sierra Club's Michael McCloskey, "In some ways the Wilderness Act fight was a very sophisticated campaign, but I think the tools or the lessons of that [campaign] really didn't get transferred very well." In his view, it was only when the Sierra Club attempted to draft and pass legislation protecting the redwoods in the late 1960s that it was introduced to the "full legislative process." Quoted in Michael P. Cohen, 326–27.

31. Richard N. L. Andrews, *Managing the Environment, Managing Ourselves: A History of American Environmental Policy* (New Haven, Conn.: Yale University Press, 1999), 190–91.

32. This was not, of course, the first time photographs had been used to influence national debates over the public lands. William Henry Jackson's photographs, which captured the nation's imagination and helped persuade Congress to designate Yellowstone as the first national park, almost certainly holds that distinction.

33. Roderick Nash, *Wilderness and the American Mind,* 4th ed. (New Haven, Conn.:

Yale University Press, 2001), 212. The essay collection, edited by Wallace Stegner, was *This Is Dinosaur: Echo Park Country and Its Magic Rivers* (New York: Alfred A. Knopf, 1955).

34. For a detailed account of the Echo Park controversy, see Mark W. T. Harvey, *Symbol of Wilderness: Echo Park and the American Conservation Movement* (Seattle: University of Washington Press, 1994), 270. For additional views on this controversy, see Nash, 212–20.

35. Andrews, 190–91.

36. Susan Zakin, *Coyotes and Town Dogs: Earth First! and the Environmental Movement* (New York: Penguin Books, 1993), 139.

37. William P. Browne, "Lobbying the Public: All-Directional Advocacy." In *Interest Group* Politics, 5th ed., ed. Allan J. Cigler and Burdett A. Loomis (Washington, D.C.: CQ Press, 1998), 355.

38. Mitchell, Mertig, and Dunlap, 20.

39. Michael C. Kraft and Diana Wuertz, "Environmental Advocacy in the Corridors of Government," in *The Symbolic Earth: Discourse and Our Creation of the Environment,* ed. James G. Contrill and Christine D. Oravec (Louisville: University Press of Kentucky), 106.

40. During debate over the Clean Air Act Amendments in 1982, Democratic Congressman Henry Waxman worked with environmental lobbyists to identify a handful of committee centrists who might be persuaded to cast their votes for strengthening the amendments. See Richard E. Cohen, *Washington at Work: Back Rooms and Clean Air,* 2d ed. (Boston: Allyn and Bacon, 1995), 35.

41. See Berry, 70.

42. According to Jeffrey Berry, citizen groups comprise about one-third of all interest groups who testify at congressional hearings. Berry argues that citizen groups have been adept at securing hearing slots for several reasons. First, they have historically depended on an "information strategy" in their legislative lobbying, and have relied heavily on mobilizing public opinion as part of their efforts to influence legislation. Secondly, citizen groups have allocated their organizational resources to stress research and the dissemination of information. Finally, citizen groups are, he argues, the primary initiators of many of the legislative proposals committees hold hearings on. See Berry, 19–21.

43. Berry, 156.

44. See, for example, Beth L. Leech and Frank R. Baumgartner, "Lobbying Friends and Foes in Washington," in *Interest Group Politics,* 5th ed., ed. Allan J. Cigler and Burdett A. Loomis (Washington, D.C.: CQ Press, 1998), 217; and Kay Lehman Schlozman and John T. Tierney, *Organized Interests and American Democracy* (New York: Harper and Row, 1986), 292.

45. Quoted in Jennifer Hattam, "Greening Capitol Hill," *Sierra* (January/February 2001): 55–56.

46. According to Ronald T. Libby, in 1985 the EPA and congressional staff members rated the Natural Resources Defense Council as the most influential environmental lobbying group. See his *Eco-Wars: Political Campaigns and Social Movements* (New York: Columbia University Press, 1998), 104.

47. Robert Gottlieb, *Environmentalism Unbound: Exploring New Pathways for Change* (Cambridge, Mass.: MIT Press, 2002), 56.

48. For a discussion of the politics of the 1977 amendments, see Bruce Ackerman and

William Hassler, *Clean Coal/ Dirty Air* (New Haven, Conn.: Yale University Press, 1981).

49. The Coalition consisted of the Sierra Club, the National Audubon Society, Friends of the Earth, Environmental Action, the Public Interest Research Group, Common Cause, the League of Women Voters, the American Lung Association, and several labor unions, including the Oil, Chemical, and Atomic Workers Union.

50. See McCloskey, 159.

51. Richard E. Cohen, 118. Much of the following discussion relies on Cohen's analysis on the 1990 Clean Air Act. See also Gary C. Bryner, *Blue Skies, Green Politics: The Clean Air Act of 1990* (Washington, D.C.: CQ Press, 1993).

52. Cohen, 45.

53. Cohen, 64. This disagreement revealed significant differences in approach among environmental groups, with EDF and the World Wildlife Federation generally being much more supportive of market-oriented solutions, while groups like the Sierra Club were skeptical. In addition, Cohen suggests that some groups distrusted EDF's motives, suspecting that the group was seeking to appease the White House.

54. Cohen, 122.

55. According to Cohen, the lobbyist quit a few days later, and went to work for the Teamsters Union. See Cohen, 115–16.

56. Cohen, 115–17, makes a convincing argument that interest group lobbying was transformed in the early 1990s. Specifically, he cites the "increased use of lobby coalitions, made possible by technological advances in communications and direct mail, which allowed groups to stay in contact with large populations." As a result, congressional offices were deluged with mail and constituent visits. In addition, members of Congress were forced to address a broad array of problems, not just local issues. And finally, echoing the arguments made by William P. Browne, lobbying "was waged far more widely" than in the past. Interest groups were lobbying everyone, everywhere. Members of Congress were contacted in the home districts as well as in Washington, and Cohen claims that these visits were often as effective as traditional office visits by paid lobbyists.

57. Cohen, 99–103.

58. Schlozman and Tierney, 150–51.

59. Walter A. Rosenbaum, *The Politics of Environmental Concern* (New York: Holt, Rinehart and Winston, 1977), 101.

60. Rosenbaum.

61. Hrebenar and Scott, 151.

62. For a discussion of presidents and the environment, see Norman J. Vig, "Presidential Leadership and the Environment: From Reagan to Clinton," in *Environmental Policy in the 1990s,* 3d ed., ed. Norman J. Vig and Michael E. Kraft (Washington, D.C.: CQ Press, 1997), 95–118.

63. Allin, 161.

64. Jacqueline Vaughn Switzer, *Green Backlash: The History and Politics of Environmental Opposition in the U.S.* (Boulder, Colo.: Lynne Rienner Publishers, 1997), 158–59.

65. Industry groups used similar tactics to encourage citizens to contact members of Congress. Callers would be connected to a central switchboard, which would then route their calls to the appropriate legislator's office. Demonstrating their ingenuity, several environmental groups encouraged their members to call the number and, when connected to

their representative's office, speak in support of environmental protection. The beauty of this approach, of course, was that their opponents paid for the phone call.

66. Switzer, 154.

67. Dana Millbank and Mike Allen, "Energy Task Force Belatedly Consulted Environmentalists," *Washington Post,* March 27, 2002, A2. See also Pete Yost, "Documents Reveal Energy Head Met No Environmentalists," Associated Press, March 26, 2002.

68. McCloskey, 86.

69. Berry, 70.

70. Berry, 63–67.

71. See Charles Davis, "Politics and Rangeland Policy," in *Western Public Lands and Environmental Politics,* 2d ed., ed. Charles Davis (Boulder, Colo.: Westview Press, 2001), 104–5.

72. Berry, 67–70.

73. See John W. Kingdon, *Agendas, Alternatives, and Public Policies,* 2d ed. (New York: HarperCollins, 1995), 127–31; see also Berry, 66.

74. Schlozman and Tierney, 150.

75. Kraft and Wuertz, 115.

76. Kraft and Wuertz, 101–3.

77. Zakin, 268.

78. Zakin, 308. The campaign was devised by Herb Gunther of Public Media Center, an advertising think tank based in San Francisco. Although groups had used direct mail prior to 1976, the baby seal campaign demonstrated again how effective it could be in recruiting new members and in publicizing environmental problems.

79. Berry, 100.

80. Zakin, 418.

81. Jennifer Hattam, "Greening Capitol Hill," *Sierra* (January/February 2001): 55–56.

82. Berry, 100.

83. Nash, 207–8.

84. Michael P. Cohen, 349.

85. Cohen, 240.

86. Cohen, 320. See also Nash, 229–37.

87. Nash, 294.

88. Zakin, 211.

89. Zakin, 355–56.

90. For a discussion of the ads, see Michael P. Cohen, 359–60, and Zakin, 165. See also Sale, 17.

91. Browne, "Lobbying the Public," 348.

92. According to Jeffrey Berry, 130, a lobbyist's chance of being sought out by journalists or having the media publicize the group's views are significantly enhanced when they are trusted. During the 1970s, he notes, when public trust in government and business was plummeting, environmental groups were seen as credible. For a discussion of public attitudes on government and business, see Seymour Martin Lipset and William Schneider, *The Confidence Gap: Business, Labor, and Government in the Public Mind,* 2d ed. (Baltimore, Md.: Johns Hopkins University Press, 1987).

93. Berry, 120.

94. Browne, "Lobbying the Public," 348.

95. Kraft and Wuertz, 113. Other celebrities who volunteered their times and services

to environmental causes included Robert Redford and Ted Danson. Both narrated documentaries, appeared at press conferences, and produced projects with environmental themes.

96. Kraft and Wuertz, 113.

97. Some dispute this conclusion, noting that EarthFirst! played an important role in several conflicts, including the dispute over an Oregon wilderness bill in 1983. Susan Zakin, for example (258), suggests that EarthFirst!'s tactics slowed down work on a logging road long enough to publicize the issue and thereby helped the mainstream groups who were also involved in the fight raise money.

98. Hrebenar and Scott, 117–19.

99. The Endangered Species Coalition, formed to stave off efforts to weaken the law, is a good example. The Coalition included the Center for Marine Conservation, Defenders of Wildlife, the Environmental Defense Fund, the Environmental Protection Information Center, Forest Guardians, the Fund for Animals, the Greater Yellowstone Coalition, Greenpeace, the Humane Society of the United States, the National Audubon Society, the Sierra Club, the Sierra Club Legal Defense Fund, the Wilderness Society, the Western Ancient Forests Campaign, and the World Wildlife Fund. The groups worked out of the Washington offices of the Audubon Society. For a discussion of the Coalition, see Libby, 178–79.

100. David Howard Davis, "Energy on Federal Lands," in *Western Public Lands and Environmental Politics,* 2d ed., ed. Charles Davis (Boulder, Colo.: Westview Press, 2001), 166.

101. McCloskey, 84.

102. As Michael Cohen has shown, for example, the Biennial Wilderness Conferences in the late 1940s and early 1950s, which were attended by leading figures from several conservation groups, were instrumental in paving the way for the Wilderness Act in 1964. In 1955, at the fourth conference, attendees began to discuss ways of writing legislation to preserve wilderness; the fifth conference tried to link the ideas of a national resources review and a wilderness system. Michael P. Cohen, 213.

103. Cohen. The groups were the Sierra Club, the Wilderness Society, Defenders of Wildlife, the National Audubon Society, the Environmental Defense Fund, the Natural Resources Defense Council, the Izaak Walton League, the National Wildlife Federation, the National Parks and Conservation Association, and the Environmental Policy Institute. Other frequent participants included Friends of the Earth, the League of Conservation Voters, the Nature Conservancy, and the World Wildlife Fund. See also Sale, 34.

104. For a discussion of the effort to protect Alaska wilderness areas, see Nash, chap. 14; Julius Discha, "How the Alaska Act Was Won," *Living Wilderness* 44 (1981), 4–9; and "Congress Clears Alaska Lands Legislation," *CQ Almanac* 36 (1980), 575–84.

105. Allin, 220.

106. Allin, 221.

107. According to Allin, 224, the coalition included the following national organizations: the Appalachian Mountain Club, the American Rivers Conservation Council, the Cousteau Society, Defenders of Wildlife, the Environmental Defense Fund, the Environmental Policy Center, the Federation of Western Outdoor Clubs, Friends of the Earth, the National Audubon Society, the National Parks and Conservation Association, the Natural Resources Defense Council, the Sierra Club, the Wilderness Society, the United Auto Workers, and the Oil, Chemical, and Atomic Workers International Union. As one might expect, a variety of Alaska-based groups were involved as well, including the Alaska Conservation Society, the Denali Citizens Council, and the Southeast Alaska Conservation Council.

108. Allin, 224.

109. Allin, 225.

110. Allin, 224.

111. For a discussion of the divisions within the environmental community, see John J. Audley, *Global Trade: NAFTA and the Future of Environmental Politics* (Washington, D.C.: Georgetown University Press, 1997).

112. David Moberg, "Brothers and Sisters," *Sierra* (January–February 1999): 46–51, 114.

113. Both EDF and NRDC also used their scientific and policy expertise to establish a foothold in the direct lobbying game. Both groups soon developed a reputation for solid research and policy information.

114. In addition to those groups already discussed, a partial list of the national groups that engage in litigation includes the Wilderness Society, American Rivers, Defenders of Wildlife, Greenpeace, the National Audubon Society, the National Parks Conservation Association, and the National Wildlife Fund. Although there are exceptions, local grassroots organizations tend not to litigate on their own, relying instead on assistance from the national groups.

115. Mitchell, Mertig, and Dunlap, 14. See also McCloskey, 23.

116. Sale, 221.

117. George Hoberg, *Pluralism by Design: Environmental Policy and the American Regulatory State* (New York: Praeger Publishers, 1992), 198–99.

118. See Lettie McSpadden , "Environmental Policy in the Courts," in *Environmental Policy in the 1990s,* 3d ed., ed. Norman J. Vig and Michael E. Kraft (Washington, D.C.: CQ Press, 1997), 168–86.

119. See R. Shep Melnick, *Regulation and the Courts: The Case of the Clean Air Act* (Washington, D.C.: Brookings Institution, 1983).

120. The following discussion is drawn largely from George Hoberg, "The Emerging Triumph of Ecosystem Management: The Transformation of Federal Forest Policy," in *Western Public lands and Environmental Politics,* 2d ed., ed. Charles Davis (Boulder, Colo.: Westview Press, 2001), 55–85.

121. Hoberg, "The Emerging Triumph," 67–72.

122. Christopher McGrory Klyza makes a similar argument, showing how the history of mining policy in the American West was for years best described as a typical subgovernment. For all intents and purposes, the issue was invisible to most Americans, and mining companies and their governmental allies made the key decisions. This began to change when environmentalists demanded access to policymaking. According to Klyza, environmental groups used a variety of tactics to increase the visibility of mining policy, including policy analysis, congressional testimony, litigation, and media campaigns. The goal was to shift policymaking from regional arenas, where mining interests dominated, to the national level, where mining is less important. This strategy required persuading members of Congress from outside the West that mining policy was flawed, and that something should be done about it. That "something" was reform the 1872 Mining Law. See Christopher McGrory Klyza, "Reform at a Geological Pace: Mining Policy on Federal Lands," in *Western Public Lands and Environmental Politics,* 2d ed., ed. Charles Davis (Boulder, Colo.: Westview Press, 2000), 124–25.

123. I am grateful to Michael Kraft for reminding me that environmentalists had experienced other bad days at the polls. In both 1980 and 1984, of course, a significant number of candidates backed by environmental groups had been defeated. In 1980, a number of allies

lost, including President Carter, Senator George McGovern, and Senator Frank Church. In the aftermath of both elections, though, environmental groups were able to block or water down many of the Reagan administration's efforts to weaken environmental policies. The groups were also able to use the Reagan administration's actions to significantly enhance their membership and finances.

124. Christopher J. Bosso, "Environmental Groups and the New Political Landscape," in *Environmental Policy: New Directions for the Twenty-first Century,* 4th ed., ed. Norman J. Vig and Michael E. Kraft (Washington, D.C.: CQ Press, 2000), 55.

125. Switzer, *Green Backlash,* 118.

126. Bosso, "Environmental Groups and the New Political Landscape," 61.

127. For an overview of the proposed policy changes, see Gary C. Bryner, "Reforming the Regulatory Process: Congress and the Next Generation of Environmental Laws," paper presented at the Annual Meeting of the Western Political Science Association, San Francisco, March 14–16, 1996.

128. Bosso, "Environmental Groups and the New Political Landscape," 58.

129. Budget figures from Bryner, 9.

130. See Bryner, 11–13.

131. Email interview with Sarah Wilhoite, Earthjustice legislative assistant, April 1, 2002.

132. Interview with Sarah Wilhoite.

133. Interview with Sarah Wilhoite.

134. Benjamin Kline, *First along the River: A Brief History of the U.S. Environmental Movement* (San Francisco: Acad Books, 1997), 131.

135. See Switzer, 122; and Kline, 131.

136. Darrell M. West and Burdett A. Loomis, *The Sound of Money: How Political Interests Get What They Want* (New York: W. W. Norton, 1998), 134.

137. Bosso, "Environmental Groups and the New Political Landscape," 55.

138. The Federal Election Commission regulates spending on political campaigns, not lobbying activities. See West and Loomis, 111–17.

139. West and Loomis, 127.

140. See West and Loomis, 111.

141. Bosso, "Environmental Groups and the New Political Landscape," 56–57.

142. Riley E. Dunlap, "Public Opinion and the Environment (U.S.), in *Conservation and Environmentalism: An Encyclopedia,* ed. Robert Paehlke (New York: Garland, 1995), 536.

143. Kraft and Wuertz, 99.

144. Robert Gottlieb, *Forcing the Spring: The Transformation of the American Environmental Movement* (Washington, D.C.: Island Press, 1993), 130.

145. Sale, 100–101.

146. Quoted in Michael P. Cohen, 436.

147. Bosso, "Environmental Groups and the New Political Landscape," 69. See also Shaiko, *Voices and Echoes,* 29.

4. ENVIRONMENTAL ADVOCACY IN THE TWENTY-FIRST CENTURY

1. www.biodiversityproject.org/more.htm.

2. Biodiversity Project, *Life. Nature. The Public. A Communications Handbook from the Biodiversity Project* (Madison, Wisc.: Biodiversity Project, 1999), 40–41.

3. See, for example, the efforts of the Bullitt Foundation, a Seattle-based organi-

zation dedicated to helping nonprofit groups educate, organize, and mobilize the public in support of the environment. http://bullitt.org/priority_results_pub.lasso.

4. League of Conservation Voters Education Fund, *Making a Difference in 2000: The League of Conservation Voters Education Fund Grassroots Program Report 1998–99* (Washington, D.C.: LCVEF, 2000), 11–12.

5. LCVEF, *Making a Difference,* 12–13.

6. LCVEF, *Making a Difference.*

7. Marshall Mayer, "Conservation Database Report: A White Paper Prepared for the Rockefeller Family Fund," October 13, 1997.

8. Mayer, 22–24.

9. WEAVE's list enhancement project is described in the League of Conservation Voters Education Fund's *Mobilize Your Members: A Simple How-To Guide for Using Lists Effectively* (Washington, D.C.: LCVEF, 1999), viii.

10. LCVEF, *Making a Difference,* 10–11.

11. LCVEF, *Mobilize Your Members,* 41.

12. LCVEF, *Making a Difference,* 10.

13. LCVEF, *Mobilize Your Members,* viii.

14. Mayer, 27.

15. Mayer, 19.

16. Mayer.

17. Michael Stein, "Environmental Defense: From Brochureware to Actionware," http://www.benton.org/Practice/Features/environmendefense.htm. GetActive Software bills itself as "the leader in online campaigns." The firm provides nonprofits with a broad range of products and services, including messaging and advocacy software, that are designed to mobilize a group's membership through email action alerts and "take action" web pages. Groups simply select which members and decisionmakers they wish to contact, and provide a lobbying message. GetActive then matches members to the targeted policymakers, delivers the responses via email, web form, or fax, and tracks response rates. In the end, groups receive detailed, real-time information on their lobbying campaigns, and gain the ability to track which and how many of their activists responded to the call for action. Theoretically, this information allows groups to learn which issues or types of messages are most effective in mobilizing their membership. GetActive is not the only application service provider offering these services to nonprofits. Convio offers a suite of products to help groups publish personalized web content and update it quickly, conduct fundraising and membership and advocacy campaigns, manage events, track their constituency, and integrate their membership and fundraising databases.

18. Telephone interview with Dennis Schvedja, Conservation Chair of the New Jersey Sierra Club, May 18, 2001.

19. Although there are limits to legislative lobbying by 501(c)(3) organizations, the groups can engage in unlimited efforts to litigate or influence agency rule making. On the other hand, 501(c)(4) organizations can engage in unlimited lobbying, and they do not have to maintain records of their spending on such efforts.

20. ONE/Northwest, "An Activists' Strategy for Effective Online Networking," www.onenw.org/toolkit/modestproposal.htm. For another perspective see League of Conservation Voters Education Fund, *Online Advocacy: Where Are We Now and Where Do We Go from Here?* (Washington, D.C.: LCVEF, 2002).

21. Ronald G. Shaiko, *Voices and Echoes for the Environment: Public Interest Representation in the 1990s and Beyond* (New York: Columbia University Press, 1999), 141.

22. Kilmer comments from email interview with Kathy Kilmer, November 21, 2001. In a November 6–7 email interview, Devin Scherubel, whose group Heartwood monitors timber sales in national forests, says that "the use of web alerts/listserv systems has increased the number of people commenting on most sales from two to three to several dozen."

23. Email interview with Amy Zarrett, November 12, 2001. For more information about the WEC online effort, see the website of ONE/Northwest, www.onenw.org.

24. Alan Cohen, "Community: E-Vironmental Activism," *PC Magazine,* September 4, 2001.

25. Alan Cohen.

26. Email interview with Kathy Kilmer, November 21, 2001.

27. Telephone interview with Alan Metrick, November 26, 2001.

28. Interview with Alan Metrick.

29. According to Devin Scherubel, Heartwood's website sees several hundred visitors most days and serves some outreach purpose, though it is difficult to judge how much. Scherubel says that most people using the alerts are referred there by the listserv, adding that there is a "trickle of memberships and requests to be on the listserve generated from the web site—one or two a week on average." Email interview November 6–7, 2001.

30. Quoted in Jon Christensen, "Using the Internet to Sell Their Love of Canyon," *New York Times,* December 13, 2000, H12.

31. Email interview with Kathy Kilmer, November 21, 2001.

32. Marc Osten and Catherine James, "Adopting Technology Case Study: Idaho Conservation League," http://www.techsoup.org/articlepage.cfm?ArticleId=333&cg=search terms&sg=idaho%20conservation%20league.

33. Christopher J. Bosso and Michael T. Collins, "Just Another Tool? How Environmental Groups Use the Internet," in *Interest Group Politics,* 6th ed., ed. Allan J. Cigler and Burdett A. Loomis (Washington, D.C.: CQ Press, 2002), 110–11.

34. www.onenw.org (emphasis in original).

35. Christensen, "Using the Internet," H12.

36. Stein, www.benton.org/Practice/Features/environmendefense.htm.

37. Stein.

38. Stein.

39. See Environmental Defense's website, www.edf.org.

40. Raymond A. Bauer, Ithiel Pool, and Lewis A. Dexter, *American Business and Public Policy: The Politics of Foreign Trade,* 2d ed. (Chicago: Aldine-Atherton, 1972).

41. Frank R. Baumgartner and Bryan D. Jones, *Agendas and Instability in American Politics* (Chicago: University of Chicago Press, 1993); see also Christopher J. Bosso, *Pesticides and Politics: The Life Cycle of a Public Issue* (Pittsburgh, Pa.: University of Pittsburgh Press, 1987).

42. Philip Shabecoff, *Earth Rising: American Environmentalism in the Twenty-first Century* (Washington, D.C.: Island Press, 2000), 233. Groups performing in a similar role were Clean Water Action and the National Toxics Campaign.

43. Telephone interview with Jon Owen, November 8, 2001.

44. Biodiversity Project, *Life. Nature,* 5.

45. Biodiversity Project, *Making a Difference* (Madison, Wisc.: Biodiversity Project, 2000), 5.

46. Email interview with Kathy Kilmer, manager of electronic communications, November 21, 2001.

47. Biodiversity Project, *Making a Difference,* 4.

48. Biodiversity Project, *Life. Nature,* 11–16. Similar themes were clearly evident in the Sierra Club's televised issue advocacy commercials, which usually concluded with an appeal to citizens to contact their legislators about some local environmental issue that was crucial: "For our families. For our future."

49. William P. Browne, *Groups, Interests, and U.S. Public Policy* (Washington, D.C.: Georgetown University Press, 1998), 85–89; see also Christopher J. Bosso, "The Contextual Bases of Problem Definition," in *The Politics of Problem Definition: Shaping the Policy Agenda,* ed. David A. Rochefort and Roger W. Cobb (Lawrence: University Press of Kansas, 1994), 182–88.

50. Biodiversity Project, *Life. Nature,* 18.

51. Bosso, "Contextual Bases," 45–46.

52. Bosso, "Contextual Bases," 9.

53. Telephone interview with Alan Metrick, November 26, 2001.

54. Robert Mitchell, "Public Opinion and Environmental Politics in the 1970s and 1980s," in *Environmental Policy in the 1980s: Reagan's New Agenda,* ed. Norman Vig and Michael E. Kraft (Washington, D.C.: CQ Press, 1984); see also Michael E. Kraft and Diana Wuertz, "Environmental Advocacy in the Corridors of Government," in *The Symbolic Earth: Discourse and Our Creation of the Environment,* ed. James G. Cantrill and Christine L. Oravec (Louisville: University Press of Kentucky, 1999), 101.

55. Biodiversity Project, *Life. Nature,* 22.

56. Biodiversity Project, *Life. Nature,* 12–14.

57. Telephone interview with Jon Owen, the group's outreach and advocacy director, November 8, 2001.

58. www.appc.penn.org/issueads/national%2-environmental%20trust.htm.

59. www.appcpenn.org/issueads/heritage%20Forests%20Campaign.htm.

60. www.appc.penn.org/issueads/M . . . Common%20Sense%20Mining%20laws.htm.

61. Telephone interview with David Yeaworth, November 20, 2001.

62. Telephone interview with Alan Metrick, November 26, 2001.

63. Biodiversity Project, *Life. Nature,* 24.

64. John Elkington and Francesa Muller, *Good News and Bad: The Media, Corporate Social Responsibility, and Sustainable Development* (London: SustainAbility, 2002).

65. Among those who claim that coalition building is more pronounced today are Jon Owen of the Washington Wilderness Coalition, Kathy Kilmer of the Wilderness Society, and Elise Jones of the Colorado Environmental Coalition. A number of scholars have noted the trend as well, notably Shaiko, 3 and 186; see also Browne, *Groups,* 147.

66. E. E. Schatteschneider, *The Semi-Sovereign People* (New York: Holt, Rinehart, and Winston, 1960).

67. George Milne, Easwar Iyer, and Sara Gooding-Williams, "Environmental Organization Alliance Relationships within and across Nonprofit, Business, and Government Sectors," *Journal of Public Policy and Marketing* (Fall 1996), 377, cited in Shaiko, 186. Telephone interview with David Yeaworth, November 20, 2001.

68. Telephone interview with David Yeaworth, November 20, 2001.

69. Sierra Club News Release, January 12, 2001.

70. Poornima Goopta, "Advertising War Launched over Arctic Oil Fields," March 28, 2001 (Reuters News Service).

71. Biodiversity Project, *Making a Difference,* 9.

72. John J. Audley, *Global Trade: NAFTA and the Future of Environmental Politics* (Washington, D.C.: Georgetown University Press, 1997), 54–55.

73. John H. Cushman Jr., "Election Day Brings Rise in Donations for Greens," *New York Times,* November 18, 2002, E19.

74. For details, see Pew's website, www.pewtrusts.com.

75. Douglas Jehl, "Charity Is New Force in Environmental Fight," *New York Times,* June 28, 2001, A1.

76. http://www.pewwildernesscenter.org/about/index.html. See also the Center's press releases of November 20, 2001, and May 24, 2001.

77. www.pewtrusts.com.

78. Jehl, "Charity," A1.

79. All information from Bullitt's website, www.bullitt.org.

80. See Shaiko, 144.

81. Christopher J. Bosso and Deborah Lynn Guber, "The Boundaries and Contours of American Environmental Activism," in *Environmental Policy: New Directions for the Twenty-first Century,* 5th ed., ed. Norman J. Vig and Michael E. Kraft (Washington, D.C.: CQ Press, 2002), 98.

5. ENVIRONMENTAL GROUPS IN NATIONAL ELECTIONS

1. See Deborah Lynn Guber, "Voting Preferences and the Environment in the American Electorate," *Society and Natural Resources* 14, no. 6 (2001), 456; and Ronald Shaiko, *Voices and Echoes for the Environment* (New York: Columbia University Press, 1999), 38. See also Deborah Lynn Guber, *The Grassroots of a Green Revolution: Polling America on the Environment* (Cambridge, Mass.: MIT Press, 2003).

2. Guber, "Voting Preferences," 464.

3. Guber, "Voting Preferences," 464.

4. Guber, "Voting Preferences," 465.

5. See as examples Mark Rozell and Clyde Wilcox, *Interest Groups in American Campaigns: The New Face of Electioneering* (Washington, D.C.: CQ Press, 1999), and Paul Herrnson, "Parties and Interest Groups in Postreform Congressional Elections," in *Interest Group Politics,* 5th ed., ed. Allan J. Cigler and Burdett A. Loomis (Washington, D.C.: CQ Press, 1998), 145–68.

6. Christopher J. Bosso, "Environmental Groups and the New Political Landscape," in *Environmental Policy in the 1990s,* 4th ed., ed. Norman J. Vig and Michael E. Kraft (Washington, D.C.: CQ Press, 2000), 66–67.

7. See Thomas Ferraro, "Friends of Earth May Shun Gore Again," *Worldwire* April 19, 2000, cited at www.enn.com/ne.04192000/reugorefriends 12164asp.; and Michelle Nijhuis, "Nader Shakes Up Western Enviros," *High Country News,* October 23, 2000.

8. Francine Kiefer, "Green Issues Alter Campaign Climate," *Christian Science Monitor,* April 21, 2000, 3.

9. See Nijhuis, and Associated Press, "Environmentalists Urge Gore Vote," October 25, 2000.

10. LCV press release, November 8, 2001.

11. *Congressional Quarterly Weekly Report,* 58, no. 44 (November 11, 2000), 2694–2703.

12. Philip Shabecoff, *Earth Rising: American Environmentalism in the Twenty-first Century* (Washington, D.C.: Island Press, 2000), 133.

13. For a discussion of the race in New Mexico's Third District, see Lonna Rae Atkeson and Anthony C. Coveny, "The 1998 New Mexico Third Congressional District Race," in *Outside Money: Soft Money and Issue Advocacy in the 1998 Congressional Elections,* ed. David Magleby (New York: Rowman and Littlefield, 2000), 135–51.

14. Atkeson and Coveny.

15. Bosso, "Environmental Groups and the New Political Landscape," 68.

16. Shabecoff, 126.

17. Christopher J. Bosso, "Seizing Back the Day: The Challenge to Environmental Activism in the 1990s," in *Environmental Policy in the 1990s,* 3d ed., ed. Norman J. Vig and Michael E. Kraft (Washington, D.C.: CQ Press, 1997), 59.

18. David B. Truman, *The Governmental Process,* 2d ed. (New York: Knopf, 1971).

19. According to Victoria Simirano, WILD PAC's executive director, the idea for the group had been in the making for over a decade. WILD PAC seeks to fill a niche in the environmental PAC community by tapping into a network of supporters and wilderness activists who have not been involved in prior elections. Their target is people who are passionate about wilderness protection but have shown little interest in conventional politics. As of April 2002, 90 percent of its contributors had never made a political contribution. The group's leaders plan to make the case that wilderness protection campaigns will have a much better chance of being enacted into law with a different, "greener" Congress. WILD PAC, which is organized like Emily's List, a PAC that contributes to women candidates, will both "bundle" contributions from individuals and make direct contributions to candidates. In the 2002 elections, the first in which the group made contributions, WILD PAC spent about $50,000 and focused on eleven races, which were carefully selected so as to maximize the group's influence and to make "a good impression." Six of the eleven candidates supported by the group won their races. In addition to contributing money, WILD PAC will focus on get-out-the-vote campaigns, and will provide campaigns with assistance with fundraising, media, organizing, and public lands expertise. Telephone interview with Victoria Simarano, Executive Director of WILD PAC, April 17, 2002.

20. Theodore J. Eismeier and Phillip H. Pollock III, "An Organizational Analysis of Political Action Committees," *Political Behavior* 7 (1985), 192–216; see also M. Margaret Conway, "PACs in the Political Process," in *Interest Group Politics,* 3d ed., ed. Allan J. Cigler and Burdett A. Loomis (Washington, D.C.: CQ Press, 1991), 204.

21. Conway, 208.

22. Frank J. Sorauf, *Money in American Politics* (Glenview, Ill.: Scott, Foresman, 1988), 103.

23. Frank J. Sorauf, "PACs and Parties in American Politics," in *Interest Group Politics,* 3d ed., ed. Allen J. Cigler and Burdett A. Loomis (Washington, D.C.: CQ Press, 1991), 230.

24. See David Cantor, "The Sierra Club Political Committee," and Philip A. Mundo, "League of Conservation Voters," in *After the Revolution: PACs, Lobbies, and the Republican Congress,* ed. Robert Biersack, Paul S. Herrnson, and Clyde Wilcox (Boston, Allyn and Bacon, 1999).

25. Personal correspondence with author, August 12, 1998. See also *Roll Call,* 22 September 1996.

26. Sierra Club Political Committee Compliance Guidelines 1995, 20, cited in Cantor, 102–7.

27. Cantor, 108.

28. Cantor, 104–10; see also Richard L. Berke, "Sierra Club Ads in Political Races Offer a Case Study of 'Issue Advocacy,'" *Los Angeles Times,* February 1, 1996, A12.

29. Mundo, 120.

30. Robert Dreyfuss, "Rousing the Democratic Base," *American Prospect,* November 6, 2000, 20.

31. In New Mexico's Third District in 1998, the LCV targeted a particular part of the district because Carol Miller, the Green Party candidate, had won many votes there in the 1997 special election, and because of information suggesting that many of the district's voters were "persuadable" in the 1998 contest. See Atkeson and Coveny, 142.

32. David Magleby, "Outside Money and the Ground War in 1998," in *Outside Money: Soft Money and Issue Advocacy in the 1998 Congressional Elections,* ed. David Magleby (New York: Rowman and Littlefield, 2000), 65.

33. All data are from the records of the Federal Election Commission. In particular, see FEC news release of April 22, 1997, "PAC Activity Increases in 1995–96 Election Cycle."

34. FEC, "PAC Activity Increases."

35. Eliza Newlin Carney, "Stealth Bombers," *National Journal,* August 16, 1997, 1643.

36. http://www.opensecrets.org/cmteprofiles.

37. All data from FEC filings.

38. FEC press release, May 31, 2001; see www.fec.gov/press/053101/pacfund/tables/pacie00.htm.

39. Rozell and Wilcox, 138.

40. John Byrne Barry, "Making the Environment Matter," *The Planet* 1, no. 4 (January 1997); see also Kim Murphy, "Oregon's New Senator Credits Environmental Vote for Victory," *Los Angeles Times,* February 1, 1996, A12.

41. www.lcv.org, www.sierraclub.org, FEC reports C00252940, C00135368.

42. Robin Toner, "Interest Groups Take New Route to Congressional Election Arena," *New York Times,* August 20, 1996, A1.

43. www.lcv.org/news/0621release_ddannounce.htm.

44. Mundo, 124.

45. www.lcv.org/dirtydozen.

46. The thirteen targets, twelve of whom were Republicans, were Senate candidates Lauch Faircloth (R-N.C.), Bob Inglis (R-S.C.), John Ensign (R-Nev.), Linda Smith (R-Wash.), Mark Neumann (R-Wisc.), and House candidates Rick White (R-Wa.), Tom Bordonaro (R-Calif.), Bill Redmond (R-N.M.), Bob Dornan (R-Calif.), Charlie Stenholm (D-Tex.), Helen Chenoweth (R-Idaho), John Hostettler (R-Ind.), and Bud Cramer (R-Ala.).

47. For a discussion of the LCV's efforts in the Nevada senate race, see www.lcv.org/dirtydozen/ensignrace. See also Tim Fackler, Nathalie Frensley et al., "The 1998 Nevada Senate Race," in *Outside Money: Soft Money and.Issue Advocacy in the 1998 Congressional Elections,* ed. David Magleby (New York: Rowman and Littlefield, 2000), 127.

48. www.lcv.org/dirtydozen/chenowethrace.

49. www.lcv.org/news/101000.html.

50. www.lcv.org/news/100800_ElectionNightRelease.htm.

51. Telephone interview with Betsy Loyless, LCV political director, November 25, 2002.

52. B. J. Bergman, "Majority Rules, and Its Green," *Sierra* (January–February 1997), 52.

53. Personal correspondence to author, August 12, 1998.

54. www.fec.gov.

55. www.sierraclub.org/action.

56. Sierra Club news release, October 25, 2000.

57. Rozell and Wilcox, 106–8.

58. Bergman, 2.

59. Sierra Club 1997 Financial Report, April 24, 1998. According to Carl Pope, the Club's executive director, the $8.5 million consisted of what the group planned to spend during the two-year election cycle plus "all of our EVEC work and everything we do that is not 501 (c)(3) or (c)(4). It has not all been raised, but if it is, it will be spent." http://www.sierraclub.org/bod/minutes/2000/mb2000520.asp.

60. Cantor, 107.

61. http://www.sierraclub.org/bod/minutes/2000/mb2000520.asp.

62. Telephone interview with Vicki Simirano, November 14, 2002.

63. Beth Sullivan, "Dear Friend" letter, October 16, 2000.

64. www.voteenvironment.org/release4 191.html.

65. LCVEF, "Debunking Environmental Myths: Unveiling How Voters Really Feel about Clean Air and Water," September 28, 2000.

66. Carl Pope, "Earth to Congress," *Sierra* (May–June 1997), 55.

67. Bergman, 52.

68. John H. Cushman Jr., "Environmentalists Ante Up to Sway a Number of Races," *New York Times,* October 23, 1996, A21.

69. Kim Murphy, "Oregon's New Senator Credits Environmental Vote for Victory," *Los Angeles Times,* February 1, 1996, A12.

70. Cushman, A21.

71. http://www.sierraclub.org/bod/minutes/2000/mb20000520.asp.

72. Sierra Club media release, November 4, 1998.

73. The boy's mother asked then Governor Bush to clean up the kiln, but the family moved away when Bush did not respond. The ad told viewers, "Texas leads the nation in cancer-causing and toxic chemicals released into the environment, in hazardous waste, in the number of factories violating clean water standards. And while federal laws are forcing states to clean up their air and water, Texas lags far behind. Even though Texas has 400,000 kids with asthma, like William Tinker, George Bush has proposed weakening the Clean Air Act. Call George Bush. Tell him to clean up Texas's air and water, for our families, and for William Tinker's future." Sierra Club news release, January 4, 2000.

74. Associated Press, "Sierra Club to Fund Congress Races," April 25, 2000.

75. Sierra Club news release, April 25, 2000.

76. Sierra Club news release, September 28, 2000.

77. Sierra Club news release, September 19, 2000.

78. Telephone interview with Margaret Conway, Sierra Club political director, November 22, 2002.

79. Interview with Margaret Conway.

80. Telephone interview with Jonathan Ela of the Sierra Club's EVEC committee, November 19, 2002.

81. Sierra Club press release, August 26, 2002.

82. Thomas Edsall, "Issue Coalitions Take on Political Party Functions," *Washington Post,* August 8, 1996, A1.

83. Ruth Marcus and Charles Babcock, "The System Cracks under the Weight of Cash," *Washington Post,* February 9, 1997, A1; see also Annenberg Public Policy Center, *Issue Advocacy Advertising during the 1997–1998 Election Cycle* (Philadelphia, Pa.: Annenberg Public Policy Center, 1999), 18–19.

84. *The Hotline,* July 12, 1996, cited in Annenberg, 18.

85. Carney, 1640–43.

86. Ruth Marcus, "Outside Groups Pushing Election Laws into Irrelevance," *Washington Post,* August 8, 1996, A9.

87. Carney, 1642.

88. Edsall, A1.

89. Annenberg, 4.

90. Richard L. Berke, "Sierra Club Ads in Political Races Offer a Case Study of 'Issue Advocacy,'" *New York Times,* October 24, 1998, A12.

91. www.sierraclub.org/planet/199901/truth.

92. www.sierraclub.org/planet/199901/truth.

93. According to Russ Lehman, the group's managing director, the ads were developed with the assistance of a Washington, D.C., media consultant, who advised where and when the ads should be aired. The groups also used polling to determine that the issues important to their "constituency" were also important to voters. In addition to its broadcast ads, the Project also worked with individual tribes to encourage registration and voting. Because Native American groups have not been actively involved in federal elections, the group's efforts attracted considerable media attention. Gorton's opponent in the race, Maria Cantwell, asked the Project not to run ads "on her behalf." In response, Russ Lehman issued a statement noting that, as a nonprofit social welfare organization, "FAEP will never call for the election or defeat of any candidate and do not and will not attempt to influence electoral politics as our primary purpose. FAEP has never coordinated its activities with any candidate or political party committee and is not working on behalf of any candidate, for any office." Information from First Americans Education Project News Release, October 2000; see also Stephen Stuebner, "Stalking Slade," *High Country News,* October 23, 2000.

94. http://www.appc.penn.org/issueads/Clean%20Air%Trust.html.

95. http://www.appc.penn.org/issueads/Democratic%20National%20Committee.htm.

96. *Greenwire,* March 6, 2000.

97. Christopher J. Bosso, "Adaptation and Change in the Environmental Movement," in *Interest Group Politics*, 3d ed., ed. Alan J. Cigler and Bardett A. Loomis (Washington, D.C.: CQ Press, 1991), 154.

98. Carney, 1642.

99. David Magleby, "Conclusions and Implications," in *Outside Money: Soft Money and Issue Advocacy in the 1998 Congressional Elections,* ed. David Magleby (New York: Rowman and Littlefield, 2000), 212.

100. Magleby, 213–16.

101. Christopher J. Bosso and Deborah Lynn Guber, "The Boundaries and Contours of American Environmental Activism," in *Environmental Policy: New Directions for the Twenty-first Century,* 5th ed., ed. Norman J. Vig and Michael E. Kraft (Washington, D.C.: CQ Press, 2002), 88.

102. Telephone interview with Betsy Loyless, LCV political director, November 25, 2002.

103. Blaine Harden, "National and State Politics Help Safeguard a Swamp," *New York Times* April 3, 2002.

104. Carl Pope, "Perot's Ghost," *Sierra* (March/April 2001), 14–16.

105. David Magleby, ed., *Outside Money: Soft Money and Issue Advocacy in the 1998 Congressional Elections* (New York: Rowman and Littlefield, 2000).

106. Bergman, 50.

107. Carl Pope, "Earth to Congress," *Sierra* (May–June 1997), 52. In a 2000 Sierra Club board meeting, Pope made this comment about the group's changing electoral role: "In politics there are voters, the media playwrights, actors, and the chorus. Environmental groups such as the Sierra Club have been part of the chorus. We commented upon what was happening but were not commented upon. We have now reached the point of important effectiveness. We are not candidates or parties but have a feature role on stage. We have more influence over the process because we got better at it. But there is also more chance for mistakes. We have to design programs that have integrity." http://www.sierraclub.org/bod/minutes/2000/mb20000520.asp.

108. John Cushman, "GOP Backing Off from Tough Stand over Environment," *New York Times,* January 26, 1996, A1.

109. Pope, "Earth to Congress," 71.

110. Mundo, 120.

111. Telephone interview with Betsy Loyless, LCV political director, November 25, 2002.

112. Sierra Club press release, November 1, 2002; interview with Margaret Conway, November 22, 2002.

113. Telephone interview, November 25, 2002.

114. www.lcv.org/news/post_election/101000.html.

115. Telephone interview with Margaret Conway, November 22, 2002.

116. www.lcv.org/dirtydozen.

117. www.lcv.org/dirtydozen/quinlan_memo.

118. www.lcv.org/dirtydozen/quinlan_memo.

119. www.lcv.org/dirtydozen/neumannrace.

120. www.lcv.org/dirtydozen/smithrace.

121. www.lcv.org/dirtydozen/ensignrace.

122. Toner, "Interest Groups," A1.

123. Marcus and Babcock, A21.

124. Bosso, "Seizing Back the Day," 63.

6. ENVIRONMENTALISM IN THE STATES

1. Like other LCV organizations, the CLCV is nonpartisan, although in recent years it has supported mostly Democrats. The CLCV is supported by thirty thousand members, and works in coalition with a wide array of environmental and community organizations.

2. The nonfederal EVECs were discussed at a Sierra Club board meeting in 2000. The Club was considering two or three EVEC sites for that election cycle. To be considered, state chapters needed to communicate to the national Club what unique factors made their race suitable for such a campaign. See http://www.sierraclub.org/bod/minutes/2000/mb20000520.asp.

3. Email interview with Ed Zuckerman, executive director of Federation of State Conservation Voter Leagues, April 16, 2002.

4. Zuckerman interview.

5. www.nylcv.org/About/about/htm.

6. www.oclv.org/greenvoter.htm.

7. League of Conservation Voters Education Fund, *Making a Difference in 2000: The League of Conservation Voters Education Fund Grassroots Program Report 1998–99*, 2.

8. LCV, *Making a Difference*, 3. See also Washington Environmental Alliance for Voter Education, "Permanent Absentee Voter Enrollment Program Progress Report, September 20, 1999, www. weave.org.

9. Telephone interview with Tony Massaro, executive director of Colorado Conservation Voters, April 11, 2002. Political Action for Conservation, another Colorado PAC, had been active in the state in the 1980s, but its influence was limited. The most the group ever raised was $19,000 in 1984.

10. According to Massaro, the group planned to spend $150,000 during the 2002 election cycle.

11. www.coloradoconservationvoters.org.

12. www.coloradoconservationvoters.org.

13. www.coloradoconservationvoters.org.

14. Telephone interview with Tony Massaro, November 18, 2002.

15. Tony Massaro interview.

16. http://minnesota.sierraclub.org/mr_flood_pulses_rivers.htm.

17. http://minnesota.sierraclub.org/mr_flood_pulses_rivers.htm.

18. Telephone interview with Victoria Simirano, executive director of WILD PAC, April 1, 2002.

19. www.cfep.org/about/how.html.

20. Typically, referenda are measures placed on the ballot by elected officials, while initiatives are placed there by citizens. Although requirements vary from state to state, sponsors of initiatives must generally obtain a certain number of signatures from registered voters. Figures on the number of states with direct democracy provisions are from Larry R. Mutter, Randy J. Virden, and N. Joseph Cayer, "Interest Group Influence in State Natural Resource Policymaking," *Society and Natural Resources* 12 (1999), 252.

21. Barry Rabe, "Power to the States: The Promise and Pitfalls of Decentralization," in *Environmental Policy in the 1990s*, 3d ed., ed. Norman J. Vig and Michael E. Kraft (Washington, D.C.: CQ Press, 1997), 36–37. For a broader consideration of initiatives and referenda, see Richard J. Ellis, *Democratic Delusions: The Initiative Process in America* (Lawrence: University Press of Kansas, 2001), and Thomas E. Cronin, *Direct Democracy: The Politics of Initiative, Referendum, and Recall* (Cambridge, Mass.: Harvard University Press, 1989).

22. Deborah Lynn Guber, "Voting Preferences and the Environment in the American Electorate," *Society and Natural Resources* 14, no. 6 (2001), 466.

23. Ronald T. Hrebenar and Ruth K. Scott, *Interest Group Politics in America* (New York: Prentice-Hall, 1982), 121.

24. Robert S. Erikson, Gerald C. Wright, and John P. McIver, *Statehouse Democracy: Public Opinion and Policy in the American States* (New York: Cambridge University Press, 1993).

25. Ronald T. Libby, *Eco-Wars: Political Campaigns and Social Movements* (New York: Columbia University Press, 1998), 91.

26. Jacqueline Vaughn Switizer, *Green Backlash: The History and Politics of Environmental Opposition in the U.S.* (Boulder, Colo.: Lynne Rienner Publishers, 1997), 134.

27. Andrew Branan, "Going against the Greens," *Ripon Forum* 30 (July 1995), 10.

28. See Libby, chap. 4.

29. Phyllis Myers and Robert Puentes, *Growth at the Ballot Box: Electing the Shape of Communities in November 2000. A Discussion Paper Prepared for the Brookings Institution Center on Urban and Metropolitan Policy* (Washington, D.C.: Brookings Center on Urban and Metropolitan Policy, 2001), 3.

30. For 1996 results, See Phyllis Myers, "Voters Go for the Green," *GREENSENSE,* Spring 1997, 3 (published by the Trust for the Public Land); for 1998 see Phyllis Myers, *Livability at the Ballot Box: State and Local Referenda on Parks, Conservation, and Smarter Growth, Election Day 1998* (Washington, D.C.: Brookings Center on Urban and Metropolitan Policy, 1999).

31. Myers, *Livability,* 1.

32. Myers, *Livability,* 3.

33. Tony Davis, "Arizona: Courting the Green Vote," *High Country News,* November 23, 1998 (http://www.hcn.org/1998/nov23/dir/Election_Hots3022.htm).

34. Dustin Solberg, "Oregon: Keep on Cutting," *High Country News,* November 23, 1998 (http://www.hcn.org/1998/nov23/dir/Election_Hots3022.htm).

35. LCVEF Handbook, 5.

36. LCVEF Handbook, 9.

37. Dustin Solberg, "Colorado: Voters Thread through the Ballot," *High Country News,* November 23, 1998 (http://www.hcn.org/1998/nov23/dir/Election_Hots3022.htm).

38. Solberg, 5.

39. Email interview with Jim Jensen, executive director of the Montana Environmental Information Center, July 9, 2002.

40. Jim Jensen interview.

41. Jim Jensen interview.

42. www.meic.org/il137victory/htm.

43. Myers and Puentes, 8.

44. Myers and Puentes, 9.

45. Berny Morson, "Growth Fight Escalates," *Denver Rocky Mountain News,* October 1, 2000, 14A.

46. Morson.

47. Morson.

48. Trent Siebert, "Voters Favor Growth Controls," *Denver Post,* October 2, 2000, 1A. The poll of five hundred registered voters was conducted for *Denver Post*/9 News/ KOA News Radio.

4 9. Michele Ames, "Two Issues Near $1 Million Mark," *Rocky Mountain News,* October 31, 2000.

50. Trent Siebert, "Voters Favor Growth Controls," *Denver Post,* October 2, 2000, 1A.

51. Kristi Arellano, "Ballot Issues Pique Interest," *Denver Post,* September 10, 2000, 1L.

52. Arellano.

53. Myers and Puentes, 35–36.

54. Bruce Finley and Peggy Lowe, "Colorado Takes the Initiative," *Denver Post,* August 4, 1998, 1A.

55. Associated Press, "Voters Approved Two-Thirds of Local 2001 Land Conservation Initiatives," January 25, 2002.

56. Myers and Puentes, 3.

57. Myers and Puentes, 7.

58. Smart Growth America, "Greetings from Smart Growth America," Washington, D.C., 2000; cited in Myers and Puentes.

59. Myers, *Livability,* 15.

60. Myers and Puentes, 24.

61. See Myers, *Livability,* 3; and Myers and Puentes, 4.

62. Myers and Puentes, 9.

63. Myers, *Livability,* 3.

64. Myers and Puente, 10.

65. See Ellis.

66. Myers, *Livability,* 16.

67. For a discussion of environmental policy in the states, see Denise Scheberle, *Federalism and Environmental Policy: Trust and the Politics of Implementation* (Washington, D.C.: Georgetown University Press, 1997); DeWitt John, *Civic Environmentalism: Alternatives to Regulation in States and Communities* (Washington, D.C.: CQ Press, 1994); and Evan Rinquist, *Environmental Protection at the State Level: Politics and Progress in Controlling Pollution* (Armonk, N.Y.: M. E. Sharpe, 1993).

68. For information about the Oregon Conservation Network, see http://www.oclv.org/ocn.htm.

69. http://www.oclv.org/olcvef.html.

70. The OLCV is not unusual. The New York League of Conservation Voters publishes a number of *Citizen Guides to Government and the Environment,* each of which discusses major issues and outlines the government, laws, public agencies, officials, and organizations that play a role in the state's environmental policy. See http://www.nylcv.org/Programs/NYCEF/nyceffactf.htm.

71. Telephone interview with Elisa Lynch, campaign director of Blue Water Network, July 3, 2002.

72. Natural Resources Defense Council press release, July 1, 2002, "Watershed Air Pollution Measure Passes California Assembly Today, Puts State in Driver's Seat in Fight against Global Warming."

73. Telephone interview with Elisa Lynch, campaign director of Bluewater Network, July 3, 2002.

74. *Sacramento Bee,* May 6, 2002, A7.

75. Miguel Bustillo and Carl Ingram, "Auto-Emission Bill Okd, Sent to Davis," *Los Angeles Times,* July 2, 2002 http://www.latimes.com/news/printedition/la-me-global2jul02012056.story.

76. Danny Hakim, "California Is Moving to Guide U.S. Policy on Pollution," *New York Times,* July 3, 2002, A1.

77. Mutter, Virden, and Cayer, 252.

78. http://www.alaleavs.org/current_issues.htm. Accessed July 11, 2002.

79. Ray Ring, "Bad Moon Rising: The Waning of Montana's Once-Mighty Progressive Coalition," *High Country News,* December 17, 2001, 1.

80. For a discussion of the factors affecting state environmental performance, see Barry Rabe, "Power to the States: The Promise and Pitfalls of Decentralization," in *Environmental Policy: New Directions for the Twenty-first Century,* 5th ed., ed. Norman J. Vig and Michael E. Kraft (Washington, D.C.: CQ Press, 2002), 34.

81. See George A. Gonzalez, "Local Growth Coalitions, Environmental Groups, and Air Pollution," paper presented at the Annual Meeting of the Southern Political Science Association, November 6–9, Savannah, Ga.; see also Evan Rinquist, *Environmental Protection at the State Level: Politics and Progress in Controlling Pollution* (Armonk, N.Y.: M. E. Sharpe, 1993), and William R. Lowry, *The Dimensions of Federalism: State Governments and Pollution Control Policies* (Durham, N.C.: Duke University Press, 1992).

82. Edward P. Weber, "A New Vanguard for the Environment: Grass-Roots Ecosystem Management as a New Environmental Movement," *Society and Natural Resources* 13 (2000), 246–47. For a different perspective, see Kent E. Portney, *Taking Sustainable Cities Seriously: Economic Development, the Environment, and Quality of Life in American Cities* (Cambridge, Mass.: MIT Press, 2003).

83. Weber, 237.

84. Daniel A. Mazmanian and Michael E. Kraft, "The Three Epochs of the Environmental Movement," in *Toward Sustainable Communities: Transition and Transformations in Environmental Policy,* ed. Daniel A. Mazmanian and Michael E. Kraft (Cambridge, Mass.: MIT Press, 1999), 4–5.

85. See Weber, 238.

86. David N. Pellow, "Negotiation and Confrontation: Environmental Policymaking through Consensus," *Society and Natural Resources* 12, no. 3 (1999), 191.

87. Weber, 251.

88. Weber, 239.

89. Daniel Kemmis, *This Sovereign Land: A New Vision for Governing the West* (Washington, D.C.: Island Press, 2001), 227.

90. Weber, 239.

91. Kemmis, 127. For a discussion of several non-western examples, see Daniel A. Mazmanian and Michael E. Kraft, *Toward Sustainable Communities: Transition and Transformations in Environmental Policy* (Cambridge, Mass.: MIT Press, 1999).

92. Weber, 256.

93. U.S. EPA, *Framework for Community-based Environmental Protection:* EPA 237-K-99–001 (Washington, D.C.: U.S. EPA, 1999).

94. Mutter, Virden, and Cayer, 253.

95. Rebecca Claren, "Hatching Reform," *High Country News,* June 10, 2002, 1.

96. Claren, 10.

97. Claren, 11.

98. Pellow, 197.

99. Applegate Partnership, Open Letter to the Environmental Community," available at http://www.hcn.org/home_page/dir/email_letters.htm.

100. Michael McCloskey memorandum to Sierra Club board of directors, reprinted in *High Country News* at http://www.hcn.org/servlets/hcn.PrintableArticle?article_id=1839.

101. McCloskey memorandum.

102. Pellow, 198.

103. Applegate Partnership, "Open Letter to the environmental community," available at http://www.hcn.org/home_page/dir/email_letters.htm.

104. http://www.hcn.org/home_page/dir/email_letters.htm.

105. Kemmis, 146.

106. See Kemmis, 130–31.

107. Michael Grunwald, "Among Environmentalists, the Great Divide," *Washington Post,* June 26, 2002, A13.

108. Email interview with William L. Baker, July 15, 2002.

109. William L. Baker interview. Because of this unsatisfying experience, the Institute has decided that it will no longer sponsor or set up collaborative groups. Instead, they shifted their focus to education and research.

110. Tim Westby, "Greens Bail on 'Bilers," *High Country News,* January 21, 2002, 6.

111. Rebecca Claren, "No Game Plan for the Public Lands," *High Country News,* February 4, 2002, 3.

112. Claren.

113. Rebecca Claren, "Ruling Ripples through Salmon Country," *High Country News,* December 3, 2001, 3.

7. CONCLUSION

1. Elizabeth Becker, "Website Helped Change Farm Policy," *New York Times,* February 22, 2004, A22.

2. "The Facts and the Farm Bill," *American Prospect,* March 11, 2002, 8. At its inception, the Environmental Working Group spent its relatively small $2 million annual budget on computer database experts, large computer servers, and salaries for its staff. The organization, which receives most of its funding from nonprofit foundations, was created specifically to provide information and policy analysis to journalists, policymakers, environmental groups, and the general public. All of its research projects are required to include plans showing how the project could appeal to journalists as well as how they could "open up" the debate over environmental issues. The EWG produces hundreds of reports each year, many of which are released in collaboration with public interest groups. See Becker, 22, for additional background on the organization.

3. William P. Browne, *Groups, Interests, and U.S. Public Policy* (Washington, D.C.: Georgetown University Press, 1998), 93. In addition to having "good issues," Browne cites a number of other advantages that contributed to the eventual success of the environmental movement. To begin, there were "respected conservation interests" that had been politically active for decades. There were also numerous conservation policies and programs already in place, such as national parks, which meant there was institutional support inside government for environmental policies, and public support for those programs. Problems in these programs were becoming apparent, and conservation lobbyists came to believe that new conservation strategies were needed. Fortunately, conservation groups had sensible, feasible solutions to recommend. In addition, conservation groups adopted a cautious approach to policy change, opting not to take on too many battles and too many "entrenched interests" at once. Finally, the presence of so many environmental organizations, focused on so many environmental issues, gave public officials different things to do and different issues to champion. In the end, says Browne, "support and rewards for a solid lobbying effort were there." See pages 170–77.

4. Cobb and Elder also note the importance of symbols in creating "stakeholders" in policy debates. The creative and effective use of symbols can enable groups to persuade

previously uninterested individuals that an issue affects them personally. The hope, of course, is that those individuals will not only take an interest in the issue, but will join the fight as well by joining the group or by communicating their preferences to policymakers. See Roger W. Cobb and Charles D. Elder, *Participation in American Politics: The Dynamics of Agenda-Building* (Boston: Allyn and Bacon, 1972), 103.

5. A third trait, according to Downs, is that the problem is not "intrinsically exciting." Consequently, news about the problem competes with other problems, and other forms of entertainment, for a share of people's time. See Anthony Downs, "Up and Down with Ecology: 'The Issue-Attention Cycle,'" *Public Interest* 28 (1972): 28–50.

6. Kirkpatrick Sale, *The Green Revolution: The American Environmental Movement, 1962–1992* (New York: Hill and Wang, 1993), 238.

7. Darrell M. West and Burdett A. Loomis, *The Sound of Money: How Political Interests Get What They Want* (New York: W.W. Norton, 1998), 21.

8. Allan J. Cigler and Burdett A. Loomis, "From Big Bird to Bill Gates: Organized Interests and the Emergence of Hyperpolitics," in *Interest Group Politics*, 5th ed., ed. Allan J. Cigler and Burdett A. Loomis (Washington, D.C.: CQ Press, 1998), 388–90.

9. West and Loomis, 217.

10. Cigler and Loomis, 390; see also West and Loomis, 30.

11. West and Loomis, 231.

12. Federal Election Commission News Release, May 15, 2001.

13. FEC Report on PAC Activity, May 31, 2001.

14. See Paul Hendried, ed., *The Big Picture: The Money behind the 1998 Elections* (Washington, D.C.: Center for Responsive Politics, 1999), 4; see also Larry Makinson, ed., *The Big Picture: Who Paid for the Last Election?* (Washington, D.C.: Center for Responsive Politics, 1997).

15. Timothy Egan, "Look Who's Hugging Trees Now," *New York Times Magazine*, July 7, 1996, 28–32.

16. www.opensecrets.org/industries/indus.asp.

17. See Robert Perks, Wesley Warren, and Gregory Wetstone, *Rewriting the Rules: The Bush Administration's Assault on the Environment* (Washington, D.C.: Natural Resources Defense Council, April 2002).

18. For details on the relationship between campaign contributions and the Bush energy plan, see Center for Responsive Politics and "The Bill That Industry Bought," available at http://www.sierraclub.org/politics/lobbying/lobbying_details.asp, viewed November 12, 2002.

19. Daniel J. Weiss and Andrew B. Art, "Take More Money . . . and Run," (Washington, D. C.: Environmental Working Group, the Tides Center, and the Sierra Club, 1997), 7.

20. B. J. Bergman, "Good Buy, 104th Congress," *Sierra* (November–December 1996), 59–60.

21. Toner, "Interest Groups Take New Route," A1.

22. Ruth Marcus and Charles Babcock, "The System Cracks under the Weight of Cash," *Washington Post,* February 9, 1997, A1; see also James Youngclaus, "All Politics Is Legal: Soft Money, Issue Ads, Non-Profits May Nationalize '98 Local Elections," *Capital Eye* 5, no. 2, 1998.

23. Toner, "Interest Groups Take New Route," A1.

24. Craig B. Holman and Luke P. McLoughlin, *Buying Time 2000: Television Advertising in the 2000 Federal Election* (New York: Brennan Center for Justice, 2001), 95.

25. Cited in Sandra Anglund and Clyde McKee, "The 1998 Connecticut Fifth Congressional District Race," in *Outside Money: Soft Money and Issue Advocacy in the 1998 Congressional Elections* (New York: Rowman and Littlefield, 2000), 163. See also Holman and McLoughlin, 41.

26. Annenberg Public Policy Center, *Issue Advocacy Advertising During the 1997–1998 Election Cycle* (Philadelphia: Annenberg Public Policy Center, 1999), 2.

27. Leslie Wayne, "Conservative Advocate and His G.O.P. Ties Come into Focus," *New York Times,* July 8, 1997, A12.

28. Annenberg Public Policy Center, *Issue Advocacy Advertising,* 4.

29. Press statement by Russ Lehman, October 3, 2000.

30. Philip Shabecoff, *Earth Rising: American Environmentalism in the Twenty-first Century* (Washington, D.C.: Island Press, 2000), 117.

31. Public Law 107-155.

32. Telephone interview with Betsy Loyless, LCV political director, November 25, 2002.

33. See Ron Facheux, "The Yes, No, and Maybe of the New Campaign Finance Law," *Washington Post,* July 15, 2002, available at http://www.washingtonpost.com/wp-dyn/articles/A8017-2002jul15.html.

34. Telephone interview, November 14, 2002.

Bibliography

Ackerman, Bruce, and William Hassler. 1981. *Clean Coal/ Dirty Air*. New Haven, Conn.: Yale University Press.

Allin, Craig. 1982. *The Politics of Wilderness Preservation*. Westport, Conn.: Greenwood Press.

Alm, Lesley, and Stephanie Witt. 1995. Environmental Policy in the Intermountain West: The Rural-Urban Linkage. *State and Local Government Review* 27 (Spring), 127–36.

Andrews, Richard N. L. 1999. *Managing the Environment, Managing Ourselves: A History of American Environmental Policy*. New Haven, Conn.: Yale University Press.

Anglund, Sandra, and Clyde McKee. 2000. The 1998 Connecticut Fifth Congressional District Race. In *Outside Money: Soft Money and Issue Advocacy in the 1998 Congressional Elections,* ed. David Magleby. New York: Rowman and Littlefield.

Annenberg Public Policy Center. 1999. *Issue Advocacy Advertising during the 1997–1998 Election Cycle*. Philadelphia: Annenberg Public Policy Center.

Atkeson, Lonna Rae, and Anthony C. Coveny. 2000. The 1998 New Mexico Third Congressional District Race. In *Outside Money: Soft Money and Issue Advocacy in the 1998 Congressional Elections,* ed. David Magleby. New York: Rowman and Littlefield.

Audley, John J. 1997. *Global Trade: NAFTA and the Future of Environmental Politics*. Washington, D.C.: Georgetown University Press.

BNA National Environment Daily. "Environmental Organizations Join Coalition to Oppose Federal Subsidies," March 25, 1993, 1–2; "Environmental Groups Launch Campaign to Counter Threats to Pending Legislation," July 8, 1994, 1–4; "Authors of Green Scissors Report Findings at Briefing," March 20, 1995, 1–2.

Barr, Stephen, and Dan Morgan. Spending Bill Deadlocks over GOP Proposal to Restrict Nonprofits. *Washington Post,* September 15, 1995, A4.

Baumgartner, Frank R., and Bryan D. Jones. 1993. *Agendas and Instability in American Politics*. Chicago: University of Chicago Press.

Bergman, B. J. 1997. Majority Rules, and It's Green. *Sierra* (January–February), 2.

Berry, Jeffrey M. 1989. Subgovernments, Issue Networks, and Political Conflict. In *Remaking American Politics,* ed. Richard A. Harris and Sidney M. Milkis. Boulder, Colo.: Westview Press.

———. 1997. *The Interest Group Society.* 3d ed. New York: Longman.

———. 1999. *The New Liberalism: The Rising Power of Citizen Groups*. Washington, D.C.: Brookings Institution Press.

———. 2002. Interest Groups and Gridlock. In *Interest Group Politics,* 6th ed. Ed. Allan J. Cigler and Burdett A. Loomis. Washington, D.C.: CQ Press.

Biodiversity Project. 1998. *Engaging the Public on Biodiversity: A Road Map for Education and Communication Strategies*. Madison, Wisc.: Biodiversity Project.

————. 1999. *Life. Nature. The Public. A Communications Handbook from the Biodiversity Project.* Madison, Wisc.: Biodiversity Project.

————. 2000. *Making a Difference: The First Five Years, 1995–2000.* Madison, Wisc.: Biodiversity Project.

Bosso, Christopher J. 1987. *Pesticides and Politics: The Life Cycle of a Public Issue.* Pittsburgh, Pa.: University of Pittsburgh Press.

————. 1991. Adaptation and Change in the Environmental Movement. In *Interest Group Politics,* 3d ed. Ed. Alan J. Cigler and Burdett A. Loomis. Washington, D.C.: CQ Press.

————. 1994. The Contextual Bases of Problem Definition. In *The Politics of Problem Definition: Shaping the Policy Agenda,* ed. David A. Rochefort and Roger W. Cobb. Lawrence: University Press of Kansas.

————. 1994. After the Movement: Environmental Activism in the 1990s. In *Environmental Policy in the 1990s,* 2d ed. Ed. Norman J. Vig and Michael E. Kraft. Washington, D.C.: CQ Press.

————. 1997. Seizing Back the Day: The Challenge to Environmental Activism in the 1990s. In *Environmental Policy in the 1990s,* 3d ed., Ed. Norman J. Vig and Michael E. Kraft. Washington, D.C.: CQ Press.

————. 2000. Environmental Groups and the New Political Landscape. In *Environmental Policy: New Directions for the Twenty-first Century,* 4th ed. Ed. Norman J. Vig and Michael E. Kraft. Washington, D.C.: CQ Press.

Bosso, Christopher J., and Michael T. Collins. 2002. Just Another Tool? How Environmental Groups Use the Internet. In *Interest Group Politics,* 6th ed. Ed. Allan J. Cigler and Burdett A. Loomis. Washington, D.C.: CQ Press.

Bosso, Christopher J., and Deborah Lynn Guber. 2002. The Boundaries and Contours of American Environmental Activism. In *Environmental Policy: New Directions for the Twenty-first Century,* 5th ed. Ed. Norman J. Vig and Michael E. Kraft. Washington, D.C.: CQ Press.

Browne, William P. 1990. Organized Interests and Their Issue Niches: A Search for Pluralism in a Policy Domain. *Journal of Politics* 52 (May), 447–80.

————. 1992. *Sacred Cows and Hot Potatoes: Agrarian Myths in Agricultural Policy.* Boulder, Colo.: Westview Press.

————. 1998. *Groups, Interests, and U.S. Public Policy.* Washington, D.C.: Georgetown University Press.

————. 1998. Lobbying the Public: All-Directional Advocacy. In *Interest Groups Politics,* 5th ed. Ed. Allan J. Cigler and Burdett A. Loomis. Washington, D.C.: CQ Press.

Bryner, Gary C. 1993. *Blue Skies, Green Politics: The Clean Air Act of 1990.* Washington, D.C.: CQ Press.

————. 1996. Reforming the Regulatory Process: Congress and the Next Generation of Environmental Laws. Paper presented at the Annual Meeting of the Western Political Science Association, San Francisco, March 14–16.

Business Week. Environmentalists: More of a Political Force. January 24, 1983, 86.

Cantor, David. 1999. The Sierra Club Political Committee. In *After the Revolution: PACs, Lobbies, and the Republican Congress,* ed. Robert Biersack, Paul S. Herrnson, and Clyde Wilcox. Boston: Allyn and Bacon.

Cantrill, James G. 1999. Perceiving Environmental Discourse: The Cognitive Playground. In *The Symbolic Earth: Discourse and Our Creation of the Environment,* ed. James G. Cantrill and Christine L. Oravec. Louisville: University Press of Kentucky.

Carr, Patrick, ed. 1989. *The Sierra Club: A Guide*. San Francisco: Sierra Club Publications.

Cawley, R. McGreggor. 1993. *Federal Land, Western Anger: The Sagebrush Rebellion and Environmental Politics*. Lawrence: University Press of Kansas.

Cigler, Allan J., and Burdett A. Loomis. 1998. From Big Bird to Bill Gates: Organized Interests and the Emergence of Hyperpolitics. In *Interest Group Politics*, 5th ed. Ed. Allan J. Cigler and Burdett A. Loomis. Washington, D.C.: CQ Press.

———. 2002. Always Involved, Rarely Central: Organized Interests in American Politics. In *Interest Group Politics*, 6th ed. Ed. Allan J. Cigler and Burdett A. Loomis. Washington, D.C.: CQ Press.

Clemens, Elisabeth S. 1997. *The People's Lobby: Organizational Innovation and the Rise of Interest Group Politics in the U.S., 1890–1925*. Chicago: University of Chicago Press.

Cobb, Roger W., and Charles D. Elder. 1972. *Participation in American Politics: The Dynamics of Agenda-Building*. Boston: Allyn and Bacon.

Cohen, Michael P. 1988. *The History of the Sierra Club, 1892–1970*. San Francisco: Sierra Club Books.

Cohen, Richard E. 1995. *Washington at Work: Back Rooms and Clean Air,* 2d ed. Boston: Allyn and Bacon.

Conway, M. Margaret. 1991. PACs in the Political Process. In *Interest Group Politics*, 3d ed. Ed. Allan J. Cigler and Burdett A. Loomis. Washington, D.C.: CQ Press, 1991.

Conway, M. Margaret, and Joanne Connor Green. 1998. Political Action Committees and Campaign Finance. In *Interest Group Politics*, 5th ed. Ed. Allan J. Cigler and Burdett A. Loomis. Washington, D.C.: CQ Press.

Cronin, Thomas E. 1989. *Direct Democracy: The Politics of Initiative, Referendum, and Recall.* Cambridge, Mass.: Harvard University Press.

Davis, Charles. 2001. Conclusion: Public Lands and Policy Change. In *Western Public Lands and Environmental Politics*, 2d ed. Ed. Charles Davis. Boulder, Colo.: Westview Press.

———. 2001. Politics and Rangeland Policy. In *Western Public Lands and Environmental Politics*, 2d ed. Ed. Charles Davis. Boulder, Colo.: Westview Press.

Dowie, Mark. 1995. *Losing Ground: American Environmentalism at the Close of the Twentieth Century*. Cambridge, Mass.: MIT Press.

Downs, Anthony. 1972. Up and Down with Ecology: 'The Issue Attention Cycle.' *Public Interest* 28: 28–50.

Dreyfuss, Robert. 2000. Rousing the Democratic Base. *American Prospect,* November 6.

Dunlap, Riley E. 1991. Public Opinion in the 1980s: Clear Consensus, Ambiguous Commitment. *Environment* 33: 10–15, 32–37.

———. 1995. Public Opinion and the Environment (U.S.). In *Conservation and Environmentalism: An Encyclopedia,* ed. Robert Pahelke. New York: Garland Publishing.

Durbin, Kathie. 1999. *Tongass: Pulp Politics and the Fight for the Alaska Rain Forest*. Corvallis: Oregon State University Press.

Dwyre, Diana. 2002. Campaigning outside the Law: Interest Group Issue Advocacy. In *Interest Group Politics*, 6th ed. Ed. Allan J. Cigler and Burdett A. Loomis. Washington, D.C.: CQ Press.

Eismeier, Theodore J., and Phillip H. Pollock III. 1985. An Organizational Analysis of Political Action Committees. *Political Behavior* 7: 192–216.

Ellis, Richard J. 2002. *Democratic Delusions: The Initiative Process in America*. Lawrence: University Press of Kansas.

Erikson, Robert S., Gerald C. Wright, and John P. McIver. 1993. *Statehouse Democracy: Public Opinion and Policy in the American States*. New York: Cambridge University Press.

Fluharty, Marlene J. 1988. The Sierra Club's Electoral Program. In *Sierra Club: A Guide*, ed. Patrick Carr. San Francisco: Sierra Club Books.

Fowler, Linda, and Ronald Shaiko. 1987. The Grassroots Connection: Environmental Activists and Senate Roll Calls. *American Journal of Political Science* 31: 484–510.

Gais, Thomas L., and Jack L. Walker Jr. 1991. Pathways to Influence in American Politics. In *Mobilizing Interest Groups in America: Patrons, Professions, and Social Movements*, ed. Jack L. Walker Jr. Ann Arbor: University of Michigan Press.

Gamson, William A. 1992. *Talking Politics*. New York: Cambridge University Press.

Gelbspan, Ross. 1998. *The Heat Is On: The Climate Crisis, the Cover Up, the Prescription*, rev. ed. Cambridge, Mass: Perseus Books.

Gonzalez, George A. 2001. *Corporate Power and the Environment*. New York: Rowman and Littlefield.

———. 2002. Local Growth Coalitions, Environmental Groups, and Air Pollution. Paper presented at the Annual Meeting of the Southern Political Science Association, Savannah, Georgia.

Gottlieb, Robert. 1993. *Forcing the Spring: The Transformation of the American Environmental Movement*. Washington, D.C.: Island Press.

———. 2002. *Environmentalism Unbound: Exploring New Pathways for Change*. Cambridge, Mass: MIT Press.

Guber, Deborah Lynn. 2001. Voting Preferences and the Environment in the American Electorate. *Society and Natural Resources* 14, no. 6: 455–69.

———. 2003. *The Grassroots of a Green Revolution: Polling America on the Environment*. Cambridge, Mass.: MIT Press.

Harrison, Kathryn, and George Hoberg. 1991. Setting the Environmental Agenda in Canada and the United States: The Cases of Dioxin and Radon. *Canadian Journal of Political Science* 24: 3–27.

Harvey, Mark W. T. 1994. *A Symbol of Wilderness: Echo Park and the American Conservation Movement*. Seattle: University of Washington Press.

Heclo, Hugh. 1980. Issue Networks and the Executive Establishment. In *The New American Political System*, ed. Anthony King. Washington, D.C.: American Enterprise Institute.

Herrnson, Paul. 1998. Parties and Interest Groups in Postreform Congressional Elections. In *Interest Group Politics*, 5th ed. Ed. Allan J. Cigler and Burdett A. Loomis. Washington, D.C.: CQ Press.

Herrnson, Paul, Ronald G. Shaiko, and Clyde Wilcox. 1998. *The Interest Group Connection: Electioneering, Lobbying, and Policymaking in Washington*. Chatham, N.J.: Chatham House.

Hoberg, George. 2001. The Emerging Triumph of Ecosystem Management: The Transformation of Federal Forest Policy. In *Western Public Lands and Environmental Politics*, 2d ed. Ed. Charles Davis. Boulder, Colo.: Westview Press.

Holman, Craig B., and Luke P. McLoughlin. 2001. *Buying Time 2000: Television Advertising in the 2000 Federal Elections*. New York: Brennan Center for Justice.

Hrebenar, Ronald J., and Ruth K. Scott. 1982. *Interest Group Politics in America*. New York: Prentice-Hall.

Inglehart, Ronald. 1977. *The Silent Revolution: Changing Values and Political Styles among Western Publics*. Princeton, N.J.: Princeton University Press.

John, DeWitt. 1994. *Civic Environmentalism: Alternatives to Regulation in States and Communities.* Washington, D.C.: CQ Press.

Kamieniecki, Sheldon. 1991. Political Mobilization, Agenda Building, and International Environmental Policy. *Journal of International Affairs* 44: 339–58.

———. 2000. Testing Alternative Theories of Agenda-Setting: Forest Policy Change in British Columbia, Canada. *Policy Studies Journal* 25, no. 1: 176–89.

Kemmis, Daniel. 2001. *This Sovereign Land: A New Vision for Governing the West.* Washington, D.C.: Island Press.

Kingdon, John W. 1984. *Agendas, Alternatives, and Public Politics.* Boston: Little, Brown.

Kingsley, Elizabeth, et al. 2000. *E-Advocacy for Nonprofits: The Law of Lobbying and Election-Related Activity on the Net.* Washington, D.C.: Alliance for Justice.

Kline, Benjamin. 1997. *First along the River: A Brief History of the U.S. Environmental Movement.* San Francisco: Acad Books.

Klyza, Christopher McGrory. 2001. Reform at a Geological Pace: Mining Policy on Federal Lands, 1964–1994. In *Western Public Lands and Environmental Politics,* 2d ed. Ed. Charles Davis. Boulder, Colo.: Westview Press.

Kraft, Michael E. 1996. *Environmental Policy and Politics.* New York: HarperCollins.

Kraft, Michael E., and Diana Wuertz. 1999. Environmental Advocacy in the Corridors of Government. In *The Symbolic Earth: Discourse and Our Creation of the Environment,* ed. James G. Cantrill and Christine L. Oravec. Louisville: University Press of Kentucky.

League of Conservation Voters Education Fund. 1999. *Mobilize Your Members: A Simple How-To Guide for Using Lists Effectively.* Washington, D.C.: League of Conservation Voters Education Fund. Available online at http://www.lcvef.org/pdf/mobilize _your_members.edf.

———. 2000. *Making a Difference in 2000: The League of Conservation Voters Education Fund Grassroots Program Report, 1998–99.* Washington, D.C.: League of Conservation Voters Education Fund.

———. 2002. *Online Advocacy: Where Are We Now and Where Do We Go from Here?* Washington, D.C.: League of Conservation Voters Education Fund.

Leech, Beth L., and Frank R. Baumgartner. 1998. Lobbying Friends and Foes in Washington. In *Interest Group Politics,* 5th ed. Ed. Allan J. Cigler and Burdett A. Loomis. Washington, D.C.: CQ Press,.

Leech, Beth L., et al. 2002. Organized Interests and Issue Definition in Policy Debates. In *Interest Group Politics,* 6th ed. Ed. Allan J. Cigler and Burdett A. Loomis. Washington, D.C.: CQ Press.

Levin, Meredith J. 1991. *Lobbying Techniques for the Nineties: Strategies, Coalitions, and Grass-Roots Campaigns.* Washington, D.C.: CQ Press.

Libby, Ronald T. 1998. *Eco-Wars: Political Campaigns and Social Movements.* New York: Columbia University Press.

Lipset, Seymour Martin, and William Schneider. 1987. *The Confidence Gap: Business, Labor, and Government in the Public Mind,* 2d ed. Baltimore, Md.: Johns Hopkins University Press.

Magleby, David. 2000. Outside Money and the Ground War in 1998. In *Outside Money: Soft Money and Issue Advocacy in the 1998 Congressional Elections,* ed. David Magleby. New York: Rowman and Littlefield.

———. 2000. Conclusions and Implications. In *Outside Money: Soft Money and Issue*

248 THE GREEN AGENDA IN AMERICAN POLITICS

Advocacy in the 1998 Congressional Elections, ed. David Magleby. New York: Rowman and Littlefield.

Matz, Mike. 2001. The Politics of Protecting Wild Places. In *Return of the Wild: The Future of Our Wild Lands,* ed. Ted Kerasote. Washington, D.C.: Island Press.

Mayer, Marshall. 1997. Conservation Database Report: A White Paper Prepared for the Rockefeller Family Fund. October 13.

Mazmanian, Daniel A., and Michael E. Kraft. 1999. The Three Epochs of the Environmental Movement. In *Toward Sustainable Communities: Transition and Transformations in Environmental Policy,* ed. Daniel A. Mazmanian and Michael E. Kraft. Cambridge, Mass.: MIT Press.

————. 1999. Conclusion: Toward Sustainable Communities. In *Toward Sustainable Communities: Transition and Transformations in Environmental Policy,* ed. Daniel A. Mazmanian and Michael E. Kraft. Cambridge: The MIT Press.

McCloskey, Michael. 1992. Twenty Years of Change in the Environmental Movement: An Insider's View. In *American Environmentalism: The U.S. Environmental Movement, 1970–1990.* Ed. Riley E. Dunlap and Angela G. Mertig. Philadelphia: Taylor and Francis.

McSpadden, Lettie. 1997. Environmental Policy in the Courts. In *Environmental Policy in the 1990s,* 3d ed. Ed. Norman J. Vig and Michael E. Kraft. Washington, D.C.: CQ Press.

Milne, George R., Easwar S. Iyer, and Sara Gooding-Williams. 1996. Environmental Organization Alliance Relationships within and across Nonprofit, Business, and Government Sectors. *Journal of Public Policy and Marketing* (Fall): 375–403.

Mitchell, Robert C. 1984. Public Opinion and Environmental Politics in the 1970s and 1980s. In *Environmental Policy in the 1980s,* ed. Norman J. Vig and Michael E. Kraft. Washington, D.C.: CQ Press.

————. 1990. Public Opinion and the Green Lobby. In *Environmental Policy in the 1990s,* 2d ed. Ed. Norman J. Vig and Michael E. Kraft. Washington, D.C.: CQ Press.

Mitchell, Robert C., Angela G. Mertig, and Riley E. Dunlap. 1992. Twenty Years of Environmental Mobilization: Trends among National Environmental Organizations. In *American Environmentalism: The U.S. Environmental Movement, 1970–1990.* Philadelphia: Taylor and Francis.

Moberg, David. 1999. Brothers and Sisters. *Sierra* (January–February): 46–51, 114.

Mundo, Philip A. 1999. League of Conservation Voters. In *After the Revolution: PACs, Lobbies, and the Republican Congress,* ed. Robert Biersack, Paul S. Herrnson, and Clyde Wilcox. Boston: Allyn and Bacon.

Mutter, Larry R., Randy J. Virden, and N. Joseph Cayer. 1999. Interest Group Influence in State Natural Resource Policymaking. *Society and Natural Resources* 12, no. 3: 243–55.

Myers, Phyllis. 1997. Voters Go for the Green. *GREENSENSE* (Spring).

————. 1999. *Livability at the Ballot Box: State and Local Referenda on Parks, Conservation, and Smarter Growth, Election Day 1998.* Washington, D.C.: Brookings Center on Urban and Metropolitan Policy.

Myers, Phyllis, and Robert Puentes. 2001. *Growth at the Ballot Box: Electing the Shape of Communities in November 2000.* Washington, D.C.: Brookings Center on Urban and Metropolitan Policy.

Nash, Roderick Frazier. 2001. *Wilderness and the American Mind,* 4th Edition. New Haven, Conn.: Yale University Press.

Opie, John, and Norbert Elliot. 1999. Tracking the Elusive Jeremiad: The Rhetorical Character of American Environmental Discourse. In *The Symbolic Earth: Discourse and Our Creation of the Environment,* ed. James G. Cantrill and Christine L. Oravec. Lexington: University Press of Kentucky.

Ornstein, Norman, and Shirley Elder. 1978. *Interest Groups, Lobbying, and Policymaking.* Washington, D.C.: CQ Press.

Paehlke, Robert C. *Environmentalism and the Future of Progressive Politics.* New Haven, Conn.: Yale University Press.

Parris, Thomas M. 1998. A Plethora of Campus Environmental Initiatives on the Net. *Environment* 40, no. 7 (September): 3.

Pellow, David N. 1999. Negotiation and Confrontation: Environmental Policymaking through Consensus. *Society and Natural Resources* 12, no. 3: 189–203.

Pierce, John C., Mary Ann E. Steger, Brent S. Steel, and Nicholas P. Lovrich. 1992. *Citizens, Political Communication, and Interest Groups: Environmental Organizations in Canada and the United States.* New York: Praeger.

Portney, Kent E. 2003. *Taking Sustainable Cities Seriously: Economic Development, the Environment, and Quality of Life in American Cities.* Cambridge, Mass.: MIT Press.

Putnam, Robert D. 2000. *Bowling Alone: The Collapse and Revival of American Community.* New York: Simon and Schuster.

Rabe, Barry. 1997. Power to the States: The Promise and Pitfalls of Decentralization. In *Environmental Policy in the 1990s,* 3d ed. Ed. Norman J. Vig and Michael E. Kraft Washington, D.C.: CQ Press.

Rinquist, Evan. 1993. *Environmental Protection at the State Level: Politics and Progress in Controlling Pollution.* Armonk, N.Y.: M. E. Sharpe.

River Network. 1998. *River Talk! Communicating a Watershed Message.* Washington, D.C.: River Network.

Rochefort, David A., and Roger W. Cobb. 1994. Problem Definition: An Emerging Perspective. In *The Politics of Problem Definition: Shaping the Policy Agenda,* ed. David A. Rochefort and Roger W. Cobb. Lawrence: University Press of Kansas.

Rosenbaum, Walter A. 1977. *The Politics of Environmental Concern.* New York: Holt, Rinehart and Winston.

Rozell, Mark, and Clyde Wilcox. 1999. *Interest Groups in American Campaigns: The New Face of Electioneering.* Washington, D.C.: CQ Press.

Sabatier, Paul, and Hank C. Jenkins-Smith. 1993. *Policy Change and Learning: An Advocacy Coalition Approach.* Boulder, Colo.: Westview Press.

Sabato, Larry, and Glenn Simpson. 1996. *Dirty Little Secrets.* New York: Random House.

Sale, Kirkpatrick. 1993. *The Green Revolution: The American Environmental Movement, 1962–92.* New York: Hill and Wang.

Salisbury, Robert H., and Lauretta Conklin. 1998. Instrumental Versus Expressive Group Politics: The National Endowment for the Arts. In *Interest Group Politics,* 5th ed. Ed. Allan J. Cigler and Burdett A. Loomis. Washington, D.C.: CQ Press.

Schattschneider, E. E. 1960. *The Semi-Sovereign People: A Realist's View of Democracy in America.* New York: Holt, Rinehart, and Winston.

Scheberle, Denise. 1994. Radon and Asbestos: A Study of Agenda-Setting and Causal Stories. *Policy Studies Journal* 22, no. 1: 74–86.

———. 1997. *Federalism and Environmental Policy: Trust and the Politics of Implementation.* Washington, D.C.: Georgetown University Press.

Schlozman, Kay Lehman, and John T. Tierney. 1986. *Organized Interests and American Democracy*. New York: Harper and Row.

Shabecoff, Philip. 2000. *Earth Rising: American Environmentalism in the Twenty-first Century*. Washington, D.C.: Island Press.

Shaiko, Ronald G. 1991. More Bang for the Buck: The New Era of Full-Service Public Interest Organizations. In *Interest Group Politics,* 3d ed. Ed. Allan J. Cigler and Burdett A. Loomis. Washington, D.C.: CQ Press.

———. 1999. *Voices and Echoes for the Environment: Public Interest Representation in the 1990s and Beyond*. New York: Columbia University Press.

Sorauf, Frank J. 1988. *Money in American Politics* Glenview, Ill.: Scott, Foresman.

———. 1991. PACs and Parties in American Politics. In *Interest Group Politics,* 3d ed. Ed. Allan J. Cigler and Burdett A. Loomis. Washington, D.C.: CQ Press.

Stanfield, Rochelle L. 1985. Environmental Lobby's Changing of Guard is Part of the Movement's Evolution. *National Journal* June 8: 1350.

Stone, Deborah A. 1989. Causal Stories and the Formation of Policy Agendas. *Political Science Quarterly* 104: 281–300.

———. 2000. *Policy Paradox: The Art of Political Decision Making*. rev. ed. New York. W. W. Norton.

Switzer, Jacqueline Vaughn. 1997. *Green Backlash: The History and Politics of Environmental Opposition in the U.S*. Boulder, Colo.: Lynne Rienner Publishers.

Tierney, John, and William Frasure. 1998. Culture Wars on the Frontier: Interests, Values, and Policy Narratives in Public Lands Politics. In *Interest Group Politics,* 5th ed. Ed. Allan J. Cigler and Burdett A. Loomis. Washington, D.C.: CQ Press.

Truman, David B. 1971. *The Governmental Process,* 2d ed. New York: Knopf.

U.S. EPA. 1999. *Framework for Community-based Environmental Protection:* EPA 237-K-99-001. Washington, D.C.: U.S. EPA.

Vig, Norman J. 1997. Presidential Leadership and the Environment: From Reagan to Clinton. In *Environmental Policy in the 1990s,* 3d ed. Ed. Norman J. Vig and Michael E. Kraft. Washington, D.C.: CQ Press.

Weber, Edward P. 1998. *Pluralism by the Rules: Conflict and Cooperation in Environmental Regulation*. Washington, D.C.: Georgetown University Press.

———. 2000. A New Vanguard for the Environment: Grass-Roots Ecosystem Management as a New Environmental Movement. *Society and Natural Resources* 13, no. 2: 246–47.

West, Darrell M. 2001. *Air Wars: Television Advertising in Election Campaigns, 1952–2000*. Washington, D.C.: CQ Press.

West, Darrell M., and Burdett A. Loomis. 1998. *The Sound of Money: How Political Interests Get What They Want*. New York: W. W. Norton.

Wilson, James Q. 1982. *American Government: Institutions and Policies,* 2d ed. Englewood Cliffs, N.J.: Prentice-Hall.

Wright, John R. 1996. *Interest Groups and Congress: Lobbying, Contributions, and Influence*. New York: Allyn and Bacon.

Zakin, Susan. 1993. *Coyotes and Town Dogs: Earth First! and the Environmental Movement*. New York: Penguin Books.

Index